The Struggle for Control of
Global Communication

THE HISTORY OF COMMUNICATION

Robert W. McChesney and John C. Nerone, editors

A list of books in the series appears at the end of this book.

The Struggle for Control of

Global Communication

The Formative Century

JILL HILLS

University of Illinois Press

URBANA AND CHICAGO

Library of Congress Cataloging-in-Publication Data
Hills, Jill.
The struggle for control of global communication :
the formative century / Jill Hills.
p.   cm.
Includes bibliographical references and index.
ISBN 0-252-02757-4 (alk. paper)
1. Telecommunication—History. 2. Globalization—History.
3. Competition, International—History. I. Title.
HE7631.H543   2002
384′.09—dc21   2002000260

To Stephanie

Contents

Acknowledgments

ANY RESEARCH that takes as long as this has accrues numerous debts. Many of those who have contributed to the outcome have no idea that they have done so. The names of others are unknown to me. Of those, I would like to thank the archivists at BT and Marconi and the two anonymous readers of the manuscript. In particular, I owe a debt of thanks to my colleagues at the University of Westminster for a working environment that is both challenging and fun and for giving me the time to complete the book. My thanks especially to Brian Winston and Maria Michalis, without whose support I could not have finished this book. During its writing, two people who have been influential in my academic thought have, sadly, died. Bo Särlvik and Susan Strange were eminent academics and a privilege to know. Finally, my family and friends have taken the inevitable sacrifices of time and energy with cynical good humor. The book is dedicated to my granddaughter, who has grown from toddler to preteen with the specter that "Granny's book" would never be finished.

Introduction

THIS BOOK ORIGINATED in an interest in the issues of the 1990s in international communications and in market structures and regulation. That interest was focused on the relations between international and national markets, on the role of multinationals in international and national political economies, and on international and national regimes of regulation. The book has been written in the belief that understanding the roots of current international arrangements and policy is important in deciding on future paths.

It was written as the World Trade Organization (WTO) agreement of 1997 and the liberalization of laws regulating telecommunications networks created private ownership of the infrastructure of domestic and international communications. The agreement has reinforced the trend of mergers by network operators and owners of information content and, through the opening of domestic markets to foreign investment, has created the opportunity for the worldwide integration of domestic and international communications networks under a U.S.-led oligopoly. The Reference Paper attached to the WTO agreement obligated signatories to create regulators of telecommunications networks that are independent of the network operator, and the paper included a number of principles that such national regulators should follow. This was the mechanism that transposed the regulation of international communications into national regulation.

Negotiators seeking international gains for U.S. multinational corporations within the WTO agreement met with two significant failures. Because no agreement was made on the worldwide liberalization of media markets, the U.S. negotiators gained no additional advantages for Hollywood. And the enshrinement of the rights of multinational corporations to invest wherever they might choose, first raised in the opening of the Uruguay Round, did not find its way into the final agreement (Hills 1994). Resurrected as the Multilateral Agreement on Investment, this multilateral agreement would have sealed by treaty the rights of private corporations over sovereign states, thereby overturning the concept of state sovereignty enshrined in the United Nations Charter. The starting point for this book, then, was this movement toward private economic power over state sovereignty, as reflected in the communications and information sectors of the last years of the twentieth century.

In pursuing this movement, the book moves backward from late twentieth-century experience to look at the period when private companies last owned the international infrastructure of communications and to examine the relationship between states and industry, between corporations and corporations, and between international and national regulation of markets. How did the major actors conceptualize international communications—as nation to nation, center to periphery, or company to company? Were the patterns of international interactions today to be found in the nineteenth century? Did corporations then hold similar power? Were the mechanisms that the U.S. government uses today to unilaterally expand domestic regulation into the international economy in fact political instruments with long histories in U.S. policy? In particular, did U.S. demands for "reciprocity" as a free-market legitimation for protectionism, noticeable both before and after the WTO negotiations of the 1990s, have an earlier history in the communications sector? Did the United States have a history of using bilateral and unilateral muscle to supplant multilateral regimes in the communications sector?[1] Were there linkages of policy running through to the nineteenth century? These were the initial questions prompting my research.

With the exception of George Codding's histories of the International Telecommunication Union (1972, 1982), together with Hugh Barty-King's 1979 and Daniel Headrick's 1981 and 1988 overviews of the commercial and strategic implications of submarine cables, when this research began there was little post–World War II material available on nineteenth- and early twentieth-century international communications. There were some specialist books, such as Rosenberg (1982), Fejes (1986), Luther (1988), and Schwoch (1990) on South America; Guback (1969), Thompson (1985), and Izod (1988) on the film industry; and a number of histories of individual corporations. Subsequently, Brian Winston (1998) and Tom Standage (1999) have written on technology. And David Puttnam and Neil Watson (1997) have provided a comprehensive international history of the movie industry.

With grateful thanks I have made full use of these and others, but this book is mainly based on primary and early secondary source material. The result is an interpretative history of the political economy of international communications from the nineteenth century to World War II, a history that uses today's power relations to explain those in the past and the past to throw light on today's.

At the beginning of the twenty-first century we have heard much of the terms *globalization* and *information society,* but we tend to forget that the introduction of the telegraph in the mid-nineteenth century was what caused the major paradigm shift in communications from national to international.[2] The introduction of the submarine telegraph cable completely transformed the mechanisms of overseas trade and investment. From a situation where ships disappeared over the horizon, not be heard from for months, the telegraph transmitted information from one end of the globe to another, first within hours, then within minutes.

As Charles Bright, the son of one of the first submarine cable consulting engineers, writing in 1898, commented, "The methods of conducting business between merchants and financiers in different countries have been completely *revolutionalised* by the telegraph cable which places the business man in touch with the money markets of the world" (1898a:171). Soon the telegraph allowed the transfer of information across international borders. In the wake of this new technology corporate empires were built on that immediacy of information. Bright continues: "The influence of this early news upon the policies of nations and the financial and commercial operation of individuals upon the fortunes—indeed, the very existence—of a great portion of the daily press of modern times, is incalculable" (1898a:174).

Information became a commodity to be bought and sold, and ownership of infrastructure became important as the means of distributing information. While the cost of transferring information decreased, its speed of transfer increased by more than ten times within thirty years. These changes mirrored those in the costs of maritime transport—both freight rates and insurance—which had also fallen by the end of the nineteenth century to a tenth of that at its beginning (Mende 1973:13).

The telegraph provided the mechanisms for reducing risk in banking, insurance, foreign investment, and commerce. It stabilized commodity prices, both nationally and internationally. Just as the Internet in the early twenty-first century is said to be cutting out the middleman, making direct contact between supplier and customer economical, so in the nineteenth century the telegraph introduced the bypassing of middlemen (Du Boff 1982:264). By allowing shippers to plan their loads in advance, it cut transportation costs and the holding of inventories. It facilitated changes in specific industries, such as shipping, allowing the growth of the tramp steamer. And its development was crucial to the safety and expansion of single-track railways and to centralization of administration.

Business gained speed, secrecy, and intelligence by using telegraph codes and private wires, the forerunners of what we know today as "leased lines," where an annual payment allows unlimited traffic. From the 1860s in the United States and the 1870s in Britain the use of these lines for internal communications between several sites advanced the growth of big business (Du Boff 1982:268; Standage 1999:162). In addition, the ease of communications provided by submarine telegraph cable and transatlantic ocean liners facilitated the spread of British capital worldwide and subsequently the expansion of U.S. companies into Europe before World War I.

The submarine telegraph cable extended the "space" of empire to facilitate the unification of territory into nation-states and to allow long-distance control of alien territories. In Harold Innis's terms "the concept of empire" is "an indication of the efficiency of communications" (1972:7). The telegraph, coupled with the printed word, altered political relations between the British government and its colonial territories, allowing more direct control. It also altered the autonomy of markets in the dominions of the British Empire, allowing London, rather than local, capital to meet demand. Had the submarine telegraph cable been laid only ten years earlier, the dominions might not have achieved such early independence from Britain.[3]

Telegraph communications, although primarily a business tool, also increased the flow of news from the white settler colonies and India, eventually influencing the public's images of colonization. Writing in 1924, John Saxon Mills suggests that

> the thrill of these newly developed nerves of communication was scarcely appreciated before the eighties of the last century. Then it was that steam and electricity began to influence the course of our Imperial history and politics. This was, no doubt, one of the many converging causes of that great outburst of "imperialism," or the sense of Empire citizenship, which has been the most striking feature of British politics of the last half century. It was that decade which saw the creation of the Imperial Federation League (1884), the proud pageantry of the Jubilee, and the meetings of the first (1887) Colonial Conference. (6)

In other words, the immediacy of news brought by the submarine telegraph increased the affiliation of the British public to geographical areas "beyond the world of known places" (Innis 1972:10). Hobsbawm and Ranger (1983) suggest that this was the period when "tradition" was invented, when the British moved from nonpageantry to a panoply of royal rituals, first in 1877 with the declaration of Queen Victoria as empress of India, and culminating in 1897 with the assembly of the empire troops and leaders for her Diamond Jubilee. In Cannadine's words, "every great royal occasion became an imperial occasion" (1983:124). As the empire became perceived as a community, the dominions of Canada, Australia, and New Zealand, with their predominantly English and Scottish emigrants, were seen as linked to the mother country by kith and kin. Helped in turn by an increasingly national, rather than provincial, press, this vision of empire as "community" was to recur throughout the early years of the twentieth century in arguments to decrease international telegraph tariffs and to promote intraempire traffic for purposes other than business. Such sentiments were what drove the first external broadcasting of the British Broadcasting Corporation in the 1930s.

The telegraph had obvious military implications. Introduced into India just before the mutiny of 1857, it is credited as having "saved" India for the British (Clarke 1927:85–86). An uninsulated cable laid across the Black Sea in 1855 for the first time provided direct telegraph communication with troop commanders in the Crimean War. And access to the British international cable network allowed Lord Kitchener to prevail over the French in the Fashoda incident of 1898 (Standage 1999:149–50). Secret British monitoring of telegraph messages began with the Boer War. The advantage that this monitoring gave to British security eventually outweighed protectionist sentiments, and foreign-owned cables were encouraged to pass through London. In contrast, in the same year the U.S. government declared war on Spain, then panicked when it found that it had no U.S.-owned cable to Cuba and had cut the wrong British-owned cable in the Philippines. That incident marked the end of cable neutrality. Access to cables and the ability to cut them became a military imperative, and the avoidance of such action became a strategic necessity.

The British governing elite saw the international telegraph infrastructure, as a strategic resource to be used for the defense of empire, although the system was owned by private companies. Britain's competitors saw it as a monopolistic power resource that gave the empire control of information, of propaganda and censorship. By virtue of its companies' ownership of the international communications infrastructure, the British government not only held direct relational power (power to enforce its decisions) in being able to decide whether messages should be passed and in what form but through its control of information also held structural power—power to set the agenda (Lukes 1974). British control of submarine cables, coupled with a monopoly within the British sphere of influence over the collection and dissemination of "news" by the Reuters news agency, skewed that reporting to British interests. By the 1890s the U.S. government was complaining of the picture of the United States that foreign, and particularly British, news agencies were presenting to the rest of the world. Such complaints about news that was disseminated in South America and China lasted until the 1920s. The French, Germans, and Mexicans aired similar complaints against Hollywood in the 1920s and 1930s. After World War I, "culture" became part of strategic relations. In Harvey's words, "power in the realms of representation" had already become something worth fighting for in the 1880s and subsequently led to external propaganda broadcasting (Harvey 1990:233).

This perception of the implications for both relational and structural power of the submarine telegraph and subsequent technologies helped fuel the resulting struggle over communications. The Crimean War was the first to be reported with an immediacy that influenced public opinion back home and resulted in Florence Nightingale's embarkation to nurse the wounded (Hudson and Stanier 1997:1–21). Censorship of news, following its introduction by the Americans in the 1890s in their war with Spain, became a legitimate mechanism of state power to be used by the British in the Boer War. However, the introduction of the radiotelegraph made such censorship from the battlefield more difficult. The experience of the Russo-Japanese War demonstrated to both the U.S. and British governments the necessity of controlling journalists within the actual theater of the war. By World War I news had become part of the propaganda delivered by telegraph.

If the communications infrastructure is a power resource, one might expect that control of international communications would reflect the dominant economic and political power structure of the day; to that extent this book tells a predictable story. The struggle between the United States and Britain from the nineteenth century into the twentieth occurred partly because British control of international communications was hindering the growing economic power of the United States. In that period private capital aligned itself with the British state to achieve domination of international communications, and British, French, and German news agencies controlled information. This book traces the technological and regulatory innovations, coupled with geopolitical gains, that allowed the United States to challenge that British hegemony.

World War II proved the turning point, and the book ends there. Although U.S. companies used the war to gain access to the British colonies, once Britain and its dominions brought international communications under state ownership, U.S. companies became the only private operators of international communications. Although the struggle for control of international communications between the U.S. government and Britain did not end with the war, in the postwar period the system of international communications controlled by private companies gave way to a worldwide structure of both broadcasting and telecommunications based on nation-states. The private control of international communications documented here was not to re-occur until the 1980s.

In sum, the book presents an analysis of power relations in the international communications sector for a span of almost one hundred years. As such it is an attempt to bring communications into the mainstream of international political economy. It demonstrates how the control of international communications was both a focus for and a contributor to shifts in economic and political power between and within states throughout that period. The book also describes the power held by private corporations in that period and the opportunity that advances in technology have given to governments and corporations to work together to alter established international power relations. The technologies involved include submarine telegraph cables, ship-to-shore wireless, broadcast radio and shortwave wireless, the telephone, and the replacement of silent movies with sound.

One reason for a tendency to look at successive technologies is that each technology has provided a power resource for competing states and their corporations. But a further reason is that domestic and international regulation has tended to be technology specific. Domestic and international regulatory regimes have regulated some technologies. Others have succeeded in fobbing off either form of regulation and instead have been allowed to "self-regulate." Only at the end of the twentieth century did regulators begin to look within the communications sector for technologically neutral rules.

Theoretical Framework

The themes of this book link international relations between states to international political economy and to domestic political economies. Treaties between states established international regulatory frameworks in the communications sector in the mid-nineteenth century in order to establish the rules for connecting national networks across national boundaries. International rules replaced private agreements between the dominant international communications companies within Europe and were originally intended to replace competition with cartelization.

The international relations literature of the 1980s first introduced the idea that these international regimes, which Krasner defined as "sets of implicit or explicit principles, norms, rules and decision-making procedures around which actors' expectations converge in a given area of international relations," were themselves a power resource of states (1983:2). At the time, in order to offset the perceived failing free-trade hegemony of the United States in world markets, U.S. theorists were looking for mechanisms that the federal government could use to perpetuate free trade. In particular, they were looking for a means to counteract the emerging power of the developing countries to the south, which was emphasized by the oil price hikes of the 1970s. Regime theorists such as Stephen Krasner (1985) argued that international regimes linked state actions in international institutions to their domestic economic and political circumstances. He claimed that the southern countries sought to gain distribution of resources by means of administrative allocation through international institutions, rather than by means of markets. Because U.S. interests were best represented by market allocation, Krasner proposed that U.S. interests were in direct conflict with the southern countries' and that the United States should disengage from such international institutions and regimes.

In direct contrast to such theorists, this book demonstrates that the linkage between international regimes, domestic and international markets, and domestic corporations has a long history in the communications sector. In both Britain and the United States in the nineteenth century the influence and alteration of international regimes were intrinsic to domestic policy. The British government, in collaboration with either France or Germany, controlled the major international regime of the International Telegraph Union (ITU). Although British adherence to free-trade ideology would not allow domestic regulation, London then used those international rules that it had formulated in order to govern the actions of British and foreign companies. International rules took the place of domestic regulation. Similarly, this intrinsic linkage between the domestic and international markets inspired the first transatlantic submarine cable. Domestic considerations also lay behind U.S. cable corporations' public rejection of international regulation, although they accepted those general rules in day-to-day operations.

In other words, this book shows that international regimes have not been stand-alone entities but part of the armory of mechanisms, including domestic regulation, tariff barriers, and bilateral agreements, that states used to delineate markets and to protect their own economies. Thus consensual international rules may be a substitute for national industrial policy. And where international regimes have failed, overtly national protectionist mechanisms may be used, as in the European movie industry in the 1920s, or unilateral regulation, as in the case of U.S. marine wireless in 1910.

Overall, international institutions have formed the meetingplace and mediating structure between domestic politics, national markets, and international markets. In these venues the policies of state delegations that include both government and company representatives reflect the shifting alliances, ideologies, and policy goals of the domestic political process. These policies in turn relate as much to the structure, scope, and process of the international institutions as to the content of the rules promulgated. Changes in the institution's structure, scope, and process can have an influence by shifting procedural and budgetary power away from one set of countries or from the institution itself and thus lead to changes in the scope and content of regulatory regimes. During the nineteenth and early twentieth centuries both U.S. and British delegations to the ITU were active in the creation and alteration of both rules and constitutions to suit their interests.

An international regime that fails to cater to its members can find itself bypassed by the unilateral imposition of domestic regulation. As this book shows, the U.S. government began this practice in the early twentieth century and has continued it to the present day. Thus the WTO agreement on telecommunications began life because of U.S. failure in the ITU, and the Multilateral Agreement on Investment was resurrected in the Organization for Economic Cooperation and Development after failing within the WTO. Similarly, in the nineteenth century the concept of reciprocity was borne out of U.S. exclusion from the original ITU negotiations and first appeared in licenses to bring submarine cable ashore.

Yet if international regimes reflect the activities of governments in pursuit of advantage for their domestic industry, the development and structure of domestic markets and the ongoing relations between domestic market and government intervention are underlying factors in those international negotiations and international expansion. The international regimes themselves affect domestic politics. The book is therefore neither simply about the politics between nation-states nor simply about their conflicts and cooperation within the ITU and other international organizations. It is also crucially about corporate strategies and the relations of corporations to governments, international regimes, and each other.

The late Susan Strange, particularly in her *Retreat of the State* (1996), suggested that in the late twentieth century private companies were one set of nonstate actors that accrued increasing power vis-à-vis nation-states. She suggested that international relations in the late twentieth century were as much about company-to-company and company-to-government relations as about government to government. She would have felt at home with the empirical research reported here. It shows that, even in the nineteenth century, communications companies were negotiating with foreign governments and with their counterparts overseas. It shows that the actions of specific companies had important political effects and affected the distribution of political power within and among states. Thus the process of "pooling" of revenue between companies led to the first U.S. regulation of submarine cable landing rights.[4] The British submarine cable companies objected to British telegraph nationalization in 1869, and when Western Union foreclosed the U.S. market to British submarine cable operators in 1911, power between the United States and Britain was redistributed.

Although these were actions taken independently of domestic government, they nevertheless were taken within a domestic market and regulatory framework that allowed such behavior. In general, in both the United States and Britain the diplomatic muscle of the home government backed negotiations with other governments and sometimes with other companies. However, that generalization has to be tempered by the recognition that in the case of certain periods and companies, their interests and those of governments diverged and that, at times, one or other government might act against the short-term interests of its corporations.

That companies had "national" identities was important in the nineteenth and early twentieth century. Only "national" companies served national interests. The incorporation of companies, coupled with increased international interaction and foreign investment, raised the 1990s question of "Who are us?" as early as 1897. At a time when financiers in London underwrote the international expansion of foreign companies, it was not enough for the funding and directors of a company to be British for it to be considered "British."[5] And much confusion resulted in the United States from attempts by various presidential administrations and Congress to exclude from market entry or to control the subsidiaries of foreign-controlled companies incorporated in the United States. Such failures led to public excoriation of those perceived as being too closely allied to foreigners. This U.S. practice of publicly denouncing companies with British links continued into the 1930s, suggesting that a weak state had to resort to public opinion to legitimate its demands on what had become large international corporations. Western Union in particular was the subject of such demonization. Before World War I the British government also publicly attacked Marconi's Wireless Telegraph Company for similar regulatory purposes.

Susan Strange's late twentieth-century suggestion is pertinent to the late nineteenth century: Within a system in which all states have lost power to private corporations, there is an asymmetry of structural power, with large states losing less power to corporate actors than small states. If the governments of poorer states then wanted communications, whether by railway or the telegraph, they had to meet the terms set by foreign companies. Transfer of technology and linkages with the outside world came only at a price. So, for example, faced with competition from wireless, the U.S.-owned Central and South American Telegraph Company cut off communications to one South American country until its government gave the company an exclusive thirty-year concession for all forms of international communications. And the American United Fruit Company, which later expanded into the radiotelegraph, accumulated vast tracts of land at low cost in the Central American "banana republics" in exchange for its railway technology. In China the Western powers and their companies built infrastructure, often without the permission of a fragmented Chinese government.

Even the British government felt itself to be weak against both its own and foreign submarine cable companies. Until after World War I it relied on international regulation to control British companies. In international negotiations, where geographical position and ownership of colonies skewed power to governments in the larger, more industrialized states, the British used the representation of company interests as a bargaining tool. For other countries not only was administrative capacity often lacking in the late nineteenth century but, although formally acknowledged as "sovereign," their vulnerable economic and political situation eroded their bargaining power, both within international organizations and in relation to major corporations in the communications sector.

The conceptual construction of the state used here follows that of Nordlinger as "made up and limited to those individuals who are endowed with society wide decision making" (1981:11). This construction sees the state as a nonunitary actor in which differing factions composed of individuals compete for power. This conceptualization allows the process of domestic policy change to be examined and explained and accepts the part played by individuals with power accrued from their positions within corporations and bureaucratic structures. Coalitions between individuals within bureaucracy and industry are seen as the root of domestic policy change. Such changing coalitions themselves reflect the influence of the international economy upon the domestic in terms of inward investment and changing technologies through which new actors enter into the policy environment. In addition, coalitions change with the changing interests of domestic companies as they become multinational and with changing perceptions of state security. In turn, as states and corporations use both domestic and international markets and control of domestic and international regulation to further their own interests, domestic politics have a bearing on stances within international negotiations and on international markets. The international permeates the domestic.

Thus this book does not use a framework that perceives states and markets as separate, as would be the case within the "realist" tradition of international relations. Rather, the view implicit in this book is similar to Lindblom's—that states construct markets, which represent the delegation of state functions to private actors (1977:171–72). Domestic and international regulation delineates markets, preventing or encouraging competition between corporations and technologies. Trust busting in one market; allowing of cross-ownership or vertical or horizontal concentration in another; fostering national champions—state-backed or -financed companies intended to dominate national or world markets—in another; separating the use of technologies by market—each of these is a policy mechanism that alters the strength of competition and the shape of markets. Detailed domestic regulatory mechanisms, in which the state takes back some of its delegated functions, in which direct authority may replace indirect persuasion, can tame the unbridled profit-seeking behavior of all corporations to more wholesome political objectives or can protect the regulated corporation from competition. But in all cases states delineate markets by making or not making decisions (Lukes 1974).

Regulation is here considered to be part of the national policy process, a matter of the continuing construction and deconstruction of national and international markets and the provision of incentives for preferred corporate behavior in both. Regulation is not construed as simply the implementation of policy, of imposing a given set of rules, but an intrinsic element of policy making (Hills 1993a). British political scientists have been debating since the 1970s whether regulation is policy making and whether the civil service and judiciary implement or make policy. The crucial element is discretion. Regulatory agencies actually require discretion in order to retain speed of action and flexibility in the face of market changes (Hills 1993a). Thus the view implicit in this book is that neither states and markets nor policy and regulation are separate entities. Regulation is part of the policy process that determines the distribution of resources between competing interests and uses the structure of the market for that distribution.

This core theme follows the argument of Mosco (1988:107–24), that regulation is one of a number of societal mechanisms that allocate the distribution of resources in a politically legitimate fashion. Legitimacy can come from the authority vested in state bureaucracy, from claims to authority gained through "expertise," from election, or from individual decisions of the market. Legitimacy in the first model comes through ownership or recourse to tradition in the relationship between state and industry. In the second model legitimacy is gained through the knowledge of those appointed. In the third it is gained through wide representation and in the market model through individual decisions made within a framework set by governments. To these models of legitimate distributive mechanisms we can add that of industry self-regulation, which has a long history in Britain. In addition, legitimacy gained through the institutional "independence" or "neutrality" of the agencies of regulation from overt political interests (which has a long history in the United States and a much shorter one in Britain), and which Mosco places in the category of legitimacy through expertise, is now of increasing salience. This book demonstrates that, at different times, governments have used different "mixes" of these policy mechanisms in the communications sector, with a predisposition to public ownership and self-regulation in Britain, to public ownership or state financing of private companies in France and Germany, to institutionally independent regulation by experts (whose appointment may be vetoed by the industry), supplemented by judicial review, in the United States.

Both Mosco and Horowitz (1989) suggest that establishing agencies for regulating industry allows only a narrow set of industrial interests to be represented in policy making. Although justified as in the "public interest," these agencies must gain the consent of the corporate interests to be regulated. Any form of regulation, whether national or international, must gain the consent of the governed, so that, as early as the 1870s, corporations were allowed into the debates of the International Telegraph Union. In contrast, the Marconi company was excluded, with the result that its hostility led to failed regulation until both the company and the British government agreed to compromise. Regulatory bodies, whether national or international, indulge in a form of microcorporatism in order to operate their divisions of the market and distribute resources, and their public legitimacy is thereby at risk through regulatory capture. Governments often establish regulatory reforms, both national and international, that are made in the interests of big business but are presented as in the "public interest" (Lindblom 1977:191).

The increased use of regulation as a political mechanism since the 1980s has made it evident that, in order to retain legitimacy, domestic regulatory agencies require wider representation of interests than do industrial customers. Where regulators are not elected, consumer representation at a formal level and informal consultations with consumer bodies have become essential tools at the national level and at the level of the European Union but are only slowly being incorporated at the international level. In the late 1990s the internationalization of communications and its decreasing cost fostered the growth of international lobbies and consumer boycotts, either to influence such regulation or to take its place in altering the behavior of companies. These protests, which echoed those of the 1930s, may be directly attributable to the undue influence of industrial interests in formulating an international regime or may constitute the citizen's answer to unaccountable "self-regulation" by industry.

At the same time, in what can be seen as a contrary move away from "accountable" regulation, there has been a demand through the WTO agreement on telecommunications for "independent" agencies of regulation. Originally proposed as a means to prevent a conflict of interest between the state as producer and its role as a regulator of potential competitors, the model has been imbued with the idea of independence from political influence, thereby assuming lack of accountability. The historical analysis presented here delineates the problems created for those companies, which the British Post Office, as operator and regulator, considered to be its competition. The analysis also shows how the independent federal agencies of the United States, lacking sufficient congressional backing or regulatory power, found it difficult to control communications companies. But the current move goes hand in hand with an attempt to portray regulation as a matter of implementing fixed rules worldwide, rather than as part of the domestic policy-making process of individual countries and therefore subject to social and cultural differences (Hills 1998a). Such attempts to constrain national governments in the type of institutions used for regulation and to set standardized rules is another illustration of the increasing importance of international regimes in the regulation of liberalized markets and their permeation of national markets. Increased international standardization of the mechanisms of nation-state control is the flip side of liberalization and distribution through the world market. Yet experience with such detailed standardized regulations for the telegraph in the nineteenth century led to its rejection in the case of the telephone. National governments wanted flexibility more than they wanted standardization.

Today, as we move away from the concept of the distributing state that controls resources and toward that of the regulating state, where private entities provide essential services, such as communications, we also move nearer to the situation of the nineteenth century. Just as, in a free global market for communications in the nineteenth century, corporations used their control of patents and of interconnection to form cartels in order to divide up world market share, today for the same reasons proprietary standards are replacing international open standards, and "strategic alliances" take the place of the "pooling" of the nineteenth and early twentieth centuries. Just as the governments of the nineteenth and early twentieth century found that they had difficulty controlling the cartelization of world markets by corporations—both domestic and foreign—today the liberalization of world markets has brought about the need to strengthen national regulation and for states to cooperate in regulating worldwide ownership.

And just as today, in the nineteenth and early twentieth century the up-front capital costs of transmission produced incentives to reduce unit costs by establishing as wide a market with as little regulation as possible. Similar incentives saw dominant operators use interconnection barriers to prevent competition. And then, as now, the economics of creation and distribution of information produced incentives for the convergence of content ownership and transmission. Bottlenecks in competitive supply could be created, both then and now, by vertical concentration of manufacturing and transmission or of content creation and distribution. Calls for an "open door" in foreign markets could mask mercantilism at home. And in the broadcast market, financial incentives within poorer countries could lead to restructuring and the relaying of foreign-produced material.

From a security perspective, although international communications in the nineteenth century were seen to benefit the British, the free flow of world-wide communications was perceived as a threat to national security. Information became a product when it was first transmitted, and as with e-mail and the Internet today, and with the telegraph in the nineteenth century, government monitoring and censorship attempted to control the flow. Much of the British government's concern in the period covered by this book involved security of communications within the empire. Economic liberalism vied with state control in a way that has been replicated since the 1980s. Particularly during wartime, the U.S. government worried about the vulnerability of its messages to interception. Legislation that has repercussions today made U.S. citizenship an important prerequisite for owning U.S. communications facilities.

The British Empire—both "formal" and "informal"—is an important background feature to the Anglo-American struggle for control of communications described in this book (Gallagher and Robinson 1953).[6] The British began to assemble their empire in the sixteenth century, and it comprised not only the dominions of Canada, Australia, New Zealand, and South Africa but the colonies of India, Hong Kong, Singapore, and numerous smaller territories. Many African protectorates were added in the late nineteenth century (Fieldhouse 1965). Its "informal" (trading) empire stretched to South America, particularly Argentina, and in the Far East to China. In contrast, the United States built its empire at the end of the nineteenth century—the Philippines, Guam, Hawaii, and Cuba (Pearce 1981). The Monroe Doctrine, which the United States cited to claim hegemony over South America; the shutting out of the United States from China; and the British government's refusal to allow U.S. companies entry to the British colonies brought the two into conflict over communications in other countries. Yet to some extent that competition between the governments was mitigated by the actions of the companies themselves, which entered into cartelization agreements during the interwar period.

To sum up, this book attempts to analyze the relations within international communications' market sectors between state and state bilaterally and within international organizations; between states and domestic and foreign corporations; and between corporations and corporations until the U.S. entry into World War II. But because the book spans almost one hundred years of Anglo-American communications, inevitably it is not comprehensive. For those interested, much more research remains.

Chapter Outline

The story told here begins in the nineteenth century, just after the repeal of the Corn Laws in Britain. A virtual British monopoly of submarine cable technology was fed by the ready supply of the insulating material—gutta-percha—from Southeast Asian plantations, by control of patents, by London financiers, and by the British control of islands around the globe. The monopoly created both political and commercial advantage. In turn, domination of world information gathering by the British news agency Reuters skewed the content of that news to British interests. U.S. responses were first to back Anglo-American transatlantic cable ventures, then to back efforts to ring the globe with telegraph cable via a Pacific route, then to attempt to reduce transatlantic tariffs by competition and to keep open through the concept of "reciprocity" the potential for U.S. companies to enter European markets. In contrast to the British, the U.S. government had little strategic concern, and private U.S. capital evinced little interest—it had far less risky opportunities for investment.

Chapter 1 also documents the beginnings of international regulation. Colonial voting (one vote for each colony) meant that the Europeans could dominate the International Telegraph Union.[7] The first regulations, designed to cartelize world submarine cable communications under national government control, were based on the existing British model of state telegraph ownership, with tariffs giving a press discount and the exclusion of "leased" lines.

Chapter 2 is concerned with the growth of security-related communications in Britain from the 1890s to World War I. These were the years when mercantilist relations became prevalent, when state-financed manufacturing and operating companies were developed in France and Germany. British companies were subsidized by the state to "follow the flag" and lay uneconomical lines to colonial outposts. The British government developed for the first time a form of domestic regulation, following that already used in the United States,which was based on control of landing rights. Free trade came into conflict with security considerations until British officials recognized that allowing London to develop as a hub for submarine cables offered security advantages.

The transiting of transatlantic cables through Britain gave the government the opportunity from the Boer War on to intercept and censor messages from the United States, a practice that continued until the 1960s. U.S. telegraph companies that had entered Britain in the 1880s came under regulation by landing license only in the 1900s, and there was no hint of demands for reciprocity when the U.S. companies prevented British companies from entering the American market. But these were also the years when the British government became frightened at its dependence on its private companies. The building of an "All-Red" Pacific cable by the British, Australian, and Canadian governments is a story of intercolonial relations, defense interests, and a means of regulating through competition a monopoly that could not be regulated otherwise.

Chapter 3 documents the similar time span within the policy of the United States. Its dependence on the British was driven home in its war with Spain, when the United States suddenly found that it had no American-owned cables to Cuba and no means of communicating from the Philippines. Its introduction of censorship on material transmitted during this war provided the precedent for the British government's introduction of censorship in the Boer War. The United States developed its landing rights policy in an attempt to unilaterally liberalize the markets of other countries. These were years of fierce anti-British feeling. But when faced with the realization that any Pacific cable had to interconnect with British-owned cables, the U.S. government allowed the interconnection, pretended that the cable was American owned, and hid the truth from the public until the Commercial Pacific Cable Company inadvertently revealed it in the 1920s.[8]

Chapter 4 looks at the competition at the turn of the century that moved into maritime radio and telegraph transmission by radio. In both the United States and Britain the navy was crucially important in introducing and developing the technology. But despite Admiralty backing, the British failed to support the global monopoly developed by the British Marconi's Wireless Telegraph Company and only belatedly backed the imperial wireless chain early in the twentieth century. The Americans and Germans set out to limit a potential British monopoly, first by international regulation and then, in the German case, by state support of the industry. The U.S. government, impatient with the failure of international regulation, proceeded to unilaterally impose domestic regulation on all foreign shipping. Later the United States used ownership restrictions, first designed for security purposes, to restrict foreign ownership of radio installations.

Chapter 5 documents competition in both infrastructure and content within South America. Despite the promulgation in 1823 of the Monroe Doctrine, which claimed South America as a U.S. sphere of influence (a claim reiterated throughout the next seventy years), not until U.S. investment bankers, and particularly J. P. Morgan, were prepared to finance submarine telegraph cables down the eastern coast of the continent did U.S. companies come into competition with the "informal" empire established by the British and French over the former colonists of Spain and Portugal. In the 1890s the U.S. government became directly involved in South America because U.S. manufacturing suffered from overcapacity and needed new export markets. But South America was still very much under Portuguese, French, and British cultural domination, so the Americans did not make inroads until World War I into the cinematic film and newspaper markets of South America. And it was not until the interwar years that the United States came to dominate the infrastructure of the major South American states or to compete with the British and French news agencies.

Chapter 6 begins with the World War I peace agreements in which the Americans fared badly. Despite the opposition of the Associated Press, the peace agreements reinstated and strengthened the cartelization of the world into the spheres of influence of the French and British news agencies. The introduction of long-wave radiotelegraphs gave U.S. companies a way to bypass the British cables. The U.S. government became increasingly mercantilist, nationalizing Marconi's U.S. assets and helping General Electric to acquire them through the company that GE formed for that purpose, the Radio Corporation of America. Private U.S. companies subsequently dominated the International Radiotelegraphic Union's conferences on the allocation of the radio spectrum.

During this period the U.S. government used another extension of cable landing rights to try to unilaterally impose liberalization of markets on U.S. companies. Although the U.S. government broke the British monopoly of cable communications in Brazil, its attempts to impose free trade on U.S.

companies were defeated by the companies' strategy of cartelization with foreign companies. During these interwar years the International Telephone and Telegraph Company (ITT) rose to control much of the domestic and international communications infrastructure of South America and Europe. The British perceived ITT as the tool of a U.S. government that was seeking a global monopoly of communications, whereas in reality Americans distrusted ITT because of its foreign ownership.[9]

Chapter 7 documents the way in which Marconi's radio transmission affected the markets of the British international cable combine and news agencies. In particular, the introduction of shortwave radio in the 1920s, with capital costs lower than submarine cable's, altered the economics of long-distance transmission. Shortwave radio also threatened the centralized control of communications in the British Empire, in which cables all led to London. The threat led to the British government's decision to protect the cables for strategic reasons and to the amalgamation of the Marconi radio-based company with the Eastern cable company to the detriment of radio. The communications company later known as the Cable and Wireless Ltd. was born, centralizing intraempire communications once more and allowing the Reuters news agency cartel to survive until 1930.

Chapter 8 looks at film and broadcasting in these interwar years. This period saw U.S. companies gradually dominating broadcast radio markets in the white dominions of the British Empire and penetration into Europe of both U.S. manufacturing companies and exports of films. Increasingly, during these interwar years the Anglo-American struggle moved from control of infrastructure to control of cultural commodities and how films represented U.S. culture and that of other nationalities. By virtue of its large home market and control of distribution in Europe, Hollywood came to dominate the interwar European markets. The British in particular saw Hollywood as undermining the culture that held the empire together and instituted quotas and protectionism. But attempts to regulate the sometimes offensive content of U.S. movies through the League of Nations failed for lack of cooperation from the companies and their government. Neither were bilateral action and market boycotts successful against Hollywood, which by the 1930s had become a global enterprise. Only eventual fear of national regulation had any effect.

Shortwave radio was to prove the means for external broadcasting. U.S. companies began broadcasting to South America on a commercial basis, while the British Broadcasting Corporation (BBC) inaugurated the state-financed World Service to bring radio to expatriates in colonial outposts. The possibility of long-range broadcasting also attracted the attention of other states and produced a massive expansion in the 1930s of state-based propaganda broadcasting. In response, the BBC began broadcasting in foreign languages, while the U.S. government orchestrated propaganda beamed at South America by U.S. companies because of the need to retain South American neutrality. The U.S. government's control of the advertising base of South American media would have the most long-lasting influence on the media organization and programming format of South American radio and, later, television.

The book ends with World War II, which proved to be a watershed in the struggle for control of international communications. The book demonstrates that the years when private companies dominated international communications were not regulation free. International regimes of regulation affected national markets, and domestic market relations affected international regimes. To a large extent the British government saw commercial gains from its companies' domination of international communications as secondary to their security implications. Much of the Anglo-British struggle for control took place on different planes. The Americans wanted commercial control, the British wanted influence and security. But after World War II the Americans dominated those communications, and the British struggled to retain markets and influence. That later period is the basis of another story.

1. Infrastructure and Information in the United States and Britain, 1840s–1890

This chapter starts with the introduction of the telegraph into the domestic economies of Britain, the European continent, and the United States. The expansion into international communications then came about largely as a result of domestic factors. At a time when it took three weeks for a letter to cross the Atlantic and six months to reach Australia, the desire for fast communications was such that, even in a free-trade era, governments were prepared to offset the risk to those entrepreneurs prepared to undertake the engineering feat of laying and operating submarine telegraph lines. Behind this public-private cooperation lay a demand for international links with major trading partners and colonial dependencies, as well as a desire to control international communications. Commercial and strategic interests joined to push the technology; by 1890, when this chapter ends, the infrastructure of the international submarine cable network had been laid, and Reuters, the British news agency, dominated economic and political news.

Throughout the period, however, tension between the international companies and their own, and other, governments was apparent. Governments attempted to regulate the companies' domestic and foreign activities and to gain ascendancy through national and international regulation. Often modeled on railway regulation, those domestic regulatory attempts were limited by the administrative capacity of governments, the financial interests of parliamentarians, and, in the case of Britain, free-trade ideology. Whereas Britain solved its domestic regulatory problems by following Continental tradition and nationalizing the telegraphs, it relied on multilateral international regulation to control international cables. In contrast, the Americans allowed a private monopoly at home but used cable landing licenses to unilaterally open up the international market, allowing cartels only where they favored domestic U.S. companies.

Domestic Development of the Telegraph in Britain

The England into which the telegraph was introduced in the late 1830s was primarily agricultural. Although the first Reform Act of 1832 had given the vote to some male property owners, hereditary peers and landed gentry still dominated the government. Manufacturing was largely based on Midlands iron and northern cotton, and there was little communication between northern and southern England (Scott 1958:18).

In fact, because the new technology was in competition with the postal services, reorganized in 1830 by Sir Roland Hill to offer a one-penny post for overnight delivery, the telegraph's widespread development under private ownership in Britain did not begin until 1843. Then its financing relied heavily on single-track railway systems and their need for signaling (Scott 1958:28). In contrast to the distance-related tariffs of private telegraph ownership, the penny post uniform tariff for any distance subsequently provided a model that linked state ownership with low uniform tariffs in the public mind.[1]

Even with the invention in its infancy, there were indications of the ideological struggle to come, between those who considered that the telegraphs should be run by the state and those who argued that private enterprise should be free to exploit the new technology (Kieve 1973:76). Although affected by voting reform that gave the growing middle class a political voice, and by political struggles to regulate the expanding railways, the concept of private property was sacrosanct in the Britain of the 1840s. Because any retrospective restriction on profits was considered an infringement of private property rights, such regulation was difficult to implement.[2] The private financial interests of members of Parliament further hampered parliamentary regulation. Large up-front fixed costs, if not as large as the railways', created similar pressures on competitive telegraph lines to form cartels to keep tariffs high. By the late 1850s the Electric and International Telegraph Company and the British and Irish Magnetic Telegraph Company had established a domestic cartel.[3]

By setting up an "intelligence service" to supply news reports to the provincial press, the Electric and International Telegraph Company attempted to convert its dominance of infrastructure into dominance over the information content transmitted. But because the service collected most of its information from the London press, the provincial papers were a day late with the news (Storey 1951:29). Although the owners of provincial papers set up their own press agency, the Press Association, they could not evade high transmission tariffs (Kieve 1973:71–72). By the 1860s demand for nationalization came from within the government bureaucracy, from chambers of commerce, and from the press.

Despite the importance of manufactured exports to its economy—cotton goods accounted for 30 percent of exports—by the mid-nineteenth century much of Britain's wealth already rested in its service and financial sectors (Foreman-Peck 1995:22–23). The financial reward available through the international linkage of stock and commodity exchanges was what would provide a major impetus to submarine cable technology. As early as 1840, Charles Wheatstone, who had patented an early telegraph with William Cooke in 1837, proposed to a House of Commons committee that England and France could be linked by telegraph across the Straits of Dover. But lack of a suitable insulation for the wire core meant that it would be ten years before that link could become reality (Scott 1958:26). By then the liberalization of agriculture following the Corn Law of 1846 had increased imports of wheat (mainly from France), making wheat importation second only to imports of raw cotton (mainly from the United States), and brought growing interest in the price of commodities.

The necessary insulating material was found in gutta-percha, a substance extracted from tropical trees in Malaysia and first used by Walter Siemens to insulate telegraph cables for the Prussian army to carry signals across the Rhine. Following this 1847 success, the German telegraph manufacturing company Siemens & Halske was established (Scott 1958:24). However, in 1848 British inventors claimed the extrusion patent for gutta-percha (Kieve 1973: 102). By 1861 Britain was importing more than one thousand tons from Malaysia each year (Lawford and Nicholson 1950:54). Control of the raw material and its extrusion patent, and lack of an alternative insulating material, created British hegemony of submarine cable manufacture.

By the 1860s four companies, all based in London, were manufacturing cables.[4] Exports of wires and apparatus rapidly expanded, so that in 1873 the total value comprised about 1 percent of British manufactured exports (Kieve 1973:117–18). Established from existing companies in 1864, and chaired by John Pender, the Telegraph Construction and Maintenance Company (Telcon) gained its dominant position by becoming the cable supplier to Pender's operating companies (collectively referred to here as the Eastern). In 1897, of the 165,000 nautical miles of submarine cable laid, 120,000 had been manufactured and laid by Telcon, including nine Atlantic cables. Its major competitor, Siemens & Halske, had laid seven Atlantic cables (Bright 1898a:154). Restructured in 1865 as the Anglo-German Siemens Brothers, from then until the early twentieth century this British-based company acted as the cable manufacturer, layer, and operator for those companies and governments wanting to compete with Telcon and the Eastern's cables (Scott 1958:51–53).[5]

Cable covered in gutta-percha had to be submerged in water to prevent deterioration of the insulation and therefore required that ships laying long lengths have large holds. In addition, sailing ships were not suitable for laying cable in straight lines for long stretches. The introduction of iron-hulled steamships by Isambard Kingdom Brunel was therefore crucial to the subsequent British hegemony of cable laying. In 1858 Brunel launched the *Great Eastern,* designed for the England-Australia run around the Cape of Good Hope. At first called the *Leviathan* because of its size, and made redundant by the opening of the Suez Canal, this ship was later to carry the successful transatlantic cable of 1866. The third important element in that hegemony was the availability of capital through the Joint Stock Company Registration and Regulation Act of 1844, which was extended to all enterprises in 1856 and 1862. It allowed entrepreneurial engineers to raise money from the public for submarine cable ventures, with each cable constituted as a company.

As early as 1845 the brothers Jacob and John Watkins Brett registered the General Oceanic Telegraph Company, the first company set up to provide "telegraphic communication from the British Islands across the Atlantic Ocean to Nova Scotia and Canada and [establish] electric communication by land and sea with the colonies." By 1851 they had already made a first unsuccessful attempt at a cross-channel cable (Garratt 1950:9). That year, a representative of Lord Palmerston, the British foreign secretary, attended the first meeting on international regulation of the telegraph that was called by Napoleon III of France. Faced with a Continental system in which the state owned the telegraphs, Palmerston is said to have threatened that, if the Bretts' second attempt were to fail, he was considering a government-owned cable across the Straits of Dover as well as laying government-owned cables to India and China (Barty-King 1979:xv).

In any event, the Bretts' second attempt in 1851, aided by the finance and design skills of Russell Crampton, a railway engineer, and by the loan of an Admiralty vessel, was successful. Horseback riders completed interconnection with the local end of the British domestic telegraph system several miles away (Lawford and Nicholson 1950:38–40). The commercial effect was immediate. "For the first time the prices of securities in Paris were known to the London Stock Exchange on the same day and within business hours" (Kieve 1973:51).

Two additional cross-channel cables, to Holland with its commercial centers of Rotterdam and Amsterdam, were laid before the engineers Charles

Tilston Bright and Edward Whitehouse succeeded in linking the cross-channel cables with the domestic telegraph from London to Manchester in 1856. By transmitting a signal over two thousand miles, they proved that transatlantic communications were possible. By 1857 the Bretts' company had established direct telegraph communications with Holland, Germany, Austria, and St. Petersburg, Russia (Kieve 1973:105). Exclusive concessions on Continental traffic had already increased the profitability of domestic telegraph companies. The Electric owned cables to Ireland and Holland and ran domestic cables in Holland. The Magnetic owned cables to Ireland and had exclusive concessions on Continental traffic carried by the Bretts' company, including a virtual monopoly on Scandinavian traffic (Kieve 1973:89).

During this period the French, Spanish, Italian, and Portuguese governments all used British-manufactured submarine cable and British engineers to lay lines to their colonies. In the mid-1850s, using Lisbon as a hub, British engineers began to lay cables successfully in the deepwater—1,600 to 1,800 fathoms—of the Mediterranean, thereby gaining the expertise necessary for long-distance submarine cables.

Before the development of specific cable-laying ships, naval vessels actually laid the cables. The British and U.S. navies also played an important role in charting oceanic waters, necessary in order to locate sudden chasms in the ocean floor that could snap the cable. Naval involvement also reflected an element of strategic concern. The Bretts marketed their new company to the prime minister, Sir Robert Peel, as offering the advantage of "immediate communication of government orders . . . to all parts of the Empire" (Garratt 1950:8). And Palmerston saw the strategic value of international cables "in affording the power of early explanation with foreign governments, on occasions when misunderstandings may have arisen" and in "the rapid conveyance of intelligence of a political and military nature from China and from our Indian and other possessions."[6]

Security considerations provided the occasion for using public-private finance initiatives to lay cable on behalf of defense interests, for example, the financing for one of the first lines between the Admiralty in London and the naval base at Portsmouth (Kieve 1973:37–38). In 1854, after the British and French governments declared war on the Russians, the British and French had the first government-owned international cable laid to the Crimea. The cable allowed the first direct contact between commanders in the field and politicians (Standage 1999:146). The Crimean War was also the first war to be covered by journalists using cable to send reports back quickly. Press criticism of British generals and the perception that the Russians gained an advantage from reading British news reports later contributed to the direct censorship of news reports during the Boer War (Hudson and Stanier 1997:19; United Kingdom 2000:3–4).

Eventually, the British government succumbed to commercial pressure and in 1869 nationalized the domestic, Irish, Channel Island, and cross-channel cables. The government paid £11 million (*$71.3 million) for the private telegraph cables, not the £2.5 million ($16.6 million) it expected. The nationalization released something like £8 million ($52 million) in private capital to be invested in submarine cables (Bright and Bright 1898:162). After the nationalization the government introduced uniform telegraph tariffs, and allowed the press substantial discounts as well as to rent lines overnight (Kieve 1973:72). These concessions to the newspapers were to cause the domestic telegraph to register annual losses until the 1920s and to bias the Treasury against further nationalization.

The model of the British telegraph nationalization was to influence the first attempts to regulate international telegraphs. The British legislation regarded "rented lines"—what we know today as "leased lines," for which companies pay an annual charge rather than a message-based tariff—as being outside the "public" network. Thus rented lines were subsequently excluded from international regulation if two states that were members of the International Telegraph Union (ITU) wished to reach such agreement. In addition, press discounts and the obligatory rental of leased lines to the press became a feature of the European agreement on tariffs, made in 1875, features that would contribute to the dominance of European press agencies. Also, the 1869 nationalization legislation did not include "oceanic" (long-distance submarine) cables. This omission, later explained as necessary because only nongovernment-owned cables would be given foreign concessions, allowed private ownership to flourish. To give the public wider access to telegraphy, the Post Office agreed to collect overseas telegrams at its offices on behalf of the cable companies. It was also important to later domestic regulatory attempts that, faced with opposition to the nationalization act from the transatlantic cable companies (Atlantic Telegraph and Anglo-American Telegraph), the Post Office agreed to continue the practice, begun in 1868, of using British-owned cable to send any telegram that entered the system with no specification of the company to be used.

At first no licenses were required to land a cable, but cable companies did need permission from the Commission of Woods and Forests. This commission was responsible from 1866 for all Crown rights to the shore and seabed. It was not obliged to consult other departments and seems not to have done

---

* All amounts for dollars and cents are in U.S. currency. Conversions are based on exchange rates provided by Economic History Services, <http://eh.net/hmit>, Feb. 28, 2002.

so, although the Board of Trade also had the power to license.[7] In fact, after it took over the cross-channel submarine cables in 1869, the Post Office paid a remittance for certain of its licenses to the commission.

The British landing-license procedure became codified only after signing the international agreements of 1875 and after an increase in the administrative capacity of the central government. Although the Anglo-American Telegraph Company's transatlantic cables were laid in 1866 and 1867, those cables and those of 1873 and 1874 were licensed retrospectively by the Board of Trade only in 1880.[8] From 1880 until 1899 cable landing licensing was the responsibility of the Board of Trade on the advice of the Post Office.

During this period the British concept of free trade prevailed, with nonexclusive landing licenses given for thirty years on any particular route. Elsewhere, the norm was for a company to seek a twenty- or thirty-year monopoly concession that might include payment to or from the destination government. Because British companies were often first in the field, they gained what economists now call "first mover advantages" from these concessions, enabling them to lock out potential competitors.

Omission of leased wires from the British telegraph nationalization created a favored position for privately run business-to-business communications that enabled new technologies to evade the Post Office monopoly.[9] Under this exemption the American Alexander Bell was first able to introduce the telephone in 1878 in the London financial district. In contrast to other European countries, where both technologies were state run, in Britain private telephone companies at first competed with the Post Office's domestic telegraph service.

To regulate these private telephone companies and to limit competition with the Post Office telegraphs, in 1882 the Treasury introduced licenses to constrain the introduction of telephony into local areas and to prevent the interconnection of private telephone lines with either the Post Office's telegraph lines or long-distance telegraph services. In addition, to keep the companies in check, the Treasury allowed the Post Office itself to establish a limited telephone service. Using a method that later became a model for regulation, the British government used competition from its Post Office to control potential private monopolies.

The licensing of telephone companies developed from a model of exclusive monopolies granted to certain companies to operate "wharves or ferry boats." These had been licensed on the basis of the concept of "common carrier," which later was extended to include those companies "affected with a public interest" (Hoida 1997:13). In addition to permitting a specific service, the licenses were intended to prevent the discriminatory treatment of third parties, but, as with the railways, "discrimination" was often difficult to prove.

Local licenses, issued for twenty-five years but subject to buy-back before that date, coupled with the threat of Post Office competition, became the primary means of regulating domestic telephone companies.[10] But lobbying by the press and chambers of commerce succeeded in engendering a liberalization of government regulation; in 1884 private companies were allowed to provide long-distance lines. This liberalization in turn led both to direct price competition with the Post Office's long-distance telegraph and, in 1889, despite government opposition, to amalgamation of the companies into the National Telephone Company.

Again, the Post Office was able to delay the effect of competition through its control of interconnection. A business renting a telephone line from the private company could not call an overseas telegram in to its local Post Office, whereas those renting a telephone line from the Post Office could do so (Kieve 1973:211–12; Hills 1993b:192). Therefore, despite the hegemony that British companies had achieved over the manufacture and laying of submarine cables by 1890, the Treasury prevented the complete integration of international and domestic communications and thereby decreased the efficiency of business. This lack of integration was the opposite of the situation in the United States.

Domestic Development of the Telegraph in the United States

The original public funding of the telegraphs in the United States contrasted with their private development in Britain. First, under article 1, section 8, of the Constitution, which gave Congress the power "to establish Post Offices and post Roads," in 1843 it appropriated $30,000 to Samuel Morse to test the practicality of a line between Washington, D.C., and Baltimore and then gave him $8,000 for a further experiment directed by the postmaster general. However, after Congress made an unsuccessful attempt to charge for use of the line, it allowed private companies to develop the telegraph (Standage 1999:55; Clark 1931:111). The change of heart is also said to have been linked to the financial interests of a former chair of the House Commerce Committee, F. O. J. Smith of Maine, who had become a director of Morse's company (Luther 1988:13; Standage 1999:106).

Unlike Britain, the United States had a predominantly local press, and it played a rather small part in the initial domestic development of the telegraph. Nevertheless, particularly during the Mexican War of 1846–48, the demand for news stimulated public awareness of the value of the telegraph

(Du Boff 1984:60). Also in contrast to Britain, the telegraph preceded the railway by several years in many parts of the United States (Du Boff 1982:254–55).

Unfettered competition led to more than fifty separate telegraph companies by 1851, not only creating problems of interconnection but leading to financial loss, mergers, and cartelization. After the 1850s the Mississippi Valley Company, which later became Western Union, began to use railroad companies to construct telegraph lines as they laid their tracks, thereby evading up-front costs of construction and allowing the company to undercut its competition and take over its rivals' lines. In 1869 William Orton, president of Western Union, defended his company's monopoly by saying, " 'Messages under this system [*of competition*] required copying and retransmission at the termini of each local line, and this process not only occupied time but was frequently the cause of errors, which rendered the service of little value' " (quoted in Du Boff 1984:57; emphasis added). As in Britain, unfettered competition led to consolidation and monopoly.

This was a period of westward expansion, and Congress was prepared to grant subsidies for the telegraph to open new frontiers. In 1860 it passed the Pacific Telegraph Act, which granted an annual subsidy of $40,000 to Hiram Sibley, a director of Western Union, to build a line from the East Coast to the Pacific (Brock 1982:81). And in the same year Jeptha Wade, later to be president of Western Union, received a $100,000 subsidy to link his California State Telegraph Company with the Western Union transcontinental line (Du Boff 1984:61). But in developing its monopoly, Western Union faced competition from the eastern seaboard.

That competition came from Cyrus Field, a paper magnate. Field was approached by F. N. Gisborne, a British engineer working in Canada who needed money to complete a landline telegraph across Newfoundland and who had a concession to lay a transatlantic cable from there. Field first envisaged linking Newfoundland to New York by submarine telegraph, which would shorten the transmission of news reports from Europe by five days (Du Boff 1982:258). After completing the New York–Newfoundland link in 1854, Field transformed his vision into a transatlantic cable that he could use to build up his newly formed domestic company, the American Telegraph Company.[11]

Field made his first attempt to lay a transatlantic cable in 1857 but did not succeed until 1866. Meanwhile, the American Civil War raised the telegraph's profile, and those companies, such as Western Union, that were on the side of the Union, prospered. In addition, until 1868 Western Union's general manager also served as chief of the U.S. military telegraph, in which capacity he oversaw the construction of fifteen thousand miles of wire. Not surprisingly, the company subsequently received ownership of those military lines. In contrast, Field's American Telegraph Company, its lines between North and South severed, was weakened by the war. The international telegraph was therefore crucial to the survival of Field's company.

The Transatlantic Telegraphs

By the mid-nineteenth century the United States was Britain's most important trading partner (with about £60 million, or $292.2 million, in annual trade) and together with India accounted for most of Britain's estimated annual foreign investment of £22 million ($107 million) (Foreman-Peck 1995:24). Britain in turn received about 75 percent of U.S. exports. That the first transatlantic cable routes ran from Ireland to Canada, not to the United States, did not reflect Canada's commercial importance but owed to matters of technology and geography. Because underwater repeaters to strengthen the signal had not been invented, telegraph signals sent more than twenty-five hundred miles by submarine cable suffered severe attenuation. The longer the distance, the slower the speed of transmission. The distance between Canada and Ireland or western England was about nineteen hundred nautical miles, whereas that between Cape Cod and Brest, France, was 3,175 nautical miles (Schreiner 1924:195). In addition, in 1853 the U.S. Navy had found a suboceanic shelf that runs from Ireland to Canada on which the cable could be laid; as a result the then fragmented territory of Canada became crucial for landing the cable.

However, Canada was also a British colony, with (somewhat unpopular) claims on British defense. In view of the British government's continued perception of threat from the United States and concomitant stationing of an albeit reduced number of British troops there, a cable from Britain to Canada also held strategic benefit (Sternbridge 1982:110). The first attempt to raise money in 1856 was made by Cyrus Field, working with the British consulting engineers Jacob Brett and Charles Tilston Bright (Garratt 1950:14).

Because most U.S. investors were putting their money into railways, Field found himself able to raise only $132,570 of the required $1.72 million in the United States (Garratt 1950:15). Field therefore contributed $432,000 himself; J. W. Brett subscribed $58,900, and "it was the merchants of Liverpool, Manchester, Glasgow, London and other British cities who only too willingly took the rest" (Lawford and Nicholson 1950:46). One of these "merchants" was John Pender, a director of the Magnetic and later chairman of Telcon, who became a director of Field's newly formed Atlantic Telegraph Company. According to Barty-King, "both British and U.S. governments agreed to pay the Atlantic a subsidy of £14000 [$68,740] a year up to the time when its dividend had reached 6 per cent, and £10,000 [$491,000] a year subsequently" (1979:12). Each government also loaned the company a warship for cable laying. In effect, the governments acted as guarantors and facilitators.

The first attempt in 1857 failed when the cable broke. Later the design, manufacture, and handling of the cable were all blamed for its failure (Joint Committee 1861). Although the cable broke again on the second attempt in June 1858, a further attempt in August 1858 was successful, and U.S. President James Buchanan and Queen Victoria exchanged messages. The cable worked for only a day or so and is said to have carried 730 messages at a cost of $1,256,250 (Johnson 1903:47). Both governments faced considerable losses.

The British government was said to have used the cable to tell troops to stay in Canada instead of leaving to quell the Indian Mutiny and therefore saved some money, but much of the U.S. press regarded the supposed success of the cable as a hoax (Kieve 1973:109). Editors argued that the Associated Press, the cooperative news agency that had negotiated a monopoly to bring foreign news via the cable, had actually produced no evidence that the cable had worked and had colluded with Field (Blondheim 1994:110–13). This suspicion of swindle or hoax permeated the midcentury speculative atmosphere surrounding submarine cables (Scott 1958:34). This cable's failure spurred the U.S. government to support a land-based alternative across the Bering Strait.

Cyrus Field tried to raise money for another transatlantic attempt. But money came in slowly from British investors and was nonexistent from U.S. financiers (Lawford and Nicholson 1950:51). As a result of the failure of the previous attempts, the British government appointed the Joint Committee of the Lords of the Privy Council and the Atlantic Telegraph Company in 1859 to review the whole process of submarine cable construction and maintenance. The public-private committee claimed that only 3,000 miles of the 11,364 miles of submarine cable were actually working but could see no insuperable problems to eventual success. Rather, committee members argued that the failures could have been avoided by better oceanic surveys and quality control of cable manufacture. In addition, they argued that capital had to be provided for duplicate cables and for repair and maintenance. The committee, which reported its findings in 1861, took evidence from academic and industry experts, thereby ensuring that all companies shared in the existing expertise (Joint Committee 1861).

The American Civil War (1861–65) intervened, but during that period the

British prime minister, Lord Palmerston—who was responding to representations from an American engineer, Col. T. P. Shaffner—allowed British naval surveys of a northern, primarily land-based, route across Iceland, Greenland, and the Davis Strait to Hudson Bay (Bright 1898a:365–66). Despite support from the Danish government and from Bright, neither this Grand North Atlantic Telegraph scheme nor a project described as the South Atlantic Telegraph via Brazil could attract sufficient capital (Bright 1898a:79). But the British government had also supported more detailed surveys of the transatlantic deepwater route. This information, along with improvements in cable manufacture, improved the prospect of success for a direct cable in 1864 when Field again tried to raise capital.

Field was once again unable to raise the money in the United States, and this new attempt was primarily financed by the construction company, Telcon. Telcon agreed to take shares in the new Anglo-American Telegraph Company in exchange for contributing more than half of the nearly $6 million (£600,000) required. Despite an initial refusal by the British government to subsidize this attempt, it later agreed to a guarantee of 8 percent on the principle for twenty-five years, providing that the cable worked. Two British, but no American, warships escorted the *Great Eastern* paddle steamer, then the largest ship in the world. When the cable broke in mid-Atlantic, sabotage was suspected (Lawford and Nicholson 1950:55–60).

Finally, a fifth attempt in 1866, again mostly underwritten by Telcon, was successful. In addition, despite the difficulty of the procedure, the 1865 cable was raised and spliced together. Cyrus Field received a unanimous vote of thanks from Congress, and the British participants received knighthoods and baronetcies (Garratt 1950:22). The American Telegraph Company's access to an international telegraph line made Field's domestic company a target for Western Union, with its virtual domestic monopoly, and the takeover took place in 1866 (Brock 1982:82).

The immediate effect of the transatlantic cable on newspapers was to reduce the time for transmitting a news story from Europe from at least eight days to a few hours (D. Read 1992:91). The cable also made it easier for British financiers to invest in the United States. According to Nier and Butrica, "the bulk of trans-Atlantic traffic . . . came during the short period each day when both the London and New York Stock Exchanges were open" (1988:216). The telegraph also linked commodity markets for cotton and corn in New York and Chicago with their counterparts in Liverpool (Kieve 1973:237). But tariffs were very high—$5 in gold per word from the United States and £20 ($138) for a minimum of twenty words from Britain—with no discount for the press (Anderson 1872:34).

Linkage of Domestic to International Communications

After the Atlantic cable had been laid and another located and spliced in deepwater investing in submarine telegraphy was no longer a speculative venture, and shares in the cable companies, although still risky, became more general investment vehicles. However, because few cable-mending ships were available, and separate companies owned each cable, investors in individual companies could find themselves with no dividend. To lessen the risk for investors Pender created the Globe Telegraph and Trust Company in 1873 to hold shares in all his cable companies.

The Globe was more than a unit trust to encourage small investors. Its articles of incorporation stated that it intended to bring about "'the acquisition and amalgamation in one Company of the principal lines of submarine telegraph and the landlines used in connection therewith'" and to make Telcon, the manufacturer, part of the new monopoly (quoted in Barty-King 1979:53). But because the proposed global network would also have involved sharing revenue with other companies, the Eastern's shareholders refused to countenance the strategy. Shareholders, whether those of the Eastern or of Western Union, favored minimum investment in infrastructure and little technological upgrading. They demanded dividends over market share. In the case of the Eastern, shareholders later would complain of Telcon's high charges to the operating company and the advantages these gave Telcon's shareholders, particularly Pender.

The Globe therefore remained a trust company, and Pender amalgamated his cable companies into three regional blocs covering Australia and Asia, North America, and South America (Scott 1958:56). The Eastern never achieved the absolute world monopoly that Pender envisaged.[12] Competition came from an Anglo-Danish firm, the Great Northern Telegraph Company, and from Siemens Brothers.

Great Northern was established in 1868, after the Danish-German war over Schleswig-Holstein had disrupted communications. Great Northern specialized in long-distance landline telegraphy. Although incorporated in London, its directors were primarily Danish government officials. The czar of Russia held a substantial stake in the company, and it gained added influence because the crown princesses of both Britain and Russia were Danish (Nier and Butrica 1988:219). Siemens Brothers was established in London in 1865, becoming a limited company in 1880. The Siemens brothers criticized Pender's company for its emphasis on profit, its failure to invest in research and development, and its attempts to become a world monopoly. In what became a publicly vituperative contest, where one company started service, the other set up in competition (Scott 1958:57).

It was not long before the high tariffs and the increased cost of obtaining U.S. news, which had risen from an average of £67 ($515) per month in 1865 to £424 ($2,862) per month in 1867, inspired Julius Reuter, of the British-based news agency, and Baron Émil d'Erlanger (a German banker) to try to introduce competition on the route with a French government–backed cable. Even before the French cable opened in 1869, the Anglo-American Telegraph Company reduced its tariffs in reaction to the competition (D. Read 1992:53). Demonstrating that a duopoly does not competition make, the French company first adopted that reduced tariff; then, in 1872 both companies switched to a per word rather than a message-based tariff. Finally, in 1873, to raise money to pay its war reparations to Prussia, the French sold their cable to their rival, the Anglo-American Telegraph Company (D. Read 1992:53).

By the 1870s there was already some understanding of the elasticities of demand associated with telecommunications traffic. In a classic statement of the advantages of restricting the output of a monopoly, Sir James Anderson, the managing director of the Eastern, complained: "Could the high tariff have been maintained one cable would have sufficed for the limited traffic, all the capital and working expenses of the French Atlantic Cable would have been saved and the Anglo-American [Telegraph] Company would now be enjoying twenty-seven per cent dividend upon a capital of £1,675,000 [$9.13 million], as against the ten per cent return that would be made on the reduced tariff" (1872:34). Some argued that, as had happened within the government-owned domestic systems of Belgium and Switzerland, substantially lower tariffs would result in an increase in residential traffic. But the Eastern did not accept that such elasticities of demand related to international operations, where at least 90 percent of all telegrams were commercial. It claimed that a much-reduced tariff might create demand that would require increased facilities at considerable additional cost (Anderson 1872:41). It saw minor reductions in tariffs as simply reducing revenue, and for many years it held out against reduced tariffs even at night, when the cables were not busy (Bright 1911:159).

By the end of 1873 five cables had been laid across the Atlantic, and three still worked. All ended in Canada and reached the United States by land. In direct response to Pender's Globe monopoly plans, the first cable intended to link the United States directly to Britain was laid in 1875 by Siemens Brothers for its own Direct United States Cable Company (DUS).[13] Reflecting its competition with Pender, and in order to get a U.S. landing license, a clause in its articles of association stated that "no working agreement would ever be made with Anglo-American" (Barty-King 1979:58). Unlike Pender's company, the DUS Cable Company recognized the skewed nature of traffic and reduced its tariffs to large users. Acting on behalf of the Eastern's competitors in 1879, Siemens Brothers also laid a French cable from Paris to New York that was financed by a banker, M. Pouyer Quertier, and known as the PQ cable (Scott 1958:42). Neither the DUS cable nor the PQ cable lasted long as a competitive entity.

The French cable suffered from its additional length and lower transmission rates. In contrast, Siemens Brothers' DUS Cable Company soon was causing problems for Pender's company (Scott 1958:40). In its first year its faster transmission allowed it to earn 11 percent on its capital, compared to the Eastern's 7 percent (Harcourt 1987:86). In response to the decline in the Eastern's shares, Pender bought the stock of the DUS Cable Company in 1877. He then overcame a legal effort by U.S. shareholders to prevent the takeover, liquidated DUS Cable, and formed another company of the same name under the control of the Globe Telegraph and Trust Company. Following Pender's takeover of the DUS Cable Company, the consulting engineers Alexander Muirhead and Herbert Taylor duplexed the cable (a single wire carried two messages simultaneously), doubling transmission rates to sixteen words per minute (Bright 1898a:123, 647). Pender's company then held a virtual monopoly of transatlantic traffic until 1881 when Siemens laid the first U.S.-backed transatlantic cable for Jay Gould's American Telegraph and Cable Company, followed by another in 1882. Faced with this competition in the mid-1880s, Pender agreed to pool the DUS Cable Company's resources with those of the Anglo-American Telegraph Company, the French PQ company, and Jay Gould's American Telegraph and Cable Company to create a transatlantic cartel.[14]

U.S. Policy after the Atlantic Cable

By 1866, when the first transatlantic cable was laid, Western Union had gained a virtual monopoly of U.S. domestic communications. In view of that monopoly, Congress debated the need for public ownership and in 1866 enacted legislation "to aid in the construction of telegraph lines, and to secure to the government the use of the same for postal, military and other purposes."[15] The act had a dual purpose—to aid private development of the telegraphs by allowing companies rights of access to public property and, if necessary, to allow public ownership in the future. The measure provided for the government to take over the telegraph lines at any time in the next five years (Clark 1931:112). Granting railroads and their telegraph partners the right to lay lines across public land, as well as financial subsidies from state governments in the South and in California, drove the expansion of the telegraph.

Western Union reached an agreement with the Associated Press that gave it a monopoly of transmitting news to all newspapers in the United States (Brooks 1976:62). As in Britain, transmission and information monopolies went hand in hand. But the inefficiency of the U.S. Post Office strengthened opposition to nationalization. By legal and illegal means, including the bribery of legislators, Western Union managed to kill any initiative that might deliver low prices and thereby allow the public to use the telegraph for social purposes. It also fought off individual state initiatives that attempted to exclude Western Union from local markets (Du Boff 1984:64).

In the view of Western Union, the U.S. government could support the private telegraph industry with subsidies but might not operate it. Despite anti–Western Union agitation, especially when it was thought to have held up transmission of the results of the presidential election in 1884, no House or Senate committee reported out a bill to nationalize the service (Josephson 1934:212; Du Boff 1984:59). But Western Union's tactics and the debate about nationalization that they engendered gave rise to arguments in the press that are still heard today: that government is bureaucratic and inefficient; tax monies should not be used to finance services that private industry could provide; regulation of such an industry should be left to the states; government ownership of such means of communication is "'communistic'" (quoted in Du Boff 1984:60).

Many of the new telegraph companies established in the 1870s and 1880s fell victim to interconnection disputes. Thanks to the financial panic of 1884, Western Union soon had only two minor domestic competitors, the Postal Telegraph and the Domestic Telegraph companies. However, by that time the telephone was beginning to compete with the domestic telegraph.

Alexander Graham Bell patented his telephone, or that of the Italian inventor Antonio Meucci, in 1876, just ahead of Elisha Gray's application for a patent. Sometime during 1876–77 William Orton of Western Union refused to buy Bell's patents, and Bell and his father-in-law, Gardiner Hubbard, formed the Bell Telephone Company as a voluntary unincorporated association in July 1877 (Brooks 1976:55). The company began renting, rather than selling, telephones to customers. Then Western Union, concerned at the potential threat to its local traffic, used Gray's technology and the inventive genius of Thomas Edison to set up the American Speaking Telephone Company, thereby infringing on Bell's patents (Brooks 1976:62).

Meanwhile, Western Union, which was controlled by William H. Vanderbilt, was fighting a takeover bid from Jay Gould, the railway magnate. The Bell Telephone Company, facing a cash flow crisis, was reorganized into two entities in 1878: the New England Telephone Company, which was responsible for franchising the rights to Bell's technology, and a new Bell Telephone Company. At the same time the Bell Telephone Company brought in Theodore Vail as general manager, and under his direction the company sued Western Union for patent infringement. Given its nationwide presence, Western Union had been able to install more telephone exchanges than Bell's company. But faced with a two-pronged battle, Western Union settled with Bell in an attempt to foil Gould. It gave up all its patents and facilities in the telephone business to Bell's company in 1879 in return for 20 percent of the rental receipts during the seventeen-year life of Bell's patents (Brooks 1976:71).

But the telephone could transmit only locally, so that even after Bell had bought out the Western Union telephone interests, the telephone company had to rely on telegraph for long-distance transmission (Hoida 1997:35; Herring and Gross 1936:46–47). The agreement between the two companies therefore ensured that all telegrams transmitted by Bell's telephone went via Western Union lines, and, because telegrams could now be delivered by telephone, Western Union's costs of delivery dropped. But in his fight to take over Western Union, Gould used international traffic.

Reflecting the growth in political concern for European export markets during the depression of 1873–78, the increased demand for transatlantic communications, and the crucial importance of the transatlantic traffic to domestic dominance, Jay Gould followed Field's example of the 1850s. He "used international telegraphic arrangements purely as a weapon in battles in the American stock market designed to press Western Union, and then to take it over" (Nier and Butrica 1988:219). There were two aspects to dominance—interconnection between the transatlantic cables and the domestic U.S. telegraph system, and access to the Canadian landlines bringing the traffic down to the United States.

At this time Western Union had an exclusive working agreement with the Great North-Western Telegraph Company of Canada, which controlled the lines of the Montreal Telegraph Company and those of the Dominion Telegraph Company to the west of the province of New Brunswick. Anglo-American Telegraph (Pender's company) also had an operating agreement with Montreal Telegraph. The American Union Company, a small domestic company, had an operating agreement with the Dominion Telegraph Company (Herring and Gross 1936:22).

Gould, together with Siemens Brothers, financed two submarine cables in

1881 and 1882 through his American Telegraph and Cable Company. Gould had already established a rival domestic telegraph company, the Atlantic and Pacific Company, which leased the lines of the Franklin Telegraph Company. Franklin, in turn, had an interconnection agreement with Pender's DUS Cable Company (Herring and Gross 1936:21). Through his takeover of the American Union Company, Gould also gained access to Canadian lines and the French transatlantic cable. Using his transatlantic cables and the American Union and Franklin Telegraph companies as a base, Gould instituted a series of raids on Western Union's stock. "As a result Western Union's business declined by two million dollars in one year," Brooks reports (1976:63).

Once Gould had secured control of Western Union in 1882, he leased his transatlantic cables to that company. This move was important because the cables altered the balance of power with Pender. They allowed Gould to broker a cartel with the British and French companies "in which every trans-Atlantic message to and from the United States passed over the wires of the Western Union" (Grodinsky 1957:475). Western Union's domestic position became almost unassailable.

Pender's strategy was understandable. Western Union now had free access to Britain and could set up its own cable offices to collect traffic for its cables. In contrast, the British company had to rely on the U.S. telegraph companies to collect its traffic in the United States. Although this dependence constituted no problem when there was only the Anglo-American's transatlantic cable, the relationship became problematic after Western Union had laid its own cables. Anti-British feeling in the 1880s, brought about by the ending of the agricultural export boom to Europe, also presented dangers to the Eastern (Williams 1969:23). Western Union could refuse to collect traffic for other than its own cables and could refuse to deliver international traffic from the Anglo-American Telegraph Company cables. To Pender's company, cartelization was essential for survival.

After 1885 Western Union's competition came from the telephone. In 1882 Bell took a large stake in Western Union's manufacturer of telegraph equipment, the Western Electric Company, and in 1885 formed American Telephone and Telegraph (AT&T) to develop its long-distance business. AT&T's certificate of incorporation stated that it was established for the purpose of "'constructing, buying, owning, leasing or otherwise obtaining lines of electric telegraph partly within and partly beyond the limits of the State of New York, and of equipping, using, operating, or otherwise maintaining the same'" (quoted in Brooks 1976:91). Because the term *telegraph* was generic, AT&T could also enter the telephone field, and it began to provide telephone long lines. Under the management of Theodore Vail, AT&T's strategy was to construct long-distance lines throughout the United States, Canada, and Mexico. So while Bell Telephone became vertically integrated, with its local operating companies procuring equipment from its manufacturer, it competed in the long-distance transmission market and competed with Western Union. But although long-distance telephone might constitute a potential replacement for the telegraph on land, no submarine cable that would carry long-distance telephone conversation was developed until the mid-twentieth century. Bell Telephone could not become independent of Western Union.

Gould's policy was to keep tariffs high. Technological developments that enhanced companies' private wires, such as duplex telegraphy and ticker-tape machines, enabled the telegraph to maintain its domestic market share. In 1884 Western Union began to lease its wires to large users. Leasing of wires became "so much more profitable than handling messages that the company had considered a suggestion that it cease to handle messages entirely and turn its entire attention to leased-wire business" (Du Boff 1983:268). Gould appreciated the potential of this large user traffic and used the transatlantic cartel to leverage higher domestic tariffs for leased lines and to raise the fixed charges for connection to the transatlantic cable (Grodinsky 1957:476). Large users dependent on transatlantic communications, particularly news agencies and newspapers, suffered.

Recognizing that Western Union's monopoly of transatlantic traffic placed his small domestic Postal Telegraph Company at a disadvantage, John W. Mackay (a banker known as the "bonanza silver king") teamed up with James Gordon Bennett, the owner of the *New York Herald,* in 1884. First they tried and failed to negotiate an independent transatlantic cable connection through Pender. They then formed the Commercial Cable Company to lay a transatlantic cable that would interconnect with Postal Telegraph and other small domestic competitors of Western Union and undercut its rates both on land and at sea. Like the British DUS Cable Company ten years earlier, but now at a time of financial panic, Commercial Cable gave discounts to large users. Western Union responded with a transatlantic price war, reducing tariffs to 12 cents per word, compared to Commercial Cable's 25 cents. But Commercial Cable kept its customers by claiming that Gould was attempting to drive it out of business. In 1886 Western Union lost money and declared no dividend (Grodinsky 1957:470–71).

This transatlantic competition lasted only as long as there were land-based competitors to Western Union, and by 1886 Jay Gould's company had bought, or destroyed through its rate war, all but Mackay's Postal Telegraph Company. In 1887 the two companies reached agreement on rate fixing within the

United States, and in 1888 they called a truce in the rates war at sea (Grodinsky 1957:475). For twenty years Gould was happy to maintain a cartel that encompassed all the transatlantic submarine cables.

Meanwhile, Congress enacted the Interstate Commerce Act of 1887, which introduced federal regulation of the railways. It outlawed "pools and required freight and passenger charges to be public, reasonable and just." Based on British legislation and coinciding with a period when Britain was also using commissions to regulate the railways and canals, the five-member Interstate Commerce Commission, which was charged with administering the new act, became the model for other later regulatory commissions (Foster 1992:23–25). The following year Congress enacted another measure, this time giving the commission powers over those companies that had received the benefits of state subsidies in terms of "lands, bonds or loans of credit." Such companies were obliged to maintain and operate the telegraph lines, and the law required them to interconnect with any telegraph companies that had accepted the conditions of the Post Roads Act of 1866.[16] But it would be twenty-two years before the commission's regulatory powers covered all telegraph companies.

The Telegraph Empire Expands East

After the successful laying of the transatlantic cable, British private investment shifted to the laying and operation of long-distance cables, particularly those to the east—to India, China, and Australasia—and to South America (then part of Britain's informal empire). In India and Australia international telegraphy appeared after the local telegraph. Introduced into India in the 1840s and functioning between all the important towns at the time of the Indian Mutiny in 1857, it was said that "'the electric telegraph saved India'" (Clarke 1927:85–86).

In view of the security implications, it is not surprising that a telegraph line to India, proposed just after the mutiny in 1857, was guaranteed a large annual subsidy from Lord Derby's government. In fact, Lord Palmerston had first broached the idea for such a line in 1851 and again in 1855 in the midst of the Crimean War. John Brett and Lionel Gisborne were the two major competitors for the 1857 Britain-India submarine cable contract, but the British Board of Trade and the Colonial Office were in favor of a government-owned line, operated by the government and the British East India Company (Cell 1970:225–26). The Gisbornes (Lionel and his brother, Francis) were distrusted by the Treasury, whose officials favored "'financial soundness, not concessions bribed from oriental potentates'" as the basis of business enterprise (quoted in Cell 1970:226). By supporting Brett in his efforts to gain the necessary concessions, the Treasury attempted to bypass the brothers, but the Gisbornes obtained a monopoly concession from Egypt. Pressured by the events of the mutiny, and Brett's lack of success, the Treasury had to agree to the Gisbornes' terms (Cell 1970:228). The line was to go overland through Turkey, then through Alexandria to Suez and on to Aden and Karachi. The British East India Company and the Treasury would split the cost of operating the line between Suez and Aden, while the British East India Company would carry the expense of laying the line from Aden to Karachi. The British government "gave an unconditional guarantee of four and a half per cent for fifty years upon the whole capital required . . . viz £800,000 [$3.89 million], thus relieving the shareholders from risk in the matter" (Joint Committee 1861).

In addition, following its practice of the time, the Treasury appointed an "official director" who had "general control over the proceedings" of the cable company. Although ostensibly private, the company was controlled by the Treasury. Because of this public-private collaboration it was not the company but the Treasury that issued the cable manufacturing contract, which contained a clause stating that the contractors could retain any cable that might remain unused (Cell 1970:233). It later emerged that the Treasury contracts had demanded only that the three separate submarine sections of the cable should work for thirty days each (Joint Committee 1861). In 1859, the year that Lionel Gisborne died, the contractors handed over the Red Sea cable in working order, but to save cable they had laid the line with too little slack, and it failed.

This failure left the British and Indian governments paying £36,000 ($175,000) per year for fifty years to the shareholders. Coming as it did just after the failure of the transatlantic cable, such risky enterprise engendered considerably less enthusiasm from the British government. Nevertheless, the Treasury paid out £30,000 ($145,800) more to an unsuccessful project to repair the cable (Cell 1970:250). Spurred partly by the perception that this cable to India would then open up Asia to the British, the U.S. government supported an American attempt to cross Siberia by landline (Clark 1931:113–15).

Following the Gisbornes' unsuccessful attempt, the first cable link to India was constructed by the British India government, which supplanted the British East India Company in 1858. The British India government then established an agency, the Indo-European Telegraph Department, to run the line. Based on landlines with a submarine section in the Arabian Sea and Persian Gulf, the cable was opened in 1865, before transatlantic communication began. The Indo-European Telegraph Department built and operated stations in Iran and Iraq and negotiated for landing rights and interconnection agreements. It built the overland telegraph system across two-thirds of Persia and ran it for the shah with British army officers stationed there. The British India government sent other British officers to run the Turkish system and its connections to Europe (Nier and Butrica 1988:218). But the Treasury had not waited for the Joint Committee report before ordering the cable, so inadequate engineering standards once more made the cable unsuitable (Smith 1891:71). Julius Reuter complained in a letter to the *Times* of London on December 24, 1866, that messages took eight to fourteen days and that, because telegraph clerks en route did not understand English, telegrams were often unintelligible (D. Read 1992:47).

Clearly, the British needed a submarine cable with British end-to-end control (Peel 1905:255). Fieldhouse comments that the coming of the international telegraph in the 1860s did little to check the despotic authority of the governor general of British India, who was also the viceroy of the Indian states (1965:274). But the viceroy's retention of autonomy may have had much to do with the technical failures of the first telegraph line.

During a period that marked the height of free-trade fervor, the British government announced that it was no longer prepared to subsidize companies laying telegraphs to Asia, despite the successful laying of the transatlantic cable. Instead, it said in 1867 that the navy would aid in oceanic surveys and in laying cables and that the government would use its good offices in negotiations for landing rights (Barty-King 1979:25). The navy and diplomacy were therefore to take the place of subsidy in easing the eastward expansion of the British submarine telegraph companies.

With British companies deterred by lack of government subsidy, Siemens Brothers raised the money for a new landline to India that opened in 1871. This line used a cable owned by Reuter's news agency that stretched from Britain "to the Prussian North Sea coast. It ran from there across Germany, a private company line in a nation where telegraphs were state enterprises, and then through vast stretches of Russia, where the same comment holds true, and then down through Iran to Tehran," where it connected with the line to India (Nier and Butrica 1988:218). The tariffs had to cover not only the capital costs of what was a considerable engineering feat but charges to interconnect with the Reuters line and to cross Germany and Russia, which together took 60 percent of the revenue (Scott 1958:53). Competition could make the line unprofitable.

It was John Pender, with his successful transatlantic cable returning an initial 25 percent on principle, and with the sale to the British government of his investment in the British and Irish Magnetic Telegraph Company, who formed the British-Indian Submarine Telegraph Company in 1869 to lay a cable from Suez through the Red Sea to Aden and thence to India. It opened in 1870 and was a direct competitor to the Siemens Brothers line. When cables from Britain to Suez were completed two years later, it became possible to communicate over an "all-British" cable between London and India. Although the submarine cable line cost almost twice as much to construct as the landline, the landline was almost five times more expensive to maintain (Peel 1905:256). Such competition for limited traffic inevitably led to losses for both lines until 1878 when Pender initiated a "joint purse," or pooling, system with Siemens Brothers and the Indo-European Telegraph Department of the British India government (Baglehole 1969:8; Peel 1905:256). This public-private form of cooperation was how a British colonial government came to enter into a cartel with two private companies.

The new cable was more efficient than the landlines and, in conjunction with the unification of the domestic Indian telegraph cable, altered relations between the Indian administration and Whitehall. Barty-King contends that "henceforth the Secretary of State exercised far more effective control over the administration of India than was the case before, and the Viceroy really tended to be a mere 'agent' of the Secretary of State" (1979:33).

India became important as a transit country for lines to Asia. The opening of the line from Madras to Singapore in 1871 was marked by the telegraphing of the results of the Oxford-Cambridge university boat race and put Singapore in direct contact with London for the first time ("Singapore" 1937). In the same year the Eastern linked Singapore with Hong Kong and, through Dutch-owned Java, with Australia. Singapore and Hong Kong were to become the "emporia of British trade in the east" (Fieldhouse 1965:289). These cables soon became commercial successes.

Australia was a different matter. Because of the desert of the interior, urbanization around ports, and the small population, the existing telegraph systems were self-contained within each of the five colonies and preceded the railways (Moyal 1984:16).[17] Pender laid the line to Australia from Singapore in response to petitions from the governments of the colonies of Queensland and South Australia. The Eastern also undertook construction of a submarine line between Tasmania and the Australian mainland and, to make the submarine cable more profitable, tried to gain control of Australia's domestic telegraph system. But the South Australian colony's government claimed construction of the eighteen-hundred-mile landline that traversed the continent and linked the colonies with the Eastern's cable in the far north. Although the submarine telegraph carried only twenty-three messages per day in the first year, as Moyal comments, its "impact . . . on the Australian colonies was immense" (1984:61). With communication time reduced to less than forty-eight hours, British capitalists and manufacturers responded to the corresponding reduction in risk (Moyal 1984:64). London replaced Melbourne as the investment center for the Australian colonies.

However, the Eastern's line had considerable problems from the beginning. Dutch operators in Java mangled messages, and the cable often failed as a result of earthquakes. In 1880, after considerable lobbying, the Eastern duplicated the cable but only in response to the promise from the Australian colonies (with the exception of Queensland) of an annual subsidy of £32,400 ($156,816). Poorer colonies had to pay for their communications.

Sovereignty and Cable—China

From the 1860s sovereignty became more of an issue in relation to communications. Whereas telegraph companies preferred end-to-end control operated by their own nationals, nation-states were eager to control their internal and external communications. Powerful countries could refuse invasions of their sovereignty, but weaker states often found the combination of a cable company backed by a powerful Western government too much to resist. One such case was China. There, following the growth of trade after the Opium Wars of 1840 and the location of Western business communities into the five treaty ports, Western merchants demanded international telegraphic communications. In addition, Admiral Matthew Perry's forcible opening of Japan to trade in 1853 and the gradual modernization of that country from the 1860s made East Asia an attractive market.

In 1854 the U.S. Navy undertook a North Pacific Ocean survey. William Seward, a former New York governor and presidential hopeful, pushed the venture as a preliminary to U.S. commercial expansion into the Pacific (Neering 1989:11). Subsequently, President Franklin Pierce was drawn into backing the explorer Perry McDonough Collins, whose vision of U.S. westward expansion encompassed U.S. foreign investment in railways and Russia-U.S. trade. In 1856 the U.S. government appointed Collins to be its commercial agent to the Amur (on the border between Siberia and China and recently invaded by the Russians); he returned to Washington in 1858 to publish his enthusiastic findings at congressional expense (Mackay 1946:190; Neering 1989:20). Inspired by the failure of the 1858 Atlantic cable, "Americans, he insisted, must build a telegraph line through the western United States into British Columbia, then through the northern British territories, across Russian America (Alaska), under the Bering Strait, south through Siberia, then along the Amur River to Irkutsk and eventually European Russia and all the countries of Europe" (Neering 1989:20). Collins's primary concern was the potential commercial exploitation of the Amur region, but his supporters were drawn by other considerations.

Given the failure of Field's 1858 transatlantic cable and recognizing that an overland route with only a forty-mile stretch of undersea cable could provide his company with the communications with Europe that it needed, Hiram Sibley, the founder and president of Western Union, was an early Collins supporter (Vevier 1959:244). He had completed his transcontinental telegraph from the east to the Pacific Coast in 1861, and he proposed to use his skilled workforce for the projected telegraph line. Congress supported the proposal twice but failed to appropriate the money to pay for it. Nevertheless, despite the ongoing civil war, Seward, now secretary of state, lobbied the British, Russians, and Swedes on Collins's behalf. The British and Russians acquiesced, but the Swedes demurred. Their government "expressed surprise that the first minister of the United States government in the midst of a great civil war had the time and disposition to employ his mind to so critical and exact a statistical and geographical examination of the subject" (Clark 1931:115).

Regarding the projected line not only as "Mr. Collins's enterprise" but "as an enterprise of the government of the United States" (Mackay 1946:194), Seward informed the Russians that "the United States government would subsidize the projected line just as it had done for the Pacific telegraph built by the Western Union . . . and felt strongly that the line would be of great commercial benefit for all concerned" (Vevier 1959:245).

On the understanding that the line would be completed within five years, in 1863 Collins gained a monopoly concession for thirty-three years from the Russians. On their side the Russians agreed to extend their telegraph lines to meet his at the mouth of the Amur River. The Russians were primarily interested in using the telegraph to increase their control over newly colonized Siberia. But they also wanted to build a line through China to link Tianjin (a treaty port) with nearby Beijing. The Chinese had rejected the proposal on the ground that the government could not protect such a line from a superstitious population (Baark 1997:72). However, in 1862, in a concession that was to influence the subsequent development of China's telegraph system, Prince Gong, the most important of the foreign affairs officers in the Chinese emperor's court, agreed with the Russians that if any other country were allowed to build telegraph lines in China, the Russians would be granted similar rights first (Baark 1997:72).

Although China refused to give Collins a monopoly concession in 1863, he did get permission from the British to use unappropriated Crown land in British Columbia (Neering 1989:24). Hiram Sibley's support then found expression in the creation of a subsidiary to Western Union and the buying out of Collins's rights (Neering 1989:25). The company announced that not only would the Russian system connect with the Indian telegraph system through Persia but that it "was projecting extensions of the line from the Russian system to China and Japan" (Vevier 1959:246). According to the company's publicity, it also had plans to connect future overland lines in Mexico and Central and South America, thereby "'concentrating the globe upon our overland lines'" (Vevier 1959:246). On July 1, 1864, President Abraham Lincoln signed a bill that gave the line a permanent right-of-way through the United States and committed the U.S. Navy to surveying the route and laying cable. Despite the terms of the concession from the British, which demanded equal treatment for its messages—representatives of the United States, British, and Russian governments were to set the tariffs—the U.S. government insisted on priority for its transmissions (Neering 1989:25).

On the orders of Seward in 1865 the U.S. minister in China proposed to the Chinese that Collins's company extend the trans-Siberian line to China, but the Chinese government rejected the idea (Vevier 1959:248). A dispute also arose with the Russians when the entrepreneurs learned that the Russian government intended that the transit traffic on the cable should cross-subsidize Russian domestic lines (Clark 1931:115). Although construction of the line continued into 1867 in the hope that Field's transatlantic cable of 1866 would fall silent, the project lost its commercial rationale. And after Western Union merged with Field's domestic American Telegraph Company in 1866, the danger of Western Union's being locked out of international traffic disappeared. Subsequently, after laying a thousand miles of landlines, Western Union discontinued work on the line in March 1867 and took the $3 million loss (Mackay 1946:211; Tribolet 1929:241). Only the line to Canada remained in operation, and it was bought by the dominion government in 1880 (Mackay 1946:214). In addition, Seward convinced Congress in 1867 "to take a stride to Asia" by purchasing Alaska from the Russians for $7 million (Vevier 1959:252).

Despite the setbacks, U.S. interest in cables to China, and particularly in a trans-Pacific cable, continued. While Pender was initiating his Globe plans, Cyrus Field, supported by senior figures in the U.S. Navy, revived the idea of a "telegraphic circuit of the globe" and wrote to Czar Alexander II of Russia in 1873. Field both advocated the laying of a trans-Pacific cable and requested the aid of the Russian government for the enterprise (Tribolet 1929:157;

Alexander 1911:52). Field followed up by visiting Russia but was unsuccessful in gaining a subsidy. However, in 1875 the Hawaiian government granted Field a twenty-year concession. That same year Congress inserted in the naval appropriations act a provision that the navy could take soundings between the United States and Japan but failed to appropriate any money for the venture (Tribolet 1929:158). At a time of depression and financial conservatism, Field tried several more times to gain a congressional subsidy but failed.

The Americans were not alone in seeking a telegraph link to China. British businesses in Shanghai lobbied the British Foreign Office to "issue demands for the introduction of railroads and telegraphs in China as part of the treaty revisions scheduled for 1868–69" (Baark 1997:56). The ensuing Alcock Convention of 1869 was intended to provide the framework for the introduction of such technologies in collaboration with the British (56). However, the main challenge to the U.S. plans came from the Danish Great Northern Company and the Russians.

After Western Union withdrew, the Russians had an even greater need to make their trans-Siberian line commercially viable by expanding their lines into China. The subsequent bid, won by the Danish company, envisaged the construction of a line from Vladivostok to Nagasaki to Shanghai and from there to Hong Kong (Baark 1997:57). But the Chinese again rejected Russian approaches for a land-based cable.

The British, helped by diplomatic pressure from the Dutch and French, and despite objections from the United States, gained a Chinese concession in 1870 (Clark 1931:115–16). On the understanding that, if the submarine cables were terminated at sea, the Russians could not argue that a cable was being laid inside China and therefore could not demand the fulfillment of their 1862 agreement with the Chinese, Thomas Wade, the British chargé d'affaires in China, secured an agreement that allowed submarine cables to terminate at stationary barges outside the treaty ports. The Great Northern Company then simply assumed that it was a party to the agreement (Baark 1997:79–81). The company went on to take its cable illegally from the agreed mooring site in the harbor by landline into the merchant area of Shanghai and, when it was damaged by locals, successfully lobbied all the major European governments to issue a stern warning to China to protect foreign companies' property (Ahvenainen 1991:61). As the Chinese foreign affairs office commented in 1870, ""When foreigners are allowed to take one step forward, they rush ahead. . . . From the sea [they will extend telegraphs] into the river; from the river into the tributaries; and from the tributaries onto the land. With galloping speed [they will] incessantly attempt to penetrate into the interior and with ever-changing ventures pursue their shrewd schemes."'"[18] As the Chinese struggled to maintain sovereignty, the issue of foreign cables disturbed them for many years.

In the case of Japan, the Great Northern Company wanted a monopoly of Japan's internal and external communications. Instead, the Japanese government agreed in 1870 that the company might operate in the southern cities of Nagasaki and Yokohama and gave it a monopoly of Japan's external communications with China and Korea (Ahvenainen 1991:40–41). Communications with the mainland opened in 1871, and, as traffic expanded, Japan too began to struggle to regain the sovereignty that it had relinquished.

The Great Northern Company's submarine cable from Hong Kong to China was opened in 1872, linking the Asiatic coast continuously between Vladivostok and Singapore via Japan and Hong Kong. It became possible for news of Britain to be transmitted to China within ten hours, rather than the previous weeks (Bright 1898a:168). The British Reuters news agency soon followed to establish its own monopoly of news collection and provision in both Japan and China.

Despite these setbacks to a trans-Pacific cable, in 1880 Cyrus Field approached the Japanese with a proposal to land a cable from the United States in Yokohama and then to link it with Shanghai. According to Baark (1997:59), the Chinese thought the U.S. plan had been shelved because of its prohibitive expense, but the concession gained from the Japanese by the Great Northern Company meant that any U.S. line would have breached its monopoly. In 1882 Field proposed to the Chinese government an alternative link between Hong Kong and Shanghai. But by then the Great Northern had gained a monopoly concession in China from one of the sections of the Chinese bureaucracy and, unbeknown to Field, had reached a secret agreement with the British Eastern company for pooling revenues on the Hong Kong-to-Shanghai line. This time it was the turn of the Chinese to reject the request from Field "with reference to the provisions in the concession to Great Northern" (Baark 1997:170–72). Basically, the United States was locked out of the Pacific area.

Although the British government and the Eastern had supported the Great Northern Company's entry into China, the Danish company's attempts to gain a monopoly concession, coupled with increasing suspicion of its collusion with the Russians, led to opposition from Western governments. In 1880, in response to Russian appropriation of land in western China (near the Amur River), and the need for military communications, the Chinese prepared to build their own domestic network. Great Northern thought that it had reached an agreement that would have prevented the Chinese government from building its own sea cables or inland telegraph line in competition with the company's (Ahvenainen 1991:68). But the Chinese wanted some autonomy. In the first example of what is a 1990s model of "build, operate, and transfer," the Chinese government contracted with the Great Northern Company in 1880 to supply technical materials, equipment, and expertise for the construction of the first Chinese telegraph lines. The Great Northern then trained Chinese personnel to take over the operation of the lines (Ahvenainen 1991:61). In 1881, in return for carrying Chinese government traffic without charge, Great Northern demanded an agreement that would give it a monopoly of submarine cables for twenty years (He 1997:58).

Both the British and U.S. governments opposed this monopoly concession. The Eastern was particularly concerned that the Great Northern Company was neglecting maintenance of the line from Shanghai to Hong Kong in order to divert traffic through Russia. Great Northern then refused to operate a joint purse arrangement, and from 1881 to 1883 the companies were in dispute. Taking advantage of legal confusion caused by competition between the Chinese bureaucracies, in 1883 the Eastern built cables from Hong Kong up the coast. Although the Chinese government originally refused the Eastern a landing in Shanghai, it relented under diplomatic pressure and the British government's offer of higher tariffs on its opium exports from British India (He 1997:59). Then the Eastern enlisted the help of the British Foreign Office to refuse cable landing licenses in Hong Kong for the Great Northern Company or any Chinese company associated with it (Baark 1997:173).

To finance their domestic telegraph expansion the Chinese used a mechanism of part public, part private joint stock companies under government control that became known in Britain as private finance initiatives in the twentieth century (Ahvenainen 1991:61). The Imperial Telegraph Administration came into being in 1882 and by 1899 had laid 27,500 miles of line (He 1997:61). Subsequently, the Chinese government wanted to construct its own international line. A new company, financed with Hong Kong Chinese capital exclusively, set out to build a line from Canton to Hong Kong. However, although the Chinese had allowed the Eastern to land on the mainland, the British colony refused to grant landing rights to the Chinese (because the new line would compete with the Eastern and the Chinese company was associated with the Great Northern Company). The Chinese company was furious with the Chinese government for not demanding reciprocity as a condition of the Eastern's concession (Ahvenainen 1991:80).

The British government's stance also met with fierce protests from British merchants in the colony who were demanding competition and lower prices. Caught between the telegraph companies and telegraph users, the

British government eventually sided with the merchants, the users. In a first regulatory move the government told the two companies to work together and to lower prices, and in 1883 the two agreed that they would pool revenue from traffic sent via Siberia or India. Eventually, despite the Eastern's contention that it held a monopoly of landing rights in Hong Kong, following its takeover by the Chinese Imperial Telegraph Administration, the Chinese company was allowed to share lines into Hong Kong.[19]

Later, in an astute maneuver the Chinese linked up their landlines with the Russians' to provide connection with Europe through Siberia (as the Americans had first proposed). In the ensuing treaty of 1893 the Chinese placated the Great Northern Company and the Eastern by agreeing to set the tariffs at the same rate as theirs, thereby not creating "competition" (Ahvenainen 1991:128). British merchants in London expressed considerable opposition to the Russian-Chinese agreement, saying that it provided no competition to the Danes and the Eastern, but the British government was unwilling to oppose an agreement between two sovereign nations, especially because the agreement followed the regulations of the International Telegraph Union that prevented competition. The U.S. ambassador to China lodged no objection to the treaty, reasoning that if the tariffs were too high, market conditions would create greater opportunities for a U.S. Pacific cable (Ahvenainen 1991:130).

The Chinese administration then funneled traffic down its own line, setting tariffs below the companies' despite its agreement with them. However, the Russian-Chinese line broke down during floods and storms, and the two Western companies' technical superiority ensured that they retained a large portion of the traffic. Nevertheless, a rate war was not to the companies' liking. Their appeals led the Foreign Office to instruct the British ambassador not to oppose the companies' position but "not to behave in any way which might give the impression that the interests of the cable companies and Great Britain were one and the same" (Ahvenainen 1991:133).

Writing from the perspective of the 1920s, Tribolet suggests that the British intention in China was strategic as well as commercial. By preventing a direct trans-Pacific cable operated by U.S. interests, the British were able to "minimize American influences in that sector of the world" (1929:266–67). But Ahvenainen's study of the official papers would suggest another explanation—that despite its desire to see trade in China expand, the U.S. government was reliant on private risk capital, and much better commercial opportunities lay elsewhere. Only after the 1890s did strategic considerations became more important to the U.S. government than commercial opportunities (Ahvenainen 1991:212).

U.S. Government Cable Policy

There seems little doubt that by the second half of the nineteenth century the U.S. government was so eager to effect telegraph communications between itself and the rest of the world that it was prepared to cooperate with other governments. But even in the 1860s it demonstrated its concern that other major powers could shut the United States out of submarine cable operation and the control of communications.

As early as the 1860s, the U.S. government tried unsuccessfully to bring together twenty-three nations to draft a joint convention for the ostensible purpose of protecting submarine cables from piracy. However, reflecting U.S. concern that allowing foreign companies to control the cables left them vulnerable to espionage, the draft convention included articles that forbade employees or agents of the states through which dispatches passed to read them. The U.S. government also proposed that "'no exclusive concession or grant of a monopoly for a submarine cable shall hereafter be made or renewed by either of the high contracting parties without the consent of the other party with whose territories such concession or grant contemplates a connection' (Art. 1)" (Clark 1931:141). The intention was to end the British monopoly by outlawing "concessions" attached to landing rights. In the words of Secretary of State Hamilton Fish, behind the draft international treaty lay the belief that the "'central position in the communication of the world entitled the United States to initiate this movement for the common benefit of the commerce and civilization of all.'"[20] However, the U.S. government's own actions undermined this approach.

In 1866 Congress granted its own monopoly concession to the International Ocean Telegraph Company for a cable between Florida and Cuba, then a Spanish-owned island important for its U.S.-owned sugar plantations. The company, founded by Capt. James Scrymser, an unemployed one-time soldier and his friend Alfred Pell, had received the Spanish concession from Horatio J. Perry, who later served as secretary to the U.S. delegation in Madrid (Ahvenainen 1996:1–3). Scrymser argued that there was a threat that the Spaniards would build and control telegraphic communications with the island and thereby control the world sugar markets (Scrymser 1915:71). The following year Congress recognized this monopoly when it gave a concession to Field's Atlantic Telegraph Company for a route to Europe that excluded the area of Scrymser's operations in the coastal waters of Florida (Schreiner 1924:40–41). Scrymser went on to gain concessions to lay cable within the West Indies, with the intention of linking these to Brazil. For this purpose in

1868 Secretary of State Seward attempted to gain a concession for Scrymser to lay a cable down the east coast of South America to Brazil but was beaten to it by Bright and his British Western Telegraph Company. Following this failure, the State Department gave up the attempt at direct competition in gaining concessions and instead began to use domestic law to ensure that Americans were not shut out of the cable-operating market (Herring and Gross 1936:30).

U.S. landing rights policy developed out of the political furor of 1867 surrounding the news agency Reuters-d'Erlanger French-backed transatlantic cable. At first pleased at the possibility of competition, and the lowering of rates, the Americans then learned that the concession granted to the French company by the French government would preclude U.S. companies from gaining landing rights in France. Lobbied by Cyrus Field to demand reciprocal landing rights, Secretary of State Fish "threatened to send a naval vessel to Duxbury, Mass., with an order to tear up the French cable, if landed without his permission" (Scrymser 1915:102). Western Union and the local Franklin Telegraph Company also opposed the landing in order to pressure the French cable to interconnect with their landlines. Field then lobbied the Massachusetts legislature, which had to consent to any landing. Because Baron d'Erlanger had served as an agent of the Confederacy during the Civil War, Massachusetts refused to sanction the landing, although the French government had revoked the exclusivity of the baron's concession.

In contrast, because transatlantic competition would decrease tariffs and thereby increase the traffic on the Cuba–West Indies cable that he owned, Scrymser was eager to see the cable laid. He therefore bribed prominent legislators in New Jersey to push through a bill to allow the cable to land there. Faced with this competition, Cape Cod legislators capitulated (Scrymser 1915:106–7).

But the issue of reciprocity and federal versus local control of cable landings did not die. In 1875, in the same year that Europeans agreed to an international telegraph convention designed to eliminate competition, U.S. President Ulysses S. Grant set out subsequent U.S. policy in his State of the Union address:

> "As these cable-telegraph lines connect separate States, there are questions as to their organization and control which probably can be best, if not solely settled by conventions between the respective States. In absence, however, of international conventions on the subject, municipal legislation may secure many points which appear to me important, if not indispensable for the protection of the public against the extortions which may result from a monopoly of the right of operating cable telegrams, or from a combination between several lines.

I. No line should be allowed to land on the shores of the United States under the concession from another power which does not admit the right of any
other line or lines formed in the United States, to land and freely connect with
and operate through its land lines.

II. No line should be allowed to land on the shores of the United States which
is not by treaty stipulation with the Government from whose shores it proceeds,
or by prohibition in its charter or otherwise to the satisfaction of this Government, prohibited from consolidating or amalgamating with any other cable-
telegraph line, or combining therewith for the purposes of regulating and
maintaining the cost of telegraphing." (quoted in Clark 1931:142–43)

Following this policy, the DUS line, laid by Siemens Brothers, was able to gain
permission to land in the United States in 1875 only because its memorandum of association precluded its working with the Anglo-American Telegraph Company (Barty-King 1979:56).

In focusing on potential cartels, Grant was reflecting the U.S. public's increasing unease at the growth of big business. In particular, the railroads'
propensity to collude in price fixing colored public perceptions. As Glenn
Porter (1973:36) explains, the railroads were the first industry to have not only
heavy sunk costs in infrastructure but also enormous debt on which interest had to be paid. Given this capital intensity and the marginal cost of carrying freight, it paid the railroad owner to push as much traffic down the line
as possible, even at a low cost. As a result price wars developed and then collusion or collapse.

The submarine cable business was not dissimilar. Each cable cost about
$2.4 million plus its associated debt. Pools, or joint purses, were a means to
protect the companies' profits at a time when traffic demand was low and
when high prices compensated for the financial risks taken in the initial investment. Shreiner points to the conditions associated with the laying of the
French PQ cable in 1879 to argue that the U.S. government's interest was
narrowly focused on the question of tariffs and pools. In its concessionary
agreement with the PQ company, the French government imposed a tax on
all foreign equipment laid in French waters or on French soil and insisted on
free use of the line. French government engineers were to have the right to
inspect the cable manufacture at the company's expense, the company had
to obtain the consent of the French government to transfer its rights, and the
agreement became void if the cable was out of action for two years. All these
conditions were set out in the landing license in addition to control of tariffs, whereas the U.S. government was concerned only about the level of the
tariff and no joint purses (Shreiner 1924:47–60).

But Schreiner rather misses the point of the submarine cable landing policy. President Grant's policy was intended to ensure that U.S. companies were not prevented from connecting to foreign countries and to ensure the development of a U.S. cable system that could be used for the diplomatic service free from foreign supervision. Although it might be anticipated that any pooling of U.S. companies' revenue on the transatlantic route would run foul of the landing rights policy, such behavior on the part of U.S. companies was seen as necessary (Herring and Gross 1936:232). Thus once Jay Gould had eliminated all but the Commercial Cable Company from domestic competition in the 1880s, his pooling arrangement across the Atlantic was able to include the foreign operators. An American-British-French pool controlled the Atlantic cables for thirty years.

In 1889, during the presidency of Republican Benjamin Harrison, the cable landing policy of the U.S. government was further extended by Secretary of State James G. Blaine, who now included "a prohibition against companies which *connected with* other companies holding exclusive concessions inimical to American interests" (Herring and Gross 1936:232). The immediate reason for this alteration was a French company's request to land a cable from Santo Domingo in South Carolina. Scrymser argued that this cable was in fact an extension of the French company's line to Brazil, where it held a monopoly concession, and was intended to connect the United States to Brazil indirectly. The secretary of state therefore altered the first of President Grant's conditions, making landing rights an explicit matter of reciprocity in third markets. In other words, any company seeking entry to the U.S. market had to allow U.S. companies comparable rights of access, not only in those markets in which the company operated but also in any markets to which it had indirect access through partner companies.

Blaine was himself not only a supporter of expansionist policies regarding export markets but "sometime during the 1870s, and perhaps a bit earlier, he had realized that the principle and practice of reciprocity offered the best of protection and free trade" (Williams 1969:33). A year before his major battle with the old-style protectionists, who were led by William McKinley, Blaine was able to put that principle into effect in his cable policy of 1889. In 1890 the protectionists were defeated when Congress adopted Blaine's strategy of protection plus reciprocity as a way to open markets in Europe and Latin America. From then on, reciprocity, used first in cable landing policy, became an integral part of U.S. trade policy (Herring and Gross 1936:233). Later, this submarine cable policy, administered on a case-by-case basis, became a potent weapon in the search for the opening of third markets to U.S. companies.

International News Agencies

As the telegraph spread, news agencies arose to market information by using the speed of telegraph transmission. The telegraph created the ability to sell information as a product, particularly to banks and trading houses. Profits went to those who got the news first. The state-owned French and German news agencies (Havas and Wolff, respectively) and the British (Reuters) all followed the expansion of the telegraph.

Julius Reuter, a German, had moved to Britain in 1851 when he was squeezed out of Paris by his Continental news service competitors. It was Reuter who first saw the potential in the collection and dissemination of information specifically for commercial clients (his first contract was with the London Stock Exchange). Business information was to pay for the collection and dissemination of political information.

Cooper (1942:7) argues that Reuter got the idea of supplying political news to the press from the Associated Press, established in New York in 1848. But in Britain daily newspapers thrived only after the stamp duty abolition of 1855 and a concomitant decrease in the cover price of newspapers created a demand for news (D. Read 1992:19). By 1859 Reuter had begun to supply his foreign news to British provincial papers through the domestic network of the Electric and Magnetic companies for £800 ($3,888) per annum.

With the establishment of a cross-channel cable in 1853, the growth of the Reuters news agency went hand in hand with the development of international submarine cables. When the first overland cable to India opened in 1857, Reuter obtained a German concession for his own cross-channel cable. This cable both gave him the basis for establishing a news agency in Germany, and after he linked it up with the Indian cable, enabled him to circumvent the cable companies' high cross-channel tariffs (Storey 1951:66–68). The Siemens Brothers Company also used the news agency cable for its Anglo-Indian traffic. The cable was successful financially, returning 19 percent on principle invested in 1868. In addition, so that his steam tender could meet ocean liners and be first with the news, Reuter joined with Siemens Brothers to build a cable in Ireland, from Cork to Crookhaven, that the Reuters news agency shared with the *Times* of London (D. Read 1992:35).

When the first transatlantic submarine cable was planned, Reuter attempted to set up his own news agency operation in the United States but was defeated by the cable's failure; he subsequently contracted with the Associated Press of New York for U.S. news during the American Civil War (D. Read

1992:33). The British followed news of the Civil War both for political reasons, particularly given the linkage to slavery, and because the British cotton industry was suffering shortages as a result of the war. News was therefore commercially important. Reuter is credited with giving an assurance of
business worth £5,000 ($34,400) per year to the Atlantic cable in 1866 but then
became shocked at the tariffs.

When the British government nationalized the domestic telegraph in 1869,
Reuter lobbied to have his German cable included in that nationalization. He
received in compensation a total of £750,000 ($4.86 million) from the British
government for the German cable and the twenty-year lease with the Indo-
European Telegraph Department; his original investment twelve years earlier
had been £153,000 ($991,440) (Kieve 1973:180). This payment may have helped
to finance his attempt to provide alternative transatlantic infrastructure.

Seeking a link that gave him preferential access to North America, Reuter
successfully backed the first French cable from Brest to Cape Cod in 1869. But
information had become a commodity whose value increased according to
the speed with which it was delivered; when the French cable proved too slow,
Reuter's company came to a large-user agreement with Pender's company,
the Anglo-American Telegraph Company. In 1876 Reuter negotiated lower
rates by agreeing to send all his North Atlantic business through the British-
owned cables (D. Read 1992:99).

In 1870 Reuter entered into a secret alliance with Havas and Wolff, the
French and German news agencies. That agreement, combined with Reuters's
monopoly on wire service news in Britain, divided the globe into "spheres
of influence" for the collection and dissemination of news. Reuter's news
agency gave up its branch offices in Germany but gained a monopoly within the British and Dutch empires. Havas gained a monopoly within southern Europe and French colonial possessions. Reuters and Havas originally
shared the Ottoman Empire, Egypt, and Belgium, while Wolff took northern Europe, the cities of Moscow and St. Petersburg, and German colonial
possessions. All three agencies could compete in other countries (Rantanen
1990:41). Despite the formal agreement, the Reuters agency's influence in
Canada was limited by the proximity of the U.S. market and the costs of telegraph transmission (Fortner 1993:90). The Associated Press, founded in 1848
by six New York newspapers and then extended nationwide, had set up its
first foreign news bureau in Canada in 1849 in Halifax, Nova Scotia, giving it
a twenty-year start on Reuters. By 1900, just before it withdrew from Canada, the AP had twenty-three hundred newspaper clients and was transmitting fifty thousand words each day.

Reuters established itself in India in 1866, when only the overland cable was in operation (Storey 1951:63). As in the United States, the telegraph stabilized commodity prices in India. Storey says that "within a few weeks no native dealer would sell a pound of cotton before he had seen Reuter's overnight quotations" for the price in Liverpool (1951:64). Once the Indian submarine cable was in service, Reuters compressed messages for third parties into codes and began undercutting the high prices charged per ten-word message. In effect, the Reuters message transmission service was the first attempt at private resale of transmission.

Whereas in the twentieth century resellers of telecommunications would buy transmission capacity in bulk from the infrastructure owner and then sell that capacity at a higher (but still below retail) price to third parties, in the nineteenth century, where infrastructure capacity was limited, the reseller made its profit by compressing the transmitted information. "By 1875 Reuter's was handling between three and four thousand telegrams to and from the East in a month; and was relying on the revenue from these private telegrams to pay for the unprofitable news service" (Storey 1951:69). In addition, it received subscriptions from governments, such as in India and Egypt, for its political news (D. Read 1992:63–64).

Although the company gained from the control of international press rates, the first regulation of international cable charges in 1877 undermined Reuters's transmission service; the St. Petersburg International Telegraph Convention of 1875 had unilaterally reduced international cable charges by international agreement (Storey 1951:91). International standardization, which introduced a word-based, rather than message-based, tariff, was based on transatlantic tariffs and may have been intended to force private competitive carriers out of the market. Reuters was forced to use increasingly elaborate codes. But it then developed a telegraph remittance business, which allowed members of the public to transfer money between India and England and between Australia and London for less than the banks charged (Storey 1951:119).

As the submarine cable expanded east in the 1870s, so did Reuters—to Singapore, China, Japan, and Australia. It also expanded to Latin America. Under the "spheres of influence" agreement made when the three news agencies followed the first cable laid in 1874, Havas and Reuters shared the cost of establishing offices in those South American countries that held the most European investment—Brazil, Argentina, and Uruguay. But the South American press was more interested in news from Havas than from Reuters, and as a result the transmission of telegrams for business became the major Reuters activity during the 1870s. A Reuters office opened in New York to handle telegrams from South America via Jamaica. But because of poor management and unreliable cables, this attempt by the company to replicate its Far Eastern experience ended in disastrous failure. It withdrew, and South America became the exclusive sphere of the French agency Havas (D. Read 1992:62).

International Regulation

Attempts to coordinate the cross-border carriage of telegraph messages came during the mid-1800s in Europe, first with bilateral treaties between Austria and Prussia (1849), then between the German states of Austria, Bavaria, Prussia, and Saxony (1850); then between France-Belgium and Prussia (1852) and all those states and France-Switzerland (1853). These treaties were then extended to Spain, Sardinia, and Switzerland in 1855. France became the link between the Latin states and Prussia and Prussia the link with other German states. These various arrangements formed the precursor to a more ambitious regional arrangement (Clark 1931:93).

When Napoleon III called together the first Electric Telegraph Commission in Paris in 1851 to discuss submarine telegraphs, Britain was the only country there whose government did not own its domestic telegraph cables. A follow-up meeting in Paris in 1865, attended by twenty Continental European powers, had the aim of establishing "a single continuous territory, to suppress zones, reduce rates, send telegrams in any language or in cipher, cause to *faire suivre*, and establish the franc as the monetary unit of exchange" (Clark 1931:94). These twenty states formed the International Telegraph Union and formulated the Paris International Telegraph Convention to regulate rates and to standardize the Morse code and other aspects of wire telegraph services across borders. But apparently because of the others' unwillingness to give credit to Napoleon III as initiator, no permanent organization was set up.

At a second conference in Vienna in 1868 member states established a permanent secretariat. By 1875 it had evolved into the International Bureau of Telegraph Administrations, located in Berne and operated by the Swiss government (Clark 1931:107). At the 1868 conference it became clear that the overall aim of the ITU was to prevent competition. The members decided that no member could institute a new charge or modification of tariffs until it had given the International Bureau fifteen days' notice. They also decided that any "alteration of rates must have for object and effect, not the creation of competitive charges between existing routes, but, on the contrary, the opening of as many routes as possible to the public at equal charges."[21] The effect was an international cartel of national telegraph agencies.

Another conference followed in 1871 in Rome, but the first major regulations were agreed to in 1875 during the St. Petersburg International Telegraph Convention. Although the United States refused to participate, saying that its telegraph industry was privately owned, the Russians twisted a few arms until the Americans agreed to send an observer (Codding 1972:42). The 1875 St. Petersburg International Telegraph Convention established a more efficient administrative organization. The rules were divided into the basic treaty (known as the convention) and the telegraph regulations. Only plenipotentiary conferences with delegates from member governments could alter the convention, but administrative conferences attended by representatives of state telegraph administrations and recognized private operating companies (companies that ran the domestic telegraph in member states) could alter the regulations. The latter conferences undertook the detailed work on regulations. As Codding points out, "Slowly but surely . . . the telegraph administrations became accepted as members of the [International Telegraph] Union on a par with 'sovereign' states that had drawn up and signed the Telegraph Convention" (1972:41).

Under the 1875 convention the signatory states agreed that they had the responsibility to ensure secrecy of telegraphic correspondence in their territory but had "'"the right to stop the transmission of any private telegram which appears dangerous to the security of the state or which is contrary to the laws of the country, to public order, or to decency, and to suspend, either generally or only on certain lines, any or all international telegraphic service . . . subject to notification thereof to the other contracting governments"'" (quoted in Tribolet 1929:10–11). This provision, reflecting the state ownership of European cables, was anathema to the Americans.

The 1875 convention also included agreements on the collection of accounts and on tariffs. The original French proposal was that each state should have only two charges for handling international traffic and that these should not be distance related—one should be an origin or destination tariff (terminal rate), and the other should be for transit traffic (transit rate). But although delegates annexed a table of rates for intra-European traffic to the regulations, these were not uniform.[22] Instead, larger countries, such as Russia, insisted on being able to charge extra according to the distance traveled (Codding and Rutkowski 1982:6). In recognition of the interests of those Continental states with large amounts of transit traffic, member states also agreed that the rates for messages sent along the whole of an international line could not be altered without the consent of all interested governments. Of most significance was the decision to standardize tariffs on a word rate rather than a message rate with its built-in minimum tariff that allowed undercutting. In addition, code words had to be no more than ten characters (Barty-King 1979:56). According to the U.S. observer, the overall concern of the conference was to protect the interests of the state telegraph agencies, not customers (Codding and Rutkowski 1982:8).

The decision about rates apparently was made without consulting the major commercial operators. In particular, John Pender is said to have expressed resentment that he could not be a delegate and that far-reaching decisions were made by people to whom he could not put his case officially. Barty-King reports that Pender was excluded from the conference room and forced to lobby in corridors (1979:54–56). But in fact the Rome International Telegraph Convention of 1871 gave private companies nonvoting rights at the discretion of the chairman. Representatives of ten private companies, including Cyrus Field, who represented the New York, Newfoundland, and London Telegraphic Company, participated in the Rome convention (Codding and Rutkowski 1982:11; Clark 1931:127). Pender's complaints about the 1875 St. Petersburg conference may have resulted from decisions about international tariffs that were made in the interests of governments, not commercial operators. According to Bright, the Eastern countered the ITU's subsequent decisions to lower international tariffs by getting the government of the colony receiving the cable to agree to make up any loss (1898a:149). In that way the companies kept control of their business processes.

Pender was certainly close to parts of the British establishment. Pender's wife is reported to have written a letter describing a dinner party given to celebrate the opening of the second Australian line in 1876 at which the colonial secretary, Herbert Samuel, had "offered to attend personally to any business that Pender might have with the Colonial Office about cables" (Harcourt 1987:86). But despite these close political connections, the Post Office was keen to see the Eastern's growing power regulated by international rules.

For the British international telegraph regimes were originally a means of ensuring interconnection via landlines through Europe to their empire's overseas territories. Because Britain's telegraph system was privately run, the British government of India was invited to the 1868 Vienna conference because it ran the Indian telegraph system. After nationalization of the domestic telegraphs, "Britain then sent two delegations to the Rome Telegraph Conference of 1871–72 and demanded that each be given the vote. 'Colonial voting' as the British action was dubbed, was incorporated in the rules of the [International] Telegraph Union at the St Petersburg conference of 1875" (Codding and Rutkowski 1982:11).[23] By ensuring that it gained votes for its colonies, Britain was always in a position where it could dominate the International Telegraph Union if it teamed up with another European colonial power. At this stage British interests were not tied directly to the commercial interests of the Eastern. Such matters as the control of rates agreed within the international regulations were advantageous to the British state in its role as user, as well as to London's financial and commercial interests.[24] The international regime regulated the Eastern in a way that the government, wedded to free-trade ideology, had difficulty doing on its own initiative.

Under pressure from its companies, the United States refused to sign the 1875 convention, claiming that to do so would have meant accepting a government's right to regulate telegraphs. Canada, China, and some other countries also refused to sign. This was a period of free-for-all by capitalists in the United States, where a persistent minority was trying to gain public control of the telegraph and its tariffs. In this business climate international regulation might be used to introduce domestic nationalization.

British companies also tried to escape the regulations. For instance, in 1883 Pender sought an exemption for the Eastern's cable between Hong Kong and China. Pender claimed that its competitor, the Great Northern Telegraph Company, did not accept the regulations and that the regulations governed communication between two contracting states and not between one contracting state (Hong Kong) and one noncontracting state (China). Until the British Post Office explained that nonadherence would allow the company to charge what it liked for government traffic and to fail to give it priority, the Colonial Office and Treasury were evidently sympathetic to the company. With few powers of domestic regulation available to his department, the postmaster general suggested that it was reasonable to "require that any Telegraph company applying for permission to land a cable on the shores of this country or any of the British possessions should accede to the obligatory clauses of the telegraph convention."[25]

Thus U.S. companies that wanted a landing license in Britain also had to abide by the convention's obligatory clauses regarding nondiscrimination between customers. In fact, private U.S. companies soon were attending International Telegraph Union conferences, accepting the regulations in practice, and participating in the revision of the regulations to which, on their behalf, their government refused to be bound (Codding 1972:43). The U.S. operators were thereby using international regulation to control their competitors.

Conclusion

In this early colonial period of the expansion of the international telegraph, the British companies gained advantages by entering the field early, controlling the patents for gutta-percha extrusion, and having readily available capital from British financiers. The original expansion from the domestic to the international was a matter of both strategic interest and commercial concern. The Indian Mutiny, the American Civil War, and the Crimean War pushed the British government to instigate expansion of the submarine cable system. For the U.S. government in the 1850s a primary concern in cooperating with the British government may have been the access it would give U.S. agricultural produce, such as cotton, to British markets as well as to the financial market. At the time both governments had privately owned telegraph companies and were excluded from the European arrangements of Napoleon III.

In the mid-nineteenth century the U.S. government was prepared to grant subsidies to see the telegraph penetrate western Europe. The British and U.S. governments cooperated, providing both financing and naval support to the initial attempt to cross the Atlantic. Both governments used their navies to survey the direct route across the Atlantic as well as alternative routes to the north and via the Pacific. During the American Civil War the British government also gave a Canadian concession to the U.S. government-financed attempt across Alaska. But border disputes on the Canadian frontier soured relations, and after the Civil War rapid industrialization and lack of capital prevented any further U.S. government subsidies.

Once the British-controlled Atlantic cable had been laid, and the British domestic telegraph had been nationalized, U.S. attitudes changed. In 1866 Congress made some provision for nationalizing domestic U.S. lines within five years, and President Grant subsequently attempted to get an international treaty to prevent monopolies. But after the British government joined the Europeans in the ITU and agreed to regulations that legitimized the interception of traffic, the U.S. government became primarily concerned at the high tariffs, lack of secure communications, and the potential for foreign-owned cartels. In contrast to the British government, which granted nonexclusive concessions even to British-owned companies, Congress was prepared to grant monopoly concessions to U.S.-owned companies. The contrasting actions reflected the free-trade ideology of the British and the developing mercantilism of the Americans.

For entrepreneurs incentives came from the potential for creating a domestic market position by controlling international traffic. In Britain the

Magnetic was the first firm to benefit in its domestic market from the control of international facilities. The high up-front costs of installing a telegraph, whether on land or sea, meant high debt, which forced the companies to recognize advantages to be gained from mergers and takeovers that would create monopolistic or dominant companies. These could then enforce high tariffs to repay high debt loads. As was to become evident in the 1990s as privatization of assets increased, the most profitable scenario for a company was to control both domestic and international communications. In the nineteenth century, when operator expertise was crucial to efficiency, this control preferably involved using domestic personnel to staff the telegraph stations in foreign countries.

Cyrus Field's envisioning of the transatlantic telegraph cable was part of his strategic plan to create a dominant domestic telegraph company within the United States. His intention was to channel international traffic from the cable down the domestic lines of his American Telegraph Company, thereby gaining competitive advantage over Western Union. The strategy did not pay off only because the submarine cable failed so many times that it weakened Field's domestic business.

Similarly, by building his own transatlantic cables, Jay Gould obtained control of Western Union through his control of international traffic. He then eliminated competition in international traffic with a cartel. Given the Anglo-American Telegraph Company's dependence on its interconnection with Western Union for collecting and delivering its traffic in the United States, it had no alternative but to join the U.S.-led cartel. The prevalence of the practice of pooling revenue, whether between commercial companies across the Atlantic or in a form of a public-private cartel, as on the route to India, suggests that international traffic may have been insufficient to sustain competition.

By the 1880s interconnection had already emerged as the dominant companies' favorite mechanism for preventing competition. Western Union attempted to use interconnection to exclude the Postal Telegraph Company, a minor competitor, from the U.S. domestic market. It also used the possibility of the denial of interconnection to control Pender's company. Similarly, the British Post Office controlled the domestic telephone companies by limiting interconnection to the telegraph.

Because the Post Office owned the domestic telegraph infrastructure in Britain, although Pender's company bought up competition such as the DUS line when it hurt profits, Pender's company could not use the same interconnection tactics against the Americans. The U.S. companies in turn took advantage of the lax British controls on cable licensing to gain collection points within Britain for their traffic. The Post Office's failure to demand reciprocity from U.S. companies in interconnection rights can be seen as not only an instance of British free-trade ideology in practice but also as a result of the Post Office's dual role as operator and regulator. In terms of operation, if the U.S. cables brought more traffic, they were to be welcomed.

The submarine telegraph business was not only expensive but initially very risky, and the British government lost millions of pounds in supporting attempts to establish telegraph communications to the United States and India. Initially willing to provide subsidies to mitigate the risk to investors, the government became increasingly unwilling to risk public money on private companies. Its first action to reduce the risk was to convene a public-private committee to review all the available evidence and gather existing expertise in one document. Then the British government moved to regulation, which it had already attempted in regard to railways. Parliament had made earlier attempts to regulate the domestic telegraph companies. Then, in the case of the domestic telephone, the government allowed the Post Office to compete with private companies. But the domestic companies had not received subsidies, and it was the payment of subsidies that opened up the possibility of other forms of regulation.

Forms of public-private cooperation developed, with the Treasury actually purchasing cable for the attempt to string cable across the Red Sea. When the Treasury's purchasing proved disastrous, alternative mechanisms of regulation were tried by appointing Treasury directors to the boards of companies receiving subsidies. Overall, the inflated cost of purchasing the domestic telegraph cables acted as a warning about the disadvantages of allowing a monopoly to develop. Thus while the Eastern was close to the British government, from the 1870s the British government's attitude was dichotomous. On the one hand, the government needed the company for strategic reasons, but on the other the government feared that the company might become a monopoly that the British government would have to buy out.

In addition, the British government had other interests to represent. As evidenced by the case of Hong Kong, the interest of the state and the company did not always coincide. When the British government told the Great Northern Telegraph Company and the Eastern to lower their tariffs, it was trying to find a third way between outright public ownership and unfettered private enterprise. But this example was perhaps the only time when the British government issued a direct order to a British company in the interests of consumers. In general it relied on the international regulations of 1875 to give it a form of regulatory control.

There were other instances where the interests of the cable companies and those of the British government diverged. The St. Petersburg International Telegraph Convention of 1875 used as its model the British domestic telegraph legislation, which not only reduced the price of cable tariffs for the press but allowed newspapers to lease lines. Yet even here, given the reliance of Reuter's news agency on its cable income, the British government's economic interest was wider than the purely commercial interest of one company. It was defending both the British monopoly of cable and its hegemony over the dissemination of news. Thus the 1875 conference both institutionalized a press rate on international lines and allowed leasing of private lines to the press—which benefited Reuters as a press agency—and decided on a word rate for tariffs—which was intended to damage Reuters as a telecommunications reseller (Bright 1898a:173). And by regulating government telegrams at half the public rate, European governments also served their own ends. As a result the International Telegraph Union was the initial attempt of governments to control international telecommunications primarily in their own commercial and security interests.

The original intention of the International Telegraph Union was to formalize cartelization involving the telegraphs of a number of countries. It was intended to end competition and to equalize tariffs. And it was for that reason that only government-owned telegraph agencies or their recognized private operating agencies were eligible for membership. Nevertheless, other international telegraph companies were allowed to attend the discussions from 1871. For governments the advantage of international regulation was that it provided a means of controlling their telegraph companies before the development of domestic regulation. In the British case, the Post Office used those regulations to prevent the Eastern from using its political connections in the Colonial Office and Treasury to evade minimum regulation. International and domestic regulation were intrinsically linked.

By 1875, when the Europeans signed the St. Petersburg International Telegraph Convention, Western Union had developed its domestic monopoly. At a time when nationalization was still on the congressional agenda, Western Union's opposition to the potential leverage that might be gained from international regulation was understandable. Then, because the U.S. government had no international regulations to fall back on, it had a greater need to formulate a domestic policy. Whereas the British did not develop a cable landing policy until the twentieth century, the U.S. government developed its cable policy in the same year as the 1875 convention. President Grant's emphasis on reciprocity of opportunity for U.S. companies, on low tariffs and no pools, was directed at both the French and British and was subsequently extended by Secretary of State Blaine to include the liberalization of third markets.

The vertical concentration of manufacturing and operation was evident not only in the case of Western Union and then AT&T but was part of the structure of financing for international cables. Telcon financed many cables. In general, there may have been an oversupply of manufacturing for the traffic available, leading to an oversupply of infrastructure. In fact, the profits of Pender's operating companies were low; it is not clear whether they were low because Telcon's costs of supplying the cable were high or because the directors were too well paid. However, lack of technological upgrading and failure to consider the needs of customers left it vulnerable to competition. As the costs of cable fell, the cream skimming of large users, noticeable in the 1980s, was also a profitable competitive strategy in the 1880s, as shown by the DUS line. The high tariffs that the Eastern charged and the manufacturing availability of Siemens Brothers encouraged competition. But even on the transatlantic route competition did not last long.

The economics of information were already evident in this free-market environment. There was early horizontal expansion from the ownership of infrastructure into the distribution of information, and from the distribution of information into the ownership of infrastructure. In Britain the British and Irish Magnetic Telegraph Company founded its own news agency with lower transmission tariffs to subscribers. In the United States, Western Union had a monopoly agreement with the Associated Press. Reuters moved from the provision of information into the provision of infrastructure—in cables to Germany and the United States—and then into undercutting the Eastern's tariffs through the innovative use of codes from India and the Far East. The European news agencies themselves cartelized the world market, helped by the discounted telegraph rates for the press formalized by the 1875 convention. In contrast, with transatlantic tariffs falling outside the convention, U.S. newspapers and agencies were handicapped by the costs of international collection and distribution of news.

Whereas the U.S. government was able to gain landing concessions from the French in response to its demand for reciprocity, other weaker countries, such as China, were less fortunate. With only concessions available as mechanisms of regulation, weaker countries first looked to monopoly agreements, which included low-priced carriage for government traffic to protect them from exploitation. But concessions given for thirty years did not give the flexibility necessary to allow for changing national interests. As the industrialization of these countries progressed, they wanted lower tariffs to reflect increased traffic and began to look for competition. Only when that strategy failed, because of joint purses and other cartelization, did they look to the replacement of private foreign control of cables with their own government control. That was when countries, such as China, began to play the foreigners off against each other to gain transfer of technology and regain some national sovereignty.

Both the U.S. and British governments were playing a two-level game. On the one hand, the official British pronouncements and the overt British cable landing policy were oriented toward free trade. On the other, the British government did nothing to prevent the Eastern from gaining monopoly concessions overseas, particularly if these were of strategic value. In their attitude toward the Eastern, splits between the bureaucracies were already evident, between Colonial and Foreign Offices on the one hand and the Post Office as domestic operator and regulator on the other. In the case of the United States, an official cable policy pressed for the abolition of monopoly concessions and demanded bilateral reciprocity in landing rights, while the government allowed U.S. companies to gain monopoly concessions and form pools. In general, Western Union's interests prevailed.

As the 1880s drew to a close, nationalism became an increasing factor in world economic relations and inevitably therefore in international communications. The British hegemony in cable manufacturing, laying, and operation saw increasing challenges from both Germany and the United States, and security became a predominant feature of international and domestic communications policy. That is the story of the next chapter.

2. Following the Flag: Cable and the British Government

DURING AN ECONOMIC DOWNTURN in the 1890s Britain's traditional free-trade ideology faced heavy pressure from chambers of commerce that were lobbying for the expansion of British overseas territory and for closer links with the settlement colonies as a way to overcome the problems of overproduction. "Overseas trade was almost the only sphere wherein a state-directed anti-cyclical policy could operate" (Hynes 1979:135). Britain was already suffering the effects of rising industrial competition. Exports increased by only 9 percent between 1880 and 1904, compared with increases of 29 percent for France, 61 percent for Germany, and 239 percent for the United States (Garvin 1905:80). Manufactured goods were particularly affected. Commentators blamed the rise in protective tariffs, not only in Europe, where Italy, Germany, and France abandoned free trade between 1878 and 1881, but also in South America, particularly Argentina (Calleo and Rowland 1973:26).

British businessmen increasingly exported their manufactured goods to countries within the empire. But as the United States and Germany built up their shipping fleets in the 1890s, the markets of Canada, South Africa, and India also became competitive (Garvin 1905:115–17; Benians 1959:217). Threatened by Continental colonialism and under pressure from commercial interests at home, the British government reverted to preventative annexations and protectorates within Africa and renewed its interest in China. In turn, reawakened enthusiasm for the empire brought a proposal from Joseph Chamberlain, the businessman and ardent imperialist who had been appointed to the Colonial Office in 1895, for a new system of intraempire preferential tariffs and further expansion into Africa and Asia (Hynes 1979:138). However, any breach in the concept of free trade and all schemes to institute a tariff bloc based in the colonies were defeated by hostility from the London financial community, with its investments in the United States and Latin America.

As the century progressed, the interest in overseas investments rather than "invisibles"—shipping and insurance—funded the British balance-of-payments deficit in manufactured goods. Investment in the United States decreased, but until 1913 Australia, Brazil, and India received large inflows (Calleo and Rowland 1973:264n.24).[1] By the beginning of World War I, Britain had invested £4 billion ($19.72 billion) abroad, whereas the combined foreign investments of France, Germany, Belgium, Holland and the United States came to £5.5 billion ($27.12 billion) (Thornton 1978:83). And a crucial factor in Britain's increased foreign investments, as evidenced by the British money flowing into Australia, was information to which investors had access following the introduction of submarine cable links.

In general, whereas British trade with the empire increased, that with the newly acquired territories in Africa remained underdeveloped. Once the economy began to pick up in the late 1890s, British businessmen lost interest in Africa and the Far East. India remained the most important of the colonial territories for trade, for its tax revenue, and for its reserve army. Yet from the late nineteenth century, in its attempt at self-sufficiency, even India imposed an import tariff against British goods.

National Policies in Submarine Cables

Inevitably, submarine cables became an industrial sector influenced by these ongoing trade and security concerns. In common with other manufacturing industries, as commercial prospects for submarine cables took second place to strategic and mercantilist considerations, other countries began to build up their own capacity. During the 1890s France, Germany, Japan, and Italy all created state-backed cable-manufacturing industries and began to lay their own cables. The French expanded their use of landing rights to promote French companies at every stage of manufacture, laying, and operation and after 1891 excluded British contractors altogether (Bright 1898b:426–27). Cooperating with the French in their desire to circumvent the British, the Germans ran a cable to Brest to connect with the 1898 French transatlantic cable and collaborated in an attempt (foiled by the British) to build landlines through Turkey to rival the British India route. The Germans also financed a cable to link with the German expatriate population in Brazil and a direct cable from Germany to Canada. As the British ambassador to Constantinople commented, although "'ostensibly the German Government have promoted their cables schemes for commercial purposes, there can be no doubt that they have long desired to free themselves as far as possible from British control, which might in time of war, be inconvenient for them.'"[2] However, because the German cable stations employed many British staff members (who were considered the best trained), the German government perceived even these German state-owned cables as unreliable (Kennedy 1971:748).

The introduction of state-supported local manufacture of telegraph cable became in turn the precursor of the state-backed national champion telephone manufacturers of the twentieth century. The virtual British monopoly of submarine cable manufacture and operation was over, but whereas in Germany from the 1880s the mercantilist ideas of the economist Friedrich List became influential, in Britain the prevailing free-trade ideology precluded overt domestic protection. Instead, a conflict arose between strategic and commercial interests, between liberal free-market ideology, with its tenet of promoting private competition, and the strategic desire for state control of submarine cables. Subsidies for defense purposes required public accountability. Yet the mechanisms of regulation remained elusive.

Censorship

The experiences of the French and Germans during the Boer War of 1895 gave them the incentive to become independent of the British. On the ground of national security, the St. Petersburg International Telegraph Convention of 1875 had sanctioned the practice of censoring telegraph messages passing through the territory of member states. And by 1891 British government lawyers had given their opinion that in time of war the government of a neutral country had the right to "stop or examine Telegrams issuing from or addressed to its own subjects."[3]

Although transmitting telegrams in code had occasionally been prohibited, such as during the Sino-Japanese War of 1895, the transmission of the belligerent's traffic by neutral cable companies became an issue in connection with the American-Spanish War of 1898.[4] Confusion about the exact obligations of the cable companies under the 1875 International Telegraph Convention was considerable.

The acting manager of the Eastern in Hong Kong wrote to the home office in May 1898 to say that the U.S. Navy, under Admiral George Dewey, had cut the Eastern's cable from Hong Kong to the Philippines. The admiral had then sent by ship to Hong Kong a "heavy batch of government and press telegrams from the American fleet" and had requested that the Eastern repair the Philippines end of the cable so that it could operate under the direction of the commander of the U.S. forces.[5] Despite pressure to restore communication with the English people in Manila, the Eastern sealed the Hong Kong end of the Philippines cable so that the Americans could not take it over. With this done the remaining question was whether U.S. naval messages should be transmitted west from Hong Kong.

The British Foreign Office wanted the Eastern to refuse telegrams about the war from both sides. But Pender's son, John Denison-Pender, who had become the Eastern's managing director in 1893, claimed that the company could do so only if the British government first notified the International Bureau of Telegraph Administrations in Berne.[6] A month later, when the Foreign Office proposed that a censor work from the company's office in Gibraltar, the Eastern insisted only that its own staff should not act in that capacity. In fact, the cable company had already been brought into plans for military censorship of cable traffic.

In 1898 a government committee devised censorship plans that would be instituted whenever the armed services were mobilized. A chief censor and his staff based in the Central Telegraph Office in London would be responsible for checking all telegrams entering or leaving Britain. The same measures were to be carried out in the colonies, and listening devices were to be attached secretly to commercial lines running to a potential belligerent's capital. Although the submarine cable companies and the Post Office were party to the plans, the censors were to be appointed and controlled by the military (Kennedy 1971:748).

Immediately after the Spanish-American War, the Post Office, acting on behalf of the Foreign Office, enlisted the help of submarine cable companies operating in Britain in determining how the United States had handled censorship during the war. The survey showed that first the Western Union and then the Commercial Cable Company and its associated French company had refused to carry Spanish government messages after the outbreak of war.[7] Also, because of its experience with the media in the Crimean War, the British government was particularly interested in a number of censorship orders made by U.S. Gen. Adolphus Greely that had prohibited "the transmission of news of the movements of American vessels or troops, even though published in the United States."[8] The Foreign Office could claim that any such British actions had a U.S. precedent.

The Boer War marked the beginning of this surveillance of cable communications and the birth of the British security agency MI5. According to Nigel West (1986:11), during the Boer War "a special unit designated Section H was established to co-ordinate inspection and censorship of mail and cables. . . . Section H was responsible for monitoring all traffic using the two main submarine cables connecting South Africa to Portugal and Aden, for maintaining strict control over the civil land-line cables and for examining the mail of suspect foreigners in conjunction with the Special Branch of the Metropolitan police." Although this blatant interference with nonmilitary traffic caused considerable local resentment, government censors opened offices at Cape Town, Durban, Zanzibar, and Aden. Traders in German East Africa and Portugal complained that they were unable to conduct their businesses, and some questioned the legality of the British action. Soon London started to receive demands for compensation, which led to relaxation of the censorship in order "to permit the use of certain selected codes and afford special facilities to foreign government messages" (West 1986:11). Nevertheless, this evidence of British power proved a major incentive for French and German attempts to promote independent cable networks.

At the end of the Boer War, Section H was taken over by a single officer, Col. F. J. Davies, who was charged with preparing contingency plans for future conflicts, including "ciphers, government telegraph codes, compensation claims, wireless telegraphy, cable censorship, press correspondence, control of the press" (West 1986:11–13). In 1906 Section H was supplanted by the establishment of a military intelligence department in the War Office (MO5, now MI5). Censorship of all cables and foreign correspondence continued under the Defense of the Realm Act, under which newspapers ran the risk of prosecution (Wedell 1968:25). Concern about censorship remained at the center of British cable policy and was to surface in a new landing rights policy in 1919.

British Cables: Following the Flag

Just as the Boer War affected German and French submarine cable policy, the Spanish-American War had a major influence on British policy. Although the British in 1898 had drawn up plans to cut foreign cables using the Eastern's cable ships, the international legitimacy of such action was in doubt. Whereas previous British policy had favored neutrality for cables in peace and war, the Spanish-American War had demonstrated that neutrality offered no defense against the strategic cutting of cables. In fact, the Post Office's survey of the cable companies' concessions found that most governments were prepared at the least to take over the cables of neutrals in time of war and at most to destroy them.[9] If Congress could authorize $10 million "for maintaining and *destroying communication,* an object in which cable-cutting would be included," the British needed to reconsider the vulnerability of British cables.[10]

During the late 1890s these strategic considerations were given voice in the new Cable Landing Rights Committee, which began to institute a more coherent cable policy. Proposed by Chamberlain after his appointment to the Colonial Office, the committee was a mercantilist response to a proposed German transatlantic cable that had been refused permission to land in Cornwall on the grounds that it was subsidized by the German government and would take traffic from British cables in the Azores. The committee's first action was to consider a renewed application from the Germans, now in collaboration with the American-owned Commercial Cable Company. They proposed to land a cable in Ireland, where it would hook up with an old Eastern cable to Germany. Unaware that technology had progressed sufficiently for a cable to be laid directly from the Azores to Germany, the committee postponed a decision on the application.

With the inauguration of the direct cable the Germans gained an independent connection to the United States, and the British belatedly agreed to the Irish link. Lord Balfour of Burleigh's 1901 Interdepartmental Committee on Cable Communications suggested that the British had effectively shot themselves in the foot.[11] Subsequently, in order to retain Britain's position as a telegraphic hub, the Post Office became an advocate of free trade in landing licenses.[12] Coincidentally, its position as a hub allowed Britain to monitor the majority of cable traffic.

Although the Cable Landing Rights Committee included representatives from the Colonial Office, India Office, Board of Trade, Post Office, Admiralty, and War Office, it became a vehicle for defense interests. As a response to both vulnerability and the potential for censorship by any country crossed by cables, enthusiasm for "All-Red" lines was growing—cables that linked parts of the empire without touching foreign soil.[13] The War Office wanted to consider the defense of each cable landing station "with reference to its being commanded by the guns of a fortress" (quoted in Kennedy 1971:744). Where such defense was not possible, that station would be cut from the transmission line in order to protect the cable (Kennedy 1971:744). New technologies created additional strategic problems. As steamships replaced sail, ports that became coaling stations gained enhanced strategic value, and islands on which submarine cables could land, such as the Azores and Zanzibar, found their relative importance had increased. Strategic and commercial interests overlapped.

Concerned at the influence exerted by the French from their base in Senegal, chambers of commerce argued that the British government should bring the rest of West Africa under British control. Just as the businessmen feared the French in West Africa, so they feared German encroachment in East Africa, particularly Uganda (Hynes 1979:129). As the idea of imperial unity became fashionable, the Eastern's fortunes became tied with defense of the empire. Even where there was little trade, government subsidies made cables profitable.

Subsidized cables down the east and west coasts of Africa, with a duplicate cable to South Africa, supported commercial and strategic ends. The initial financing for these cables was partly provided by the Portuguese and the South African colonies, but the Treasury, which followed its long-time practice of appointing directors to the companies, provided operating subsidies. By the late 1890s the main coastal cities in Africa were ringed with cable, for which the Eastern had received subsidies of £1,337,000 ($6.5 million) (Barty-King 1979:103).

Meanwhile, the high charges of the Eastern's service to South Africa provided the incentive for Cecil Rhodes to propose a land-based five-thousand-mile cable cutting through the center of Africa to Egypt. The proposal had first been put forward in London by Sir James Sivewright in 1878 but then had been dropped because the Eastern, responding to the potential threat to its interests, had completed the east coast line to Durban. The proposal had also met considerable opposition on the grounds that native populations would attack and steal the line and that malaria would kill white staff members (Weinthal 1923:211–13). Rhodes revived the proposal in the late 1880s. By 1888 he had gained control of the Kimberley diamond fields and 90 percent of world production. In 1889 he presented the British government with a plan to develop the areas north of the three Boer republics of Transvaal, Natal, and the Orange Free State. Part of that plan involved extending the railways and telegraph to the Zambesi River. He also wrote a confidential letter to the foreign secretary proposing to take the line through German East Africa and up to Egypt, for which he wanted the British government's help in gaining the German concession.

Rhodes gained a royal charter for the venture in 1889 and formed a company in 1892. But of the initial £140,000 ($681,800) capital required, only £46,000 ($224,000) came from the general public. Rhodes contributed the rest himself. By 1899, although one section had been destroyed in a Mashonaland rebellion, the line had reached the southern end of Lake Tanganyika, and Rhodes eventually received the kaiser's permission to cross German Africa. However, the financing of the cable relied on Rhodes's finding a rumored golden reef that would attract investors. His failure to do so meant that the cable never reached Uganda (Weinthal 1923:217).

Although Rhodes's plan was to undercut the Eastern's rate of nine shillings and sixpence ($2.31) per word by charging two shillings and sixpence (61 cents), the Eastern's executives were not worried. As Sir James Anderson, the managing director, pointed out, "'The natives who do not wear clothes are not in the habit of sending telegrams.'" The Eastern would continue to carry commercial traffic from the coast to the interior (Barty-King 1979:91). The Eastern proved correct in its assessment. Owing to diminishing receipts, Rhodes's company was placed in liquidation in 1911, and World War I led to its demise (Weinthal 1923:217).

Of more concern to the Eastern was the public backlash after the Boer War. During the prelude to that war the cables down both coasts of Africa were out of action for several days. Both were laid in shallow waters, and a warm water worm had destroyed their insulation (Lawford and Nicholson 1950:74). Although an effective preventative had been discovered ten years earlier, the Eastern apparently did not apply it to the African cables. As a result between 1894 and 1896 the east coast cable to the Cape of Good Hope was down for 209 days and the west coast cable for 151 days. Just after the Jameson Raid, an invasion of the Transvaal in December 1895 by an employee of Rhodes, the east coast cable went down, and the west coast cable was blocked. For two days neither the British government nor the London financial district, with "millions invested in the Rand," received news from South Africa (Hurd 1896:902). Hurd paints a picture of "her Majesty's Secretary of State . . . though ill from exhaustion, leaving his home and waking the echoes of the City at dead of night in search of news" (902).

In strategic terms the vulnerability of the shallow-water African cables had been recognized a decade earlier and reemphasized by an interdepartmental commission in 1898 (Kennedy 1971:734). Yet a third cable was not laid until after the Boer War of 1899, this time in deepwater from Cape Verde to Cape Town via Ascension and St. Helena. That the cable was delayed for several years was a direct result of standoffs between the company and the government of the Cape Colony, which for the first time demanded concessions on rates from the Eastern in return for landing rights, and between the company and the British Treasury, which objected to the cost of cable subsidies. Hicks Beach, then Chancellor of the Exchequer, wrote a strongly worded memo attacking those who argued ""that no communication of the kind is satisfactory which touches foreign soil, though that soil may belong to a nation with which we are not likely to be at war, or even to a nation who would almost certainly be our ally in the event of war. And, further, existing cables are destructed which are laid in shallow water, or landed in undefended places. If these views are to be accepted, I see no limit to the demands which may be initiated by a body like the Colonial Defence Committee . . . which is not likely to have the slightest regard to the cost.""[14]

The dispute centered on a spur to the cable that the British government wanted laid to link Ascension with Sierra Leone for strategic reasons. The

Eastern demanded a subsidy of £5,000 ($24,300) for five years. The Treasury threatened that unless the line were laid without a subsidy, the company would be unable to obtain British landing rights, but eventually, faced with an obdurate company, the government had to agree to a subsidy of £4,500 ($21,870) per year.[15] This incident created greater determination within the British government to control the Eastern.

Despite the Eastern's global dominance and its subsidization by the British government, John Denison-Pender wanted more. In 1899 he proposed that in return for a general reduction in rates to all British colonies and possessions, the empire should give the company a guarantee of landing rights for any additional cables that the Eastern might consider necessary and that in all parts of the British Empire the Eastern should be placed "on terms of equality with any other Telegraph Administrations that might be competing against them."[16] In effect, by trading regulation for monopoly, Pender was responding to the establishment of the Second Pacific Cable Committee in 1899 to further consider the Canadian proposal for a state-owned cable from Canada to Australia.

The Post Office was eager to see a reduction in tariffs and argued that the company's proposals would give the government more control than it had previously, but neither the War Office nor the Admiralty was prepared to allow the Eastern a guarantee of landing rights. They argued that the government must retain the right to have a cable laid by a route that it thought strategically necessary. The Colonial Office wanted to encourage "any attempt to compete with the Company which might prove beneficial to the public interest," and to use landing rights to gain concessions from the company.[17]

And the Treasury was not pleased with the form of regulation that the company proposed. The Treasury argued that "the machinery which the Companies propose to adopt is not novel. The principle of a sliding scale of charges, based on a minimum revenue having relation to the cost of the cables, has been before their Lordships in the negotiations with regard to the new cable to South Africa. It would be difficult, in applying the principle throughout the whole of the Companies' system, to apportion the cost of cables to the various descriptions of traffic." In other words, almost a century before the matter of how to distribute common costs arose in relation to domestic telephone operations, the major question of regulation in the 1890s revolved around how to define those "costs" on which a rate of return on investment and subsequent tariffs would be calculated.

But regulation as a form of government intervention did not yet have public legitimacy. The Treasury commented that it also did not like the idea that the government might be seen to sanction even reduced rates.[18] Nor was it happy that the company was not prepared to discuss the details of regulation before its proposals were accepted in principle. Finally, the Cable Landing Rights Committee pointed out that it had no authority over the dominions, so it rejected outright the idea that the company should be given a kind of roving commission to lay cables wherever it pleased.[19]

That Pender felt that he could make such demands on the British government reflects the Eastern's position at the turn of the century. Of the inhabited British territories, only those of minor strategic or commercial importance, such as Fiji, British Honduras, Tobago, the Falkland Islands, Turks Islands, and New Guinea, were without a cable (Morris 1979:60). By 1892 the British controlled 66 percent of the world's cables; the United States, 15.7 percent; the French, 8.8 percent; the Danish, 5.2 percent; and others, 3.9 percent. And to achieve this preeminent position on behalf of the British state, by the end of 1900 the Eastern had received subsidies of £2.9 billion ($14.2 billion) from the British and colonial governments (Balfour Committee 1902:78–79).

Meanwhile, further prolonged breakdown of the cables from South Africa between 1899 and 1900 raised questions about what the Eastern had been doing with its subsidies. High tariffs were another popular complaint. State ownership was on the agenda once more. In May 1900, when a member of Parliament, Sir Edward Sassoon, moved that legislators should formally inquire into the commercial and strategic defects of imperial telegraphic communications, the government responded by setting up an interdepartmental committee under Lord Balfour.

The committee's brief covered strategic considerations, regulation, and tariffs. It was empowered to consider how the existing telegraph network should be supplemented, to investigate what control the government had over the cable companies and what policy it should adopt in the future, and to determine whether international tariffs were "fair and reasonable." Public opinion at the time favored "All-Red" cables, but the Balfour Committee concluded that the best protection against cable cutting was having several alternative routes to any one place, rather than all-British lines, which "public opinion has tended to over-rate in importance."[20] The committee argued that every important colony or naval base should be connected to Britain by one "British" cable but found it difficult to strike a balance between strategic and commercial considerations (Balfour Committee 1902:15–16).

In considering the mechanisms by which the state could exert control over the companies, the committee commented that "many of the witnesses who came before us did not seem to realize how limited is the control exercised by the State over private cable companies." It concluded that the state had the power to make stipulations when granting a subsidy; to use public funds to encourage competition; to grant or withhold general cooperation; to allow or withhold use of the cable for government messages; and to determine which company should receive "unrouted" telegrams (those that did not specify the operator to be used). The committee argued that the government's most effective power came through the granting or withholding of landing rights.

The Balfour Committee recommended that, in order to make London the center of the telegraphic world, the traditional policy of a "free trade" in cables was correct and that permission to land a cable should be withheld only for reasons of "national interest," not to protect the existing companies. It recommended that the government not require payment for those landing rights. However, it suggested that "the real function of these concessions is to furnish opportunities of correcting any marked unreasonableness on behalf of the companies" and that landing rights should be granted only for a "medium term," which would give the government sufficient opportunities to review the company's behavior. To ensure better regulation through this mechanism, the committee recommended that the Cable Landing Rights Committee should be strengthened and report to the Treasury, rather than to the Board of Trade—a suggestion not implemented.

On the question of tariffs the committee (dependent on the company for information on "costs") concluded that, bearing in mind the need to provide investors with a return on their capital, only the line to Nigeria was overpriced. The committee defended subsidies to the Eastern on strategic grounds and came down heavily against the purchase of the Eastern cables by the state, a move that the committee estimated would cost £25 million ($122 million) and result in uneconomic demands for increased wages and lower tariffs. However, in order to increase the use of the international telegraph for residential, rather than business traffic, it urged the adoption of deferred rates (lower rates for nonimmediate transmittal) that would allow people to send telegrams overnight, just as they could on domestic lines.

Perhaps in anticipation of the committee's findings, in 1900 the Post Office apparently began to use landing license renewals to extend regulation. In 1900 and 1901 it requested a delay in the renewal of a license for the British and U.S. transatlantic cables so that it could renegotiate terms for a domestic leased line.[21] In addition, in the case of Western Union, the Post Office suggested that the "British Government might not unreasonably take advantage of this opportunity to impose a special condition for the protection of the 'all-British' route to the West Indies from Halifax (Nova Scotia) via Bermuda." Whereas by virtue of its pooling arrangement the U.S. company had previously been able to insist that its Canadian facilities should handle all traffic to the West Indies, now the Post Office made it a condition of its landing license in Cornwall that the company hand over its traffic to the British-owned Halifax and Bermudas Cable Company.[22] This company had been established in 1889 under a British government contract to link two naval stations, and it received an annual subsidy.

This license provision (which the British could insist on because the United States was not a member of the International Telegraph Union) was joined by one that forced Western Union to accept the International Telegraph Convention's regulations in the operation of its transatlantic cables (but not Western Union's domestic U.S. system). A similar clause formed part of the license granted to the Commercial Cable Company. In addition, the Post Office limited the licenses to ten years, and both companies had to accept the provision that they could be taken over by the government in time of war. Landing licenses were starting to become instruments for protecting "British" cables.

But these efforts at regulation contained provisions about tariffs that did no more than ensure that the company could not charge more to Britain than to any other European country and that the government should not pay more than any other European administration. Even this latter provision was modified for the Commercial Cable Company, which had a preexisting agreement with the German government to carry traffic at half price.[23] And the landing licenses made no provision for regulating tariffs paid by the public.

Nor does the Post Office seem to have tightened its regulation of the U.S. companies' collection of traffic. On one landing license an official commented that "it appears from the Company's notifications to the public that they collect Telegrams at London, Liverpool, Dundee, Bristol, Bradford, Edinburgh, Glasgow, Leith, Manchester and Newcastle, though they do not rent private wires to the last eight towns named." Another Post Office official wrote a margin note in response: "They have never been authorised to collect telegrams at the places in question."[24] The ensuing license contained no specific permission to do so, but it seems that the practice was allowed to go on. Nor did the Post Office demand reciprocity for British companies.

The British government could not implement a number of the mechanisms for domestic regulation that the Balfour Committee suggested. Because the government had made an agreement with the telegraph companies before nationalization that any telegrams that did not specify a distribution company should be handled by the Eastern, it could do nothing about this preferential treatment. Membership in the International Telegraph Union (ITU) also precluded the government from demanding that tariffs to the Far

East be reduced if that reduction would affect intra-European or transit tariffs agreed upon by the ITU. For the same reason the government could not introduce a system of "deferred" rates for night-time transmission if other European states opposed the practice, and it took until 1912 and the persistence of Herbert Samuel, then the postmaster general, for the system to be introduced. Samuel was also said in 1914 "to be taking steps towards the control of cable rates with the renewal of landing licences" (Bright 1914:141). But World War I intervened, and further attempts at regulation took place in the 1920s in a different political culture.

Nevertheless, the debate about cable rates and state ownership did not end with the Balfour Committee's 1902 report. The press called for a national cable policy (*Times,* June 29, 1902). Critics of the companies argued that tariffs should allow for a proper rate of return on investment but should have a fixed maximum and that government traffic should be carried at half rate (Peel 1905:287). However, technologies had begun to change, and by the time that the Balfour Committee published its second report in 1902, Marconi had developed long-distance wireless signals. Despite the findings of a report by Oliver Lodge, an eminent physicist, and the Post Office's chief engineer, Sir William Preece, that "nothing [in wireless] . . . would tend to disturb the predominance of cable enterprise in the international communications of the world" (*Electrician,* May 9, 1902), the potential of wireless competition began to frighten cable company shareholders. And even as the Balfour Committee was paying its respects to the cable companies, the British government opened its first state-owned submarine cable in direct competition with the Eastern.

The All-Red Route of the Pacific Cable

On the surface the story of the state-owned All-Red cable from Canada to Australia is one of initiative on the part of the Canadian government and particularly of one individual, Sandford Fleming. But it also demonstrates how bureaucratic interests and alliances changed over twenty years. The united position of the Post Office and Colonial Office once meant triumph for the Eastern, but the appointment of Joseph Chamberlain to the Colonial Office changed the balance of power. His desire for lower tariffs, combined with the strategic interests of the War Office, brought the All-Red cable to fruition despite the best efforts of the Post Office and the Eastern to block it.

The All-Red cable proposal came out of Canada, where problems that the British-financed Canadian Pacific Railway had in laying its railroad through the Rocky Mountains led to the decision to link east to west by telegraph independently of the railroad. This telegraph line, which ran on the U.S. side of the border, was completed at the end of the 1870s. Until that moment the commercial focus of Canadian enterprise had been the Atlantic seaboard, with its telegraph communications to Britain. But once the telegraph reached Vancouver, the chief engineer on the railway, Sandford Fleming, began to envision telegraph communications across the Pacific to parallel the proposed new steamship line with Australasia. The original reason for the Pacific cable was therefore to stimulate trade on the Canadian Pacific coast.

Yet the idea arose contemporaneously with the state's takeover of the domestic telegraph in Britain and the subsequent lowering of tariffs. That experience led Canadians to equate state ownership with low tariffs. The scheme was not simply a means of periphery-to-periphery communication and increased trade but contained an underlying vision of the future—that state ownership and low tariffs would promote integration within the empire (Earl of Jersey 1894:141). In addition, the concept of a state-owned system of international cables, of which the Pacific would be the first, was also intended to push the issue of state-owned telegraphy onto the political agenda in Canada, whose cable market was dominated by private U.S. operators.

As in the case of the lobby to nationalize the private telegraph companies in the United Kingdom, the proponents of empire-owned submarine telegraph cables at first argued that high tariffs kept traffic demand low. Then, as the preoccupations of the times changed, the emphasis of the Canadian arguments changed from commercial-cultural-social unification of the empire to greater concern about imperial defense. Inasmuch as what became known as the All-Red route was to be state owned, touching only those countries that were British, it was in tune with the strategic outlook of the times.

As Sandford Fleming outlined in a June 1880 letter to Canada's governor general, his original concept was for a submarine cable that would cross to Japan and would land at one of the Kurile Islands, which he suggested should be transferred to the British Crown (Johnson 1903:14) However, the British Foreign Office was not happy at the prospect of making such a request and as a substitute suggested a guarantee from Japan to protect the cable (15). Other delays followed.

The Canadian Parliament granted Fleming a concession in 1882, but the cable was delayed by the British government's refusal to undertake the necessary oceanic survey. Although Fleming lobbied in London in 1886 at an unofficial colonial conference organized by the Imperial Federation League, he came up against direct opposition from Sir John Pender and lack of enthusiasm from the dominions and the British government. But by the time of the first official Colonial Conference in 1887, held to coincide with Queen

Victoria's Golden Jubilee, the British government had begun to recognize the importance of the telegraph to the isolated dominions, and the conference invitation letter mentioned that "'the promotion of commercial and social relations by the development of our postal and telegraphic communications could be considered with much advantage by the proposed conference'" (quoted in Johnson 1903:52). But Australian concerns dominated the conference, particularly the high costs of mail, and Pender's close relations with the Foreign and Colonial Offices biased their reactions. Post Office officials raised technical difficulties, contending that parts of the Pacific were thirteen miles deep.

Only Henry Cecil Raikes, the postmaster general, was sympathetic to the idea of All-Red cable (Johnson 1903:56). He felt that "'it would be . . . absolutely impossible for the English people, or for Her Majesty's Government, to recognise any monopoly, such as seems to be claimed by any company, however deserving their enterprise may have been.'" Nevertheless, on the ground that it would be difficult for the British government "'to constitute itself a competitor with existing commercial enterprise carried on by citizens of the British Empire,'" he was not in favor of the state construction or ownership of the cable (quoted in Johnson 1903:58–59).

In complete contradiction to his previous sentiments and almost as if to demonstrate the benefits of potential competition, Sir John Pender then offered to reduce the rates from Australia to four shillings (97 cents) per word (from nine shillings and sixpence, or $2.30) in return for a guarantee of half of any loss that the company might accrue from introducing the lower rates. Accepting that lower rates would increase demand, Pender suggested that the deficit that the Australian colonies would be asked to make up would soon diminish and perhaps disappear. His suggestion that "'if the government are going to begin to lay cables on their account, they must deal with companies who have laid cables'" implied a threat (quoted in Johnson 1903:65). No formal resolutions were allowed at the conference, but to the chagrin of the Colonial Office the delegates passed informal resolutions in favor of the All-Red Pacific cable and of undertaking an oceanic survey.

Then, a complete breakdown of the Australia-to-Java lines in both 1888 and 1890 increased enthusiasm for the project (Peel 1905:270). On visiting Australia in 1893 the Canadian minister of trade and commerce and Sandford Fleming found that two colonies, Queensland and New Zealand, had entered an agreement with a French company to subsidize a cable to New Caledonia because it would form part of a Franco-German Pacific cable.[25] There was considerable suspicion that the Eastern was behind this new means of undermining the idea of a state-run Pacific cable. In fact, the Eastern's rival,

Siemens, which the Eastern had beaten for the contract between Tasmania and the mainland, now was trying to raise the money to link the French line to a Pacific cable via Fiji and Hawaii (Harcourt 1987:87).

However, the Eastern's behavior aroused Fleming's suspicions. Following up on its proposals to the 1887 conference, in 1889 the Eastern had laid a further cable from Java to western Australia. The company agreed to reduce tariffs to four shillings (97 cents) per word on payment of a subsidy. Two colonies had paid the Eastern more than £50,000 ($242,500) per year in 1887 and 1888, but because traffic had not increased sufficiently to pay for the reduced tariff, these colonies then learned that the Eastern had raised the tariff back to four shillings and ninepence ($1.15).[26]

Fleming found the Eastern not only well entrenched in Australia but backed by Whitehall. On hearing that the Canadians were about to visit Australia, the Colonial Office had sent two documents to the colonial governments. The first, a letter from J. C. Lamb of the Post Office, estimated the cost of the Pacific cable at £3 million ($14.55 million) and the annual loss to be made good by subsidies at about £157,164 ($763,817) a year. The second, a seven-year-old report by the hydrographer of the Admiralty, stated that the lengths of the section between Vancouver and Fanning Island, together with the depths, islands, and hills in the unsurveyed Pacific Ocean bed, made the route unsuitable for a cable (Johnson 1903:116–18). Further, preventing the possibility of alternative Australian-owned submarine cables to the east, in 1893 the Eastern announced (inaccurately) that the company had been granted a twenty-five-year monopoly of landing rights in Hong Kong (Johnson 1903:305).[27] With matters stacked against it, the Canadian government called a conference in Ottawa of all the dominion premiers for 1894.

In the meantime Fleming was not above attempting a bit of land grabbing in order to obtain a landing point nearer to Vancouver than the thirty-five hundred nautical miles to Fanning Island. Having unsuccessfully requested that the British government annex the then unclaimed Necker Island (an uninhabited rock off Hawaii) for a cable landing station, he sent an agent to do so privately. But he reckoned without the British Colonial Office and Foreign Office, which, unwilling to risk offending the U.S. government, informed the Hawaiian government of its interest in the island for a cable landing station. Before Fleming's agent could act, the Hawaiian government, suspicious of a British warship said to be undertaking "maneuvers," planted its own flag on the island. Fleming's agent returned empty handed (Johnson 1903:121–48; Alexander 1911:60).

By the time of the Ottawa conference in 1894, the Australian colonies and New Zealand had passed new resolutions in favor of the All-Red cable. The arguments had altered slightly in that, in addition to the potential commercial opportunity of trade between the dominions, delegates now emphasized the importance of the cable to the defense of the empire. Whereas the cable fitted into the general Canadian predilection for increasing trade between the dominions, the Australian colonies were worried that their telegraph communications to England relied on a single Mediterranean cable that could be cut at Alexandria or in Portugal.

In Ottawa the premiers complained that the Admiralty had started, then stopped, the Pacific Ocean survey. Suspicion was cast on Sir John Pender, who was reported to have said of the proposal in an 1894 letter to the governor general of Canada that "first, . . . it cannot be built; second, if built it will not pay; and third, if it is to be built, he [Pender] wants to build it" (Johnson 1903:137). Delegates also were concerned by the activities of the French. In particular, the Australians wanted to prevent "any other nation [from] becoming dominant in the Pacific" (127).

But proponents of an All-Red route were divided. Some wanted cables that would bypass unreliable countries and were under British control. Others wanted the lower rates that a government-owned cable could provide (Hurd 1896:908). Nor could they agree on the route that the cable should follow, whether private enterprise or the governments should build it, or whether it should be extended to South Africa. Instead, they unanimously agreed that the Canadian, Australian, and British governments should jointly pay for the nautical survey and should explore the possibility of using the Hawaiian Islands as a landing point (Hurd 1896:906).

Because Siemens Brothers assured the premiers that the cable could be laid without further detailed soundings, they agreed that the Canadian government should call for bids and should act as the secretary to the conference. Subsequently, a member of the British Colonial Office and Fleming visited Hawaii to request a lease for a neutral landing ground for the cable so that it could still be "all red." The Hawaiian government, bound by its reciprocity treaty with the United States, refused. The British contingent then took up the matter with President Grover Cleveland, whose reaction was favorable, but in view of congressional hostility the proposal was dropped (Tribolet 1929:169). However, the process of bidding for the laying of the cable continued to exert pressure on the British government.

In addition, pressure from elsewhere began to build in favor of the All-Red route. Several books by military personnel pointed out the problems of the existing cable system, and chambers of commerce began to lobby for an "All-British" cable to Asia (Baglehole 1969:12). This increased commercial interest came with the discovery of gold in western Australia in 1893. International traffic from Australia rose by 118 percent in 1893–94 and by 700 percent in 1894–95. By 1896 the Canadian government had received bids for the cable, and the governments of Canada and Australia had each pledged to share the cost with the British government—a cost estimated at £1.5 million ($7.3 million, not the £2.75 to £3 million [$13.4 to $14.6 million] estimated by the Post Office). But still lacking was a commitment by the British government.

Bowing to increasing pressure and as a result of Chamberlain's appointment to the Colonial Office in 1895, the Pacific Cable Committee was constituted in June 1896 in London. The six members were divided equally between the British government, Australia, and Canada. Fleming acted as adviser, not only to the Canadian delegation but on an informal basis to the committee. The committee consulted experts in cable manufacture and laying; cable operators; potential users from banks, finance houses, Lloyd's of London, and traders; and the Eastern, as well as officials from the Post Office. Of these, the only witnesses against the project were the Eastern's representatives and the two Post Office officials, W. H. Preece, the chief engineer, and J. C. Lamb, the third secretary.

They argued that the cable would be unfair competition to the Eastern and that the proposed tariff of three shillings (7 cents) was too low to be reasonable. Preece had to acknowledge that his previous estimates had been too high but argued that a full survey must be done before the cable could be laid. Lamb argued that in addition to being too expensive and upsetting the government's relationship with the Eastern, the cable would reduce telegraph tariffs for U.S. traders and would ease market access to Australia and Asia for U.S. companies.

The report, completed by March 1897, deemed the cable to be practicable, but it was not published until 1899, just two months after Chamberlain wrote a strong memo in favor of the project that was supported by the Admiralty and War Office. Opposition from the Post Office and the Eastern continued, and in 1899 Chamberlain cabled the governor of Canada to say that the imperial government had decided that it would not take an active part in laying or working the line and would be responsible for loss of revenue only up to a maximum £20,000 ($97,200). Outrage from the press in Canada, Australia, and New Zealand eventually produced a change of heart and a formal partnership agreement between the governments on the last day of the century (Johnson 1903:431, 435). But continuing opposition from the Eastern, the Post Office, and the Treasury led to the appointment of another Pacific Cable Committee.

Finally, the Eastern's own actions provided the required impetus. In 1900 the Eastern approached the Australian colonies with a proposal to build a cable from South Africa to western Australia and to reduce the tariffs immediately from four shillings and ninepence ($1.16) to four shillings (97 cents) per word, with a press rate of one shilling and sixpence (37 cents). Further, the Eastern proposed that if its traffic from Australia averaged £350,000 ($1.7 million) annually in 1899–1901, the company would reduce tariffs further, to be followed by further reductions every three years if traffic kept up. In return, the Eastern wanted to be allowed to open offices in the chief towns in Australia and to advertise for its own traffic.

The Second Pacific Cable Committee concluded, "We are of the opinion that these facilities would enable them [the Eastern] to obtain a larger portion of the traffic than they would otherwise get, and so far as the interests of the Pacific cable are concerned, we should accordingly deprecate their being given."[28] The committee did not, however, suggest that the colonies should be forbidden to accept the Eastern's offer, which would create problems later. Instead, although the committee recognized this approach by the company as a tactic designed to prevent construction of the Pacific cable, it responded by proposing that the tariffs on the proposed cable should undercut those of the Eastern and that the cable should be run at an initial loss. The committee also proposed that the cable be run by a board in London consisting of two members from Canada, two from Australia, one from New Zealand, and three, including the chair, from Britain.[29] Finally, in 1901, despite the continued opposition of the Treasury, an act of Parliament—the Pacific Cable Act—"'to provide for the construction and working of a submarine cable from the Island of Vancouver to New Zealand and to Queensland'" was passed, and work on the project started early in 1902 (Peel 1905:271). Perhaps to placate Denison-Pender, the contract went to Telcon. The cable, which was eight thousand nautical miles long, ran from Vancouver to Fanning Island, then to Fiji, Norfolk Island, New Zealand, and Australia. It was the longest in the world (Baglehole 1969:13).

Although the Australians in particular had lobbied hard for the Pacific cable on the basis of competition for the Eastern, it seems likely that the considerations in its construction primarily involved the security of a deepwater Pacific cable that was not vulnerable to potential enemy action (Barty-King 1979:94). The British government had not intended that the cable be state owned but had been pressured by the dominions, and for some time the Post Office mourned the disruption that this caused in relations with the Eastern. Yet competition by the state in order to regulate private companies had been used previously in the domestic telephone market, so it was not something new. In the same year that the act was passed, as a spoiling tactic the Eastern connected the Cape of Good Hope with Australia and New Zealand and reduced its tariffs.

Placed under a board of management—the Pacific Cable Board—the state-owned cable worked in conjunction with landlines across Canada. According to Peel, the 30 percent reduction in tariffs that went with the opening of the cable did not result in a corresponding increase in traffic, so both the Pacific cable and the Eastern saw losses in 1903–4 (Peel 1905:272). In the early 1900s the Eastern suggested a "joint pool"—the sharing of revenue—between the two cables—a move that the Canadians saw as an attempt to take over the cable. But in the longer term, despite its inauspicious beginnings, the deepwater cable turned out to be commercially viable and came into its own during World War I. During the first twenty years the cable accumulated sufficient reserves to pay for its duplication in the 1920s (although the duplicate touched Honolulu) (Tribolet 1929:169–71).

International Regulation

The provisions of the Rome International Telegraph Convention of 1871 were intended to regulate international communications on the basis that these were separate from domestic communications. Because international communications ended at national borders except for through traffic, the convention did not consider the interaction between international and domestic state-owned systems. Where domestic competition existed, there were problems that the ITU could not address. So, for instance, after the inauguration of a state-owned cable between Tasmania and the Australian mainland, the Eastern found the interconnection rates demanded by the Australians discriminated against its cable. Although the company argued that such discrimination was against ITU regulations, in fact nothing in those regulations prevented such discrimination. The company then attempted to persuade the British government to agree to a blanket regulation preventing such discrimination within the empire—failing to understand that Britain did not control the dominions. Eventually, diplomatic pressure caused the Australians to retreat.

The international regulations themselves hampered the lowering of tariffs by ensuring that the countries crossed by cables had equal rights to those where the cable began and ended. This provision meant that tariffs could be reduced only if all interested parties in a line agreed. In the early years of the twentieth century, the Post Office was under pressure from business to reduce the tariffs to India. But, reflecting the conservatism of state-owned telegraph administrations and concerns about potential loss of revenue, the German and Russian governments, whose territory the landlines crossed, refused a lower tariff. The British government of India became so incensed that it proposed to put forward an amendment to the regulations at the London conference of 1903 along the lines that the international regulations should no longer apply to intracolonial traffic.

But the Germans and Russians were not the only problem. As a reprisal against the Pacific cable, the Eastern refused to contemplate a tariff reduction. In this case, the amendment proposed by British India, which was backed by the British Treasury and the Balfour Committee of 1901, seems to have galvanized the British Post Office into more intense negotiations with both the governments and the Eastern. The Post Office even considered refusing to renew the company's British landing rights. Eventually, as a result of a guarantee from the British that its transit rates would not be reduced, the Russian government capitulated in 1902 and reduced by 30 percent its 1886 charge of four shillings (97 cents) per word.[30]

Although such negotiations created incentives for "British" cables touching only British territory, Treasury resistance meant problems in lowering tariffs on the state-owned cross-channel cables. And the question of how to regulate the Eastern's monopoly remained. In this regard the International Telegraph Union conventions were the venue where the British government felt it could apply pressure to the Eastern. Thus the British delegation's report to the government on the 1896 conference stated: "In our relations with the Companies . . . we endeavoured while defending their legitimate interests, to obtain such concessions as they might reasonably be expected to make in favour of the public."[31]

At a time when the telephone began to challenge the hegemony of the telegraph, European telegraph administrations and treasuries were not eager to forgo telegraph revenue and undertake new capital expenditure. The Germans were the most eager to use international regulation to control competition from the new technology. At the 1885 Berlin Telegraph Conference at Germany's behest "five general paragraphs dealing with the telephone" were added to the regulations (Codding 1972:32). But because of the opposition from other European governments, which argued that the telephone was a new technology and its development could be hindered by strict regulation, national telegraph agencies had almost total freedom to decide the technical characteristics of the equipment, tariffs, and interconnection charges. "The only regulation of a substantial nature set the time-unit for charges and a limit to the length of conversations in cases where there were other requests for the use of the line" (Codding and Rutkowski 1982:9).

Although the first London-to-Paris telephone cable was laid in 1890, telephone regulations did not become a recognized part of the work of the ITU until the London conference of 1903. A special committee was established to draw up regulations. These were similar to the telegraph regulations, but they remained rudimentary. Perhaps because telegraph agencies were wary of the International Bureau of Telegraph Administrations in Berne, which was seen as "showing the tendency . . . to tighten its control" over the telegraph network, they were not obliged to interconnect their telephone lines to form a European network until 1925 (Codding and Rutkowski 1982:9).[32]

Conclusion

The period from 1890 to 1914 was a period of growing mercantilism—between European countries, the United States, Russia, and South America and even within the British Empire. With the increase in protectionist tariffs, Britain came to rely increasingly on its formal and informal empire for exports of capital and goods. The Spanish-American War of 1898 raised suspicions of the United States, which were replaced by distrust of German intentions in the early twentieth century. This growth of distrust between nations and efforts to expand colonial possession were replicated within the communications sector.

In particular, after the experience of France and Germany in the Boer War, when they had been unable to communicate without permission from Britain and without censoring their messages, both countries built up their own cable-manufacturing industries and operating companies. This was the period in which dirigiste industrial policies created national champion companies. Britain lost its hegemony in the manufacture of submarine cables but not its overall dominance of their ownership.

Whereas the British cables laid before the 1880s were primarily laid to commercial centers and along trade routes at the instigation of individual consulting engineers such as Bright and Brett, those laid in the 1890s tended to reflect British government priorities about colonial possession, wars, and strategic interests. Although the policy of All-Red cables was justified as a strategic necessity, it not only became very expensive in terms of subsidies but, because the British government used only one company, placed the empire in a position of dependence. When rising costs demanded a trade-off between economic realities and strategic interests, the government found that controlling or regulating the company was difficult.

The dominions had the problem of the Eastern's high tariffs and monopoly position. By the turn of the century public opinion in Britain also called for a lowering of tariffs. Yet the British government had difficulty separating its interests from those of the Eastern, and divisions of opinion brought conflict within the policy-making elite. The Post Office, the Foreign Office, and the Colonial Office (before Chamberlain's appointment) had close links to the company and defended its interests. In view of the costs of subsidies, the Treasury was much less enthusiastic and would have welcomed competition that would lower tariffs. But attempts at private competition, such as the Rhodes plan for Africa, were ill conceived. Yet the idea of government regulation of private enterprise was not publicly accepted, nor, as the 1901 Balfour Committee pointed out, were the mechanisms available to undertake it.

The Treasury appointed personnel to the Eastern's boards, but this seems to have had little effect. And the scheme of regulation submitted by the Eastern, which involved a form of "rate-of-return" regulation linked to tariff levels on different routes, failed because of the difficulty of estimating the company's costs and their distribution across routes. The scheme was much more complicated than the rate-of-return regulation adopted in the 1930s in the United States and suffered not only from the government's dependence on the Eastern for information about costs but also from the vertical linkage between the Eastern and Telcon that could inflate the costs of construction.

During the early years of the twentieth century, the Treasury viewed state-owned competition as a means of regulating the private domestic telephone companies. This model was expanded to the international level in the case of the Pacific cable. However, laying the state-owned cable took twenty years of lobbying by the Canadians. It was an example of a cable that originally was proposed as an adjunct to commercial interests and eventually laid for strategic interests. Partly paid for by the dominions, it gave the indirect benefit of introducing competition to the Eastern and thereby gaining lower tariffs. But because of the opposition of the company and its bureaucratic and political allies, it took the strong personality of Joseph Chamberlain, in alliance with military interests, to win its acceptance. Nevertheless, the cable and its regulatory board provided an indication of a more collaborative spirit by the British toward the dominions on whose markets Britain was becoming increasingly dependent.

At the beginning of this period the British government was still inclined to use its bargaining power over the Eastern, which it gained by representing the company's interests within the international conferences. And the institution of the Cable Landing Rights Committee in 1899 allowed protectionist sentiment to be clothed in strategic language. After the Balfour Committee reports, it became evident that retaining London as a hub for international cables also served potential strategic interests of censorship, but the Post Office once more reverted to free trade in landing licenses. Following the committee's second report, the Post Office also began to use landing licenses to regulate both the Eastern and some U.S. companies. It was possible to insert clauses in those licenses to regulate behavior on interconnection in Canada by Western Union and to bargain to gain acceptance of the government's terms for private wires within Britain. But the Post Office did not tackle the question of tariffs for the public. It was primarily when government-owned lines were affected that the Post Office acted in its own interests in using the issue of landing licenses to bargain with the companies.

In fact, in this respect the international regulations, which insisted on prior notification of changes in tariffs to Berne and that all countries crossed by a line agree to any such changes, were a handicap to national regulation. The ITU members delayed even the introduction of lower tariffs for night-time use for many years after their introduction in Britain. Nor did the ITU regulations in any way deal with the refusal of interconnection practiced by the U.S. companies against the British or the discriminatory rates for interconnection imposed by the Australians.

In the spirit of the times the ITU was still an organization devoted to cartelization, not competition, and was specifically concerned with government interests, not those of private companies. It seems evident that the British government and others gradually came to find the detailed regulations for the international telegraph, and the failure to allow competition, to be a handicap and the perpetual negotiations with other governments difficult. That Britain and other member states rejected international regulation of the telephone in preference to national regulation may have reflected a combination of factors—a desire to evade the inflexible bureaucracy of Berne, a growing nationalism in the early twentieth century, or the prevalence of private telephone companies in Britain until 1911. A reliance on national regulation allowed each European telephone agency to build up its own national manufacturers using national standards. For similar industrial policy concerns, the mantra first chanted in 1885—that the telephone was a "new technology" and therefore would be hampered by regulation—has become a predictable refrain in relation to each new technology that has evolved since.

During this period it is evident that the British concern was primarily to expand the empire's cable network for security reasons rather than commercial ones. Fear that a cable could be cut in time of war led to a preoccupation with routes that avoided potentially unsympathetic governments. Deepwater cables prevented the possibility of sabotage, while control and staffing of stations with British personnel meant that in time of war, censorship of telegrams could go on without hindrance. Although All-Red lines were expensive, as the Balfour Committee acknowledged, reaching a compromise between security and commercial interests was difficult.

The dependence of the British government on the Eastern was emphasized at the start of World War I. Although the government feared the Eastern's monopoly, the company itself was part of the strategic power of the British state. Cables primarily linked center to colony, so that London was the centralized hub of a vast web of cables under the control and censorship of the British government. During World War I cable cutting and censorship became resources that Britain, but not Germany, could call on; unlike the United States, Britain emerged from that war with a stronger cable system.

3. Wireless and the State

IN THE EARLY PART of the twentieth century the conflict between the United States and Britain over the wireless telegraph was essentially a conflict about a worldwide monopoly developed through proprietary standards. Maritime radio—the transmission of Morse code by wireless to ships—was the first application of the new technology. Introduced at the end of the nineteenth century, wireless seemed to provide the possibility of a technology that the United States might use to break the British monopoly of international communications.

But by being first in the market, the Italian-born entrepreneur Guglielmo Marconi was able to create a de facto global standard for wireless telegraphy. By refusing interconnection and by enforcing its patent rights, Marconi's British-based company, Marconi's Wireless Telegraph Company, was able to impose its standard worldwide, despite attempts by the British government to subvert it. As with submarine cables, the Americans attempted to break the British (Marconi company) monopoly. Acting in collaboration with the Germans, the U.S. government first attempted to use international multilateral regulation to prevent Marconi's expansion; when that proved ineffective, it resorted to the unilateral imposition of domestic law. Similarly, reflecting its close relationship with cable and other wireless companies, together with a desire to protect its existing investment in fixed line telegraphs and fear of a private monopoly, the British Post Office sought to prevent the success of the new technology.

The early history of wireless once more demonstrates the close interplay between domestic and international markets and between domestic and international regulation of those markets. Domestic politics influenced the stances of national delegations in international forums, and the prospect and outcomes of international conventions influenced domestic policy. But throughout the period navies regarded the technology of wireless as a strategic weapon, and these strategic considerations vied with other commercial and regulatory priorities. Ironically, the period ended with British Marconi and German Telefunken in a joint venture to supply the German merchant marine and with the U.S. government's nationalization of the Marconi Wireless Telegraph Company of America.

Early Maritime Wireless in Britain

Following a lack of interest by the Italian government in his invention of wireless transmission of the Morse code, the young Guglielmo Marconi took his invention to Britain, where he patented it in 1896. In Britain, Marconi was sponsored by William H. Preece, the chief engineer of the Post Office who had been experimenting on the basis of Gustav Hertz's 1887 discovery of electromagnetic waves. Because of skepticism from established scientists who argued that electromagnetic waves would not follow the curvature of the earth, Marconi had a credibility problem. Inasmuch as he was not a qualified scientist or electrical engineer, his patent came under immediate attack from such figures in the scientific establishment as Oliver Lodge, who had already worked on Hertz's waves. Whereas Preece considered that Lodge's equipment would not stand up to patent litigation, Lodge was convinced that his work on a tuning device—a "coherer"—had contributed substantially to Marconi's system. Once "'Mr Marconi's success was assured,'" said Henry Jackson, a cruiser commander in the Royal Navy, "'Dr Lodge at once patented every device he could conceive of for improving and, at the same time, obstructing the Marconi system of wireless telegraphy'" (quoted in Jolly 1972:90).[1]

In addition, after Marconi's Wireless Telegraph Company rejected an offer by the Post Office of £10,000 ($48,500, later upped to £15,000, or $72,750) for its patents, the Post Office regarded it as a competitor. Using equipment borrowed from the company, the Post Office proceeded to conduct experiments on wireless communications with France from which it excluded Marconi (W. Baker 1970:36). Only when the experiments were unsuccessful was the Marconi company once more invited to take part (Jolly 1972:49).

Other companies in Germany and France were also developing wireless equipment. The German equipment, manufactured by Allgemaine Electricitäts Gesellschaft (AEG), was said to be an improved copy of Marconi's (Hall n.d.:4). But it would be another ten years before Marconi's company was strong enough financially to sue for patent infringement (Wedlake 1973:22).

As Winston argues, navies were now equipped with ironclad battleships that needed radio communications to prevent collisions at the speed of steam. Semaphores were no longer enough (1998:71). But the Admiralty challenged Marconi's patents, arguing that its own communications expert, Jackson, had developed equipment that preceded Marconi's (Goodwin 1996:4). Jackson himself disagreed.[2] After the fleet engaged in exercises using sets loaned by Marconi, Jackson recommended that the fleet be fitted with wireless and its sailors trained to use it (Jolly 1972:67).

That was in 1899, the year that the Post Office moved against Marconi's Wireless Telegraph Company. The Post Office claimed that a monopoly of public telegraph systems under the 1868 Telegraph Act included wireless. As a result Marconi's company could not use the Post Office's system to transmit public telegrams. As soon as Marconi had developed effective radio technology for communications between ship and shore, the Post Office widened its domestic monopoly to include three miles offshore. Marconi's company was unable to sell equipment without breaching the Post Office monopoly.

In response to these events, company policy changed in 1899 to one of leasing equipment. Because the 1869 act specifically exempted intracompany lines (i.e., private lines), Marconi's company could argue that by renting equipment and wireless operators to ship owners and transmitting free of charge, the service represented intracompany communications and was not subject to the Post Office monopoly. Inasmuch as investment in ground stations had to be made up front, while rentals, primarily to passenger ships, produced little income, the strategy was expensive. But the policy had the advantage of allowing the company to specify that shore stations should communicate only with ships using its equipment. Marconi's Wireless Telegraph Company therefore established a subsidiary, Marconi International Marine Communication Company, to handle all marine activity (Goodwin 1996:7).

The marine company demanded annual royalties of £100 ($486) and met with considerable resistance. The Admiralty regarded the price as preposterous. Instead, it "invoked the provisions of the Patents, Designs and Trade Marks Act of 1883, which gave the Crown the right to manufacture and employ an invention on terms settled by the Treasury, if that patented invention was needed urgently for national defense. Thus the Admiralty itself began to manufacture their own equipment based as far as possible on the Marconi design, with Henry Jackson in overall charge" (Goodwin 1996:5).

In turn, because the Admiralty's own designs proved deficient, rather than challenge the legality of Marconi's patents in court, Jackson suggested that the government should negotiate with the company to get a reduction in the "exorbitant royalty" that it was demanding (Jolly 1972:91). Jackson scotched a suggestion from H. M. Hozier, the secretary of Lloyd's of London, that the Admiralty and Lloyd's should both buy German Braun equipment and another from the Post Office that it should buy the equipment from Lodge's company. In both cases, Jackson argued, the technology infringed on Marconi's patents.

The Boer War proved the turning point. Marconi's contract with the British army was for five mobile stations to maintain contact between the shore and supply ships. However, when the equipment arrived in South Africa, the army, which had no personnel qualified to use it, changed the plan. The army mounted the wireless transmitters on horse-drawn carts and sent the Marconi company's employees into the field, only for the antennas to fail in the high winds. Marconi publicly blamed the War Office for that failure and for not supplying the besieged towns of Ladysmith, Kimberley, and Mafeking with wireless before hostilities began (Jolly 1972:98). The Boers had also seen the potential for radio and ordered equipment from Germany, but it arrived too late to be of any value (Howeth 1963:33).

The War Office's immediate response to Marconi's criticism was to withdraw the mobile stations and to hand the sets over to the Admiralty, which then established shore stations at Durban and Delagoa Bay (Jolly 1974:120). Naval officers found the invention useful, not only for maintaining the blockade but for arranging shore leave, and their enthusiastic reports swung Admiralty opinion (West 1986:10–11). It placed an order for thirty-two sets in 1900 but continued to pirate the equipment and "subsequently had fifty copies of the Marconi set made by Edisan's and refused to pay any royalties at all on them" (Geddes 1974:13).

The Marconi company faced further problems from Lloyd's. Hozier had set up his own company in wireless telegraphy using equipment that copied Marconi's; in exchange for arranging a contract with Lloyd's, Hozier demanded that the Marconi company buy his company in exchange for cash and shares in Marconi's Wireless Telegraph Company (Jolly 1972:93). Lloyd's lobbied the government, which in turn made unsuccessful "special efforts . . . to secure the abolition of the veto of the Marconi Company on communications with non-Marconi ships."[3] Eventually, in 1901 Marconi Marine signed a fourteen-year contract under which it would equip ten of Lloyd's signaling stations and would allow Lloyd's to operate them to provide marine information to ships (Aitken 1976:235–36). But the company was short of cash and obliged to accept a clause in the Lloyd's contract that required the Marconi company to give Lloyd's the right of first refusal on future ship-to-shore stations in certain areas. Hozier then received his payment (Jolly 1972:94).[4]

In 1901 Marconi's Wireless Telegraph Company applied to the Post Office for "an exclusive licence for the practice of wireless telegraphy between England and ships at sea, between England and foreign countries, and between England and the British colonies" (Jolly 1972:136). It also requested that its telegrams be collected at Post Offices, as were those of the cable companies. The Marconi company was attempting to move its status from that of a supplier of intracompany communications to that of a carrier for the general public and to interconnect with the Post Office's existing domestic services. Much of the company's argument for a monopoly was based on the need to control the use of frequencies and for international long-distance telegraphy to be integrated with the domestic telegraph system (Jolly 1972:136, 138). But the company was handicapped in these negotiations because transatlantic service was not yet in regular operation.

Long-distance signaling began in 1901 when a signal from Marconi's research station at Poldhu in Cornwall was received in Newfoundland. But Marconi's company then faced opposition by the Post Office and the Eastern to the development of a commercial service. In Britain the Post Office had deferred the company's application for a landline link to London. In Newfoundland the company had run up against the Eastern's claim that its landing rights concession extended to all technologies. Marconi's company had had to move its transmitter into Canada. From there King Edward VII and President Theodore Roosevelt exchanged messages by long waves (Wedlake 1973:76). But when ice brought down the antenna, an initial attempt to provide a limited news service for the *Times* of London ended after nine days (Geddes 1974:21).

The service was erratic and slow and, despite the company's advertising it as a commercial service in 1902, the Marconi company did not institute a full-blown commercial wireless telegraph circuit between Glace Bay in Canada and Clifden in Ireland until 1907. Based on long waves, the service relied on high-power transmitters to push the signal through the transatlantic static. Because no technology available could provide the continuous waves that the system needed, it tended at first to be slow and unreliable. It was also handicapped by the overloading of the landline into New York, which the cable companies refused to ease by increased investment in infrastructure. Therefore, Marconi's company at first could not compete with the cable companies in terms of delivery speed. Mainly, the service carried news for the New York newspapers. It was 1914 before new stations in New York and Wales obviated the landline problem.

Aware that the British government could commandeer its patents, the company kept all the relevant information in house. In turn, Post Office officials made every effort to get their hands on the technology so they could set up their own transatlantic service. Perhaps they were not intentionally attempting to drive the company into bankruptcy, but certainly they appeared not to care if they did so. The issue was to bias Post Office policy for the next twenty years.

Successive postmaster generals refused the license application, first on the ground that the request required new legislation, then on the ground that Marconi's equipment might interfere with that of the Admiralty, then on the ground that the government could do nothing that might prejudice the 1903 international conference called by the kaiser in Berlin. The Marconi company was perhaps unlucky that Austen Chamberlain, a friend of Oliver Lodge's, became postmaster general while the second secretary to the Post Office was J. C. Lamb, an avid believer in public ownership. Lodge was also close to Arthur Balfour, the prime minister from 1902 to 1905.

In 1903 Chamberlain publicly attacked the Marconi company for looking for a national monopoly.[5] The company interpreted this attack as meaning that the government wished "'to remain in a position to take the whole thing over without paying compensation to us when they can work it successfully themselves, or to shut the whole thing up if it suits their convenience for naval purposes or because of the cable interests,'" as H. Cuthbert Hall, the managing director of the Marconi company, put it (quoted in Jolly 1972:137). At one point the Post Office, which had once used Lloyd's shipping offices to collect mail, seemed to deliberately misinterpret the Lloyd's contract with the Marconi company as giving the insurer unlimited rights to Marconi's patents. The Post Office intimated that it would give a license to Lloyd's rather than Marconi's company.[6]

In 1902 the Cable Landing Rights Committee had its responsibilities broadened to include determining specifically which system of wireless technology the Admiralty should use and what response the British government should make to the German proposal for an international conference.[7] The Admiralty supported the Marconi system and argued that the technology could be developed only if the company were given a national monopoly. The newly appointed first sea lord, Admiral Sir John "Jackie" Fisher, had begun to modernize the British navy in response to the building program of the German Fleet Law of 1900. The modernization required that the Admiralty collaborate with the Marconi company. Wireless allowed a smaller number of craft to control larger distances, making it a tool crucial to naval supremacy.

After Fisher's appointment, in 1903 the Marconi company received another contract from the Admiralty under which Marconi's Wireless Telegraph

Company licensed the use of all its patents for ship-to-shore wireless and the use of its long-range transmitting facilities for twenty minutes each day until 1914 (United Kingdom:1906b).[8] The Admiralty could thereby reach its ships in the Mediterranean and mid-Atlantic, and by 1905 all British naval vessels were equipped with wireless (Wedlake 1973:94). But the contract contained a confidentiality clause that prevented the Admiralty from divulging information about Marconi's long-distance transmitters to the Post Office. This provision was to cause conflict between the company and the Admiralty.[9]

Early Marine Radio in the United States

Marconi created a U.S. subsidiary of his British company, Marconi's Wireless Telegraph Company, in 1899, but for many years the Marconi Wireless Telegraph Company of America remained little but a sales office. The first demonstration of his technology in the United States came in 1899, when he reported the America's Cup yacht races for the *New York Herald.* This immediately created a perception among the press that wireless presented potential transatlantic competition to the high-priced cables (Douglas 1987:25). But it was not the newspapers but the U.S. Navy that was the dominant influence in the early history of wireless in the United States, and it was slow to adopt the new technology. Douglas (1985:119–21) suggests that the major reason for this lack of interest stemmed from the navy's failure to modernize from sail to steam and from ship commanders who were jealously guarding their autonomy. But the failure of Marconi to include a tuner in his early demonstrations led naval officials to believe that he promised more than he could deliver, and relations between the company and the navy broke down. This distrust was exacerbated by Marconi's demand for a minimum order and annual royalty and the company's policy of not interconnecting with landlines. As one naval official noted, "'Such a monopoly will be worse than the English submarine cable monopolies which all Europe is groaning under'" (quoted in Douglas 1985:130).

However, in the early 1900s no one else was able to deliver such apparatus. Reginald Fessenden, a former college professor, was then experimenting through the U.S. Weather Bureau and established the National Electric Signalling Company only in 1902. Although Lee De Forest, later the inventor of the Audion vacuum tube, had formed his Wireless Telegraph Company (after Marconi declined to hire him), it had no resources. A second De Forest company founded in 1902, the American De Forest Wireless Telegraph Company, was little more than a stock market fraud. The navy therefore employed a retired naval officer resident in Europe to review the systems available.

Douglas reports that this officer, Cmdr. Francis M. Barber, was suspicious of all non-Americans and particularly loathed Marconi, whom he reported as working on stolen technology. Barber evidently rejoiced in the conflict between the Marconi company and Lloyd's of London. According to Barber, in 1902 the secretary of Lloyd's thought that "'Marconi had never yet got a signal across the Atlantic or 2,000 miles at sea either. The whole thing is a stock-jobbing operation worked in the interest of "a lot of Jews"'" (quoted in Douglas 1985:135).

On the basis of this antipathy, after trials in which the Marconi of America refused to take part unless guaranteed a contract, the U.S. Navy chose the German Slaby-Arco (Telefunken) equipment (Douglas 1985:140). Later the U.S. Navy behaved as the British Admiralty had and had Fessenden's technology copied for a lower price by the American De Forest Wireless Telegraph Company and Telefunken. Only three court actions, a contempt of court ruling, and legislation finally stopped the practice in 1911.

By 1903, and the first international conference on wireless regulation, there was increased recognition of the threat posed by German imperial ambitions. A commensurate buildup in the U.S. Navy took place, but it still had only eight enlisted men capable of taking charge of a wireless station. Nevertheless, U.S. naval personnel, including Barber, fueled by antipathy toward the Marconi company, dominated the U.S. delegation (Baer 1994:39; Douglas 1985:148).

The International Radiotelegraphic Conference of 1903

The potential worldwide monopoly of Marconi's company over wireless technology held a strategic threat to Germany, which was already vulnerable to British domination of submarine cables. Marconi's Wireless Telegraph Company was about to cut off an alternative. In addition, there were commercial implications. The high-profile German ocean liners then competing with the British on the transatlantic crossing used wireless contact with people ashore to attract passengers. Matters were brought to a head in 1902, when a brother of the kaiser, traveling on a German transatlantic liner equipped with German wireless equipment, found himself unable to communicate with the Marconi International Marine Communication Company's shore stations.

The initial German response was to order that German military and civilian wireless stations should use only German equipment and to bring the German manufacturers together in a state-backed alliance to market the Telefunken system (Douglas 1987:120; W. Baker 1970:33, 96).[10] Then the German government enlisted the diplomatic help of other foreign powers "to assist in overthrowing, or in preventing the establishment of this [Marconi's] monopoly" (Hall n.d.:6). Citing "the preservation of world peace and free enterprise as the primary reason for the meeting," Kaiser Wilhelm II called the International Radiotelegraphic Conference, the preliminary session of which was held in 1903 in Berlin (Douglas 1987:120). Put simply, the interests of the German manufacturers were to compel the Marconi company to share its network with their equipment. Their goals were the enforcement of free interconnection by international treaty and global standardization of equipment.

Opening the conference, the Germans called for interconnection between all systems of wireless telegraphy, "in the interests of world shipping." Delegates from the United States, Argentina, Austria-Hungary, France, Russia, and Spain supported them. The Germans were also successful in gaining a resolution that required the sharing of technical information to allow this interconnection to take place. The U.S. delegation, incensed at the refusal of a Marconi-equipped ship to speak to a U.S. naval vessel, went further and proposed compulsory interconnection for ship-to-ship as well as ship-to-shore communications. But this proposal, requiring direct regulation of ships, was rejected as impractical. Together, the British and Italian delegations proposed unsuccessfully that coastal stations communicating with a different system should be able to charge an additional 50 percent of the normal telegram rate as an interconnection surcharge.

Finally, the delegates agreed to a protocol under which governments would license stations, train and certify operators, and forbid the jamming of signals (Clark 1931:171; Wedlake 1973:40). Britain and Italy refused to sign the protocol, citing existing contracts with the Marconi company and no domestic legislation under which to enforce the treaty. But the British delegation (made up mainly of Post Office officials) was actually in favor of the principle of nondiscriminatory interconnection. The way had been paved by an alteration in the Marconi Marine company's contract with the Admiralty, the 1903 version of which provided for compensation if the noninterconnection policy were breached. Yet the Admiralty and War Office were opposed to compulsory interconnection.

Among the British delegation was Col. F. J. Davies, who was responsible for Section H. He was particularly concerned at the German government's backing for Telefunken's long-distance wireless research and, by implication, the effect that its access to Marconi's technology would have on the German ability to challenge the British hegemony of submarine cables (West 1986:11–12). In terms of security interests it was therefore prudent for the British to defend Marconi.

From the perspective of Marconi Marine, if implemented, the protocol carried the implication that the Marconi company would be forced to share its patents and team up with the German manufacturers. To the company the protocol also "contemplated in effect a wireless telegraph organisation—world-wide—for carrying on the business of a public telegraph company; which organisation would be made up of a number of ship stations controlled by the different shipping companies, and of coast stations controlled by governments or private companies" (Hall n.d.:8–9). However, as in most international law, the protocol contained no provisions for enforcement. At this point the conference lacked even a secretariat.

After the conference the Marconi company came under increasing pressure from governments within the United Kingdom that wished to sign the protocol. "Among other measures adopted was an attempt still longer to withold [*sic*] inland telegraph facilities in the United Kingdom for collection and distribution of wireless messages, and active opposition to any arrangement between the colonies and the Marconi Company not involving adherence to the Berlin proposals" (Hall n.d.:12). In addition, the British government excluded the company from government contracts for cross-channel communications and from supplying equipment to the army and informed the British government of India that the preferred suppliers were the Lodge-Muirhead Syndicate, using technology developed by Alexander Muirhead of cable duplexing fame, and the De Forest company (Jolly 1972:150–51).

Britain needed domestic legislation so that it could ratify the 1903 protocol, and the ensuing Wireless Act did not give the Marconi company the de jure monopoly that it desired. In introducing the 1904 act the postmaster general stated that "its principal objects were, by regulating wireless telegraphy, to make it more useful for purposes of defense and general communication, and to provide against the growth of a monopoly in the hands of any one Company."[11] However, in the explanatory memorandum accompanying the bill, the government cited security issues and the international protocol as its justification, and license applications rejected after the bill's passage suggest that the government continued to grant a de facto domestic monopoly to the company.[12]

In August 1904, just four days before Parliament passed the act, the Marconi company signed a contract with the Post Office. The agreement specified that in return for an eight-year license for the company's ship-to-shore stations, and a fifteen-year license for its long-distance service, it would "accept (without prejudice to their patent rights) the obligation to interchange messages with ships and shore stations in the United Kingdom respectively equipped with other apparatus" (clause 10). This clause authorized the company to collect a surtax or "additional rate," for seven years beginning in July 1904, when exchanging correspondence with stations not equipped with the Marconi system. If the international convention would not sanction such additional interconnection charges, the government would pay them (United Kingdom 1906a). In other words, the British government had decided to ratify the Berlin convention and was prepared to pay the Marconi company in order to have the freedom to do so. The agreement also relieved the Admiralty and Lloyd's of their contractual obligation to the Marconi company to refuse interconnection with other companies' equipment.

As for the Post Office, for the first time it agreed that telegraph messages to and from ships at sea (Marconigrams) could be relayed through the domestic telegraph and that the company would be given substantially the same facilities as the cable companies. The company became a "common carrier"—it stood ready to carry the message of anyone who cared to pay for its transmission. The company credited a 1903 change in personnel at the head of the Post Office, from Sir G. H. Murray to Henry Babington Smith, as the catalyst for this agreement. Nevertheless, H. Cuthbert Hall, the managing director of Marconi, reported that certain permanent officials and members of the government "were going around breathing out vengeance against him" (Jolly 1972:139). Because the domestic legislation could not enforce interconnection outside British waters, the Marconi company seemed to have lost little and gained much.

Bilateral Pressure on the Marconi Company

In the meantime, having learned of U.S. common carrier legislation from the U.S. delegation to the convention, the German government complained to the U.S. government that German liners could not communicate with the Marconi–*New York Herald* system on the Nantucket lightship. This lightship was twenty hours from New York by steamship, and Marconi had had an installation on it for three years. Shortly before the 1904 U.S. presidential election, the German government sent a diplomatic note that pointed out to the U.S. government that Marconi's noninterconnection policy breached U.S. legislation that required interconnection with all systems. The note probably was referring to legislation enacted in 1888, which imposed interconnection on telegraph companies receiving grants of lands from the federal government.[13] The German government asked for action against the company.

The Commercial Department of the British Foreign Office declined to support the company. And, after it refused to obey U.S. government instructions to exchange traffic on a nondiscriminatory basis, the Marconi company lost the Nantucket lightship in 1905 (Hall n.d.:13–14). The U.S. Navy took the station over and subsequently had Telefunken compete with the French in bidding for the contract, which Telefunken won (Douglas 1985:141).

The Russo-Japanese War of 1904–5 delayed a further session of the international convention to work out detailed wireless regulations. This war was also the first in which wireless played a considerable part in the relative military capabilities of the protagonists (Douglas 1987:123). Some explanations of Japan's naval victories over Russia "centered on the superiority of Japan's Marconi wireless system over the Russian Navy's German-made equipment," but others pointed out that the Russians failed to encode their messages (Sidak 1997:16; Wedlake 1973:90). However, the American De Forest company, not Marconi, in collaboration with the *Times* of London, received a license from the British government to erect a station at Weihaiwei, the British naval base leased from China, from which it could cable reports back home (Jolly 1972:148–49). In turn, the reporting of the war by wireless caused massive interference to the warring Japanese and Russian wireless systems. Seven different wireless systems were said to be operating at once (Sidak 1997:17). Even before the war ended in 1905, these problems of interference led President Theodore Roosevelt to establish the Interdepartmental Board [on] Wireless Telegraphy, known as the Roosevelt Board, to study the U.S. wireless position.

Neither were the lessons of the war lost on the British Admiralty. As the British delegation's stance was being decided before the next session of the international convention, which was to be held in Berlin in 1906, the Admiralty put forward the view that compulsory interconnection would cause chaos and it would be better to have no convention at all. Instead, the Admiralty wished "to see Marconi Stations established throughout the Colonies, so that stations on a uniform system would be available at all strategic points for Naval use in time of war at practically no cost to the Admiralty."[14] It suggested that if the government wished to accept the principle of interconnection for the public international service, it should do so by providing new or government-owned stations.

Eventually, a compromise was reached; the British government would propose to the convention that governments should reserve the right to exempt certain stations from the general principle. In this way the Post Office could force the Marconi company to interconnect with other systems where its stations had little traffic, but busy stations could be exempted. The British delegation would then argue in favor of the untried policy of effecting interconnection through new or government-owned stations. At a meeting before the convention the French agreed to support the amendment.[15]

The compromise opened up the possibility that the Post Office could use international regulations as leverage in its domestic campaign for state ownership. Although its 1904 agreement with Marconi was to end in 1912, before the 1906 International Radiotelegraphic Conference the Post Office issued standard wireless licenses that were to end on December 31, 1909, thereby making it possible to nationalize on that date. The new licenses demanded adherence to the terms of the 1906 International Radio Telegraphic Convention and were similar to those of the cable companies in providing for government business at half price and in empowering the government to take the stations over in an "emergency." The new licenses differed from cable licenses in obliging wireless companies to employ only British subjects—a provision that excluded Marconi, who had kept his Italian citizenship.[16]

The differential treatment that the British government accorded the cable companies was evident in their being allowed representation at international conventions, whereas the Marconi company was not (*Marconigraph,* July 1912:113). The company made itself unpopular by attempting to lobby conference delegates. J. D. Tomlinson reports that a Marconi representative accosted delegates on a weekend trip to Hamburg and was handing out leaflets "as though they [the delegates] were members of the British parliament" (1945:295). In contrast, backed by the German government, Telefunken was able to take advantage of the conference to hold an exhibition and to provide delegates with demonstrations of long-distance transmission.[17]

Because of hostility to the Marconi company, particularly from the United States, members of the British delegation reported that whenever it was evident that they were speaking in the interests of the company, such as in favor of an additional charge for interconnection, their proposals were defeated. However, H. Cuthbert Hall gained entrance to later meetings of the conference as the representative of Montenegro. On more than one occasion he voted against the British delegation. Its members commented that, in doing so, he had made their task of appearing separate from the company's interests considerably easier. The delegation was successful in negotiating the acceptance of its formula on interconnection and in preventing the adoption of a specific anti-Marconi proposal from the Germans for a boycott of companies operating in countries that did not sign the convention. But although the British delegation defeated the U.S. proposal to make interconnection between point-to-point land-based stations compulsory, it was unable to prevent the acceptance of a late U.S. proposal to reintroduce the principle of obligatory interconnection between ship-to-ship traffic.[18] The U.S. proposal appeared in the Annex to the Final Protocol, to which Britain, Italy, and Japan entered a reservation.

The Germans used another mechanism at the convention in order to undermine the Marconi company. The conference prioritized military and government interests and for the first time assigned wavelengths to services. The conference agreed on a wavelength range of 600 meters to 1,600 meters for naval and government use and 300 meters to 600 meters for merchant ships and commercial stations. U.S. naval interests, seeking military control of the spectrum within the domestic arena, supported the requirement that amateur radio operators be limited to wavelengths shorter than 300 meters (Douglas 1987:140). The British delegation had been given autonomy to decide the British position on wavelengths and similarly favored government interests.

In effect, the long waves that carried farther were to be off limits to shipping and commercial ship-to-shore stations. Wavelengths longer than 1,600 meters were set apart for long-distance land-based point-to-point communication. As a result Marconi's private ship-to-shore service would be limited to wavelengths shorter than 600 meters except for naval purposes, whereas the German state-owned ship-to-shore stations would be able to use any wavelength. The immediate effect on the company would be to end long-wave transmission to shipping from its Poldhu (Cornwall) station.

The final convention and regulations, signed by twenty-seven countries, contained Britain's watered-down version of the principle of obligatory interconnection between ship and shore stations. It also set out detailed provisions on wavelengths to be used for specific services, required the registration of frequencies with the Berne secretariat of the International Telegraph Union, determined technical standards (including a limitation on the power of shipboard transmitters), regulated tariffs—setting a maximum charge to be breached only under specific circumstances for ranges greater than 800 kilometers—and agreed that SOS should be the international distress call (J. D. Tomlinson 1945:26). As Fortner points out (1993:85), the three principles (reserved frequencies for services, avoidance of interference, and registration of frequencies) have formed the basis for regulation of international wireless communications since 1906. However, there appears to have been little appreciation that if interconnection was obligatory and wavelengths were specified, governments would need to regulate independent shipping owners to ensure that they upgraded equipment and kept to their wavelengths. In battles between shipping interests, governments, and broadcasters, this weakness in the regulation of the spectrum was to return repeatedly during the next forty years.

The newly elected British government wanted to ratify the Berlin convention, but because of the Marconi company's lobbying of Parliament, the

House of Commons appointed a select committee in 1907 to consider the effect on the national interest of of adhering to the convention. The Marconi company argued that the major beneficiary of this international regulation was Telefunken, which would now have free access to Marconi's shore stations. It pointed out that the convention had evaded the question of interconnection costs by simply denying their existence. In any event, the Select Committee agreed to ratification, but to get that result the Post Office was obliged to state that the Admiralty was now in favor of compulsory interconnection.[19] The Marconi company continued to lobby the new Labour government up to cabinet level. But the postmaster general, Sydney Buxton, continued to recommend ratification, claiming that backtracking on his agency's decision might damage British influence at future conferences (the next one was to be held in London).[20]

Then in September 1909 the Post Office "made clear that . . . Marconi's licences to operate the stations would certainly not be renewed when they expired in what was by then only four years time" and forced the company to sell its shore stations and license its ship-to-shore patents to the Post Office. In the same year Marconi was awarded the Nobel Prize for Physics (Wedlake 1973:41). In 1910 Marconi's Wireless Telegraph Company paid a dividend for the first time, and Godfrey Isaacs became managing director of the company. He was to become a major influence in redirecting the company's strategy into suing its competitors for patent infringement. In 1911 Sir Oliver Lodge received an extension of his "tuning" patent of 1897, thereby threatening Marconi's key patent; to strengthen Marconi's position, Isaacs bought Lodge out for £15,000 ($72,900) and hired him as an adviser (Geddes 1974:29). Although part of the agreement required that the Lodge-Muirhead Syndicate cease to operate, it did not prevent Lodge from using his position of influence in the scientific establishment to continue to attack Marconi in private.[21]

U.S. Response to the Convention

In a climate that was antipathetic to government control of private industry and distrustful of Kaiser Wilhelm II, the Foreign Relations Committee of the U.S. Senate refused to recommend ratification of the 1906 treaty, despite its delegation's leadership in demanding obligatory ship-to-ship communication (Luther 1988:18). Up to that time wireless technology had mainly been developed by amateurs, who fought to keep the government out of the sector on the basis that it tended to support large-scale business and "monopoly interests." By 1910 U.S. amateur stations outnumbered commercial and government stations by 4 to 1 (Douglas 1987:207).

The question of ratification came hot on the heels of controversy generated by the recommendations of the Roosevelt Board. After being sworn in in 1902, President Theodore Roosevelt had established the board to examine the relationship between wireless and government. In view of ongoing conflicts between the navy, the Weather Bureau of the Department of Agriculture, and the U.S. Army Signals Corps, Roosevelt, a naval supporter, weighted the board in favor of the navy. Its 1905 report recommended that the navy establish a series of coastal stations around the United States and the Panama Canal Zone and that these should be protected from the interference of private stations in their vicinity. Also, to "'prevent the exploitation of speculative schemes on a public misconception of the art,'" it recommended that the Department of Commerce and Labor license all stations (Interdepartmental Board, quoted in Sidak 1997:18). But its report immediately ran into opposition from the press, which was incensed that government might establish control over the fledgling technology and was scathingly critical of the competence of the navy.

Despite the opposition of the U.S. wireless companies, the navy acted on the recommendations of the Roosevelt Board and went ahead with building up a wireless network; with De Forest equipment it established naval stations in Florida, Puerto Rico, Cuba, and Panama (Douglas 1985:147–49). Meanwhile, both Fessenden and De Forest became embittered because the navy had been pirating their patents. Fessenden lobbied hard for a change in the law, and eventually, in 1910, Congress passed a measure that allowed the owners of patents to sue the government if they were used without permission. The navy could no longer pirate equipment (Douglas 1985:153).

The two related issues of increasing interference from amateur operators and of shipboard safety were brought home by a harbor collision in 1909 in which interference was deemed to have played a part. Congress came to agree with Roosevelt that some regulatory action was needed. But what transpired in legislation was limited. The Wireless Ship Act of 1910 was a security-based measure directed primarily against the Marconi of America. In effect, the U.S. government used extraterritorial legislation to force the Marconi company's compliance with the 1906 convention.

The act required that all passenger ships carrying fifty or more people, leaving from U.S. ports, and plying between ports two hundred or more miles apart should be equipped with radio apparatus capable of sending and receiving signals for one hundred miles and specified that such equipment would not be legal unless "'the company installing it shall contract in writing to exchange . . . messages with shore or ship stations using other systems of radio-communication'" (quoted in Luther 1988:18). In an example of

Congress's using domestic regulation to liberalize the international market, this provision applied to foreign ships calling at U.S. ports as well as to U.S.-owned ships (J. D. Tomlinson 1945:28).

The immediate effect of the 1910 measure was to increase the United Wireless Telegraph Company's sales to shipping. Luther reports that "this company had taken over De Forest's company in 1907 and the equipment was based on the Telefunken design which the Navy had adopted" (1988:18). However, a financial panic in 1907 had raised public concern about stock promotion activities in wireless companies, and in 1910, after numerous complaints, the Justice Department charged De Forest's company with fraud. The company was placed in receivership, and, after Marconi's Wireless Telegraph Company filed a successful lawsuit alleging infringement of its patents, in 1912 United Wireless became part of Marconi of America. The former De Forest company brought with it seventy shore stations and several hundred shipping installations. Following the recapitalization of Marconi of America, the merged company became the largest wireless operating company in the United States (W. Baker 1970:130). Thus congressional attempts to break Marconi's market dominance through domestically imposed safety standards (later recognized as a nontariff barrier to trade) were limited in their efficacy. By the end of 1915 Marconi of America owned and operated the radio apparatus on more than four hundred ships of the U.S. merchant marine (Herring and Gross 1936:77).

Marine Wireless Allies with Cable

Meanwhile, Marconi Marine had decided to cut the costs of global expansion by extending its ship-to-shore telegraph business along the routes of submarine cables and by collaborating with the Eastern. Marconi Marine proposed that the Eastern pay for the erection of six stations in Gibraltar, Malta, Aden, Colombo (Ceylon), Singapore, and Hong Kong and that the companies share revenue on an equal basis. For its part the Eastern had applied unsuccessfully for a license within Britain to move into ship-to-shore radio and now took on the task of selling the collaboration with Marconi to the British government.[22]

The Cable Landing Rights Committee's strongest objection to the scheme was that it strengthened the Eastern's monopoly. But it recognized that the existence of the proposal suggested that the two technologies were not likely to compete in the near future. In addition, the colonial governments concerned had already rejected government ownership of what would be uneconomical stations. Despite objections by Lloyd's, which cited its previous agreement with the Marconi company, the committee recommended four-teen-year licenses with a buy-back clause after ten years.[23]

The committee also agreed that a special clause in the licenses should place the rates charged under government control and that any dispute regarding what constituted "reasonable" rates should be referred to the committee. This was the first time that anyone had suggested that the British government directly regulate international tariffs through the mechanism of a license.[24]

The first station licensed, in the Cocos Islands in the Indian Ocean, opened in 1911. Malta followed in 1912. Bust elsewhere the companies met with problems. In Aden, the British government of India decided to provide wireless communications. In Gibraltar the companies withdrew because of competition based in Morocco. Then a dispute arose that involved the companies, the Admiralty, and the War Office regarding Singapore and Hong Kong, where the Admiralty was in the process of establishing high-power stations. The intention of the Admiralty, to offset the cost of the stations by competing with them for commercial work, was unacceptable to the companies.[25] The Cable Landing Rights Committee refused to contemplate a subsidy to the companies, and Downing Street directly vetoed the companies' demands. By the time World War I broke out, government-owned stations were planned for but not erected in Gibraltar, Singapore, and Hong Kong.[26] The collaboration had brought little benefit.

Marconi's Relations with the Admiralty

Meanwhile, pressured by the Post Office, the Admiralty had decided to approach Marconi's company about removing the "confidentiality clause" in its 1903 contract and ensuring that the Admiralty was informed of the Marconi company's new inventions within a specific period.[27] The Marconi company's dispute with the Admiralty regarding its 1903 contract had already had an effect on the company's business. In revenge the Admiralty had registered its ships with the International Bureau of the Telegraph Union in Berne as having been fitted with wireless apparatus but had not specified that the apparatus was made by Marconi. In contrast, the German government had registered every one of its ships as using the Telefunken system and then had circulated the Berne bureau's figures to show that Telefunken had the largest share of the world market. In addition, although Marconi's subsidiary in Australia had spent thousands of pounds to build trial stations and demonstrate its system to the Australian government, the Admiralty approved adoption of the Telefunken system. A follow-up mission by the Admiralty to help the Australians, who got into financial difficulties, led the Marconi company to insist on adherence to the confidentiality clause of its 1903 agreement.

The company also claimed that it had received only a small number of public contracts and that the Admiralty and the Royal Engineers had pirated its equipment designs on a number of occasions. Finally, the company interpreted its agreement with the Admiralty to mean that after its contract ended in 1914, the Admiralty would no longer have the right to use any of the company's patents. In view of this history the company proposed a comprehensive agreement with the British government, covering the use of its patents by all departments, for which a royalty would be paid. It also proposed that it should receive purchasing preference over other firms and support from the government similar to what the Eastern received.[28]

Faced with these demands, the Admiralty decided to await the outcome of legal action that Marconi's Wireless Telegraph Company had brought against the British Radio Telegraph and Telephone Company regarding a master patent for "tuning." Because the government had been using the British Radio Telegraph company when the judgment went in Marconi's favor in 1911, something like panic seized the British government. There was talk of invoking the provisions of the Patents Act of 1907 to allow the government to use Marconi's patents, with a payment to be adjudicated by the Treasury. But from the Post Office's point of view, this provision would not get it the information that it wanted on long-distance wireless communications, so the government tried another tactic, this time holding out the possibility to Marconi's Wireless Telegraph Company of an imperial wireless chain—licensing the company to provide intraempire long-distance wireless communication.[29]

From the company's point of view, its easier financial position allowed it to bring other lawsuits. By 1912 successful patent actions had given the Marconi company a virtual monopoly of maritime communications in the United States and France. But action against the German Telefunken company was hampered by the active backing for that company by the German government.

Anglo-German Alliance

Although the British government signed the 1906 Radiotelegraphic Convention of Berlin, which took effect in 1908, Marconi Marine continued its practice of refusing interconnection to German equipment, other than for distress calls. With the nationalization of domestic stations in 1909 the Marconi company's remaining stations were in foreign countries and on foreign ships, so the British government could do little. The company justified its actions by pointing to the "the Telefunken Wall" of state subsidy and export financing against which it had to compete (W. Baker 1970:131).

In 1910 the competition between Marconi and Telefunken came to a head when the German government declared that no foreign wireless apparatus would be permitted aboard German vessels (Sturmey 1958:53–54). Faced with this loss of business, the Marconi company compromised with its German competitor. A new Anglo-German-Belgian company, registered in Germany, was created in 1911, with the approval of the German government. The new company, Societé Anonyme International de Télégraphie sans Fils (SAIT), in which Telefunken held 55 percent of the shares, took over the wireless business of the whole German merchant marine and later that of Austria as well. It delivered free intercommunication between ships fitted by partners in the combine. Despite objections from the British Post Office, the practical effect was not only to establish a monopoly within Germany but also to freeze out other British companies, which were denied interconnection with German stations.[30] The German company was later reconstituted so that Belgian banks owned one-third of its capital, and the remainder was split evenly between British Marconi and Telefunken (W. Baker 1970:133). In effect, the two companies agreed to share the world market for marine wireless, and the British government could do little to regulate the combine.

1912 International Conference

The situation changed with the sinking of the *Titanic* in 1912. Although radio secured the rescue of seven hundred passengers, many of the fifteen hundred who died would have been saved if the ship nearest the stricken liner had picked up its distress calls. Both Marconi and his wife had been invited on the *Titanic*'s maiden voyage. Because of business commitments Marconi had taken an earlier passage, and his wife missed the sailing because their child was sick (Geddes 1974:29–30). In the immediate aftermath of the disaster Marconi found himself lauded in the United States for his invention of ships' wireless, which had saved so many lives.

But the meeting of the signatories to the 1906 convention, held in London three months after the *Titanic* disaster, was less laudatory. Only signatories to the 1906 International Radiotelegraphic Convention were eligible to attend. To avoid exclusion the U.S. Senate reconsidered the 1906 treaty and recommended ratification in April 1912, just before the sinking of the *Titanic* (Luther 1988:19).[31] Strongly affected by the loss of the great ship, the conference began with the decision by Britain, Italy, and Japan, the three states that had previously signed reservations, to accept the protocol of 1906, which imposed interconnection on ship-to-ship communications. Although lack of interconnection had not played a part in the loss of life on the *Titanic*, the Marconi company responded to public sentiment by announcing that the company would implement interconnection to all makes of wireless equipment.

In contrast to the 1906 conference, sixteen representatives of eleven wireless companies, including Marconi and Siemens from Britain, four French, and two German companies, were in attendance (*Marconigraph*, July 1912). Given the U.S. weakness in wireless, the sole U.S. company represented was the German-owned Telefunken Wireless Telegraph Company.

Because the ship nearest the *Titanic* had had only one wireless operator, who had gone off watch at the time of the disaster, the conference discussed such issues as the obligatory installation of radio equipment on ships, where aboard ship the wireless installation should be placed, the provision of emergency batteries, and the problem of how to ensure a continuous watch. Commercial rivalry once more intervened. Marconi had developed apparatus for an automatic alarm, but it required the addition of a dash to the Morse code for the SOS sign. The French and Germans objected to this alteration of the Morse code because Marconi's equipment competed with the equipment that their companies were developing. The defeated proposal was not revived for fifteen years, by which time the patents on the Marconi equipment had almost expired and more effective apparatus had been invented (J. D. Tomlinson 1945:34–35; W. Baker 1970:116).

The 1912 conference also recognized that the problem of ensuring that shipping lines installed wireless required further international regulation. Although Britain was a major shipping nation, it had implemented the 1906 convention only as far as it needed to wrest marine wireless from Marconi and had imposed no regulation on its merchant fleet. Subsequently, the International Convention on Safety of Life at Sea took effect on June 20, 1914. This convention was based on the 1910 domestic U.S. legislation and required all ships carrying fifty or more people to be fitted with radiotelegraph equipment.

Yet ship owners' reluctance to invest in wireless equipment meant that by 1914 British regulations demanded only the minimal provision of one wireless operator on ships weighing more than sixteen hundred tons. Even that minimal regulation involved a government-sponsored crash training program for operators by the Marconi company (W. Baker 1970:160). Not until late in World War I were British merchant ships carrying more than fifty people properly equipped or did many British sailors come to appreciate wireless (Wedlake 1973:113).

Point-to-Point Services

By the time of the 1912 International Radiotelegraph Convention, the Marconi company had had a monopoly of long-distance point-to-point telegraph communications for five years. The company had operations in the United States, Canada, Argentina, Brazil, France, Spain, and Italy (Herring and Gross 1936:79). The De Forest company had received a license for transatlantic transmission from a remote site in Scotland but gave up when it hit difficulties. The same company also experimented with long-distance radio communication over land within the United States, but the service was more experimental than commercial. The only substantial French company, France Maritime et Coloniale de T. S. F., was under the control of Marconi. Only Telefunken of Germany, then about to open a transatlantic link from its Nauen transmitter to New York and radiotelegraphic services to the German colonies and Brazil, provided competition to the Marconi company. Thus the Belgian Congo's proposal at the 1912 international conference for regulation of long-distance wireless communications was primarily aimed at the Marconi and Telefunken companies.

The French, German, and British delegates met before the conference to agree on their countries' positions. All agreed that point-to-point and aerial wireless services should not be on the agenda. The French were less convinced of the wisdom of this course than the Germans and British, who argued that point-to-point services had more in common with cable telegraphy, that long-distance services were few, and that the technology was new. They contended that "regulation should follow experience, not precede it," and decided that the matter could be settled if those countries chiefly interested in regulation were to make any necessary arrangements among themselves. The three sets of delegates expected that, faced with their opposition, the Belgian Congo would withdraw its proposal.[32]

But at the conference the Belgians failed to withdraw the proposal, the Germans backtracked on the previous agreement, and, supported by the French and Americans, the Germans put forward an amendment proposing that interconnection should not be withheld because a different system was in use. Following its success during the 1906 convention on ship-to-ship interconnection, the United States had it put to a vote and won. But the British managed to introduce wording that did not imply a general principle of obligation. Instead, the resolution gave complete freedom to each country to organize services between fixed points (J. D. Tomlinson 1945:36). The British signed the ensuing convention.

Because of opposition from the Americans and Germans, the proposal to merge the International Telegraph Union and the International Radiotelegraph Union also failed.[33] No organization was set up to monitor or enforce the radio regulations. Instead, the Berne Bureau of the International Telegraph Union was designated as the secretariat for the new International Radiotelegraph Convention. Members were to pay dues, which would cover the expenses of the organization, and countries were divided into six classes, with each country choosing which class it would enter (Clark 1931:175). The two unions did not merge under one convention until 1932.

The U.S. Radio Communications Act of 1912

The United States had belatedly ratified the 1906 International Radiotelegraph Convention and similarly ratified that of 1912. That it did so was primarily because of the U.S. Navy. But another reason was that because false messages of rescue had been received during the *Titanic* disaster, the press had now swung behind legislation that would prevent the amateur radio community from broadcasting on wavelengths used for shipping. By now the Marconi Wireless Telegraph Company of America had also altered its stance and was in agreement with regulation to control the interference coming from amateur stations (Douglas 1987:235).

Congress acted first to revise the 1910 act to require ships carrying fifty or more people to have two skilled operators and an auxiliary power supply for the ship's wireless. Then, to ensure that all passengers would have access to wireless if no commercial station existed within a one-hundred-mile radius of a ship, the 1912 act made the navy responsible for transmitting and receiving commercial messages. In turn, the new responsibilities required additional naval reorganization, which promoted the use of radio within the fleet and necessitated the upgrading of shore stations. Radio became part of U.S. Navy operational systems after Rear Adm. Charles J. Badger, a member of Roosevelt's 1902 Interdepartmental Board on Wireless Telegraphy, became chief of the Atlantic Fleet in 1913, and as a result of the efforts of a naval officer, Stanford C. Hooper (often called the father of naval radio), before the United States entered World War I (Douglas 1985:154). The act both boosted the position of the navy and for the first time gave the president the power to seize any apparatus in time of war, a power he was soon to use.

The 1912 international agreement also included a commitment by each signatory to regulate radio within its territory, "a position which found little support among United States policy makers" (Luther 1988:19). Nevertheless, the mechanisms necessary to comply with the two conventions were written into the Radio Communications Act of 1912. The act introduced licensing of wireless stations and empowered the secretary of commerce to change wave bands and to revoke licenses for "good cause." The weakness of the legislation was that the secretary of commerce was obliged to issue a license to suitable applicants on request, thereby nullifying the purpose of regulation. Despite attempts to allocate wave bands, there was chaos of interference until Congress passed another measure in 1927.

As the international convention required, the 1912 act restricted radio transmissions to those portions of the radio spectrum agreed in London. For the first time nongovernment stations were restricted to wavelengths above 1,600 meters or below 600 meters, and amateurs were limited to the portion of the spectrum then thought unusable, below 200 meters. (The international convention specified 300 meters, so the U.S. legislation was more restrictive.) Despite these restrictions, the act failed to quench the enthusiasm of amateur radio operators; when their activities were shut down in 1917, eight-five hundred amateurs had been licensed to transmit (Wedlake 1973:73). Ironically, the limiting of amateurs to shortwave aided the development of that technology in the postwar world.

To prevent foreign agents from transmitting messages in time of war, the navy urged Congress to restrict foreign ownership so that "'such license shall be issued only to citizens of the United States or Porto Rico, or to a company incorporated under the laws of some State or Territory of the United States or Porto Rico.'"[34] Although trade concerns entered the debate, Sidak (1997:25) argues that the foreign ownership provisions in the 1912 act were primarily intended as a national security matter. In contrast, Douglas (1987:235) states that they were introduced because United Wireless had testified during congressional hearings in 1910 that it had had difficulty gaining overseas licenses. Marconi of America opposed the licensing provisions in general, and Republican members of Congress, then in the minority, opposed the foreign ownership restrictions, particularly because they applied to Canada. The Republican leader in the House—James Robert Mann of Chicago—argued that the foreign ownership provisions would encourage Canada and other countries to refuse licenses to U.S. firms (Sidak 1997:25–26). He proved correct in that the restrictions were to be the first step in eighty years of U.S. economic protectionism.

But the restrictions, which took effect in August 1912, did not prevent the takeover of United Wireless by Marconi of America at the end of 1912. Nor, despite its being a subsidiary of a foreign company, did the measure prevent the 1912 licensing of the Atlantic Communication Company, a subsidiary of Telefunken, to provide transatlantic service from Long Island to Germany. The question of the licensing of this company prompted the outgoing Taft administration to ask the attorney general for an opinion on the 1912 act. The attorney general concluded that because the Atlantic Communication Company was incorporated in New York, the secretary of commerce and labor was required to license it. The attorney general said that the secretary of commerce had no discretion in the matter and determined that the license could not contain any demand for reciprocal rights for U.S. companies in Germany. The opinion specifically contrasted the discretion allowed to the president to demand reciprocity on cable landing rights, where there was no federal legislation, and that allowed in the case of radio, where Congress had acted.

Sidak suggests that the Taft administration sought this ruling after election day in an effort to hobble the incoming Democrat, Woodrow Wilson, and that it represents a victory for the outgoing free-trade Republicans (1997:29–30). In taking this precaution, the Republicans may have known that Wilson would appoint Josephus Daniels to be secretary of the navy; until his retirement in 1921 Daniels "actively promoted a governmental monopoly in radio under the control of the Navy Department" (Rosen 1980:21). Although some of his underlings, such as Stanford C. Hooper and William H. G. Bullard (who would later become an admiral), opposed Daniels's views—they argued that the navy should control only coastal stations, not high-power transmission—the secretary's views would become important during and in the immediate aftermath of World War I (Rosen 1980:22).

The Imperial Wireless Chain

In 1906, even before the Atlantic service was in commercial operation, the Marconi company suggested to the Colonial Office that it should be given a contract to build a chain of high-power stations to link the empire with Britain. The Colonial Office, traditionally hostile to the company, was unsympathetic. For its part, the Post Office was concerned that if the company were given permission to erect radio stations in the colonies, the effect would be to allow it a virtual monopoly of long-distance radio communications within the empire. Postal officials also saw in the company's application the means of gaining entry to its long-distance technology. In the words of Marconi's Godfrey Isaacs:

> as a result of an application made some time back by this Company to the Colonial Office for the right of construction of certain stations in different

Crown Colonies, the matter has been referred to the Post Office and the Post-master General has suggested to us that we might place at the disposal of His Majesty's Government in confidence particulars as to the working of Transatlantic Service, proposing to us that one or more representatives of that Department might be stationed for sometime at our Clifden Station and the Company's staff be instructed to allow them to follow the working from day to day and afford them full information on practical details.[35]

The company had refused the request, and in 1910, as part of Isaacs's plan to stabilize company finances, he submitted a further proposal for an imperial wireless chain.

The company's later plan was to link twenty-two stations throughout the empire (West 1986:14).[36] It claimed that such a chain would link the whole of the empire directly to London by a British-owned system; that existing rates would be cut in half, thereby stimulating trade; a less expensive rate for the press would create better news reporting within the empire; more settlers would be able to keep in touch with their families, thereby encouraging migration to the colonies, rather than the United States; and the government's telegraph bill would be reduced and all naval ships could be in direct touch with the Admiralty. The company suggested that after twenty years the government could take over ownership of the chain.[37] In effect, the Marconi company was proposing a build, operate, and transfer scheme with a twenty-year monopoly within the empire.

But the Cable Landing Rights Committee feared that the cable companies might be driven into bankruptcy by the undercutting of their rates. Instead, the committee wanted a state-owned imperial wireless system under which, the Post Office suggested, it might be possible to arrange a cartel with the cable companies: "The State could then regulate the competition between the new means of communication and the old in such a way as to secure for the public reasonable reductions of charges without imperilling the highly developed system of the British Cable Companies."[38] This proposal was to surface again almost twenty years later. In the meantime the Marconi scheme was submitted to the Committee on Imperial Defence.

Other countries already were beginning to use wireless for point-to-point communications to link up with their colonies. By 1911 Marconi had brought into service a 500-kilowatt station in Italy whose signal could reach Italian Eritrea, twenty-four hundred miles away, and it had a monopoly of Spanish colonial and domestic communications (W. Baker 1970:137). The company was becoming experienced in long-distance transmission, was in a stronger position on patents, and consequently was more bullish in its relations with the British government.

Sir Matthew Nathan, the new Post Office secretary, met with Marconi officials in January 1911 and made it evident that his main concern was to get access to the long-wave technology. In his own words, he "reminded Mr Isaacs that we [the Post Office] had applied for permission to examine the working of the Clifton Station so that we might be satisfied that the proposals of the Company could be efficiently carried out," but the company was not prepared to "part with their secret" without a definite agreement. Nor, at this stage, was the company prepared to cooperate with the government in developing a system of long-distance stations. Rather, Marconi officials suggested that the company might be forced to collaborate with Telefunken in developing the worldwide system of long-distance wireless communications that the German company was proposing.[39]

The threat to collaborate with the Germans, together with potential embarrassment at the impending imperial conference (New Zealand had given notice that it intended to put forward a proposal in favor of a state-owned imperial wireless system), induced a sense of urgency in the deliberations on the Marconi proposal. The new Post Office regime was inclined to deal with the company "in a more liberal spirit in view of the large sums of money that the company had expended in bringing their system to its present state of efficiency" and took the threat of its collaboration with the Germans seriously.[40] The Post Office had also changed its mind about a state-owned system, first because of the risk to capital involved and second because the system would be in competition with the Eastern's cables and most likely would be forced by "public agitation to charge an unremunerative tariff." In fact, the threat of wireless had brought cable rates down by half on plain-text telegrams, and because wireless could transmit only about ten words per minute as against the thirty per minute on cable, a wireless system was probably not viable. Additionally, following the company's successful patent action, the government could not use Marconi patents without approval. But particularly because the Treasury was prepared to consider the financing of a state-owned system, the members of the Cable Landing Rights Committee were not persuaded.[41]

Instead, the committee turned to the Admiralty to build and operate the chain. But the Admiralty then made clear that it would require exclusive use of the stations during maneuvers, which would wreck the commercial scheme.[42] The only possibilities remaining were either to agree to Marconi's becoming a private monopoly or to ask the Marconi company to act as a contractor for a state-owned scheme and to pay it royalties on the traffic.

The company agreed to act as a contractor, asking £70,000 ($340,200) for each station, a one-time payment of £250,000 ($1.2 million), and royalties of one halfpenny per word on all messages for each terminal and transit station.[43] Given the cost of £1 million ($4.9 million) for the whole chain, the Cable Landing Rights Committee then proposed that only six stations should be built—Cyprus, Aden, Bombay, Singapore, and Perth. This proposal was put before the Imperial Wireless Conference of 1911.

West (1986:14) suggests that "official reluctance about the plan was eventually overcome when the British Ambassador in Berlin reported, coincidentally, on a German scheme to link the main transmitter at Nauen to several German colonies. Apparently, Nauen had already established a permanent link with Atake-pame in Togoland and the British Consul in German South West Africa claimed that Telefunken were in the process of erecting stations at Windhoek, Tabora and the Caroline Islands in the Pacific." In addition, news that the French had "built a station atop the Eiffel Tower to communicate with three sites in French West Africa" lent strength to Marconi's proposal (West 1986:15). Also, the Eastern's manager in Shanghai had earlier reported U.S. attempts to provide a wireless service from Shanghai and Hong Kong to the Philippines and Singapore.[44]

Marconi's Wireless Telegraph Company obtained the imperial communications contract in 1911 for which it was to be paid £60,000 ($291,600) for each station and a 10 percent royalty on gross traffic receipts for twenty-eight years, a sum considerably less than that requested (W. Baker 1970:137). In return, it had to agree neither to build stations for a foreign government nor to enter into any arrangement with a foreign company without the British government's consent. Much of the capital for the project was to come from the dominions. The Treasury's main concern was to keep the cost down.

In the meantime, the Marconi company, now stronger financially and having settled the German maritime radio conflict with Telefunken, began successful patent litigation against Telefunken's British representative, Siemens. It also sued the Australian government and Telefunken. The matter was settled with the creation of an Australian company to purchase the Australian Marconi and Telefunken interests in which Marconi held two-thirds of the shares, the Australians 28 percent, and Telefunken 5 percent. Litigation between the two companies eventually ended in 1912 with an agreement for an exchange of patents, past and future (W. Baker 1970:134–35). The result was that Marconi's technology would contribute to the German war preparations.

However, the imperial wireless chain was not built until after World War I. Before the work could be started, a scandal blew up concerning insider trading in the company's shares by David Lloyd George, then chancellor of the Exchequer; Herbert Samuel, the postmaster general; and Sir Rufus Isaacs, the solicitor general and brother of Godfrey. These individuals had bought shares in the Marconi Wireless Telegraph Company of America, whose capital had been expanded by public subscription in order to finance the takeover of United Wireless, De Forest's company. The investors subsequently concealed their purchase of stock. The political capital made by opposition Unionists against the Liberal Party leaders was reinforced by commercial opponents of the company and by those who favored state ownership of an imperial wireless system (Jolly 1972:193–96). The insider trading charges were eventually found unproved but led to a parliamentary committee that revisited the award of the contract.

Although the committee considered the Marconi technology to be the only one with a track record of success, the delay to allow the committee's work meant the contract was not awarded until 1913 and only two of the stations, one at Oxford and one at Cairo, had been started by the outbreak of war. The Post Office canceled the company's contract in December 1914 and rejected a request for payment of compensation (W. Baker 1970:148). However, the company went on to finish the powerful long-wave station at Leafield (Oxford) for the Post Office and within a period of five weeks erected a high-power station at Cairo for the British Admiralty so that it might communicate directly with its naval forces.

In contrast, the Germans had constructed a series of high-power radio installations that transmitted from Germany to the United States and Germany's colonies in Africa; the Nauen transmissions to the United States kept Germany from isolation when the British government ordered the cutting of the German transatlantic cables.

Marconi and Reuters

Just as Reuters had moved earlier from supplying information into providing its own infrastructure, Marconi followed the British and Irish Magnetic Company of the 1850s by moving from providing infrastructure into providing information. It capitalized on its wireless infrastructure to evade Reuters's cable-based monopoly of news collection and dissemination.

In November 1899, while traveling back to Britain after the U.S. Navy trials, Marconi published a shipboard newsletter aboard the *St. Paul* as an experiment (Howeth 1963:33). Then, in 1903, after Marconi was able to demonstrate that transatlantic liners equipped with his system were never out of touch with shore, the Cunard line became the first to start a regular shipboard newspaper, which became a feature of transatlantic liner crossings. By 1913 at least thirteen shipping lines were producing such shipboard newsletters

(Wedlake 1973:41). In 1910 Marconi established the Wireless Press Ltd. to publish ships' newsletters and books and papers relating to wireless telegraphy, which gave the company an interest in the news agency business.

When World War I began, the Admiralty took over the Marconi transmitters at Caernarvon and Towyn. Except for the transatlantic service from Ireland, the use of wireless by civilians was forbidden. Private wireless equipment was confiscated, and all wireless stations were shut down as a matter of national security (Wedlake 1973:101). Then the navy was alerted to wireless communications' potential lack of security and for the first time monitored overseas wireless communications and appointed a chief censor of radiotelegraphy (West 1986:27). All commercial cables sent by wireless went from Marconi's Wireless Telegraph Company through the censor's office. Attempts to completely ban the use of codes for commercial messages met with resistance. In a compromise the government allowed "certain reputable firms . . . [to] lodge copies of their private ciphers with the Board of Trade and continue to code their messages" (West 1986:28). In late 1915 the government paid Marconi to intercept wireless traffic between Germany and the United States (fifteen thousand words per day) and to translate and edit the messages. These intercepts of German propaganda were then distributed to government departments and given to newspapers in a press release entitled "Admiralty Intercepts per Wireless Press."

When the war began, newspapers needed rapid reception of official communiqués that the Axis governments were disseminating by wireless and approached Marconi's Wireless Press. According to an internal Marconi company memo,

> Enemy communiques being already available, the Wireless Press arranged for the transmission and reception of the official and semi-official communiques of all the Allied Governments. Italy as a result of the efforts of Senator Marconi was induced to radiate her communiques and the Russian and Roumanian Governments similarly agreed. . . . France sends her official and semi-official communiques by the private wire of the Embassy to the Wireless Press, and this agency after translating the messages into English and editing them, hands them to the Marconi Company for radiation to America and neutral countries via Caernarvon.[45]

Through its wireless links on the European continent, the Wireless Press became a news agency receiving stories from special correspondents in Russia, Italy, Switzerland, Holland, and France, the latter through an exclusive arrangement with the Agence Radio.

Reuters claimed that "under the protection of the Admiralty Marconi had been allowed a monopoly of news received by wireless. This gave Marconi's Wireless Press an advantage since Marconi could pick up enemy news direct from the Continent, while Reuter agents had to send the same news by cable" (D. Read 1992:155). Marconi contracted with the Admiralty to distribute a daily news message of six hundred words to the Royal Navy and to all vessels chartered by the Admiralty for the duration of the war. Marconi's Wireless Press also offered for a subsidy of £100 ($493) per week, offset by any profits made on the U.S. service, to distribute propaganda messages to Scandinavia, Holland, Russia, Italy, Spain, and Portugal and to distribute more complete messages to the U.S. press than the existing news agencies were sending.

Whereas the Wireless Press flourished, Reuters began to lose money. When Roderick Jones became general manager in 1915, Reuters was in financial trouble, and the following year Godfrey Isaacs signaled the Marconi company's interest in buying it. Although his brother Rufus, the solicitor general, had been exonerated in the Marconi scandal of 1912–13, Lord Robert Cecil, a Conservative on the investigating committee, had considered the evidence given by Godfrey Isaacs "not satisfactory."

By 1916 Cecil was serving as foreign undersecretary in the wartime coalition with responsibility to promote British propaganda overseas and was determined to prevent Godfrey Isaacs from gaining control of Reuters. According to Donald Read, "Rather than allow this the Government would have intervened openly" and would have blocked Marconi's bid "using its powers under the Defence of the Realm Act" (1992:123–24). Backed by a loan guaranteed by the British government, Roderick Jones and Mark Napier (then chairman of Reuters) moved in with an offer of £11 ($54) per share to top that of the £10 ($48) per share made by Godfrey Isaacs. The purchase was made in the names of Napier and three others "willing to lend themselves as foreign office nominees" (D. Read 1992:124). The Foreign Office held one "public-policy" share that allowed it to nominate a director with powers to veto the appointment of any other director, veto any share transfer, and exercise a veto on questions of public policy. The definition of "public policy," as stated in a letter to Napier from Cecil of December 16, 1916, suggested that

the FO [Foreign Office] should be able both to prevent the Company from taking any action which might be contrary to public policy (such as the dissemination of reports prejudicial to the national interest, the employment of undesirable correspondents, or other employees, the undertaking of undesirable contracts with other news agencies, or the admission of undesirable persons as shareholders or directors) and also to secure that the Company's operations and actions are in conformity with public policy or the national interest, and that information of national importance is properly collected and circulated. (D. Read 1992:124–25)

In effect, although much denied later, Reuters kept the appearance of being a privately owned company while moving into state ownership. However, the appearance of Reuters's independence was important to the government. Donald Read quotes a Department of Information official as saying in 1917 that ""the work done is that of an independent news agency of an objective character, with propaganda secretly infused. . . . It is essential that independence should be preserved"" (1992:127–28).

The agency's falling private income was then supplemented by the distribution of news and commentary prepared for the Foreign Office and its Department of Information. By the end of the war Reuters had become financially viable again. Reflecting the strong linkage to the government, in 1917 Sir Roderick Jones was placed in charge of cable and wireless propaganda in the Foreign Office's Department of Information; he worked part time and was not paid (Cooper 1942:29). But when in 1918 Jones was appointed the director of propaganda in the newly established Ministry of Information under Lord Beaverbrook, he was forced to resign after a suggestion of conflict of interest (D. Read 1992:129). Nevertheless, at the end of the hostilities Jones was able to use his political connections to campaign hard and successfully to prevent Marconi's Wireless Telegraph Company from being allowed to combine the functions of a news agency with those of a wireless carrier, and Jones was able to reestablish Reuters's dominant position in Britain (D. Read 1992:146, 155).

Wartime Policy

Whereas the technology of point-to-point wireless communications languished during the war years in Britain, the Marconi company not only manufactured wireless for the military but developed new applications. Of these, direction finding, which fixed the location of enemy ships and spotter planes, was used extensively, and the military began to use wireless communications between aircraft and land. Marconi, an Italian, served in the Italian military and redeveloped an interest in shortwave transmission, which was to come to fruition in the 1920s.

When Britain and Germany declared war, President Woodrow Wilson had immediately declared the United States to be neutral. After the British and French cut the German submarine cables, German wireless communications with the United States were its major link to the outside world. The powerful British and German transmitters in the United States could be used to direct attacks on shipping from submarines. Because of these factors the U.S. presidential decree included censorship and neutrality regulations.

To ensure that Wilson's neutrality regulations were followed, the navy barred the transmission of all coded messages and dispatched censors to foreign-controlled long-distance stations to monitor all incoming and outgoing traffic. At first the navy made an exception for the Germans because without code they could not send diplomatic messages; the navy allowed them to use codes, so long as they gave the navy copies. But Navy Secretary Daniels was eager to have the navy control the foreign-owned stations. First the navy took over the station at Tuckerton, New Jersey, which had been built by a German firm for a French state-owned company, reasoning that the station had not been formally registered before the outbreak of war and under the Hague Convention of 1907 could not be licensed to a belligerent. The navy removed the German equipment in August 1914 and installed equipment made by the American-owned Federal Telegraph Company of California. The navy then used the station to handle news and diplomatic and commercial messages (Douglas 1987:270–71). And, despite its protests that it was "American," Marconi of America's station was also closed down for several months on the ground that it had breached neutrality.

Coinciding with an outbreak of U-boat activity in the Atlantic in the spring of 1915, the sudden trebling of the strength of the German-owned station at Sayville, Long Island, brought public disquiet. The sinking of the *Lusitania*, in which 1,198 died, followed by the sinking of the *Armenian*, led to the suspicion that messages in plain English or German were in fact coded messages and that this wireless station was the center of a spy network (Douglas 1987:273). In the one month after the German station's power was upgraded from 35 kilowatts to 100 kilowatts that spring, the gross tonnage of British shipping lost to enemy action almost quadrupled (Sidak 1997:38). Critics argued that upgrading the station made Sayville a new station that could not be relicensed, and it was transferred to the navy on July 9, 1915. But in the month after the takeover British losses of merchant shipping increased by almost 300 percent, to 1,488,464 tons (Sidak 1997:42). Between 1915 and 1917 the two high-power stations allowed the navy to monitor traffic between Long Island and the German transmitter at Nauen; as a result the U.S. government seized a considerable amount of German property within the United States and German-owned shipping (Tribolet 1929:202n). However, German engineers released from Sayville were later found to have spent the war in Mexico, operating a long-range transmitter for the Axis powers against Allied shipping.[46]

Josephus Daniels, the navy secretary, used breaches of neutrality in 1916 to argue "that no censorship of radio stations can be absolutely effective outside of complete government operation and control" (Douglas 1987:274). Such breaches could also be used as a public justification for a restriction on foreign ownership. In addition, the use of wireless to distribute propaganda by both sides in the European war increasingly led the U.S. press to regard the airwaves as national property to be defended from foreign penetration (Douglas 1987:275–76).

Playing to these concerns, the chair of the Interdepartmental Radio Committee, Capt. W. H. G. Bullard, drafted a new radio regulation bill to enforce U.S. government control. Under the provisions of what became known as the Alexander Bill (after Joshua Alexander, chair of the House Committee on Merchant Marine and Fisheries), U.S. government radio stations would be able to undertake commercial business; the government through the navy would be empowered to purchase any coastal station that the owner wished to sell; the frequencies to be used for commercial and ship-to-shore traffic would be restricted; only a limited number of shore stations would be licensed; and those so licensed would be prevented from changing equipment. Believing that it was the target of the Alexander Bill, the Marconi Wireless Telegraph Company of America condemned this naval scheme as "'evidence of a desire to limit private enterprise'" (quoted in Howeth 1963:314–15).

The measure was intended to eliminate commercial interests in ship-to-shore radio and for the first time would limit the amount of stock that foreigners held in any operating company. "The proposed restrictions would prohibit alien officers and impose a maximum one-third limit on alien directors and stockholders. In addition, the bill would prohibit the granting of radio licenses to foreign governments or their representatives" (Sidak 1997:39). According to John W. Griggs, president of the Marconi Wireless Telegraph Company of America, Captain Bullard and Commander D. W. Todd (a leading figure in naval radio development) admitted during hearings on the bill that the purpose was "'to give the Navy Department unlimited authority to do commercial business in competition with these gentlemen who have put their money into a mercantile venture, and to so conduct the Government end of it that eventually in five years, we would be glad to sell out'" (quoted in Sidak 1997:40). The bill was not reported out of committee.

On April 7, 1917, the day after the United States entered the war, President Wilson placed all radio stations in the United States, except for those of the army, under naval control. "The Navy suddenly had five high-powered stations (two Marconi, two German and its own at Arlington [Virginia]) plus the entire network of private stations, most of them American Marconi, at its disposal" (Douglas 1985:168). With the naval takeover of Marconi's coastal stations, Marconi abandoned its rental system for shipping in favor of out-right sales (W. Baker 1970:180). Then, early in 1918, the U.S. Shipping Board asked the navy to arrange to purchase all the radio equipment on the vessels that it owned or operated. These ships all used Marconi equipment leased from the company; seeing the writing on the wall, the company refused to allow the navy to buy the equipment without also buying the Marconi shore stations. The navy paid $798,500 for all the company's low-power stations and three high-power stations in Alaska and Astoria, Washington, but did not buy the Marconi stations used for long-distance transmission (Howeth 1963:251).

In addition, in May 1918 the navy bought the Federal Telegraph Company, which held the patents to the technology of arc transmitters developed by Valedesnaar Poulsen, a Danish resident of the United States. The oscillating currents of these transmitters were important to telephone development. The navy acquired these patents, together with three high-power and five coastal stations, for $1.16 million. Congress reopened its hearings on the Alexander Bill just after the armistice in 1918; Daniels's testimony was self-congratulatory:

> "The Navy department now owns all of the Radio Stations in the United States and its possessions formerly used for commercial radio traffic, with the exception of sixteen privately owned commercial stations. . . . This purchase means that the Marconi Co has gone out of the business of handling ship to shore radio messages, and this business has been turned over to the Navy Department, by whom it will be handled in the future. The Navy will have the advantage of using not only its coast stations previously established, but also the Marconi stations now purchased . . . as well as the stations recently purchased from the Federal Co. . . . The great increase, present and prospective, in the number of vessels on our coasts and the consequent increase in radio communication on many different wave lengths, continues to demonstrate the necessity for unified control under the navy Department of all radio communication to prevent interference. The recent purchase will go far toward accomplishing this end so far as ship to shore communication is concerned."[47]

But some members of Congress were not amused by Daniels's activities. U.S. Rep. George Washington Edmonds, a Republican from Pennsylvania, attacked Daniels, pointing out that ""after this committee refused to bring out a bill to purchase wireless apparatus, you utilized the government's money to purchase this wireless apparatus and took over the commercial systems without the consent of Congress""" (quoted in Howeth 1963:317). The midterm elections of 1918 reversed the control of the Senate and House, and in January 1919 the House Merchant Marine and Fisheries Committee unanimously tabled the bill. It was never reconsidered, and navy officials, with the exception of Daniels, switched support from outright public ownership to the idea of a U.S.-controlled communications company (Howeth 1963:317).

However, as the major purchaser of radio equipment from 1914 to 1918, the U.S. Navy played an important role in the development of radio technology. In return for the navy's patronage, Stanford Hooper was able to insist that the manufacturers—General Electric, Western Electric, De Forest, and AT&T—share their patents and standardize their technology. As a result of this concentration on research and development, considerable strides had been made by the war's end in the development of continuous wave technology (Douglas 1985:169). The postwar resumption of competition in international communications between the United States and Britain then built on this advantage.

Conclusion

The history of marine and long-distance wireless before World War I illustrates how domestic and international considerations were closely tied in a predominantly mercantilist system of relations. The negotiations and outcomes of international conventions were but one part of complex strategies of government-company relations. As in the case of submarine cables, first in marine wireless and then in point-to-point long-distance wireless, a British company dominated the world market. Marconi's wireless hegemony came from de facto standardization and a refusal to share the technology that would allow other companies' equipment to be compatible with its own. In this respect, its market dominance was similar to that of IBM a half-century later. The difference lay in the financial weakness of the Marconi company and its inability to protect its patents through legal means in the first years of its existence. Its refusal to interconnect with other companies' equipment was a way to protect its capital investment in shore stations and to gain the market dominance that it could not reach through legal means.

The international market dominance of the British Marconi company was the incentive for the German inauguration of radiotelegraphic conferences. The German government feared a British monopoly, and antipathy to the Marconi company gave the Germans an ally in the U.S. naval delegation. But the success of the Germans in gaining their demands for access to Marconi's technology and compulsory interconnection between systems also relied on the conference outcome's feeding into the domestic interests of the British Post Office, also determined to develop its own wireless service. However, whereas the British interests were primarily about using the convention to regulate the company, the Germans and Americans were predominantly concerned with strategic interests.

For the Germans those interests included those of German manufacturers and technology. For the Americans the close collaboration between government and industry evident in the United States in the postwar years had not yet developed in wireless. Rather, there was hostility. Because both the U.S. and British navies disregarded patents and pirated wireless inventions, they had no need for private companies in the early years. For the U.S. naval personnel at the conferences the issue was not only to undermine the Marconi monopoly but to create the legitimacy for an increase in naval control of wireless within the United States itself.

In turn, the domestic position of the Marconi company was intrinsically linked to British policy within the international conventions. By 1903 the Post Office's antipathy to the company had already been made evident in its withholding of a license, its refusal of public contracts, and opposition in the colonies. The intention then had been to place the company in the position where it would sell its technology at a low price to the government. Because of the company's insistence on confidentiality concerning its long-distance technology, even the company's support from the Admiralty was ambivalent. That the British government in 1903 was prepared to pay additional interconnection charges to the company for it to accept international regulation of interconnection may have been due to a determination to appease the Germans, but it is just as likely to have been linked to the fear of another unregulated monopoly that would have to be bought out. However, the evidence is conflicting. That the British government began to license other British companies only after 1906 suggests that its private policy was at odds with its public statements.

The 1906 clash between the Admiralty's concern for strategic interests and favorable attitude toward a worldwide private British monopoly and the Post Office's desire for international regulation to control the company led to a different approach. The 1906 convention demonstrates how international regulation can be used in domestic politics. The resulting compromise on compulsory interconnection, sold first to the French and then to the international convention, gained the Post Office the domestic legitimacy it needed. It was able to issue new licenses (which, coincidentally, demanded the employment of British personnel and therefore the exclusion of Marconi himself) and subsequently to nationalize the company's ship-to-shore business. In addition, on the ground that only governments could use long wave for transmission to shipping, the wavelength allocation agreed to by the Post

Office–dominated delegation could be used as an argument for public ownership. Then, even when the convention became the subject of domestic conflict, the Post Office was able to sell it as a fait accompli to a new government eager not to lose international status.

In the same way, even though the U.S. Congress did not ratify the 1906 convention, the navy was able to use it to advance its domestic and international agenda. At home the Wireless Ship Act of 1910 forced interconnection on ships using U.S. ports. As in the submarine cable market, Congress was prepared to impose extraterritorial regulation on foreign interests. The Marconi company used the public reaction to the sinking of the *Titanic* in 1912 to announce its compliance with the decisions of the 1906 treaty. But U.S. observers might well have argued that it was the federal government's decision, to take unilateral action in forcing interconnection on any ship using U.S. ports, that was the decisive factor in gaining that compliance.

In fact, although the 1906 convention set out the principles of subsequent international radio regulation (frequency allocation to services, avoidance of interference, and registration of frequencies), it demonstrated that international regulation is effective only so far as the member states implement that regulation. It is evident that the British did not implement the 1906 regulations on shipping interests. Nor did they regulate Marconi's activities in third markets. Nor did the Germans. As soon as the Marconi International Marine Communication Company joined with the Belgian and German manufacturers, they jointly operated a policy of noninterconnection and were supported by the German government.

However, by the 1912 convention the British had brought the Germans as well as the French into preconference discussions, and together the European powers agreed that long-distance point-to-point communications should not be regulated. Together they controlled the conference through colonial voting, so that despite efforts by Belgium and the United States, the eventual outcome (despite some interim backtracking) was as the trio of nations had intended. In effect, the United States could be successful only if it was collaborating with one of the major European delegations. The U.S. delegation's successful opposition to a joint radiotelegraphic and telegraph convention coincided with the interests of Germany.

The Marconi company had taken successful legal action to defend its patents both in Britain and the United States, and its successful transatlantic service on long wave—technology still not available to the Post Office—placed the company in a more powerful position in relation to the government. It was represented at the 1912 convention in London for the first time, and it could enter the discussions. In turn, this shift in power and the company's potential collaboration in long-distance wireless with Telefunken threatened British cable and security interests. The Post Office moved from punitive national regulation to financial incentives for regulating the company's actions. Reflecting a change of personnel and attitude, through the imperial wireless scheme the Post Office used public purchasing contracts with the intention not only of gaining access to the technology but also of preventing links with a foreign company. That the scheme failed to materialize and that Marconi and Telefunken entered a patent-sharing agreement was solely the result of the domestic political debate about public ownership of the imperial wireless chain. For almost twenty years in the British case, international conferences and the development of wireless throughout the colonies were therefore little more than addenda to the more important business of domestic conflicts regarding public ownership.

In the U.S. case, it would have been unusual for Congress, so subject to lobbyists' pressure, to go against the declared interests of business. Ratification of the 1906 treaty would have coincided with an election year at a time when Theodore Roosevelt's antitrust activities already had antagonized big business. Congress later ratified the 1903 and 1906 conventions because of the fear that the United States would otherwise be excluded from all discussion. In particular, the 1906 convention played to domestic naval interests by excluding amateurs from all but a small portion of the radio spectrum.

By 1912 the U.S. commercial companies, dominated by Marconi of America, were in favor of regulation and were not disposed to oppose the strong views of senior naval personnel. Additionally, at a time of uncertainty "national interest" plays well. The Radio Communications Act of 1912 allowed the navy to enter into commercial wireless transmission, which would later be used to subsidize the press. And whether for protectionist or security reasons, the 1912 act introduced the provision that licenses could be issued only to U.S. nationals or U.S.-registered companies. This provision later proved ineffective against German-owned, U.S.-registered companies but marked the beginnings of a protectionist stance against foreign investment in radio.

Despite congressional opposition, the same U.S. naval interests that bought out Marconi's ship-to-shore stations in 1917 backed the Alexander Bill and used U.S. neutrality at the start of the European war to expand naval control of wireless. They were also responsible for nationalizing Marconi of America in the postwar period and for establishing the Radio Corporation of America. Those naval interests, in alliance with a much-expanded merchant marine and the enhanced relevance of radio to shipping, were to ensure that U.S. shipping interests became an increasingly important player in the postwar period in international negotiations for dividing the radio spectrum. For several decades the international regulation of wireless was to see a conflict between different forms of users. Shipping interests, supported by the United States and Britain, fought off continental European broadcasting interests for retention of the airwaves that they already occupied.

4. The United States, Trade, and Communications, 1890s–1917

WHILE BRITAIN RETAINED its adherence to free trade, the United States in the mid-nineteenth century was mercantilist and nationalist. The leading U.S. economist, Henry Carey, denounced free trade as Britain's policy to gain world supremacy and to reduce all agricultural states to tribute payers (Calleo and Rowland 1973:26). But as the United States became increasingly industrialized, by the 1890s its ideology had moved toward what Rosenberg terms "liberal developmentalism" (1982:10). Adam Smith's tenets of economic and political freedom through free trade were linked to the expansion of overseas markets and to "the mental and moral development" of populations in Asia and Latin America (Williams 1969:361).

Whereas British business in this period saw overseas expansion as the means to allow an anticyclical government policy that forswore protectionist policies at home, the United States backed its arguments for "equal access," or an "Open Door," for trade and investment with the mechanism of reciprocity to gain such access. Demands for reciprocity could be encompassed within a model of liberal protectionism in which the openness or otherwise of a foreign market, determined on a case-by-case basis by the U.S. government, was the instigator of protectionist measures. This ideology, first implemented in the 1890s by Secretary of State James G. Blaine, runs through to the twentieth century (Williams 1969:327).

After the Civil War the U.S. economy changed drastically. By the 1890s mechanization of agriculture had increased production and exports of cotton and wheat (Rosenberg 1982:18). In manufacturing the introduction of mass production before the depression of the 1890s led to decreasing costs and increasing exports for those firms that were selling new products such as typewriters, sewing machines, and cigarettes or processed foods. The depression then decreased production costs further, thereby making products more competitive in world markets (Becker 1982:20). A big jump in the exports of manufactured and semimanufactured goods came between 1894 and 1900 (Williams 198:360). Then, between 1900 and 1913 annual exports almost doubled to $2.5 billion, with the value of manufacturing exports exceeding the values of agriculture and raw materials (Kaufman 1974:4; Becker 1982:1).

A reorganization of the State Department in 1890 first heralded the desire to promote U.S. business overseas and the "recognition of the importance of controlling the means of global communications as a key element in both domestic and global expansion" (Schwoch 1990:25). But the bank failures and panic of 1893, followed by a deep depression and social unrest, brought big business in the northeast to the same conclusion that farmers had reached in the 1880s and had been lobbying for ever since: the need to open foreign markets (Rosenberg 1982:39). Although Europe still was the most important U.S. export market, taking 75 percent of all U.S. exports in 1900, the rise of European tariff barriers increased the political pressure to open up alternative markets. The European threat to the China market brought about more U.S. government intervention in support of exports. The State Department established its Bureau of Foreign Commerce in 1897, thereby institutionalizing diplomatic support for exports. A State Department memorandum the following year stated that the "'enlargement of foreign consumption of the products of our mills and workshops has . . . become a serious problem of statesmanship as well as of commerce . . . and we can no longer afford to disregard international rivalries now that we ourselves have become a competitor in the world-wide struggle for trade'" (quoted in Rosenberg 1982:40).

Responding to business, Congress created the Department of Commerce and Labor in 1903 and organized the Bureau of Manufacturers within that department to provide detailed reports on market opportunities overseas. As U.S. industry grew more concentrated, big business itself came to dominate the export trade. In 1913, 81 percent of manufactured exports came from industrial sectors (food, drink, tobacco; metal manufacture, machinery) in which sixty-seven of the one hundred largest corporations were to be found (Becker 1982:13)

Although the United States continued to be a net importer of capital until World War I, U.S. companies and capital began to invest overseas in the 1890s to gain access to raw materials. U.S. industry and capital became more important in the Caribbean and Central and South America, and by the end of the nineteenth century, to get around high tariffs, U.S. manufacturers had established twenty-eight plants in Europe, followed by fifty more in the next decade (Southard 1931:xiii).

During this period direct foreign investment in the United States continued to rise, from $1.4 billion in 1870 to $3.6 billion in 1900, much of it going into railroads but also into land and food processing (Porter 1973:76). Once the capital needs of the railroads had been satisfied and personal savings increased, a market for industrial shares developed, and capital became available for developing large holding companies (Porter 1973:77–84). This development of large-scale industry, aided by the growth of newspaper advertising to foster demand, challenged the American dream of a land of individual opportunity and fueled political opposition to big business. U.S. agrarian antipathy to cartels and big business and the demand for regulation led first to state regulation, then to passage of the Federal Act of 1887, which established the Interstate Commerce Commission to regulate railroads, and the Sherman Anti-Trust Act of 1890. Ironically, the legal interpretation of the latter, which outlawed cartels and provided an incentive to mergers, led to even bigger businesses and to the advent of virtual monopolies, such as Western Union.

The United States used its military power to support the expansion of markets.[1] Only a belief that opening countries to U.S. goods would also give the inhabitants political freedom could justify direct colonization by a country with an anticolonialist ideology. In 1898 President William McKinley attributed to God his decision to take the Philippines from Spain (Braisted 1958:55). And Theodore Roosevelt, elected president in 1901, argued that when the U.S. government fought wars "'with barbarous or semi-barbarous peoples,'" it was not violating the peace but merely exercising "'a most regrettable but necessary international police duty which must be performed for the sake of the welfare of mankind'" (quoted in Rosenberg 1982:41).

The United States therefore began the twentieth century as a colonial power with interests stretching from Puerto Rico in the Caribbean into Hawaii, Samoa, the Philippines, and Guam in the Pacific and with a Monroe Doctrine (see chapter 5) that claimed South America as its own sphere of influence. In 1914 U.S. companies had $250 billion invested overseas.[2] By then U.S. trade had diversified, with 25 percent going to North America and 6 percent to South America (Kaufman 1974:4, 6–7).

As the British had shown earlier, military (particularly naval) power, financial power, foreign investment, and trade went hand in hand. But they all depended on communications, and in this regard the United States was weaker than Britain. In particular, the growing power of AT&T and its monopoly of the telephone skewed U.S. domestic and foreign policy.

U.S. Cable Policy

Following the laying of transatlantic cables by Jay Gould's American Telegraph and Cable Company and John W. Mackay's Commercial Cable Company during the 1880s, additional U.S. transatlantic cables were laid in 1889 for Western Union and then, following the financial panic, in 1894 for Commercial Cable (Scott 1958:70). The period that began in 1893 was one of free trade in cable landing licenses. "During President Cleveland's second administration [from 1892], Secretary of State [Walter Q.] Gresham and later, Secretary [Richard] Olney held that there was no inherent power in the Executive to regulate landing licenses, and they refused to exercise any powers in relation to submarine cables" (Herring and Gross 1936:230). As a result of this interpretation of their powers, Pender's Anglo-American Telegraph Company was able to lay another transatlantic cable in 1894.

But in 1896 the resurrection of the 1889 proposal for a French cable from Haiti to New York led to a restatement of the earlier U.S. policy of refusing interconnection or landing rights to companies that operated monopoly concessions in third countries. When the French government–backed Compagnie Française des Câbles Télégraphiques built a submarine cable from Cuba to Haiti to New York that hooked up with its line from Brest and London to New York, its initial strategy was to become independent of both Western Union and Mackay's Postal Telegraph Company by establishing its own U.S. network. Arguing that there was no U.S. law to prevent it, the French company laid six underground wires between New York and Boston and a number between New York and Washington, D.C., and planned a U.S. domestic network that was based on stringing wires along Western Union's poles.[3] However, it subsequently linked up with the Postal Telegraph and Commercial Cable lines. As with the French proposal of 1889, the point of U.S. contention lay with the lack of reciprocity. Because the cable would link New York with Brazil via Haiti, U.S. concern lay with the monopoly concessions of the French in Venezuela and down the east coast of South America. Meanwhile, the French government was also becoming increasingly dirigiste. It had specified that the cable must be manufactured in France using only French engineers and that only a French ship could be used to lay it (*Electrical Review,* Oct. 9, 1896). The new McKinley administration therefore informed the French ambassador that the company "would land the cable at its peril" and that the cable must be operated under "such regulations and restrictions as this Government may prescribe" (*New York Herald,* June 28, 1897).

In 1896 the U.S. government filed suit against the French cable company and its associated companies, alleging that "the corporations are combining and conspiring to monopolize part of the trade and commerce between the United States and foreign countries, to the irreparable injury of the people and business interests of the United States."[4] The government obtained an injunction, but it had been based on the contention that the U.S. company to which landing rights had been given was really a French company and American in name only. The injunction was lifted after the company produced an affidavit that the company that intended to control and operate the Haiti cable—the United States and Haiti Telegraph and Cable Company— was American owned. In fact only the part of the cable landed in the United States and ten miles offshore belonged to the American company; the rest belonged to the French company. The cable was opened in August 1898 amid much fanfare and presents to President McKinley from the French.[5] But the U.S. government forced the Compagnie Française and the Haiti company to maintain separate offices and would not allow the line from Brest to Cuba to operate as one line, thereby making it uneconomical (Ahvenainen 1996: 146). The declaration that the Haiti company was not a subsidiary of the French company would soon backfire on the French company.

Upon the declaration of the Spanish-American War in 1898, the U.S. Army was about to be dispatched from Florida to Cuba when the military realized that it had no means by which the president could communicate with his troops. The U.S. government at first proposed to buy a British cable running from Panama to the West Indies and Cuba but then recognized that under international law the British could not sell to a belligerent. The United States was in a quandary. Called in to advise, James Scrymser (who held the Florida concession) then suggested that, on the basis of the 1896 affidavit from the United States and Haiti Telegraph and Cable Company that it was American, the government should requisition its cable. Only through this requisition was McKinley able to take direct control of the fighting in Cuba. Scrymser himself was appalled at Washington's lack of planning for communications during the war (Scrymser 1915:95–98).

Following this debacle, the acting attorney general summarized the basic principles underlying the U.S. cable landing policy during congressional hearings in 1898:

"1. The President, in exercising control over the relations of the United States with foreign powers, has the duty of seeing that in the exchange of comities among nations the United States gets as much as it gives. He, therefore, must not permit a cable to land upon our shores under a concession from a foreign power which does not permit our cables to land on its shores and enjoy there facilities equal to those accorded its cable here.

2. A submarine cable is of inestimable service to the government in communicating with its officers in the diplomatic and consular services and with the army and navy when abroad. The President, therefore, should demand that precedence in the use of the line be given to government communications, those of the United States equally with those of foreign governments.

3. Treating a cable simply as an instrument of commerce, it is the duty of the President, in the absence of legislation by Congress, to impose such restrictions as will forbid unjust discriminations, prevent monopolies, promote competition, and secure reasonable rates." (quoted in Herring and Gross 1936:231–32)

This statement was later approved by Attorney General John Griggs (Herring and Gross 1936:231–32).

By the late 1890s, then, the acknowledged primary principle behind the U.S. cable landing policy had become that of reciprocity. Other principles—that the U.S. government should be treated with status equal to others' in the rates charged and that there should be competition to gain "reasonable" tariffs— were of lesser importance. Yet despite this policy, two U.S.-dominated cartels ruled transatlantic communications.

On the one hand, the first transatlantic German cables, laid in 1898, formed one pool with the Postal Telegraph and Commercial Cable companies and the Canadian Pacific Railway. In 1894 Compagnie Française des Câbles Télégraphiques withdrew from this pool. The Anglo-American Telegraph Company and the DUS Cable Company, together with Western Union and the Great North-Western Telegraph Company of Canada, formed the other (Bright 1911:169). In the long term the French policy of eschewing domestic interconnection does not appear to have been successful. Bright (1911:174) suggests that, because the French cables were not closely allied with either of the two domestic U.S. companies, collection and delivery problems meant that the French cables took only a small proportion of the transatlantic traffic. On the other hand, the rapid spread of the telephone in the United States and the rise of AT&T increased the vulnerability of foreign cables to the refusal of interconnection.

The Commercial Cable Company gave evidence to the Balfour Committee in 1901 (see ¶1615) about its methods of collecting traffic in Britain. The company had its own stations in three of the four cities from which it leased private wires from the Post Office to interconnect with its cable, but its manager explained that "in all other provincial places we have to depend upon putting ourselves before the telegraphing public." Unless customers specified the name of a carrier for their telegram, under a previous agreement by the

Post Office all "unrouted" traffic went to British companies.⁶ Advertising was therefore crucial to the U.S. cables.

In contrast, because British companies could not advertise for business in the United States, they relied on their U.S. partners to share the outgoing traffic (Peel 1905:252). The matter came to a head with the takeover of Western Union by J. P. Morgan's AT&T.

Morgan acquired control of AT&T in 1907 after a fight with Mackay's Postal Telegraph Company; Morgan reinstated Theodore Vail, who had resigned in 1885, as president. Following the financial panic of 1907, Vail was under pressure to reduce costs, raise revenue, and gain a monopoly of the field. As a result AT&T refused to interconnect its telephone long lines with small local independent companies, thereby putting them at the mercy of J. P. Morgan and leading to their takeover by AT&T. The policy gave AT&T 80 percent of the domestic market. Vail and Morgan then won control of Western Union.

Despite the domestic growth of the telephone, the telegraph was still the primary means of long-distance and international communication. When AT&T took full control of Western Union in 1910, it immediately connected its domestic telephone lines with the international cables. A new, faster cable—the first AT&T–Western Union transatlantic cable—was completed in the fall of 1910. And despite a delay of six months by the British Post Office, perhaps because transatlantic radiotelegraph service had been started in 1907 and competition was beginning to affect the cable companies, the British landing license contained no clause regulating tariffs (Bright 1911:173).

For the first time it was possible to send a telegram from Britain to a U.S. resident by using one carrier and the telephone at each end. However, following the merger, Western Union's policy toward other transatlantic cables changed, so that if the U.S. sender did not specify the telegraph company, all such telephoned traffic was immediately turned over to Western Union's international cables (Danelian 1939:74–76). Although this mirrored the British practice, this AT&T policy, coupled with the inability of the British companies to advertise for their own traffic, rendered them completely vulnerable to AT&T's terms of interconnection. Vail set out his strategy in a letter to John Moon in January 1919. Vail states:

> "My efforts towards an intranational and international communication system
> are of long standing. The whole development of the Bell Telephone system from
> the beginning was based on comprehensive intercommunications systems by
> wire. When the American Telephone and Telegraph Co., bought the Western
> Union, its first attempt was to secure trans-Atlantic cables by laying one and

leasing several. . . . It was our intention to develop this system and ultimately bring the United States into focus with the great arterial cable systems throughout the world. The combination was not then countenanced by the Government." (quoted in Tribolet 1929:214n)

Western Union's refusal to collect traffic for the British-owned transatlantic cables meant that the British had to lease their cables to the Americans (Schreiner 1924:106). In 1912 all five of the transatlantic cables owned by the Anglo-American Telegraph Company and that of the Direct United States Cable Company were leased to Western Union for ninety-nine years. Although Vail presented the agreement to the British press as not meaning "an amalgamation of rival concerns, but rather a community of interests," in effect the British were frozen out of the transatlantic route by denial of interconnection (Bright 1911:172).[7] By World War I the American-owned Western Union and the Commercial Cable Company controlled all thirteen transatlantic cables and transatlantic tariffs, impeded only by Marconi's competition (Bright 1914:136).

Vail's words to Moon suggest that he intended some further alliance with the Eastern companies and that the Democratic administration of Woodrow Wilson refused to allow it, but that refusal may have been indirect in that domestic antitrust developments were soon to remove Western Union from AT&T control. One year after Western Union leased the British cables, the U.S.government instituted an antitrust investigation of AT&T through the Interstate Commerce Commission. Pressure for AT&T to interconnect with independent telephone companies and to stop buying them up had increased after Wilson's inauguration in 1913. That was also the year that J. P. Morgan died; his acquisitiveness had been a major factor in AT&T's monopoly aspirations. Vail agreed to the "Kingsbury Commitment" of 1913, by which AT&T agreed to divest itself of Western Union, to stop buying up independents, and to interconnect them with its long lines (Brooks 1975:136). But that agreement did not regulate the actual interconnection charges, and it was possible for both AT&T and Western Union to be discriminatory.

The Interstate Commerce Commission (ICC) acted under the Mann-Elkins Act of 1910, which had made some provisions of the Interstate Commerce Act of 1888 applicable to interstate commerce by wire or wireless. Mann-Elkins applied the term *common carrier* to telecommunications for the first time. It defined *common carrier* as including "'all persons, natural or artificial, engaged in such transportation or transmission . . . as common carriers for hire'" (quoted in Herring and Gross 1938:211). Such common carriers could classify services and apply differential rates, but those rates had to be just and reasonable and nondiscriminatory between persons. Because most landline telephone services at the time were intrastate, the commission was primarily concerned with telegraph and wireless (Herring and Gross 1938:210–12).[8] Although in 1913 the ICC imposed a uniform accounting system on companies, it ran into problems with how to account for depreciation of network infrastructure and, because companies were under no legal obligation to file or publish their tariffs, or to submit them to the commission other than for information purposes, the commission's rate jurisdiction was limited. It lacked the power to investigate proposed changes in tariffs. Only when it received a complaint could it adjudicate.

In 1915, in response to such a complaint, the ICC ruled against Western Union in a case brought by the Commercial Cable Company involving discriminatory interconnection fees for its international traffic. In what was the first case of its kind, the ICC said that it was entitled to rule on interconnection for international traffic because such traffic comprised three segments—the originating segment, the international segment, and the termination segment—and each produced a tariff. International traffic was not, as Western Union contended, seamless "through" traffic and therefore outside ICC jurisdiction, the ICC found. The commission ruled that if the termination segment involved interconnection with another company's lines, that interconnection fell within its purview. The ICC ordered that Western Union cease its discrimination (Herring and Gross 1936:224–25). The analysis contrasted starkly with the situation in Britain, where the Post Office's interconnection charges (which were said to discriminate in favor of its own cross-channel cables) could be challenged only at the political level.

In the intervening period, in order to make full use of its infrastructure AT&T had developed a leased-line telegraph service for big business, in competition with Western Union and the Postal Telegraph Company. Two years later the ICC found that the charges by AT&T and other telegraph companies for private wire telegraph and telephone service were "'unreasonably low'" and that the companies were "'furnishing the more valuable service at a relatively lower charge contrary to recognized principles of classification'" (quoted in Herring and Gross 1936:221).[9] In other words, small businesses and residential telephone customers were subsidizing large users' leased lines. But by the time the decision was published in 1918, AT&T had been nationalized, and the commission entered no order.

Public hostility to large corporations and the appointment of Albert Sidney Burleson as postmaster general in the Wilson administration resulted once more in a discussion of government ownership. Vail had dismissed such talk in 1912 as "not likely to become anything more than academic, at least for the present." Burleson believed that the telegraph should be part of the government-run postal service, and members of Congress began advocating the "postalization of the telephones and telegraph." Vail argued that while "all monopolies should be regulated, Government ownership would be an unregulated monopoly" (Brooks 1975:148–49). However, the takeover did not occur until the United States entered World War I.

The Pacific Cable

Direct communication with China had been a goal of U.S. cable policy since the unsuccessful efforts of Cyrus Field in the 1860s, and events there had increased the need for such communication. Given the influence of railway interests in a Pacific submarine cable, the newly strengthened U.S. Navy surveyed the route between San Francisco and Honolulu in 1891–92. However, the laissez-faire beliefs of the Cleveland administration clashed with the need for government backing for U.S. firms in competition with European banks and companies. Only after business leaders persuaded the Cleveland administration to host the visit of China's elder statesman, Li Chang Hung, in 1892 did the United States become more proactive.

After the railways had spanned the country in the 1880s, U.S. railway magnates such as James J. Hill pushed for expansion of exports to Asia. He proposed filling his westbound railway wagons with East Coast wheat for the Asian market, even going so far as to have wheat cookbooks printed and distributed in various Asian languages (Rosenberg 1982:16). Despite Hill's close association with Cleveland, neither he nor cable interests, led by Scrymser, were able to get legislation through Congress during the early 1890s (Alexander 1911:54). In fact, competition between the two American consortiums, the International Pacific Cable Company headed by Col. Z. S. Spalding and the Pacific Cable Company of J. A. Scrymser, was instrumental in ensuring that neither was successful. The fiercely anti-British Scrymser lobbied heavily in Congress, arguing that Spalding's company was under the influence of Pender's Eastern.

Meanwhile, the balance of power in the Far East was changing. The Sino-Japanese War, won by the Japanese in 1895, had given that country informal control of Korea and brought it into conflict with a Russia that was expanding into Manchuria through the Trans-Siberian Railway. In a depressed domestic market, and concerned lest business opportunities be lost, the U.S. representative in China was given permission in 1896 to use all his personal and official influence on behalf of any reputable U.S. businessman (McCormick 1967:74). Despite the overarching influence of Russia, which was backed by French financiers, by 1897 U.S. trade figures showed a first-ever surplus with China—mainly in manufactured cotton, kerosene, woolens, metals, and yarn (McCormick 1967:85). But lack of direct communications was an impediment to trade.

The 1898 Spanish-American War brought home to the U.S. government its dependence on British cables. Despite previous U.S. attempts to get an international treaty protecting "neutral" cables, in response to refusal by the Spanish authority in the Philippines to allow each belligerent to send messages, Adm. George Dewey planned to cut the Eastern's cable linking Manila to Hong Kong. In fact, he cut a tributary cable to another island, and messages from the Spanish government in Manila continued to get through. Washington called in Scrymser for advice on what to do. He suggested that the United States appeal to the British government for cable neutrality; as a result the Eastern then sealed the Hong Kong end on the advice of the British government. Neither Spanish nor American messages could get through.

The U.S. government then attempted to make a confidential arrangement with the Eastern to use the cable and, when refused, applied for permission to land a U.S. cable from Manila on a barge outside the harbor at Hong Kong—a request that Lord Salisbury's government also refused. Admiral Dewey would send messages by dispatch boat to Hong Kong, then had to rely on the good nature of the manager of the cable station for their transmission to Washington, D.C. (Braisted 1958:32–33). In fact, lack of cable communications worked to the advantage of the United States. Although the peace protocol was signed on August 12, fighting (which the Americans won) continued in the Philippines until August 16, 1898.

The cable reopened at the end of that month with the agreement of both belligerents, and the Eastern promptly filed for $36,000 in damages against the U.S. government. It claimed it was due that sum for submarine cable interruption, for a breach of its monopoly concession in the laying of military cables within the Philippines, and, following the transfer of the Philippines to U.S. ownership, for the U.S. government's failure to honor the contract of the Spanish government for a $21,825 annual subsidy for the use of the Eastern's domestic and submarine cables (Tribolet 1929:251–52). The case dragged on until 1912 when a U.S. court ruled against the Eastern.

During the war the U.S. government's consideration of a Pacific cable focused on the desire for any proposed cable between the United States and the Philippines to land only on soil under U.S. sovereignty. According to Howeth, "The cable company was completely in agreement, but insisted that the Navy department lend full assistance and backing in the acquisition of the necessary islands, either by peace treaty with Spain or by purchase. In order to provide one of the landings the *U.S.S. Bennington* was sent to occupy unclaimed Wake Island in the name of the United States Government. Additional naval assistance was provided by hydrographic survey West of Hawaii" (1963:13). For this reason the U.S. government at first claimed the Caroline Islands against German demands in the postwar division of spoils. But it then decided that buying the entire Philippines archipelago, together with ownership of the islands of Midway (acquired in 1867) and Guam, would provide a Honolulu-Manila link (Braisted 1958:55–57; Rosenburg 1982:43). The U.S. government intended to access China from the Philippines.

However, the Eastern had other ideas. Only a few months before the outbreak of the Spanish-American War, the Eastern had signed a monopoly cable concession with Madrid for a cable from the Philippines to China (Tribolet 1929:267). This agreement, which the McKinley administration was not aware of in 1898, lasted twenty years. As a result, even though the United States bought the Philippines as a naval base and stepping stone to China, the earlier concession prevented the United States from establishing its own communications with China via Manila.

While the U.S. government was fighting Spain, China's internal government began to collapse. Germany, France, Russia, and Britain each gained a sphere of influence and commercial concessions, so in 1899 McKinley's secretary of state, John Hay, sent his first "Open Door" note, asking all nations to respect the principle of equal commercial opportunity in China (Esthus 1967:6). A year later, fearing that the Boxer Rebellion might lead to outright European colonization, Hay sent a second note asking nations to respect Chinese territorial integrity. The principle of the "Open Door"—noncolonization of China and equal commercial access—became the foundation of an economic diplomacy in the Far East that reflected primarily the U.S. government's interest in the commercial opportunities available (Williams 1969:409; Becker 1982:17).

In his 1899 State of the Union address, McKinley called congressional attention to the need for a Pacific cable to link with the Philippines (Alexander 1911:68). For a year the islands had been under a U.S. military government that set out to "civilize" the Filipino people and fought the Filipino independence movement. The 1899 decision to use English in schools, made when Gen. Arthur MacArthur was in command, became law in January 1901. The legislation reflected William Howard Taft's belief that "'English is the language of free government; it is the language through which Filipinos can read the history of the hammering out by our ancestors of the heritage of liberty which they have conferred upon us,'" and it involved recruiting one thou-

sand U.S. teachers of English (quoted in Bresnahan 1979:65). Such immigra-
tion, together with a military government and civil war, demanded telegraphic communication. Yet there was no direct means of communication between
the Philippines and the United States. Nor was there direct communication
with Hawaii or Guam. And despite the increase in diplomatic influence heralded by John Hay's Open Door letter, lack of direct communications weakened the U.S. position in China. Reflecting these different pressures, between
1899 and 1901 no less than eighteen bills containing proposals to construct a
Pacific cable were introduced in Congress. All foundered on the question of
cost and subsidy. Congress was adamant that the cable should be "American" but was not prepared to give subsidies, and private investment had
found more profitable areas elsewhere.

In 1901 the new president, Theodore Roosevelt, asked Congress to address
the "crying need" for a cable to Hawaii and the Philippines, to be continued
to Asia. Because the war against the Filipino independence movement was
still dragging on, the cable was "'demanded, not merely for commercial, but
also political and military considerations.'" The president suggested that
either a government cable should be laid or a private cable "'giving like advantages to those accruing from a Government cable'" (quoted in Tribolet
1929:181). Eight more bills were introduced in Congress in the following year,
all unsuccessfully.

Finally, after more than fifty congressional bills over almost thirty years,
the "American" cable was eventually constructed in 1902. The catalyst may
have been the impending British state-owned "All-Red" Pacific cable, and it
came about through the actions of one of the transatlantic entrepreneurs,
"Bonanza King" John W. Mackay, who had laid the first U.S. Atlantic cable
in 1884 and then established the Postal Telegraph Company. He bypassed
Congress under the existing Postal Telegraph Act of 1866 on the basis that
the cable to Hawaii and the Philippines connected places within the United
States and was therefore a "domestic" cable. Mackay's enterprise incited congressional hostility and led Scrymser to the extreme of arguing for a government-owned cable. But Mackay agreed to abide by maximum tariffs and
promised that his company would never accept exclusive privileges from a
foreign government or enter any agreement to regulate rates, except for interconnection.

However, because the Eastern and Great Northern companies owned the
concessions from the Philippines to China and within China itself, Mackay
had to bring them in. Not surprisingly, given the nationalist sentiment around
the issue, the agreement by which these two owned 75 percent of the equity
in the "American" company, although known to the president and the at-

torney general, was kept secret by the company and the U.S. government and did not become public knowledge until 1921 (Tribolet 1929:181–87). The cable was laid as far as the Philippines in 1902–3 (Brown 1927:23). Competitive to the end, the British All-Red Pacific cable opened for business on January 1, 1903, one day ahead of the "all-American Pacific cable" (Alexander 1911:71).

As a result, although the telegraph played an important strategic role in U.S. diplomacy before and during the Russo-Japanese War (and figured in the final treaty), throughout Theodore Roosevelt's presidency White House telegrams went via British cables. After the Russo-Japanese War, the U.S. Pacific cable was extended to Shanghai in 1906, but a plan to extend the cable from the Philippines to Japan met with the opposition of the Japanese government. The cable later linked up at the island of Yap (west of Guam) with the German cables built just before World War I as part of Germany's own imperial system. From Yap one German cable ran to Guam, another to Shanghai, and a third to the Dutch East Indies. The German cables were to serve as alternate routes for U.S. traffic in an area subject to the interruptions of earthquakes and would be seized by the Japanese during World War I.

In fact, the Pacific cable was to be a disappointment to those concerned with China. Whereas the U.S. government anticipated that commercial opportunities in China would follow the Russo-Japanese War, the cable company was predominantly interested in the traffic from Japan, with its burgeoning exports (Esthus 1967:117).[10] In addition, the reluctance of the Japanese military to withdraw troops from China coincided with the Japanese commercial appropriation of mining and communications opportunities. Britain complained formally in March 1906 about the limitation of commercial trade and Japan's refusal to grant telegraph facilities and railway transport in Manchuria to British companies (Esthus 1967:119). Then in 1907 Japan signed a treaty with France that recognized that each held special interests in China and a secret treaty with Russia in which each undertook not to seek concessions for railways and telegraphs in each other's spheres of interest in Manchuria (Esthus 1967:126, 257). Thus despite its formal political status as part of China, Manchuria became divided between a northern section under Russian commercial control and a southern section under Japanese.

In any case, once the domestic market began to recover from the depression of the 1890s, U.S. exporters lost interest in China (Esthus 1967:124). "By 1907 . . . manufacturers and other businessmen sensed the difficulties of doing business with people of strange customs and peculiar buying habits where political intrigue and power politics made the conduct of commerce precarious at best" (Kaufman 1974:53). And in view of the rise of Japan, the U.S. "vision of a vast export of cotton, machinery and buckwheat cakes" through the Open Door became increasingly unrealistic (Garvin 1905:99). A resurgent Japanese presence added to, rather than created, investment uncertainty in a geographical sphere where the United States had one colony and no client states.

With U.S. approval, rumored at the time to be a quid pro quo for Japanese assurances that it would not attack the Philippines, Japan fully occupied Korea. Having already laid a military cable to Korea during the Russo-Japanese War, the Japanese immediately set about linking Korea more firmly to Japan. Citing security needs, they bought the Great Northern cable between Korea and Japan and built another to Formosa (now Taiwan). Later the Japanese laid a cable to Shanghai and another to Siberia (Tribolet 1929:224). In effect, as industrialization and imperialist expansion affected the Japanese government, it became determined to have its own government cables linked to the mainland. When negotiations with the companies for lower tariffs failed, Japan eventually achieved what it wanted by organizing through traffic to Europe via Russia (Ahvenainen 1981:210). Thus the Russo-Japanese War signaled a shift in the balance of power in the Far East, reflected in the control of international communications.

The Advent of War

In the case of AT&T, the U.S. declaration of war in 1917 brought further threats of a government takeover. "Newspaper editorials urged a wire takeover, and Post Office officials spoke about eliminating all telegraph offices and substituting post offices for them" (Brooks 1975:150). Unlike the radio acts, which gave the president the authority to take over private radio companies, no such legislation governed the wireline telegraph and telephone sector. But even before the United States entered World War I, it had recruited AT&T for national defense preparations.

Once the European war began in 1914, censorship meant that round-trip transatlantic transmission that once took forty minutes now required seven hours.[11] President Wilson then placed all the transatlantic cables under the control of Newcomb Carlton, president of Western Union, on behalf of the U.S. government—a form of nationalization that the rival Commercial Cable Company protested. The British immediately expressed consternation at the breach of sovereignty that would occur if U.S. cable companies, with the right to operate on British soil, were U.S. government owned, so the president backtracked and instead placed the companies under an obligation to share traffic and operate the cables as efficiently as possible.[12]

After the United States entered the war in 1917, the Bell system shipped to

France large amounts of equipment in order to establish a complete U.S. network there, and the Signal Corps battalions of the American Expeditionary Force subsequently recruited fourteen thousand Bell employees. Eventually, in July 1918 Congress began hearings on a resolution designed to give the president the authority to assume control of all telephone and telegraph systems. The measure was backed not only by the postmaster general but also by the secretaries of war and the navy. The secretary of the navy argued that government control was "'the only absolutely safe way in which the government may insure the dispatch of its messages and the secrecy of its business'" (quoted in Brooks 1975:151), and Wilson issued a proclamation assuming control in July of that year. However, the contract between AT&T and the government, signed in October 1918, was finalized only one month before the armistice.

The agreement stated that "the government got rate-setting powers but would consult the judgment of AT&T in exercising them; it agreed to maintain the property and eventually to return it in as good condition as received" (Brooks 1975:152). The financially generous settlement included payment of all taxes on the property seized. The government also pledged to allow AT&T to inspect the books and even to maintain the current $8 annual dividend to its stockholders. The Post Office established the Wire Control Board, which then appointed an operating board on which AT&T executives sat. In effect, AT&T ran its own system for the government (Brooks 1975:152–53).

The government takeover proved a disappointment to those who assumed that government ownership would reduce tariffs. As Vail had suggested, government ownership became "an unregulated monopoly." So, whereas in the prewar years state public utility commissions had prevented Bell companies from forcing new subscribers to pay a connection charge, the federal government introduced the charge within four weeks of taking over. This charge never disappeared. In addition, faced with inflation, the government raised long-distance tariffs by 20 percent in January 1919. Two months later it increased Bell's tariffs for local calls. Protests from subscribers ensured that the legal challenge would go to the Supreme Court, but the Court upheld the increases. In all, the one-year period of public ownership increased costs to subscribers to the Bell system alone by more than $42 million per year, and in July 1919 Congress ended the arrangement (Brooks 1975:158). The unfortunate experience was to bias public opinion against public ownership and to herald a decade of laissez faire.

International and Domestic Regulation

Throughout this period the U.S. telegraph companies continued to refuse to be constrained by international regulation. That there was sometimes a division of opinion between them and the U.S. government was evident because, although the U.S. government was not a signatory to the convention, it actually notified the Berne Bureau concerning its censorship of telegraphs during the Spanish-American War of 1898.[13] And although the U.S. companies castigated the regulations of the International Telegraph Union (ITU) as intended to prevent competition, their own pooling had the same effect. In 1905 it was less expensive to cable India from Britain at 2.55 pence (5 cents) per mile than to cable the United States at 3.4 pence (7 cents) per mile (Peel 1905:258–59). In fact, once U.S. companies owned transatlantic submarine cables, they were more profitable than the regulated European companies because the U.S. companies remained outside the ITU agreements. Even before Western Union took over the British cables in 1911, its cables earned £50 ($244) per mile per year, whereas the Eastern's earnings averaged only £35 to £39 ($170 to $190) per mile (Balfour Committee:¶602). The difference in profitability was at least partially because of the ITU's regulations.

The detailed regulations included maximum charges not only for traffic within Europe but outside Europe and regulated the traffic of those companies whose home countries were signatories to the convention, even if the cables were transmitted between nonsignatories. The regulations set tariffs and added to company costs by regulating which parts of the message were chargeable to the customer. In particular, the U.S. companies objected to regulation that would prevent them charging customers for the "service" part of the telegram, such as the address or the time of filing. The regulations had the effect of increasing the "dead time" on telegrams to about 17 percent.[14] In addition, the regulations required the company to make multiple copies of telegrams at its own expense. Also, the convention accepted that the routing specified by the sender should be honored, whereas the U.S. companies argued that to do so "'would compel private enterprise to place the use of their property at the service of competing concerns on the same terms as they are employed for our own business purpose'" (quoted in Tribolet 1929:14). In other words, the specification of a route by the customer implied interconnection with other company's cables, the sharing of traffic, and lower profits.

In addition, the European countries agreed that telegraph transmission should be inexpensive for the press, whose messages were uncoded and therefore easier to transmit, and that night-time leased lines should be available to newspapers. In contrast, the U.S. cables were run as a purely commercial enterprise. As Cooper (1942:11) pointed out sixty years later, "Only the American-owned cable companies refused to follow the others in making practical rates for news transmission; rates attractive enough to encourage the export of news from the United States."

So although the U.S. companies argued that they could not accede to the international regulations on the principle that the U.S. telegraph system was run by private companies, the driving force behind their objections was primarily a matter of profitability. They gained legitimacy for their objections by suggesting that the U.S. system, run by Western Union and Commercial Cable, was competitive, rather than cartelized, and that it therefore differed from the monopolies of state ownership in Europe (Peel 1905:258–59). In the later words of Clarence H. Mackay, who had succeeded his father as president of the Commercial Cable Postal Telegraph Company: "'We do not wish to be mistaken as opposing the international convention in so far as its regulations are designed to maintain a uniform method of dealing with international traffic, but to compel us to be strictly bound by rules and regulations which are created more in the interests of the European Government-owned telegraph systems will not only destroy the enterprise of competitive service but reduce the private companies to the conditions of Government ownership.'" [15]

It may be that successive U.S. administrations also believed that the unilaterally applicable landing-rights policy, which gave each president discretionary power, was a more effective tool for regulating foreign companies than the international convention and offered more possibilities for gaining U.S. entry to monopoly markets. Although the policy was ignored in secret deals with the Eastern over the Pacific cable, it was an effective bargaining tool that did not rely on alliances in international forums with one or other European power. Certainly, by the start of World War I the U.S. government had had more success in the field of communications by pursuing its interests through unilateral legislation and bilateral deals based on reciprocity, where its burgeoning economic power could be used effectively as leverage to open markets.

The one issue that the U.S. government did attempt to tackle on a multilateral basis beginning in 1860 was the protection of submarine cables from attack. But whereas the government advocated the neutrality of all cables in the 1860s, by the time of the nationalistic 1890s it considered neutrality only in relation to times of peace. Given that the United States had itself attacked the neutral cables of the Eastern in the Philippines during the Spanish-American War, and had failed to make compensation, it lost the moral high ground. Clark states that at the peace conference in 1907 at the Hague it was agreed that "'submarine cables connecting an occupied territory shall not be seized or destroyed except in case of absolute necessity. They must be likewise restored and compensation fixed when peace is made (Art. 54)'" (quoted in Clark 1931:162). Under article 54 Japan cut the German cables in the Pacific at the outbreak of war in 1914, just as Britain and France cut them in the eastern Atlantic. None of the cables was restored to Germany (see chapter 6). Thus the only prewar international law concerning submarine cables and involving the United States proved ineffective.

Conclusion

From 1890 to 1914 war demonstrated the importance of communications to the U.S. government. Growing mercantilism within a rapidly industrializing country led to attempts by successive administrations to rid the United States of dependence on the British. Despite the free-market laissez-faire ideology propounded in the Open Door notes against the perceived corporatism of the Europeans, the U.S. government also used its communications companies when it could. It backed them in order to expand its influence and supported their efforts to break the European hold over the cable market. Despite this liberalizing zeal abroad, at home the nationalistic tone of debate, and demands that U.S. companies might not interconnect their cables with those of the British, led eventually to the exclusion of the British from the U.S. market. This exclusion took place not because the U.S. companies were denied access to the British domestic market but because the Eastern held monopoly rights in third markets. Thus the concept of bilateral reciprocity in landing rights could be stretched to allow countervailing measures on a case-by-case basis. And, as before, the antagonism to pooling did not involve regulation of U.S.-dominated transatlantic pools.

Despite the government's desire for a U.S.-owned Pacific cable, the failure of Congress to provide subsidies and the small financial incentives for such a scheme limited U.S. communications to the Asian Pacific during the nineteenth century. Although the United States was victorious over Spain and purchased the Philippines, U.S. communications had to travel over British lines. Given that the Pacific cable's eventual British ownership contradicted all the aspirations of successive entrepreneurs, it seems hardly surprising that the provenance of the cable was kept secret for almost twenty years. Its owners' decision to concentrate on the Japanese, rather than Chinese, market reflected commercial rather than political priorities and demonstrated the weakness of successive U.S. governments in directing private companies. That weakness contrasts with the ability of British governments to gain their demands for security-related cables by using subsidies.

The period also demonstrates the importance of interconnection between domestic and international networks. AT&T's denial of interconnection to the British cables replicated its domestic behavior with independent local telephone companies and ensured AT&T the majority of transatlantic traffic as well as domestic. Domestic antitrust regulation, which split AT&T from Western Union in 1913, seems to have prevented AT&T from expanding further into the international sector. In contrast to Commercial Cable, which successfully applied to the Interstate Commerce Commission after being treated in a discriminatory manner, the British companies could appeal to neither domestic nor international regulation.

In the domestic market, despite the antitrust decision against AT&T in 1913, tariffs and interconnection charges were virtually uncontrolled. The regulatory powers of the Interstate Commerce Commission were too weak for it to be effective and limited it to interstate, rather than intrastate, communications. Although states set up their own regulatory authorities during this period, AT&T became a virtually unregulated monopoly from 1911 until its breakup in the 1970s. In general, with minimal domestic regulation of either the telegraph or interstate telephone, the commercial interests of first Western Union and then AT&T prevailed. At home both were allowed to provide leased lines to large users below cost, and after taking over the British cables, Western Union and AT&T also provided private lines across the Atlantic.[16]

In addition, the domination of international communications by these companies meant that the information sector fed the companies' profits. U.S. news agencies, while competing with Reuters within North America, had to contend with the high tariffs of transatlantic pools and with poor cable communications to the south. Only in a war situation did information and propaganda begin to gain political salience.

Nevertheless, when war came and with it the nationalization of AT&T, the ensuing price hikes led to the perception that a public monopoly was even less regulated than a private one. As chapter 7 shows, in the postwar world U.S. politicians and the public were less than prepared to accept any further public ownership of communications technology. And, in general, in the immediate postwar world the U.S. government felt itself to be even weaker in its control of communications.

5. South America: Prewar Competition in Infrastructure and Information

THE AMERICANS competed most fiercely with the British and French in the Caribbean and Central and South America, beginning in the 1880s. During the early nineteenth century South America had become Britain's "informal empire." Argentina had an English trading community in the 1830s, before independence (Barty-King 1979:46). And British influence in the 1820s largely persuaded the Portuguese monarchy, exiled in Brazil since Napoleon's invasion of the Iberian Peninsula, to agree to Brazil's independence. By 1897 Britain had more than twice what France—and six times what the United States—had invested in Latin America.[1] Latin America primarily provided raw materials and opportunities for construction companies. Although in the mid-nineteenth century Britain attempted to expand its influence in Central America, British interests were mainly centered in British-controlled Guiana and the West Indies, for their sugar; in Argentina, from which it exported meat and wheat; and in Brazil, with its raw materials of wild rubber and coffee. U.S. interests were concentrated in the Caribbean, in Mexican railroads and mines, and in Cuban sugar plantations (Fejes 1986:16; Petras et al. 1973:54). But by the turn of the century U.S. influence in South America had begun to increase.

In the 1890s the fast industrialization of the United States produced the need for markets, so its claim to hegemony over the whole of Latin America became more pronounced. Promulgated at a time when Latin America was gaining its independence from Spain and other European powers were threatening to intervene, the Monroe Doctrine of 1823 consisted of a declaration that interference by any European power in the newly emerging Latin American republics would be considered an unfriendly act toward the United States

(Pearce 1981:8). Before the Mexican War of 1846–47, President James K. Polk expanded the doctrine in 1845 to forbid diplomatic interference by European powers and the voluntary ceding by Latin American governments of any territory to a European power. The United States then seized vast areas of Mexico, including Texas and California (Petras et al. 1973:62). After the American Civil War, as industrialization and commercial activity increased, politicians began to conceive of the U.S. role in Latin America not as military conqueror but as industrialized supplier of goods. The role of the military was to back up U.S. commercial interests.

In 1889 Secretary of State James G. Blaine proposed a customs union (free-trade zone) for Latin America by which the "'United States, supplanting Europe, should become the industrial provider of the agricultural nations in Latin America'" (quoted in Petras et al. 1973:62). Blaine's proposal, made at the first conference of the International Union of American Republics, was given legitimacy by appeals to Pan-Americanism, and anti-imperialist rhetoric, but was not accepted.[2] Blaine subsequently negotiated bilateral agreements with Brazil and Cuba based on reciprocity and involving preferential tariffs for their coffee and sugar exports in return for the opening of their economies to U.S. exports (Garvin 1905:104). Unrest in Brazil as a result of the agreement was met by U.S. naval intervention.

In 1895 the Olney Declaration, made by Secretary of State Richard Olney, claimed the whole continent as American:

> "Today the United States is practically sovereign on this continent, and its fiat is law upon the subjects to which it confines its interposition. Why? . . . It is because, in addition to all other grounds, its infinite resources combined with its isolated position render it master of the situation and practically invulnerable as against any and all other powers. All the advantages of this superiority are at once imperiled if the principle be admitted that European powers may convert American states into colonies or provinces of their own." (quoted in Petras et al. 1973:63)

Olney's declaration came in response to Britain's attempts to expand its influence in Venezuela. In a message to Lord Salisbury, President Grover Cleveland asserted that U.S. predominance in the western hemisphere was "'important to our peace and safety as a nation and is essential to the integrity of our free institutions and the tranquil maintenance of our distinctive form of government'" (quoted in Williams 1969:379). From this time on the British implicitly recognized the U.S. sphere of influence. U.S. military intervention followed with the invasion of Cuba, ostensibly to free it from the Spanish but also on behalf of U.S. sugar interests. After the Spanish-American War of 1898, Cuba became a U.S. protectorate, with part of it leased for a U.S. naval base; the United States also annexed Hawaii and bought Puerto Rico from Spain.

In 1904 the Monroe Doctrine took another twist as Theodore Roosevelt, responding to demands of mining, railroad, and banking interests, promulgated what came to be known as the Roosevelt Corollary: "'Chronic wrongdoing or an impotence which results in a general loosening of the ties of civilized society, may in America, as elsewhere, ultimately require intervention by some civilized nation, and in the Western Hemisphere the adherence of the United States to the Monroe Doctrine may force the United States, however reluctantly, in flagrant cases of such wrong doing or impotence, to the exercise of an international police power'" (quoted in Petras et al. 1973:65). This corollary, based again on appeals to moral obligations and U.S. destiny, "incorporated the concept of preventive intervention in order to undercut European expansionism in favor of United States interests" (Petras et al. 1973:65).

The Roosevelt Corollary, then, justified extensive intervention to support U.S. financial interests. The U.S. military intervened to back an independence movement that separated Panama from Colombia, gaining in return the lease in perpetuity of a strip of land across the isthmus in order to create the Panama Canal. Because the naval fleet was no longer split between Atlantic and Pacific, the canal, completed in 1914, was of prime strategic importance to the U.S. Navy, but it also acted as the incentive for an increase in the merchant marine and brought Australia closer to the eastern seaboard of the United States than to Britain.

By the turn of the century both the U.S. penetration of markets and the imposition of tariffs by the Latin American republics had begun to affect British commercial interests. Garvin (1905:103) reports that in 1905 the "preferential rebate upon imports from the United States ranges from 20 to 40 per cent" in Cuba and that U.S. moves to impose heavy tariffs on Indian rice would kill off India's rice trade in favor of U.S. rice. From 1898 to 1908 total U.S. investment in Latin America had tripled to $1.06 billion. As U.S. exporters lost interest in the China market, their interest in Latin America increased; the 1912 Lodge Corollary to the Monroe Doctrine served commercial interests. Occasioned by a Japanese corporation's interest in buying a harbor in Mexico, the corollary "extended the exclusionary non-colonization principle by asserting that foreign companies, as well as foreign governments, were now prohibited from acquiring land in the Americas" (Petras et al. 1973:68).

But despite these claims to hegemony, a small merchant marine handicapped the United States until World War I. Its goods and passengers went to South America via Britain. News about the United States took the same route to South America's Portuguese- and Spanish-speaking communities, where European culture dominated. Few submarine or overland cable routes operated between the United States and South America, and those that existed were often unreliable. In turn, the South American republics were happy to be able to play the European powers off against the United States. The prewar period, then, was one in which the U.S. government, companies, and military conquered Central America but struggled against European influence in South America. Despite attempts to create a Pan-American union under U.S. control, by the start of the war in Europe the venture had not been successful. However, at the beginning of World War I the Americans were rewarded with a vacuum into which they were prepared to step commercially.

The Telegraph and Latin America

The introduction of the domestic telegraph to Latin America came about primarily as an instrument for government. Crucially, as Baur points out, most Latin American countries at the time had "no centralised administrative structures with stable sources of revenue," and the domestic telegraph "provided a means to work toward this consolidation" (1994:11). Within economies that came to depend primarily on the export of raw materials, connecting the interiors to ports by railway and telegraph was of crucial importance. The extension of the telegraph internationally served both these primarily foreign commercial interests and those of the republics' governments.

Early concessionaires in the 1860s demanded subsidies from the Central and South American governments. These concessions gave governments the right to send traffic up to the value of the subsidies but with no reduction in tariffs (Stewart 1946:122). The later concessions, such as those given by Brazil in the 1870s, either allowed the government to use the cable as a leased line, paying only for the time used, or allowed a 10 percent or 20 percent rebate on government traffic. In addition, the Brazilian government insisted that government employees transmit its telegrams.[3] Because of the wildness of the internal terrain and the concentration of population around ports, submarine cables could also serve domestic traffic by linking one port with another, such as down the coasts of Brazil, Uruguay, and Argentina. But problems occurred when the Brazilian government built its own landline network.

Before the cable manufacturer Telcon became the designated supplier to the Eastern, it financed the first international cable within South America. This cable connected the capitals of Argentina and Uruguay and was opened in 1866 during the War of the Triple Alliance against Paraguay (Barty-King 1979:23).[4] Brazil was the first of the South American republics to establish its own domestic telegraph cable, in Rio de Janeiro in 1852, and to have its own government telegraph department from 1863. In the 1870s internal rebellions and external security threats spurred other republics, such as Argentina and Chile, to expand their networks using government subsidies (Berthold 1924:18).

Brazilian entrepreneurs attempted to raise local financing for the construction of international cables, but in view of the sums required, British capital dominated. Where local capital developed long-distance landlines, as in Uruguay, these were subsequently taken over by the Eastern's subsidiaries in order to create an embryo regional network (Bright 1898a:127). Similarly, concessions granted to locals found their way into the hands of British companies. In the mid-1870s the Brazilian government was not happy that Argentineans André and Pedro Llamas had to move to London to find financing for their Platino-Brazileira Company. They had a concession to construct submarine cables down the South American coast, from Pernambuco on the most easterly tip of Brazil south to Uruguay and Argentina and north to French Guiana. Despite Brazil's objections, the Llamases' company became a subsidiary of the Eastern called the London Platino Brazilian Telegraph Company (Bright 1898a:127). The Eastern operated these interport monopoly concessions in Brazil in conjunction with the first international submarine cables from Brazil to Lisbon.

The first concession for a South Atlantic cable to Brazil had been granted to an Italian engineer, M. Pier Alberto Ballestrini, in 1864 but lapsed for lack of money and because of the opposition from an American, Horatio J. Perry, who had secured a concession for a cable over a similar route from the Spanish government. Then, in view of the failure of the transatlantic cable in 1865, in 1866 the governments of France, Italy, Portugal, Spain, Brazil, and Haiti granted a concession "for a line via Lisbon, the Canary islands, the Cape Verde islands, Cape San Roques in Brazil and the West Indies." Because financiers judged that there was only enough traffic for one transatlantic cable to be commercially successful, this scheme for a South Atlantic cable also collapsed because of the 1866 success of the North Atlantic route.[5] Later the Brazilian government transferred Ballestrini's concession to one of Brazil's top bankers, Vicomte de Mana, who in turn joined forces with Telcon in 1873 to establish a cable via St. Vincent and Madeira to Portugal. One provision of the concession from the Portuguese government was that the cable must touch no foreign land between Madeira and Lisbon; this reflected the deteriorating relations between Portugal and Spain. Again illustrating the control that governments could exert by using landing licenses, the Portuguese government set out the tariffs to be charged and provided for both a proportionate reduction in charges and an additional cable (laid in 1884) if traffic increased.[6]

In turn, the two Brazilian cables were linked from Argentina west with a seven-hundred-mile landline to Valparaiso, Chile. At first they linked up in the north and shared traffic with a cable that joined Brazil to British and French Guiana and to the British, Dutch, and French West Indies (Bright 1898a:126). This British-owned West Indies system, laid by Sir Charles Tilston Bright, was joined to the United States by James Scrymser's cable from Cuba to Florida. Scrymser originally intended to link the West Indies with Brazil; he had gained concessions from Horatio Perry and laid cables within the British West Indies and from Jamaica to Panama. But when, despite the intervention of James Seward, the U.S. secretary of state, the concession for the cable north from Brazil went to a British company, Scrymser handed his West Indian concessions over to the British and established joint traffic agreements (Scrymser 1915:74). In contradiction of its free-trade stance, although the British government demanded that concessions in the West Indies should be nonexclusive, it was prepared for a British company to negotiate monopolistic concessions from Brazil.

However, the cable from Brazil to the West Indies repeatedly failed and was abandoned in 1876. Its failure both opened that route to the French and left the West Indies reliant on the U.S. company and the Spanish government in Cuba. Following the threat of war with the United States in 1884 over mineral rights in Venezuela, in 1889 the British government financed a strategic cable from Halifax, Nova Scotia, to Bermuda (the Halifax and Bermudas Cable Company), extending it in 1899 to Jamaica to bypass Cuba and ensure "All-British" communications.[7]

Although the British Admiralty and the Cable Landing Rights Committee of 1902 advocated extending the line to St. Lucia in the eastern Caribbean, the Admiralty changed its mind and began to pull its forces out of Halifax. In turn, the advent of this government-subsidized cable, coupled with the poor economic situation in the region and the rapid rate of deterioration in cables on a volcanic sea bed, meant that the existing subsidiary of the Eastern lost its Jamaica traffic. It failed to declare a dividend until its stock rose at the prospective opening of the Panama Canal in 1913 (Bright 1898a:138; Peel 1905:262–63; Barty-King 1979:122). This was an example of British security considerations' undermining private commercial interests.

British companies had demonstrated little interest in the Pacific coast of South America. Although Telcon and U.S. entrepreneurs (including Cyrus

Field) collaborated on plans for a cable from Panama—then part of Colombia—to Peru during the 1860s and had the backing of the British government, they shelved it because of the depression of the 1870s (Stewart 1946:121). The only British-financed subsidiary was a Telcon cable that ran down the west coast of South America to Lima and Valparaiso in 1876. This cable was linked via a landline to Argentina and the international cables in the east. Therefore, all messages from the west coast of South America to the United States had to go through London and back to the United States via the transatlantic cables, at the cost of $7.50 per word, with New York counted as two words (Scrymser 1915:78).

Reflecting U.S. financial interests in sugar, mining, and railroads, U.S. telegraph development was originally centered in Central America. In the 1860s first Florida and then Congress had given Scrymser a fourteen-year monopoly concession for an international cable from Florida to Cuba. His company, the International Ocean Telegraph Company, was partly financed by Western Union and joined to Western Union landlines. He subsequently entered into an agreement to share traffic with Cyrus Field's American Telegraph Company, which then amalgamated with Western Union. Scrymser's company was itself taken over by Jay Gould in 1878 (Scrymser 1915:74). Because the British blocked Scrymser from extending down the west coast of South America, and only the banker J. P. Morgan encouraged him, Scrymser moved on to Mexico to institute a plan that had been delayed for seven years because of the refusal of the U.S. government to recognize the revolutionary government of President Porfirio Díaz.

According to Baur (1994:14), "In Mexico the development of telegraph lines was directly related to the European invasion and French occupation of the country in the early 1860s. Once republican forces regained control from the French, private telegraph lines were consolidated into a state company." In the 1870s this domestic telegraph monopoly was linked to the United States through the telegraph lines of Western Union. These connected by cable under the Rio Grande. The connection was regularly disrupted, and Western Union found it unprofitable (Scrymser 1915:76). In 1879 Scrymser gained the concession to lay submarine cables across the Gulf of Mexico; this would provide a more reliable connection to the Western Union network in Galveston, Texas, and allow Scrymser's company (the Mexican Telegraph Company) to benefit from Porfirio Díaz's decision to expand the domestic network for administrative purposes.

Using British-made cable and manufacturers to lay the line, but U.S. capital raised by J. P. Morgan, Scrymser then extended the Mexican cables by landline across Mexico and, following the route once proposed by Telcon, down through Panama and along the west coast of South America to Peru (Bright 1898a:133). This company, the Central and South American Telegraph Company, immediately cut the telegraph rates from the west coast of South America to between one-half and one-fifth of what it had cost to go through London (Scrymser 1915:78, 82; Herring and Gross 1936:31).

But in establishing his new Central and South American Telegraph Company, Scrymser reports that he faced opposition from Jay Gould, who by then not only owned the Havana-Florida cable but had taken over Western Union. When Scrymser learned that Gould had attempted to have his Mexican concession rescinded, Scrymser retaliated by gaining a concession from the Spanish government for a cable from Havana to Mexico (Scrymser 1915:88). Faced with this potential competition, Western Union eventually backed down, and in 1897, when Western Union emerged victorious from a fight with the Postal Telegraph Company over Mexican traffic, the two companies entered a formal agreement to interchange traffic with the Mexican government (Herring and Gross 1936:17).

In the late 1860s the Mexican railways had been allowed to provide a telegraph service for their internal use and in the 1880s entered into an agreement with the American Postal Telegraph Company for the exchange of international traffic—perhaps the first "liberalization" of international traffic by large users. Despite complaints that the order was contrary to the Mexican Constitution and constituted a restraint of trade, the Mexican government prohibited the railroads from handling international messages. Eventually, Western Union emerged with a monopoly that effectively precluded competition for more than twenty years, and in 1899 President Díaz restricted the use of telegraphs to railroad-related business.[8]

Scrymser became determined to enter Brazil. He therefore extended the Peruvian cables by landline to Chile and bought up a local company that operated between Chile and Argentina. But because the British concession prevented Scrymser's network from entering Brazil, it ended in Argentina. Scrymser, backed by the U.S. government, set out to remedy the situation. In his memoir Scrymser thanks nine secretaries of state for their recognition of "the political and commercial value of an independent American cable communication" and their assistance in its establishment and extension (1915:93).[9]

Until the 1890s, then, the British had a monopoly of European traffic from Brazil, but relations between the three subsidiaries of the Eastern and the Brazilian government deteriorated during the 1880s. The companies sometimes deliberately sought to undermine the host country's sovereignty. The problem was that as the Brazilian government built its own landlines, the

Eastern's subsidiaries began to compete for domestic traffic. Whereas their concession prevented the government's landlines from undercutting the companies' submarine tariffs, it did not prevent the British companies from setting their tariffs to undercut the landlines. Objections by the Brazilian government in the 1880s were met with the offer of a pool arrangement. Initial rejection turned into acceptance in 1890 after a change of government, but the company's behavior led to problems with the renewal of its concession in 1892 and to Brazilian sympathy for the developing competition from French, U.S., and other British companies (Barty-King 1979:96).

The French extended their government-backed colonial telegraph network to their Caribbean and French Guiana colonies and to Venezuela during the 1880s, linking these to the Eastern's cables to the south and Scrymser's Cuban cable (Bright 1898a:137). Further expansion of French communications to South America coincided with the 1891 decision of the French government to build up its domestic cable manufacturing and operation. Eager to rid itself of dependence on the Eastern, the French laid a cable from Senegal to Brazil in 1891 and connected its Venezuelan cable to the Brazilian government landlines. In addition, in 1890 the French gained a thirty-five-year concession for an east coast cable connecting Brazil to Haiti and the United States (Tribolet 1929:44).[10] Although this cable was to prove unreliable, the concession prevented other companies from using this route to link Brazil with the north.

In 1892 the French government also persuaded the Portuguese that for "political" reasons, despite Portugal's extension of the concession to the Eastern for cables between Lisbon and Brazil, the contract for another Lisbon-to-Brazil cable should go to the French company. But the French company could not lay the cable in the stipulated time, so the Eastern laid the additional line in 1898 (Brown 1927:18–19; Barty-King 1979:97). The Eastern's high tariffs also provided the incentive for competition from the Spanish, who were working with Telcon, the Eastern's cable supplier. In 1892 a Telcon-backed company took advantage of the end of the Eastern's concession to lay another cable from Senegal in West Africa through the island of Fernando de Noronha to Brazil to connect with a cable that it had laid from Cadiz for the Spanish government. This new entrant charged fourpence per word less than the Eastern's rate (Barty-King 1979:96).

In 1893 John Pender, the Eastern's chairman, reacted to these developments by merging the three operating companies in Brazil, Argentina, and Uruguay into the one company, the Western Telegraph, a subsidiary of the Eastern, and created a new landline from Buenos Aires across the continent to Chile in 1894. This regional system covered thirty-one thousand miles (Brown 1927:18).

Despite competition from Scrymser's company from its base in Buenos Aires, and opposition from the U.S. ambassador, in 1893 the Eastern gained a further twenty-year concession on traffic to Uruguay and Argentina from Brazil, effectively blocking Scrymser's entry for another twenty years (Tribolet 1929:47).

At the outset of competition from the U.S. company, the British story is that Western Telegraph attempted to set up an agreement to interconnect with Scrymser's network. The U.S. story is that the British, who collected traffic in Brazil, charged Brazilian customers more to go via Scrymser's lines to the United States. According to Herring and Gross (1936:32), "On all messages destined to be transmitted to the United States via the Pacific they [the companies] levied a charge, in addition to the charge for local messages between Brazil and Argentina, high enough to force the Brazilian business to go to the United States via England." Thus the British used the U.S. company's lack of collection rights within Brazil to impose high interconnection charges, or what were described by the British Post Office as "blocking rates," to limit U.S. competition. Scrymser's company in turn used those same blocking rates to keep the Eastern out of Ecuador and Colombia.[11]

Nevertheless, once the Americans had entered Latin America, the British company came under increased pressure. At a time when it was negotiating for the Panama Canal, the U.S. government was embarrassed by poor communications to Central America. As a result in 1905 Congress voted to finance a cable linking the United States and Panama. The contract was the first to include a buy-American preference (later to be a feature of all defense contracts); the cable was to be built by an American company, provided that the successful U.S. bid was no more than 10 percent more expensive than foreign companies'. The tariff was also fixed per word, with reduced rates for the press and government traffic.[12] Thus in its control of tariffs, the regulation of this line was more severe than the British Cable Landing Committee's licenses of the time.

The Scrymser company, the only U.S. company with cable ships, won the contract and linked New York and Colon (Panama) directly—a case of a strategic U.S. cable.[13] Additionally, the new cable speeded up transmission from South America to Europe by connecting with the U.S. cables in New York; this enabled Scrymser's company to take more of the Argentinean traffic (Herring and Gross 1936:32). In response, despite German opposition, the Eastern then built a cable to connect Buenos Aires to Ascension, thereby also speeding up Argentinean traffic to North America via the Azores, where it connected to the American Commercial Cable Company.[14]

In 1911 the prospect of the Panama Canal began to concern businessmen in Britain. The increasing incursion of U.S. interests in South America, the prevalence of press reports antagonistic to British interests, and the prospect that the opening of the Suez Canal would strengthen the U.S. communications companies led the Birmingham Chamber of Commerce to lobby the Foreign Office in 1911 for British cables to encircle the South American continent. The Post Office vetoed the idea.

In view of Scrymser's monopoly concessions down the west coast of South America, the Post Office could see no possibility of a British company's wanting to undertake the project. And unless British cables were likely to develop important traffic, the Post Office could see no point in encircling South America with British cables. It suggested that the increased traffic engendered by the canal would be mainly with North America, Europe, and the Pacific coast of South America, not Brazil. Further, if a new cable was to be provided north from Brazil—and the Germans were contemplating such a scheme— the Americans had "obtained promises that their wishes [for a direct Brazil-U.S. cable] will be met in so far as lies in the power of the Brazilian government."[15]

The Post Office hoped that, if the Eastern decided to collaborate with the Americans in providing a link to Brazil, it would choose either Western Union or Commercial Cable, both of which needed landing licenses in Britain, rather than Scrymser's company, over which the Post Office held no leverage. Post Office officials, more concerned with German than U.S. influence, viewed the Eastern's direct cable between Buenos Aires and Ascension as important and its monopoly of the Brazil-Argentina traffic as effectively keeping the Americans out. Despite competition from French and German cables to Europe, Post Office officials still considered the Eastern line the most efficient. In an interoffice memo that reflects the wounds of the Pacific cable, Post Office officials poured scorn on those politicians who wanted low rates and state competition with private companies, when the government actually needed private companies to collaborate with it.[16]

During the early 1900s the Brazilian government began testing the Eastern's concession by granting alternative concessions to one of the Eastern's former employees. Then, in 1913, as the Eastern's concession on Argentina-Brazil cables ran out, Scrymser's company presented a proposal to establish a separate line from Buenos Aires to two Brazilian ports not covered by the Eastern interport concession and that would give Scrymser's company access to 75 percent of the Brazilian traffic. According to the concession, the Eastern subsidiary was entitled to the first option to lay the lines, but when approached by the Brazilian government, the company demurred and proposed that the matter should go to arbitration. Instead, the Brazilian government continued the Eastern's existing interport concession until 1933 but awarded Scrymser the concession that his company had sought (Tribolet 1929:48). At this point the Eastern attempted to cartelize the South American market with Scrymser's company—a move rejected by the State Department—and then made an unsuccessful agreement with Western Union to prevent Scrymser's interconnection within the United States, a move also blocked by the State Department.

In a further attempt to keep the Americans out, the Eastern then took the Brazilian government to court. The case lasted for five years; in 1919 the court ruled in the Brazilian government's favor, and Scrymser's lines were laid. Coincidentally, in that same year the Eastern opened a cable from Rio to Ascension, giving it additional speed in communications to North America, and dropped its tariffs by 20 percent (Brown 1927:18; Tribolet 1929:48).

The Brazilian government was not alone in struggling against foreign cable companies that meddled in domestic politics. For instance, in 1900 in Venezuela the French cable company was shown to have colluded with U.S. and French commercial interests in attempting to overthrow the government, and the dispute dragged on until 1908.[17] Therefore, when wireless held out the prospect of a technology that could be controlled without diminution of sovereignty, the Central and South American governments found it attractive.

But because wireless technology was primarily the property of the Marconi and Telefunken companies, it threatened the existing cable companies. One potential response was to renegotiate international concessions in a way that would shut out the wireless technology. When in 1904 Mexico became one of the first countries to contract with Telefunken for two wireless stations designed for both domestic and ship-to-shore traffic, Western Union reacted so strongly that the Mexican government told the 1912 International Radiotelegraphic Convention in London that, because of its contract with Western Union, all international traffic had to go via cable.[18] In Colombia, where Scrymser's company had a concession until 1904, the prospect of competition from Marconi led it to sever its cable in order to force the government to give it a monopoly of all technology.[19] In Ecuador Scrymser's Central and South American Telegraph Company renegotiated its concession to exclude the Commercial Pacific Cable Company, which was attempting to expand into Ecuador and Peru.[20] And in Venezuela, despite action by the British government to gain the support of the French government for wireless communications between Venezuela and Trinidad, the French cable company emerged from its dispute with the Venezuelan government with rights over wireless.[21]

Within Central America, where the U.S. government wielded influence, the

United Fruit Company established a preeminent position in wireless telegraphy. The company was formed in 1899 by an amalgamation of interests in the shipping of bananas to the United States and the construction of railroads in Central America. The new company owned 112 miles of railroad and 212,394 acres—61,263 acres in banana production—and had financing of $11,230,000. It bought land in Santo Domingo, Honduras, Guatemala, Panama, and Cuba and additional acreage in Nicaragua, Jamaica, and Colombia. These Central American "banana republics" were eager to sell land inexpensively in return for port and railroad facilities (May and Plaza 1958:5–7).

United Fruit also began its own shipping fleet in 1899 (it became the Tropical Fruit Steamship Company in 1904) but was handicapped by the lack of cable communications. Messages from the United States went via cable to Mexico, then via landline through Costa Rica and Nicaragua for delivery at United Fruit's office at Port Limón. These messages were then "entrusted to natives, who would make the trip in a canoe on the open sea between Port Limon and Bocas del Toro in from 30 to 60 hours, depending on weather conditions" (Douglas 1987:95). In view of these inadequate communications, "as early as . . . 1904 United was one of the first commercial companies to put radio on board their ships and to establish the Tropical Radio Telegraph Company" (May and Plaza 1958:18). The company erected land stations at New Orleans and Boston and in Central America, but the tropical static on the De Forest equipment made radio communications difficult. Subsequently, in 1908 United Fruit bought Fessenden's equipment, which United Fruit representatives had heard transmitting between the naval stations in the Caribbean (Douglas 1987:161). In 1910 uninterrupted communication between the United States and Central America was formally established, and in 1913, when its stations were opened to the public for commercial messages, the Tropical Radio Telegraph Company was incorporated as a subsidiary of United Fruit and became a common carrier (Herring and Gross 1936:78).

Despite cable company opposition, by 1910 South America had about fifty wireless stations and several hundred by 1914.[22] Some, such as that at Punta Arenas in Chile, could transmit two thousand miles, while a station in Brazil could converse with Washington, D.C., more than three thousand miles away. By 1911 Germany's radio penetration of South America had become of strategic concern to the British, and the Colonial Office was prepared to use its influence to back the Marconi company in an attempt to prevent contracts from going to the Germans, as in Chile.[23] But Marconi also faced U.S. opposition.

An indication of U.S. government thinking is given by a 1915 circular from Secretary of State Robert Lansing to all U.S. embassies in Latin America stating that the State Department was concerned that radio stations in South America should be owned by Americans (Clark 1931:239). In particular, Lansing states that the control of radio communication in the Americas "'should not pass beyond this hemisphere and into European or Asiatic hands.'" Instead, "'the Department would accordingly be inclined to look with favor, and believes that other American governments share this view, upon any mutually acceptable agreement whereby the control of this vitally important method of communication between the American continent might rest wholly in sympathetic and disinterested hands, thus realizing another conception of broad and beneficial Pan-Americanism'" (quoted in Fejes 1986:19).

In 1914 the U.S. Navy took over all radio communications in Panama for the duration of the war. Gradually, at the behest of Secretary of the Navy Josephus Daniels, U.S. policy swung toward promoting government ownership of radio communications within Latin America in order to prevent European expansion (Clark 1931:240; Schwoch 1990:36–37). Under the guise of military security, in 1916 the United States outlined a plan to Latin American governments for the organization and construction of a Pan-American system of radio communication that the United States would lead. The intention was to prevent foreign private ownership by emphasizing "the need for governmental systems to prevent violations of neutrality and to guarantee national safety" (Hogan 1977:140). The U.S. Navy advocated a government-owned integrated radio system throughout the region and a "special inter-American committee to devise the regulations necessary to combine the radio services of all American republics" (141). The State Department in turn circulated to its embassies a plan for a wireless network centered in the Panama Canal Zone, with relay stations in Washington, D.C., Cuba, Guatemala, Paraguay, and Argentina. Although these naval stations were established in Panama, Cuba, Florida, and Washington, D.C., at a cost of $4 million, initially these stations, according to Scrymser, were failures (1915:85). Because the Latin American republics lacked enthusiasm, nothing came of the idea. Nevertheless, government ownership and monopoly of radio facilities in Latin America, based on Daniels's views, remained U.S. policy until the mid-1920s (Fejes 1986:19–20; Schwoch 1990:52n.33).

The U.S. State Department exerted particular influence over Brazil. In its rivalry with Argentina, and its "pretension to a moral hegemony over South America similar to that exercised by the United States over the Caribbean," Brazil looked to U.S. friendship (Connell-Smith 1974:125). Partly because of U.S. opposition, a Brazilian concession seemingly granted to Marconi Wireless Telegraph Company of America in 1913 was delayed because of competition from the Federal Telegraph Company, which was backed by the U.S.

government. Franklin D. Roosevelt, then an assistant secretary of the navy, argued that U.S. support should go to "'corporations which have no foreign connections, and which can furnish completely apparatus of purely American manufacture'" (quoted in Schwoch 1990:39). Schwoch comments that as the U.S. subsidiary of a British company, Marconi of America "had become a paradox, at odds with the long-range ideology supporting the global expansion of American corporations" (1990:39).

But there were also splits within the Brazilian administration. Its foreign secretary was prepared to contemplate concessions to overseas companies to run international communications. But in view of its problems with the cable companies, the Brazilian Telegraph Administration was so determined to run wireless telegraph and telephone itself that in 1913 it expropriated a private wireless company established in the Amazon by the U.S. Rubber Company (Schwoch 1990:18). In order to assuage Brazilian nationalism, Marconi of America set up a local company. The Federal Telegraph Company was then advised by the U.S. government to follow suit (Schwoch 1990:38). When, after a debate in the Brazilian parliament, Marconi appeared to be the front-runner for the license, the U.S. State Department sent a diplomatic *note verbale* to the Brazilian ambassador in 1916 advising that the English cable companies were "in practice nothing but the extensions of the telegraphic systems of the European powers" and arguing "the necessity of not granting facilities to European wireless concerns." Instead, the State Department advised the Brazilian government to delay a decision in order to allow Western Union to present its "extensive scheme" that would "surely be considered advantageous to the Americas."[24] The "Western Union scheme" involved its unsuccessful attempts to buy Scrymser's Central and South American company.

The following year the State Department approved the formation of a joint company by Marconi of America and Federal Telegraph—the Pan-American Wireless and Telephone Company—to exploit South America "on the assumption that complete American control of the combine was assured" (Hogan 1977:141). As Admiral William S. Benson pointed out, the project permitted U.S. interests to control the Marconi system in South America, "'pending implementation of the Navy's plan for an integrated radio network under government control'" (quoted in Hogan 1977:141).[25] Once the British Marconi company had sold its rights in Latin America to Pan-American Wireless, the Brazilians awarded the concession to Pan-American (Schreiner 1924:154).

Throughout the war both the British and Americans monitored closely potential breaches of neutrality within Latin America by German radio transmitters. The State Department deciphered messages from one such transmitter in Argentina and leaked them to U.S. and Argentinean newspapers in 1917.[26] But German-manufactured transmitters flourished under the revolutionary Mexican government, in Peru and Brazil, and in the Danish West Indies, some operated by German staff and others serving the needs of local German populations for German war news.[27] By the end of the war German radio interests in South America were stronger than U.S. or British.

Telephone Development

Although the telephone was introduced into Central and South America in the 1880s, it never achieved the political saliency of the telegraph. Telephone technology originally limited it to a radius of twenty miles and allowed fragmentation between competing systems. And when the technology advanced, governments were not prepared to allow telephone long lines to compete with state telegraphy (Baur 1994:16–18).

But the telephone provided a means of entry into the domestic markets of the Latin American countries for U.S. and Canadian companies. The Continental Telephone Company, an offshoot of AT&T with a license on Bell's patents within Latin America, received its charter in January 1880, and by 1885, when the Tropical America Telephone Company, registered in New Jersey by the same people who backed Continental Telephone, acquired all its rights in Central America, it had companies in Colombia, Venezuela, Chile, Peru, Ecuador, Bolivia, and the West Indies but not Cuba. Subsequently, it entered Brazil and the remaining countries of South America (Rippy 1946). It is not clear whether AT&T used its domestic policy of licensing local interests and supplying them with equipment in return for equity in the local company, but, as in the case of the telegraph, little local capital was available and the lack of local manufacture of equipment opened local companies to pressure from suppliers. With some exceptions, local and European capital was at first driven out.

By 1890, although Guatemalan interests had a small investment in Guatemala and a few Uruguayans may have invested in the Uruguayan company, the only British interests in telephony were in Venezuela and Uruguay (Rippy 1946). In Argentina, U.S., British, and Belgian companies formed a joint venture in 1890 to drive the only local company out of the market, but large users countered by forming their own regional company (Petrazinni 1995: 106–7). In Brazil, German interests in Bahia and Rio later succumbed to U.S. interests (Berthold 1922).

The one independent European equipment supplier established the most successful European company in Mexico. Because of American Mextelco's high tariffs and slow expansion, and, because allowing a private monopoly would have violated the Mexican Constitution, in 1903 the Mexican government licensed a Hungarian American entrepreneur for Mexico City. Two years later he sold out to a Swedish consortium led by the equipment manufacturer L. M. Ericsson. To provide a demonstration network in Latin America, Ericsson formed Mexikandra Telefon AB Ericsson (Mexeric) in 1907. Whereas Mextelco was taken over by the government in 1915, Mexeric remained privately owned throughout the Mexican Revolution period of 1910–17 (Attman et al. 1976:186).

However, with the exception of Ericsson, the Bell factories in Belgium and Britain dominated European production of equipment, and with networks under the control of governments, there was no European domestic base from which to export equipment nor the expertise in establishing networks. Nor were the fragmented telephone networks, which were often denied interconnection with the state telegraphs and even (as in the case of Brazil until 1919) denied timed local calls, particularly profitable investments in risky, unstable political environments (Berthold 1922). Nevertheless, it seems that British capital had reappeared in the Latin American telephone sector by the 1920s.

The Advent of War: News Agencies

World War I handed the United States an opportunity to begin to replace European influence within Latin America. Disruption of Latin American trade with Europe allowed U.S. firms and financial institutions the space to expand their Latin American activities in line with what had been U.S. policy since the 1890s. Seven of the twenty-one Latin American republics—including Argentina, Mexico, and Chile—remained neutral throughout the war, and U.S. interests could trade on the fact that the United States did not enter hostilities until 1917.

Initial U.S. neutrality was effective in the news field. Even before the start of the war, German expatriates in South America were complaining that Havas sent no news from Germany. The initial period of the war, during which the French news agency refused to report German military successes, then exacerbated those complaints.[28] The war therefore presented an opportunity for the entry of the Americans into what had been a French news agency monopoly in South America.

But the Associated Press was handicapped by its agreements with Reuters. In 1893 the U.S. news agency had joined the European triumvirate. As Storey (1951:187) explains: "Under the new Treaty (of 1893) the European Agencies were barred from selling their news direct to any newspaper, or Agency, other than the Associated Press, in the United States, just as the Associated Press was similarly barred throughout the territories exclusive to Reuters, Havas and Wolff."

Under this quadrilateral agreement, made at a time when German influence within Victorian Britain had waned, "Reuters had Great Britain, including all the colonies and dominions and Egypt, Turkey, Japan, China and what might be called the suzerain states, or those in which England exerted a sphere of influence. Havas . . . controlled the French Empire, Switzerland and all the Latin countries, including Italy, Spain, Portugal and those in South America. To Wolff fell the Scandinavian states, with Russia and all the Slav nations. Austria also came under jurisdiction of the German agency" (Cooper 1942:17–18). The Germans and Americans were therefore excluded from South America, which Havas claimed wholly as its territory (Rantanen 1992:12).

In 1902 the Associated Press renegotiated the agreement to give it exclusive rights within the United States and a free hand in Canada, Mexico, Central America, and the West Indies. The agency's contemplation of expansion into Central America was dependent on the easier telegraph communications to those countries from the United States brought about by the enterprise of James Scrymser. However, the AP's entry into South America did not move forward until after the United Press Association opened foreign bureaus. This agency was founded by E. W. Scripps in 1907 to directly compete with the Associated Press, but it had no access to foreign news because of the AP's exclusive agreement with Reuters and Havas. So United Press (UP) began appointing its own foreign correspondents and selling its news to all comers. Reporting directly to the parent agency, UP's foreign correspondents emphasized immediacy and mass appeal (Rantanen 1992).

According to William W. Hawkins, who was president of United Press in 1921, when World War I began, no U.S. news agency had attempted to deliver news to South America. The statement was not entirely true. The AP supplied U.S. news for South America to Reuters, but because Reuters handed it over to Havas before it was cabled to South America, the AP had no control over the editing or dissemination. Hawkins told a congressional committee in 1921 that "'an examination of the Brazilian papers by the UP in the fall of 1914, showed that over a period of 30 days, there appeared about six small items. . . . These were chiefly about lynchings, railroad wrecks and fires, and events that would more or less cast reflection on the United States rather than help it any.'" The hegemony of Havas meant that "'all South America could be blanked out on anything not pro-French—the only entire continent that could be treated thus by any single news agency'" (quoted in Schreiner 1924:176). Because its agreement with Reuters and Havas precluded it from entering the Argentinean market, the AP's failure to reply to a request from *La Nación,* the major Argentinean newspaper, opened the way in 1916 for United Press to begin supplying European war reports (Rantanen 1992:15).

According to Melville Stone, then the manager of the Associated Press, after war was declared in Europe the U.S. government "'felt that it was of very grave consequence that we should establish more intimate news relations with South America. There was also a very urgent demand on the part of the commercial interests of the United States for more intimate relations.'" Stone was invited to Washington, where the State Department suggested that he "'should employ the editors of almost every leading paper in South America on handsome salaries as correspondents of The Associated Press, and . . . was told that (he) could pay them handsome amounts whether they sent us any news or not and that the government would recoup us for anything that we paid'" (quoted in Cooper 1942:48–50). At the time the U.S. government was embroiled in a military invasion of Mexican territory and wanted "some sort of illuminating service from the United States to indicate that this country is not money-grabbing or territory grabbing" (Cooper 1942:51).

Then, once the United States entered the European war, the federal government wanted some form of propaganda that would rival what the British were putting out, because U.S. officials felt that the United States was not being given due credit for its war efforts (Cooper 1942:47). After the AP turned down the opportunity to be a propagandist, the U.S. government looked for alternatives. Woodrow Wilson created the Committee on Public Information under ex-journalist George Creel. And as part of its wartime propaganda campaign, the administration actively encouraged and supported the efforts of the United Press to expand its activities in South America. The United Press representative went to South America in 1918 with a letter of introduction from President Wilson himself (Cooper 1942:89). At the same time the Scrymser company, whose president now was John L. Merrill, became actively involved with the State Department in enlarging cable traffic to South America and provided a news service to some South American newspapers.

"At the behest of the State Department the American-owned cable from New York was beginning to give reduced rates from New York to Buenos Aires for American clients only" (Cooper 1942:65). The rate between the two cities had become sixteen cents a word and only two cents a word for each ad-

ditional city en route at which messages would be copied. These cities included Panama, Guayaquil, Lima, Valparaiso, and Santiago. Whereas the British
cable to Argentina was busy with war traffic, and the French news agency had
to pay twenty-five cents a word to have its news sent from London or Paris
to Buenos Aires, the United Press was able to send news directly from New
York at the lower rates (Cooper 1942:80). By 1918 the United Press was threatening to displace Havas in South America.

Sensing the danger, the Associated Press negotiated a change in the agreement with Havas in 1918 (Fejes 1986:24). The AP gained a free hand in South
America but undertook to reimburse Havas if the latter lost income through
the transfer to the AP of its members in Brazil, Uruguay, Paraguay, and Argentina. Havas was also allowed to continue to use AP reports about the
United States in South America in competition with the AP itself (Cooper
1942:79). By 1919 the AP was competing against a weakened rival because
Havas's loss of its government subsidy had led to poorer quality service, and
the membership of the AP grew to include twenty-five of the major newspapers in South America (Cooper 1942:81–82). The Associated Press contract
with Havas was weakened further in 1921 and 1922 when Havas agreed that
it would send only its own news to South America (not the AP's, as previously) and that it would no longer expect compensation if South American
papers joined the AP (Cooper 1942:114–15). In turn, the AP's aggressive tactics hit the United Press's South American business. United Press began to
recover only when it began to submit news of Europe to its South American
clients (Rantanen 1992:19).

Nevertheless, as late as 1921 both Congress and U.S. reporters continued
to see coverage of the United States in South America as unsatisfactory. But
whereas Sen. Frank B. Kellogg, the Minnesota Republican, and his committee (a subcommittee of Interstate Commerce) saw this situation as resulting
from malice by the British and lack of cables, newspapermen tended to see
it as a matter of lack of interest. The acting general manager of the AP commented that "'you cannot force news, the stream of news uphill. . . . South
American countries have shown that they do not want our news'" (quoted
in Schreiner 1924:179).

In the immediate postwar years the British were also concerned at their
loss of influence in South America and Reuters's reliance on Havas. The
French news agency did "not go to any particular pains in the adequate or
accurate representation of British policy" (Taylor 1981:63). Reuters itself was
subsidized by the British Foreign Office for a contract entitled "Agence Service Reuter." The contract made Reuters responsible for disseminating news
and official communiqués. It ended in 1919, replaced with an agreement that

compensated Reuters for the additional cost of sending messages that would not have been sent on a commercial basis (Taylor 1981:58–59). But given Reuters's lack of efficacy in South America, the News Department of the Foreign Office cabled material for translation to its embassies in the form of a "London Letter," which was distributed free to the local press. According to the Foreign Office, these news releases were "'not intended to be merely commercial propaganda—to boost British trade—but are rather to keep South American countries supplied with reliable British news in order that this country may not be relegated entirely to the background in consequence of self advertisement carried on by the other important powers, efforts which sometimes take the form of deriding British policy and achievements'" (quoted in Taylor 1981:62). But the cables to South America were extremely expensive, so that it was less expensive to send news through New York than directly to Buenos Aires (Taylor 1981:99). Given the state of the British economy during the 1920s, the British Treasury cut the subsidy for these cablegrams to South America. In effect, by 1920 the British government had ceded its influence in South America to the Americans.

Movies Go South

U.S. influence in South America was also enhanced by the expansion of the movie industry. World War I, and the constraints that it imposed on European filmmakers and distributors, allowed Hollywood to increase its export of films to South America. Before the war, because the British tended to concentrate on distribution rather than production, Britain was the center for the re-exportation of U.S. movies to the European continent, to the formal British colonies, and to the informal colonies of South America and the Far East. Often, for a small additional sum the British rights for a film would include rights outside the United States and Canada. Regular shipping runs from Britain to South America, made in order to supply coal, eased transportation problems, and South American distributors found films less expensive to obtain from London than directly from the United States. However, the length of the war and the difficulties of exporting from Britain instigated direct distribution to national markets through the U.S. companies' own agents and linked distributors. Although the U.S. government had used the Sherman Anti-Trust Act to break up control of film distribution in 1915, the U.S. distributors were able to replicate their prewar vertical integration in other national markets.

In Latin America the war helped the U.S. companies oust the French film company Pathé, which had maintained distribution offices in Buenos Aires,

Rio de Janeiro, Havana, and Mexico City. The Hollywood companies that would form the 1920s oligopoly of Famous Players–Lasky, Universal, Goldwyn, and Fox all expanded overseas. Fox was first into Argentina and Brazil and by 1919 had offices, or representation, in every Latin American country except Colombia (Thompson 1985:72). Direct distribution from the United States was said to account for 60 percent of Argentina's imports in 1916 and for a rise in Brazilian film imports in both 1915 and 1916. Penetration of the Argentinean and Brazilian markets then filtered down to the smaller markets such as Chile and Peru. U.S. shippers promised regular South American runs, and Thompson quotes reports shortly after the war ended: " ""Leading South American film men declare they will never go back to dependence upon European markets, as they have found the American firms greatly superior to European productions"" " (1985:80).

Increased penetration of U.S. movies and news became linked with advertising for U.S. manufactured products. Even during World War I, agencies within the government encouraged the U.S. advertising industry to develop its activities in Latin America in order to create product markets and to replace both the influence and markets of Europeans. In 1917 the Department of Commerce surveyed advertising within Latin America and found it underdeveloped; the U.S. government encouraged advertising agencies to move in (Fejes 1986:26).

Thus whereas at the beginning of the period international communications were viewed as a means of distributing news and of making commercial transactions more efficient and government relations easier, within a short time U.S. business saw international communications as the means to create markets for products. In the postwar world international communications policy was no longer a matter of conveying information as a simple product but became the means to a mass overseas market for private enterprise.

Conclusion

At the end of the nineteenth century the French and British largely dominated South America, either by formal colonization or by wielding political influence through trade and investment. In 1905, in order to compete more effectively with the British naval buildup, Germany stopped trying to expand its influence in the area. Despite the hegemony that the United States claimed over the whole of Latin America through the Monroe Doctrine, U.S. influence was largely confined to Central America because of poor shipping and communications links. But during the first years of the twentieth century, the need for export markets and raw materials expanded the interest of the U.S. government, bringing it into competition with the Europeans.

The conflicts that arose in the expansion of international communications and the penetration of South American markets reflected this larger political environment. Because of the dominance of British capital and expertise, the submarine cable monopoly concessions that were granted from the 1870s on went to British companies. The French then challenged the British in the 1890s with state-backed manufacturing and operating companies, to be followed by the Americans moving south from their base in Mexico and Cuba. Although the introduction of the telephone allowed entry to AT&T, and Western Electric as its supplier, it appears that much of the later investment capital was also British. And, in competition with domestic state-owned telegraphs, the telephone companies remained fragmented and relatively unimportant.

The ownership of international telegraph cables was crucial in the distribution of foreign influence. And by the World War I that ownership in South America largely followed the foreign investment patterns of the United States and European powers. Scrymser's Central and South American Telegraph Company held monopolies of international communication in Mexico, Salvador, Nicaragua, and Ecuador.[29] It also held a monopoly on the Colombian Pacific coast for cables running south and a monopoly on cables running north from Peru. French companies held exclusive concessions in Venezuela and Dutch and French Guiana. The British held a monopoly concession in Uruguay, preferential rights in the Argentine Republic, and preferential rights in Brazil for cables connecting the major ports and for those connecting Brazil with Uruguay and Argentina. In British Guiana the British were the only operating company but without exclusive rights. In Panama, Peru, and Chile the Americans and British competed with each other.[30] In addition, the British had cables within the British West Indies and a cable linking those islands to Canada, while the Americans had cables linking the United States to Cuba and Bermuda. These monopolies were strengthened by control of interconnection. Each used high interconnection charges to prevent a competitor from entering its territory.

Because of their thirty-year monopolies, the cable companies became domestic political and economic actors of considerable power. Not only could they alter the domestic balance of power during revolutions but they also could effectively cut off a whole country from external communications, thereby provoking wars (as Scrymser claims he did), or they could undercut the tariffs of the state-owned telegraph company. With concessions given for such long periods of time, it was impossible for poor nation-states with little administrative expertise to set out terms and conditions within the licenses to allow for changing circumstances. And those governments that challenged the power of the cable companies often found themselves overthrown, as in Venezuela. Even in the 1870s the relative lack of sophistication of the landing licenses given by South American republics contrasted with those given by the Portuguese, which set out preconditions on tariffs and investment if traffic increased.

Given the companies' power, even when wireless was introduced for marine and point-to-point communications, it failed to provide the nation-states of Central and South America with the sovereign control of international communications that they required. Instead, either the cable company demanded control of the new technology or it was provided and controlled by foreign investors, such as Western Union, United Fruit, and Marconi of America. Throughout the period successive U.S. governments intervened in order to shift the control of communications away from the Europeans. U.S. cable competition with the British was most intense in Brazil. In the 1870s the secretary of state backed a bid by Scrymser's company to gain entry to Brazil—and did so again in the first decade of the 1900s and again ten years later. The company finally gained entry in 1919. A strategic cable from Panama to the United States, financed by the U.S. government, not only created a reliable communications link for the future site of the Panama Canal but also speeded transmission from Argentina, putting competitive pressures on the British. In contrast, the British government was content with its company's monopoly in Brazil, despite commercial unease at growing U.S. influence. So in 1911 it was not prepared to consider subsidizing cables around South America to parallel those around Africa.

But in the years immediately before World War I, German wireless expertise and the state backing of Telefunken opened up South America once again to German influence and propaganda, thereby increasing the continent's strategic importance. Only then were British consulates enlisted in the cause of pressing Marconi's case on domestic governments. But the allocation of concessions, as in the case of Brazil, was often delayed because of U.S. diplomatic support for U.S. companies. In this respect Marconi of America, although registered in the United States, was considered a British firm. The strength of U.S. government influence eventually obliged the company to enter a joint venture with Federal Telegraph to develop Latin American markets, a joint venture that was acceptable to the U.S. government because it believed that Federal Telegraph controlled the joint company. Outside Brazil, U.S. policy evolved around the ideas of Josephus Daniels. Instead of allowing European companies to take control of wireless on the continent, national governments were to be encouraged to own the facilities themselves. Government ownership of radio therefore became U.S. policy in the region until the 1920s, by which time a state-backed U.S. radio company, the Radio Corporation of America, had been established.

During World War I the U.S. government also was active in the field of propaganda, attempting to alter Latin American perceptions of the United States. In view of the domination of the French Havas news agency in the region, and the Associated Press's arrangement with that agency, the U.S. government actively supported United Press in penetrating South America. In turn, the Scripps agency's activities forced the AP to loosen its connection to the worldwide news agency cartel and into more aggressive transmission of U.S. news. This news agency expansion was itself dependent on subsidies to the press organized by the U.S. government with the Scrymser cable company. Yet the relative lack of success of both the U.S. and British governments and news agencies in interesting the South American public in their news contrasts with the success of the U.S. movie industry. Forced to distribute directly, rather than through Europe, Hollywood quickly filled the vacuum left by the French and opened the way for U.S. radio and advertising interests in the postwar period. Therefore World War I was the primary factor in altering the overall balance of political and economic power in South America and in thereby bringing about the liberalization of international communications in the region. The postwar story is told in the next chapters.

6. The United States: Competition for Infrastructure in the Interwar Years

WORLD WAR I began the process of redistribution of power between the European states and the United States. In Galbraith's words: "It shattered a political structure that had been dominant in Europe for centuries. And it greatly altered the position of the United States on the world economic scene. From being an addendum to, even an afterthought in, economic discussion, the United States became the centerpiece" (1994:10).

After a slight dip in the early months of the war, U.S. exports climbed rapidly, reaching a peak in the late war and early postwar periods. The increase came from supplying Allies with foodstuffs and munitions and from moving into markets that Europe could no longer supply. Beginning in October 1914 the U.S. government allowed private banks to finance the British war effort, and, following U.S. entry into the war, the United States also extended credit to its allies. So whereas in the period 1914–17, of $7 billion of goods bought by the Allies from the United States $2.4 billion was on credit, in the period 1917–18 the United States exported $10.3 billion of goods to the Allies, of which $7.3 billion was on credit. There was "a massive inflow of gold to pay for the purchases of the friendly European belligerents. . . . These [gold flows] and the loans they could sustain would . . . establish the United States in general and New York City in particular as the world financial center" (Galbraith 1994:30–31).

World War I produced, perhaps for the first time, an appreciation of strategic resources within the Wilson administration. Dependence upon foreign powers for fuel, investment capital, and communications was "considered tantamount to political dependence and a potential threat to the nation's security" (Tulchin 1971:v). The Great War also eased U.S. expansion into Latin

America and the extension of U.S. capital, exports, and strategic influence throughout the western hemisphere. Led by the bank of J. P. Morgan, the New York banking houses set up a South American "group" that was "to act as a unit in handling the governmental or semi-governmental securities offered from the leading South American countries" and, as the United States became the center of financial loans to South America, it became more dominant in trade (Tulchin 1971:8).

The postwar period also saw the increase of U.S. companies' penetration of Europe and elsewhere. A 1930 survey by the U.S. Department of Commerce found that U.S. investments in Europe, both direct and indirect, were valued at $1.352 billion among twenty-five countries, of which Britain received about $500 million, Germany received $250 million, and France $125 million. But of a total of worldwide investment of $7.478 billion by U.S. investors, only about 18 percent went to Europe (Southard 1931:194). By 1929 thirteen hundred U.S. companies were doing business in twenty-eight countries (Southard 1931:xiv).

Because of the high interest on postwar U.S. loans to Britain, U.S. exports and investment in Europe were met with hostility. As Southard comments, "When one recalls that Europe is prone to regard the United States as a commercial and industrial colossus—a creditor surrounded by a tariff wall which serves to increase the difficulties of debt repayment—it is not surprising that much of the force of the prevailing nationalistic spirit is directed against this country" (1931:129). The Anglo-American Agreement on trade, designed to improve political relations between the two countries, with Britain agreeing to take an increasing share of U.S. exports, was not signed until 1938 (Drummond 1972:114). U.S. companies active in the telephone and radio markets in Europe found it necessary to hire local management in order to circumvent national hostilities. They entered domestic government-backed cartels intended to preserve local supply. And they were sometimes so successful at establishing domestic credentials (such as the British subsidiary of International Telephone and Telegraph) that their ownership did not become an issue.

Because the control of communications lagged behind the ongoing change in power within the global political economy after World War I, the competition between the United States and Britain for control of international communications—both the means of transmission and the content—intensified. That competition encompassed technologies, information markets, and international regulation and continued the prewar pattern of involving the third markets of South America and China. But the Great Depression of the late 1920s and 1930s also affected this competition, bringing overcapacity in international infrastructure and cartelization by operators. This chapter and those that follow explain how the struggle for control of international communications developed in these interwar years.

Peace Negotiations and Submarine Cables

In 1914 the British had cut the two German-owned transatlantic cables, to the United States and Brazil, in the English Channel and six hundred miles off the U.S. coast. Then, when the United States entered the war in 1917, the U.S. ends were also cut, perhaps, as Clark (1931:164) suggests, to fix them as spoils of war. One cable was diverted to Canada, thereby providing an all-British state-owned transatlantic cable run by the British Post Office at both ends (Barty-King 1979:174). The U.S. government allowed the transfer of the other to the French government, a decision that it later regretted (Schreiner 1924:197). In the early part of the war Germany was forced to rely on the Nauen radio station and on two transatlantic cables. The German foreign office routed its telegrams through its embassy in Stockholm to Buenos Aires and over the cable used by the U.S. State Department from Copenhagen. Both cables went through a relay station in England where messages were copied to the Admiralty and Foreign Office in London (Wedlake 1973:79; West 1986:68).

The entry of the United States into the war was itself precipitated by an intercepted telegram from the German foreign minister to the German ambassador in Washington, D.C., that offered the Mexicans a piece of the U.S. landmass in return for neutrality should the United States enter the war (Fortner 1993:105). Because the U.S. State Department could not be alerted to either the interception of its traffic or the breaking of its diplomatic code, the British had to leak the cable in a way that would not betray their actions. Although suspicions led Washington to establish an encryption unit in 1917, the Americans found it almost impossible to evade British penetration (West 1986:66–68). Tulchin (1971:206) reports that, "because the British had broken American codes, a 'top secret' message to Argentina had to be sent down the All America company line through Mexico, down the west coast, and then on land lines over the Andes Mountains to Buenos Aires." But there were no U.S.-controlled cables to Rio de Janeiro over which to send such messages.

Before the United States entered the war, the British government was able to monitor and regulate all the news sent from Germany to the United States. By arrangement with the Marconi company, the British also were able to use wireless to reach neutral countries. Overall, the British propaganda effort, run toward the end of the war from the Ministry of Information and the Department of Propaganda in Enemy Countries under the direction of two newspaper proprietors, Lord Beaverbrook and Viscount Northcliffe, was considered successful (Stuart 1920). In contrast, because telegrams went via landlines, the propaganda put out over the telegraph by the U.S. Committee on Public Information would sometimes arrive in South America after the mailed dispatches (Tulchin 1971:208).

As World War I ended, a primary consideration for the Americans was how to undercut the submarine cable hegemony of the British. Traffic overload on the cables in wartime had afforded the Eastern the opportunity to abolish the general press rate, charging high prices to U.S. newspapers (while subsidizing British ones) (Mills 1924:115). Overt British wartime censorship continued into 1919, and U.S. businessmen believed that such censorship had more to do with commercial intelligence than national security (S. Baker 1923, 3:doc. 62). The U.S. Shipping Board, which was in charge of the merchant marine, was so worried about British censorship that it devised its own cable code, which could not so easily be deciphered (Hogan 1977:107). This U.S. desire for secrecy ran up against the British desire for control. A number of English admirals argued in 1919 that the Treaty of Versailles should include a clause "forbidding countries to use any code for international messages that was not known and recognized" (West 1986:75). In other words, the British wanted to hold the key to all communications. In 1919 the renewal of both Western Union's and the Commercial Cable Company's landing licenses obliged them to agree to hand over copies of their cables to the British government.[1] And in 1920 a clause in the British Official Secrets Act made this provision obligatory in all subsequent cable landing licenses (West 1986:75).

Although the Eastern had been forced to lease six of the thirteen cables between the United States and England to the U.S. telegraph companies in 1912, because all traffic to other parts of the world had to pass through England, the Americans perceived themselves as dependent on the British for communications beyond the Atlantic (S. Baker 1923, 2:468n). With the transfer of the transatlantic German cables to Britain and France, and the seizure of the German cables from Guam by the Japanese, the U.S. government regarded itself as ending the war weaker, rather than stronger, in communications (S. Baker 1923, 2:466).

As a result U.S. negotiating tactics at the Paris Peace Conference moved from first demanding the restoration of the German Atlantic cables to their former owner to then arguing for the cables to be held jointly by the five Allied powers and managed under the terms of an international convention (S. Baker 1923, 2:481). Woodrow Wilson was influenced by Walter Rogers, the communications expert of the U.S. Commission to Negotiate the Peace, who in order to promote a "more orderly, efficient and integrated world network," supported the inclusion of the U.S. cable companies under the International Telegraph Convention. Wilson attempted to put the issue of the international regulation of cables and, particularly the lowering of tariffs, on the conference agenda (Hogan 1977:109). Rogers had worked out a free-trade program for cables in which all members of the League of Nations were to "abolish discrimination in rates and exclusive landing concessions, and to grant free exchange of business, the establishment of inland extensions of cables, and freedom of transit for messages without scrutiny or interference" (S. Baker 1923, 2:476). In other words, the Americans were looking to the Europeans to liberalize their international communications.

In addition, of particular concern to the Americans was that the Japanese had seized the Pacific cables of Dutch-Niederlandische Telegraphengesellschaft, a German-Dutch company. In the prewar period the company, which was subsidized by the German and Dutch governments, had run cables from Guam to Yap and from there south to the Dutch East Indies and north to Shanghai. Clarence Mackay's Commercial Pacific Cable Company had operated the Guam end under contract to the German-Dutch company and had linked it to Commercial Pacific Cable's cable to the Philippines and China, thereby providing an alternative route in case its cable failed. The seizure of the German cable by the Japanese and its diversion to one of the Japanese islands prevented Mackay's company from using it. [2] Delays became commonplace. So poor were postwar communications across the Pacific that the State Department's Bureau of Foreign and Domestic Commerce commented that "'if the present system continues it will render futile the efforts of the Shipping Board, the Federal Reserve Bank, the Bureau of Foreign and Domestic Commerce, (the) banking houses which are establishing branches in foreign countries, the corporations formed under the Webb-Pomarene law, and many other agencies, to promote American commerce in the Far East'" (quoted in Hogan 1977:106). Because of the strategic importance of Yap to U.S. cable communications, Woodrow Wilson proposed unsuccessfully that the island should be excluded from Japanese control and should be subject to an "international commission in control of the cable lines" (S. Baker 1923, 2:480).

But the British foreign secretary, Arthur Balfour, refused to contemplate including cable regulation within the negotiations. He told Woodrow Wilson that the U.S. government needed to nationalize the U.S. telegraph companies before complaining about rates. Wilson then had to accept an amendment that allowed the German cables to be used, for the time being, by the British and French. Faced with opposition to international regulation from the U.S. cable companies, which resented being forced to share transatlantic traffic, Walter Rogers built a communications policy based on that of government ownership of radio. This was the policy that Josephus Daniels had developed to stop European expansion in South America. As a means of undercutting private cable rates, Rogers argued within the U.S. delegation in favor of a policy of proactive development of radio in which "each of the nations should nationalize its radio facilities, and . . . the nations of the world acting together develop a truly world-wide service" (S. Baker 1923, 2:487). Rogers is said to have convinced Woodrow Wilson of the virtues of the policy by suggesting that international collaboration in radio would provide the means to publicize Wilson's League of Nations (Luther 1988:21).[3]

In general, the U.S. position in the peace conference was to foster international political cooperation through the League of Nations but to operate an Open Door policy in economic matters. Although that policy was rather vaguely expressed in the phrase "commercial equality," Wilson seems to have interpreted it to mean that the Allies would give each other most-favored-nation status, along the lines of the subsequent Pan-American Agreement of 1933.[4] But faced with protectionist Republicans in Congress, and a British campaign to translate his idea of commercial equality into a multilateral commercial treaty, Wilson backtracked from committing the United States to free trade.[5] Instead, it was agreed that the Covenant of the League of Nations should include a provision in Article 23e " 'to secure and maintain freedom of communications and of transit and equitable treatment for the commerce of all Members of the League,' " while article 24 provided for placing international bureaus, such as the International Bureau of the Telegraph Union, under the direction of the League of Nations, if "the parties to such treaties consent" (quoted in S. Baker 1923, 2:417). Congress never consented.

At this point navy officials on the U.S. negotiating team developed the concept of a private radio company to carry forward U.S. government aspirations for communications hegemony. The overall intention of the U.S. Navy became to develop "a new system with the United States as the center" (Luther 1988:20). To bypass Telcon's virtual monopoly, the Department of Commerce began researching the possibility of developing submarine cable–manufacturing capacity in the United States. And the U.S. Post Office Department looked at the possibility of consolidating and subsidizing the private cable companies in return for placing them under government supervision (Hogan 1977:107–8).

The negotiators in Paris accepted Wilson's proposal for an international congress to be called by the "Five Allied and Associated Powers . . . as soon as possible . . . to consider and report on all international aspects of telegraph, cable and radio communication with a view to providing the entire world with adequate communication facilities on a fair, equitable basis" (S. Baker 1923, 2:483). The original plan was for a conference to which all nations would be invited, to be preceded by a preliminary conference among the five Great Powers that would establish the agenda and allocate the German cables (Tulchin 1971:212). But the British and French, not wishing to give up the German cables, delayed the preliminary conference until November 1920.

The intention of the preliminary conference was to simplify communications by bringing all methods of electrical communication under the same rules as far as was practicable. The proposed convention, pushed by Britain and France and following the same outline as that adopted in 1875 at St. Petersburg, brought together radio and cable communications. Showing the influence of the League of Nations structure, it provided for a universal "Electrical Communications Council" of representatives from the United States, France, Britain, Italy, and Japan and four other representatives of the signatories and proposed a universal communications union that would include telegraph and radio. But the U.S. telegraph and radio companies objected to the provision that a two-thirds majority of signatories could alter international regulations, thereby bringing them under the power of foreign governments (Tribolet 1929:16–18). To meet the demands of Western Union, AT&T, and Commercial Cable that they be excluded from regulation, the U.S. government proposed that it should sign a separate protocol. But the other powers were not prepared to accept this device (J. D. Tomlinson 1945:48). In addition, despite initial support from the British and Italians, U.S. proposals for an end to monopoly concessions and for reciprocity in the award of cable landing licenses were ignored (Hogan 1977:110).

The disagreement that the preliminary conference engendered led to a further delay in the calling of an international conference to review the radio regulations. It eventually took place in 1927, by which time interference between stations and services, both within the United States and internationally, had become a considerable problem. The intervening years also allowed the companies to organize themselves to influence government policy, under the leadership of RCA's Col. A. G. Davis and the AP's Kent Cooper (Renaud 1985:13). Also, once Republican Warren Harding was inaugurated in 1921, Rogers's influence declined, and the power of the companies increased (Schwoch 1990:289–97).

After a reaffirmation at the Paris Peace Conference of the importance of the Monroe Doctrine to the United States, in the immediate postwar period U.S. complaints focused on the British cable monopoly in Brazil, which the Eastern was then defending in the Brazilian courts (S. Baker 1923, 2:314–39).

But undermining the U.S. position on liberalization were the monopoly concessions held by All America Cables, Inc. (Scrymser's former company), in Central and South America. The company defended itself in a statement to the U.S. delegation to the 1920 conference:

> "It has been argued that the Government of the United States should not concern itself with the destruction of the British monopoly in Brazil because All-America Cables (Inc) has monopolies on the west coast of South America. It is true that All-America Cables has monopolies on the west coast but this fact does not lessen the injury which will be done to American commerce and American diplomacy if they are to be denied communication with northern Brazil except over British lines. . . . We must either fight with every resource diplomatic and commercial against preponderance of British communications wherever encountered or we must give up all hope of making headway against it." (quoted in Schreiner 1924:136–37)

Frustrated at the lack of progress in gaining a U.S.-dominated communications system, mercantilist hostility in Congress became directed at Western Union for its actions in South America.

When the Eastern failed to prevent the Brazilian government from granting All America Cables a concession to enter Brazil from Uruguay, it first responded by suggesting the recognition of "spheres of influence." The U.S. companies would keep the west coast of South America, and the British would retain Brazil and the east coast. When, at the instigation of the State Department, this proposal was rejected, the British company allied itself with Western Union.[6] The intention was to lock All America Cables out from interconnection with Western Union for local deliveries within the United States and to route all Western Union's traffic from Europe to South America through the subsidiary of the Eastern, Western Telegraph.

In 1919 Western Union agreed to bring a cable down from Miami to Barbados to join one owned by Western Telegraph that ran up from Brazil, so that the two companies would operate a joint telegraph service down the east coast of South America. The U.S. company justified its actions as responding to a request made by the secretary of the treasury, William McAdoo, in 1917 (Tribolet 1929:53n.13). However, Western Union decided not to install a cable itself, because wartime scarcity made it too expensive. Instead, because the British still had a monopoly of the major ports in Brazil and might decide to bypass the United States by installing a cable from Barbados to Canada, Western Union agreed to work with the British company. Western Union's justification for its actions implied that the U.S. government was at fault for allowing the British to take the transatlantic German cable—which gave Western Union the incentive to establish a cable from Brazil to Canada. But Western Union also needed its British cable landing licenses renewed in 1919 and therefore was predisposed to come to an arrangement with the Eastern.[7] The U.S. War Department approved the plan, but the State Department did not.

All America Cables retaliated by asking the government to withhold permission for the landing of the proposed cable in Miami until the British agreed to relinquish their monopoly in Brazil. U.S. Marines then took up position in and off Miami to prevent the landing of the cable. At this point Western Union took the matter to court, challenging the legality of the U.S. denial of landing rights.

The company pointed out the discriminatory way in which the Wilson administration had acted. Whereas the Commercial Cable Company interconnected with the Eastern in the Azores, and Mackay's Commercial Pacific Cable not only interconnected with the Eastern but was 75 percent owned by it, Western Union was denied the right to interconnect with the Eastern in the Bahamas. In reality the administration was protecting the interests of All America Cables, which had strong ties to government. In testimony to the House, the company's legal representative, Elihu Root Jr., argued in 1921 that "'if the British company succeeds in breaking down the system in South America . . . it will be true that with the exception of one line across the Pacific and two French lines across the Atlantic, . . . we will have no cable line connecting us with any continent which does not either pass through British territory or relay over British lines" (quoted in Tribolet 1929:52n.12). As a result Congress accused Western Union of having "some unbiblical connection with something British," and the company had to defend its U.S. credentials. Subsequently, Western Union became so alienated from the Wilson administration by its branding as a "British" company that it had its interests represented by the British delegation at the 1927 and 1932 International Radiotelegraphic Conferences (Tribolet 1929:51n.11).

As a direct result of Western Union's legal challenge, Congress enacted legislation in 1921 that "gave the President considerable powers in the granting of licenses for cable landings on American soil, as well as for the obtaining of concessions for the United States in other parts of the world" (Wilshaw 1939:9). The legislation echoed the 1875 sentiments of President Ulysses S. Grant and gave the incoming Harding unchallenged authority to negotiate on the basis of reciprocity. The Kellogg Cable Landing Act of 1921 enabled "the President to insist on equal rights" for U.S. companies overseas, and U.S. negotiators were able to hammer out an informal understanding with the British (Hogan 1977:110). In effect, bilateral reciprocity replaced international multilateral negotiation. After a stand-off between the State Department and the Foreign Office, in which the State Department demanded that Western Union should control the whole cable, the matter was settled by the companies themselves. The British gave up their monopoly in Brazil, and All America Cables gave up its monopolies in Central America (Herring and Gross 1936:234; Hogan 1977:111–17).

Herring and Gross consider the act to have been successful:

> Largely as a result of this policy, during the first eight years after the passage of the Act, in six countries provisions contained in cable concessions granting rights in the nature of a monopoly were terminated, notably the monopolies of the Western Telegraph Company in Brazil, Uruguay, and the Argentine; and those of All America Cables in Colombia, Ecuador, and Peru. In three other cases, monopolistic concessions were not renewed upon their expiration, as in the case of the monopolies of the French Cable Company in Haiti, in Santo Domingo, and Venezuela. In addition, applicants for landing licenses have been forbidden to associate with any cable company that possessed exclusive rights by reason of which American cable companies would be barred from foreign territory, this also resulting in the cancellation of certain monopolistic concessions. (1936:236)

But while the effect of the act was to end monopoly concessions, simply refusing landing rights to foreigners could not produce incentives to invest.

Failure to improve the situation in the Pacific led to a proposal for a government-owned Pacific cable, subsequently vetoed by Harding (Hogan 1977: 108). Eventually, in 1922 the Americans signed a bilateral treaty with Japan. Yap was to remain a Japanese mandate with a U.S. cable landing station to which the United States was to have equal access. There was to be no censorship of cables, and U.S. nationals were to have the same rights in radiotelegraphy as in cables (Clark 1931:165). But the concept of reciprocity did not extend to gaining the U.S. companies entry to China, and relations between them and the Harding administration deteriorated (Tulchin 1971:224).

In administering the 1921 act, subsequent landing licenses came to be based on a model license, which took the place of U.S. adherence to the convention of the International Telegraph Union (ITU) and also transferred some of the provisions of the Interstate Commerce Act to the international sphere. This model license gave U.S. government telegrams precedence over all others at preferential rates. Licensees were forbidden to discriminate among the general public in regard to rates, order, or transmission, although they could classify telegrams into different categories with differing tariffs. The rates themselves had to be just and reasonable, and licensees were forbidden "to lease, transfer, assign or sell" a cable or to "consolidate, amalgamate or combine" with another party without the consent of the secretary of state. Nor could they "enter into any agreement with any other cable or communications company or any foreign government either for regulating rates or for any other purpose" without the consent of the Department of State (Herring and Gross 1936:236). Even the technology was specified. So licensees had to use cable and appliances "modern and manufactured in accordance with the latest approved methods," and there had to be an ample repair service. In addition, the president was empowered to take over the cables in time of war and to rescind the licenses at any time (Herring and Gross 1936:236–37).

The model license was not to the liking of the U.S. cable companies. They objected to the provision requiring that they gain government approval before making agreements with foreign firms holding monopoly privileges. They wanted to seek approval only after they had worked out an agreement. And, because they were allowing the Mexican government to transmit its messages for free, they objected to what they called the "dead-head" clause giving the United States most favored government rate privileges, which might lead to similar demands (Tulchin 1971:227). But eventually they were obliged to give in to the government.

Whereas Wilson's policy of nationalization had been followed by the Harding administration's initial mercantilist policy of "active encouragement" of "the extension of the American owned and operated cable and radio services," from 1921 the Harding administration shifted to a position where it became intransigent in its demands for a free market (Tulchin 1971:228–29). Gradually, the administration's separate complaints concerning company strategies of cartelization were fused into a single brief against all monopolies until, at the end of 1921, the U.S. government announced its commitment to the "open door in cables and its policy of opposition to all monopolies," a policy that was then applied to U.S. as well as foreign companies (Tulchin 1971:223).

Relations between the State Department and the companies perhaps reached their lowest ebb during this period when a conflict took place with the British over landing rights in the Azores (Tulchin 1971:230). Because the Portuguese Azores were under the informal control of the British, Harding's policy of encouraging U.S. cable companies to lay new lines could be achieved only with British concurrence. In 1919 the Commercial Cable Company proposed a new line to the Azores, which would connect there with a new German cable from Emden. Western Union signed a similar agreement with another German company and with an Italian group. The intention was that the cables from Europe should take both U.S. and South American traffic, which would then go by landline to link with the U.S.-controlled west coast route to South America. Such traffic would bypass the east coast cable of the Eastern company in South America, and this diminution in its South American traffic caused the British company to pressure the Portuguese government to block the landing licenses.

The Eastern's John Denison-Pender was supported by the Foreign Office, the Post Office, and the British Admiralty, all wishing to prevent an independent route from Europe to South America that would bypass British censorship (Hogan 1977:120). Not that the British were about to admit to such a concern. "'This is not a consideration we could use openly,'" explained Rowland Sperling of the Foreign Office, "'least of all to the United States Government who may complain that we are hampering a legitimate form of United States enterprise'" (quoted in Hogan 1977:121–22). The British Foreign Office attempted to use potential U.S. entry to the Azores as a lever to help the Eastern keep its monopoly in Brazil. Both sides tried to use financial pressure. The Americans discussed tying funding arrangements for the British debt and financial assistance to Portugal to cable rights in the Azores, and the U.S. companies "were trying their best, through favors to Portuguese officials, to buy their way into the Azores" (Hogan 1977:123). The British discussed the possibility of the Eastern's making a loan to Portugal while, much to the State Department's displeasure, the Commercial Cable Company offered to float a loan for Portugal on the U.S. market (Tulchin 1971:231).

Concerned about the loss to U.S. commerce in Europe from the delay, the standoff between the State Department and the British Foreign Office led the Commerce Department to enter the fray. The British suggested that the companies be left to settle the matter among themselves, and over State Department protests the Commercial Cable Company broke ranks and came to an agreement with the Eastern to transfer all the South American traffic from Germany to the Eastern's South American cable. And when it seemed in 1922 that Western Union might construct a direct line from Italy via the Canaries to South America, a compromise agreement was reached with the Eastern, overseen by the Foreign Office. In effect, the companies drew back from competition and reached a market-sharing agreement instead.

Pender and the Foreign Office then withdrew their opposition, and in early 1924 the Portuguese government gave landing licenses to both U.S. companies. The State Department did not oppose the agreement but simply refused to help companies that were considered to have betrayed "patriotic considerations" (Hogan 1977:127). Secretary of State Charles Hughes's view was that "'if American companies desired to accept less than (the) Department has endeavored to obtain, they are at liberty to do so and must accept (the) consequences and assume responsibility for their action'" (quoted in Hogan 1977:127). But holding to its Open Door principles, before the State Department would agree to licenses at the U.S. end, both U.S. companies had to agree to allow equal opportunity in the future to other U.S. interests. In 1925 Western Union's cable to Italy and Spain via the Azores began operation and in 1927 so did that between the United States and Germany. And in 1925, so that traffic was interchanged over a U.S. network, both U.S. companies allowed each other entry to previously exclusive agreements with foreign companies.

The U.S. State Department then drew back from attempting to impose competition on the private companies, or an Open Door in communications. But by then competition with shortwave wireless had replaced the need for regulation. This new threat brought U.S. and British cable companies together in research and development. They looked to increase the traffic capacity (and therefore lower the unit cost) of their cables and to develop a submarine cable that could carry speech over long distances.

Research on carrying speech via submarine cable centered on finding a better insulation material than gutta-percha and a more conductive material than soft iron for the core. Both AT&T's Western Electric and Telcon produced new alloys for the core, which were introduced into "loaded" cables in the mid-1920s. "Loading" cables, based on a principle pointed out by the physicist Oliver Heaviside at the turn of the century, involved improving the strength of a signal by increasing the transmission capacity of the core. The technique of winding metallic tape around a copper conductor was introduced in 1910 by Siemens of Germany (Lawford and Nicholson 1950:89). It was first used for telephone transmission but proved practical in increasing transmission speed for the telegraph. In 1924 trials of a joint Western Electric (AT&T), Telcon, and Western Union "loaded" cable with a new alloy core worked at a speed of 380 words per minute compared to the thirty per minute on an old-style cable. Western Union first introduced the new technology in its transatlantic cable of 1924. Loaded cables were only 15 to 25 percent more expensive than the old ones and provided six channels that could be used simultaneously. Introduced commercially during the mid-1920s, they altered the economics of cables. The capital cost of the cable no longer was the major outlay; the major costs became those of operation, especially collection and delivery. Postal delivery, first tried by the wireless companies, came to be seen as a cost-effective alternative to the traditional telegraph-boy delivery service (Brown 1927:86–88).

But until 1926 the cable companies were not able to place repeaters under water. This new technology made redundant some of the island repeater stations and allowed submarine cables to interconnect with each other. It therefore helped cut staffing at a time when cost cutting became essential to compete with shortwave radio.

During this period, to increase the distance that cable could carry speech, AT&T's Bell Laboratories had been experimenting with compounds to replace gutta percha. Because AT&T did not manufacture cables, it offered the resulting patented material, "paragutta," to Telcon for experimentation. Telcon found that the properties of paragutta were so good that an Atlantic telephone cable would be possible. "Detailed designs were worked out and costs considered, but by this time the depression had begun to fall on America and all schemes were abandoned" (Lawford and Nicholson 1950:103). Because of the depression, the decrease in transatlantic traffic, and the competition with radio, a transatlantic telephone cable had to wait almost thirty years (Lawford and Nicholson 1950:103).

RCA: International Wireless and Cables

Marconi's early experiments with radio had suggested that wireless could transmit international telephone traffic. But the technology had been lacking until World War I. In 1913 the demonstration of radiotelephony occurred in London between two buildings (W. Baker 1970:151). The following year Marconi himself gave a successful demonstration of wireless telephony over a distance of forty-five miles (W. Baker 1970:171). During a visit to the United States in 1914 Marconi had inspected a new device, the "Alexanderson alternator" developed by General Electric, and had recognized its potential to provide a continuous wave of sound for transmission by high-power wireless stations. In 1918 the British Marconi company set out to buy the patent. But ownership of the patent would have consolidated British hegemony over both radio and cable, and the U.S. Navy and the Commerce Department, both intent on countering the British dominance in cables, opposed the sale (Luther 1988:22). The director of the U.S. Bureau of Foreign and Domestic Commerce, Burwell S. Cutler, was convinced that "'the Departments of Commerce, State and Navy should take united action'" and "'give the necessary assistance to some private corporation which may be selected to operate more or less in silent partnership with the Government as the provider of purely American wireless communication throughout the world for the benefit of American commercial and military interests'" (quoted in Rossi 1985:32–52). These views reflected those of the U.S. delegation at Versailles.

There the U.S. Navy was represented by Adm. W. H. G. Bullard of the U.S. Naval Communication Service, and Bullard's superior, Navy Secretary Josephus Daniels, both of whom had been behind the 1918 Alexander Bill to gain naval control of wireless (see chapter 3). Because U.S. domestic political opinion was against a naval monopoly, the U.S. delegation began to consider the possibility of a private radio company that the government could support in diplomatic negotiations (Barnouw 1970:144). Because Daniels could not accept a potential private monopoly, according to Fleet Adm. Chester W. Nimitz, Bullard and Stanford C. Hooper became the main driving forces behind the idea (Howeth 1963:xiv).

During the Paris Peace Conference, Owen D. Young of General Electric attended a series of meetings in which it was agreed that the alternator patent would not be sold to Marconi. Young later reported his meeting with Admiral Bullard:

> "Admiral Bullard said . . . that the president had reached the conclusion, as a result of his experience in Paris, that there were three dominating factors in international relations—international transportation, international communication and petroleum—and that the influence which a country exercised in international affairs would be largely dependent upon their position of dominance in these three activities; that Britain obviously had the lead and the experience in international transportation—it would be difficult if not impossible to equal her position in that field; in international communications she had acquired the practical domination of the cable system of the world; but that there was an apparent opportunity for the United States to challenge her in international communications through the use of the radio; of course as to petroleum we already had a position of dominance. The result of American dominance in radio would have been a fairly equal stand-off between the United States and Great Britain—the United States having the edge in petroleum, Britain in shipping, with communications divided—cables to Britain and wireless to the United States." (quoted in Rosenberg 1982:94)

However, because Daniels would not support the negotiations of Bullard and Hooper, and Daniels refused to sign the agreement to establish the new company, the amalgamation of radio interests into the Radio Corporation of America took place without direct government backing. Howeth blames Daniels's failure to support his subordinates for the subsequent rapid diminution of the navy's control of national radio policies. The records reflect no further official correspondence requesting naval support, and within thirty months Owen Young was complaining about the lack of a coherent government policy (Howeth 1963:358).

Formed in 1919 under the direction of Young, RCA was conceptualized as a subsidiary of General Electric. The navy transferred the Marconi Wireless Telegraph Company of America to the new company. In effect, the United States first nationalized, then forced the sale of British Marconi radio interests. RCA took over the staff of Marconi of America, but the old company retained its corporate identity, so that only the name on the paycheck changed. RCA gained access to the Marconi patents, the high-power stations, the contract with the U.S. Shipping Board, the American market of the Wireless Press subsidiary of Marconi, and three-eighths of the stock of the Pan-American Wireless Telegraph and Telephone Company—the company set up by Federal Telegraph and Marconi of America to establish radio circuits in Central and South America (Howeth 1963:359). RCA entered a long-term contract with British Marconi that gave RCA all radio traffic between the United Kingdom and the United States, and RCA bought the rights to Marconi's radio service between the United States, Hawaii, and Japan. This latter service had operated for only a few weeks in 1917 before the navy had taken it over (Sobel 1982:61; Tribolet 1929:208).

RCA's articles of incorporation reflected naval concerns with ownership and the provisions of the 1910 Wireless Ship Act. They prohibited the election of foreign nationals as directors or officials and prohibited foreigners from holding more than 20 percent of its stock. To prevent abuse foreign-held share certificates were to carry "Foreign Share Certificate" printed on their faces. In addition, RCA's articles of incorporation allowed the government to participate in the company's affairs, and in 1922 James G. Harbord, a retired Marine Corps general, served as its president (Howeth 1963:359; Barnouw 1970:144).

But good relations between the navy and the company did not last long. Whereas in inaugurating RCA the intention of the navy was primarily to create a top-flight company to promote a worldwide U.S. radio monopoly, according to Aitken, among the handwritten notes in Owen Young's papers one word was unmistakable: *loot* (Aitken 1976, cited in Luther 1988:163n.56). As the chief of naval operations, Adm. W. S. Benson, commented, the "'object of paying dividends'" was more important to RCA than a worldwide U.S. wireless system (quoted in Rossi 1985:36). RCA immediately followed the practices of the day, which favored international cartels. It entered a market-sharing agreement with British Marconi that gave that company the exclusive right to supply radio equipment to the British Empire outside the western hemisphere but allowed free competition in Asia (Schwoch 1990:60).

The new company entered into negotiations with AT&T, which held some patents that RCA needed, bought half the stock of the United Fruit subsidiary, and formed an attractive prospect to Westinghouse, which faced a postwar drop in the government procurement of radio equipment.[8] The resulting combine, controlled by four co-owners, each already active in radio communications and hardware manufacture—General Electric, Westinghouse, AT&T, and United Fruit—ended competition in the domestic radio-manufacturing industry. RCA's ownership structure represented an accommodation of existing power groups. This formula was to be repeated first in Britain in the 1920s, at the beginning of broadcasting, and again in the United States in the 1960s when Comsat was established to control satellite communications (Barnouw 1970:209).

When RCA began, communications across the Pacific were either by the slow Mackay cable, naval radio from California to Hawaii, or army radio from Alaska to Japan. From Hawaii messages could be transmitted by radio to Manila and then from the Philippines to the Far East or via Guam, Samoa, and Fiji to connect with the All-Red British cable to Australia and New Zealand. A radio station within the U.S. legation in Peking was used to pick up U.S. news and broadcast it to the press in China (Tribolet 1929:133).

As a direct result of pressure from the Associated Press, which had claimed that foreign control of cables was prejudicing U.S. interests in the Asian Pacific, in 1912 Congress had ordered the army and navy to open their Pacific radio circuits to the press (Renaud 1985:12). The inexpensive service allowed the Associated Press to supply newspapers in Alaska, the Philippines, Puerto Rico, and Hawaii. The AP claimed that the service was uneconomical at commercial rates of transmission and that its reports were serving the national interest by being distributed for free from Manila to the press associations in Japan and China (Tribolet 1929:210n.73). In fact, in allowing the Japanese and Chinese press free access to its copy, the AP was effectively breaking the terms of its agreement with Reuters. Obviously, it could afford to give copy away only if communications were inexpensive, so naval radio was cross-subsidizing the AP's expansionary tactics.

In February 1920 the naval stations and those of the army operating in Alaska were turned over to RCA. However, the Associated Press in particular was unhappy at this privatization. In view of congressional concern at the lack of representation of U.S. ideas abroad, RCA allowed the naval stations to continue to serve the press until 1922, but David Sarnoff, then commercial manager of RCA, would allow them to charge rates less expensive than RCA's only over the Pacific.[9] However, with backing from the State Department, U.S. newspapers were able to evade RCA's transatlantic charges. In 1920 they formed the American Publishers Committee and in 1921 set up their own radio station at the terminus of the British submarine cables in Halifax, Nova Scotia. In 1924 the original service to Britain was extended to France and Italy (Gross and Herring 1936:89).

The effect of RCA's focus on profitable routes was to allow the navy to continue to service the less profitable. The Radio Act of 1927, which established the Federal Radio Commission under Admiral Bullard, allowed the navy to use its stations worldwide for the reception and transmission of messages from U.S. newspapers and news agencies, and from newspapers published by U.S. citizens in foreign countries. It also allowed the use of naval stations in Alaska for all kinds of commercial traffic. The major constraint upon the navy was that it could operate only where RCA had no regular stations. Thus the U.S. taxpayer subsidized the transmission of news on "thin" routes under the navy budget. In addition, despite objections from RCA, the Federal Radio Commission allocated twenty shortwave frequencies to the American Publishers Committee. Later, a public utility corporation formed by the U.S. press, Press Wireless, Inc., carried the bulk of traffic, so that to a large extent during the interwar period U.S. news agencies and newspapers controlled their own means of transmission and had low-cost access to Europe (Gross and Herring 1936:90).

One of the first actions of RCA after its inauguration in 1920 was to agree to carve up the South American market with its British competitor, Marconi. The British company had already gained a concession and set up an Argentinean subsidiary to erect a transmitter in competition with Telefunken. In particular, the U.S. State Department was eager for the RCA combine to build a transmitter in Argentina to preempt the Germans. But there were problems. Ostensibly, the Marconi company delayed construction, supposedly incensed by the details of the agreement with RCA, which gave the U.S. company a majority of directors in the joint company. But in fact the shareholders of the Argentinean subsidiary were not prepared to sell out at a loss to the joint company, and after investigation the British government concluded that the British Marconi company had gained the original concession without intending to erect a transmitter, and the whole enterprise had been something of a stock market scam at the expense of the Argentinean investors.[10]

Eventually, in order to avoid duplicating infrastructure in what were still underdeveloped markets, the two companies agreed that they should collaborate with their French and German competitors. Then, in December 1921, RCA, Marconi, Compagnie Générale de Télégraphie sans Fils, and Gesellschaft für Drahtlose Telegraphie m. b. H agreed to form a trust, to last until 1945.[11] Under the agreement the partners were to hold equal shares in the trust, but RCA was to appoint the chair, "'thus carrying the principle of the Monroe doctrine into the field of communications in the Western Hemisphere and giving the Americans effective leadership.'"[12]

The intention was to form national companies in each of the South American countries south of Panama "for the conducting of their international communication service" and headed by a national of the country (Tribolet 1929:61). In the first such agreement the companies agreed to allocate wavelengths for long-distance international communications, and they adopted a policy of noninterconnection with stations in South America that belonged to other companies.

Eventually, both the State Department and the Commerce Department repealed the Daniels South American circular of 1916 that advocated government ownership and agreed to back the combine. And with the backing of Herbert Hoover, the new secretary of commerce, the navy also lent its support (Schwoch 1990:297). Although RCA held only 25 percent of the stock, the combine was designated an "American" company, which entitled it to government support (Hogan 1977:144–45). By 1925 the company had stations in Argentina, Brazil, Colombia (previously a British station), and Chile, and U.S. government policy had moved to a commitment to "private ownership and management" and private capital as the best means by which to improve radio communications in the hemisphere (Tribolet 1929:69; Hogan 1977:145).

The South American agreement did not cover either the manufacturing of equipment or ship-to-shore communications. However, the companies also agreed to set up an international wireless trust (the Commercial Radio International Committee), which allowed each to use the patents of the others, "thus providing each member undisputed control within its own country of the production of wireless apparatus" (J. D. Tomlinson 1945:57). In effect, the combine had cartelized the worldwide production of wireless equipment.

Soon after its creation RCA also tried to organize a similar international radio consortium to divide up routes from China; the catalyst for this move was the need to replace the slow and expensive Mackay cable. Financed by Japanese government loans, Japanese Mitsui Bussan Kaisha had obtained a thirty-year build-and-operate monopoly concession for wireless telegraph from the Chinese Ministry of Navy in the spring of 1918 to establish a high-power transmitter for communications with the United States, Japan, and Europe. Then, in 1919, British Marconi agreed to set up, with the Chinese Ministry of War, a joint company for the manufacture of wireless equipment. It also gained a monopoly concession for domestic wireless telegraphy. Although under their 1919 traffic agreement RCA had ceded China to British Marconi, it had done so on the ground that Marconi would have a monopoly of wireless communications in China. But then the Japanese began to build their station, and Federal Telegraph reached agreement with another part of the Chinese bureaucracy, the Ministry of Communications, for a "joint partnership" to establish direct wireless communications between

China and overseas (Tribolet 1929:99). In turn, the Danish government protested on behalf of Great Northern and the British government on behalf of the Eastern and Marconi, while the U.S. government cited its principle of the Open Door as justification for its support for Federal Telegraph (Kirwin 1953:274). RCA saw the clash between these various interests as providing the opportunity for its own entry into China (Tribolet 1929:98n.38). But recognizing that, with 50 percent of its trans-Pacific traffic coming from Japan, the company could not afford to offend the Japanese government, RCA's Owen Young put forward the idea of a consortium that brought together the Americans, English, French, Germans, and Japanese under Chinese chairmanship to provide international wireless communications for China. However, the proposed agreement ran afoul of Hoover's commitment to the Open Door policy and an administration in favor of market competition.

On the ground that doing so would test British support for an Open Door in China, the U.S. State Department backed the Federal Telegraph Company of California.[13] The U.S. legation in China was instructed to put its weight behind the Federal's bid. Chinese hesitance in the face of British and Japanese objections then provoked arm twisting in relation to the upcoming Washington conference on arms limitation of 1922. The U.S. government prevailed. The Federal Telegraph Company signed a $4 million contract with the Chinese Ministry of Communications (Rossi 1985:38).

At the conference RCA's Young tried to round up support for his consortium proposal. The French delegation proposed a resolution supporting the cartel, but the U.S. government amended it, claiming that competition was the "American" way and coordination the "European" way. Subsequent attempts by the British government to settle the dispute failed to move the Harding administration.

The conference eventually agreed to Chinese government demands that all radio stations within China should be owned by the Chinese government. Where foreign stations within legations were allowed to remain, it was agreed that they should transmit only official business and would agree on wavelengths with the Chinese government (Tribolet 1929:130–31). This agreement meant that the U.S. legation's radio station could no longer be used to disseminate news to the Chinese press to counter Japanese influence.

Yet because the Chinese government was in danger of defaulting on loans, Federal Telegraph lacked long-distance wireless experience, and RCA was operating its existing Pacific service at a loss, even the backing of the State Department, Commerce Department, and President Harding could not secure for Federal Telegraph the financing it needed from the sale of Chinese government bonds. When Federal Telegraph proved unable to finance the contract, the State Department and the U.S. Navy proposed that RCA join Federal Telegraph in its China bid. Renaud (1985) concludes that the incident was yet another example of big business's exerting its power and pursuing its own interests, rather than those of the United States.

However, although the two companies set up a subsidiary in 1922, the Federal Telegraph Company of Delaware, the transmitter was never built. According to an RCA official, speaking in 1928, "as everyone else knew, the Federal Company had contracted for an unnecessarily expensive equipment in China, so naturally the Chinese didn't push the project" (Tribolet 1929:139). Both the British and Japanese objected to the RCA-Federal concession. And although the State Department did eventually agree to an arrangement with the British that would reserve most of the U.S.-China traffic for RCA, the Japanese opposed the arrangement. Because the Chinese government had refused to pay for the Mitsui transmitter, which had proved to be unsatisfactory, the Japanese wanted a "four-power monopoly of all China radio business, one that would take in their unprofitable and inefficient Mitsui station, near Peking" (Hogan 1977:152–53).

During this standoff the Japanese used their stations within Manchuria for broadcasting, while a French-owned radio station continued to operate from a hotel in Shanghai. Although the Chinese government turned a blind eye to these violations of its sovereignty, it refused to allow the importation of radio sets. In 1927 at the International Radiotelegraphic Conference in Washington, D.C., the Chinese renewed their opposition to foreign radio stations in the leased territories, railway zones, or legations (Tribolet 1929:148–49). In effect, the Chinese used international telegraph conferences to strengthen their sovereignty.

The Marconi company was about to sell a shortwave transmitter to the Chinese government when its amalgamation with the Eastern in 1927 and the station's potential competition with cables put an end to the transaction. Meanwhile, filling the gap left by the British and U.S. companies, in 1927 Telefunken sold to a pro-Japan Chinese warlord a shortwave transmitter that could transmit to Berlin. Although RCA would not recognize the Chinese station by communicating directly with it (because it still wanted to complete the Federal contract), the company was prepared to receive traffic from the station via Berlin (Tribolet 1929:145). As a result of this confusion, during the 1920s all traffic from China to the United States went either by British cables or German radio.

Because the majority of trans-Pacific traffic was with Japan, RCA chose to concentrate on this profitable route, despite the lack of communications channels across the Pacific. RCA opened service to Hong Kong and "thin" routes to the Dutch East Indies and French Indochina only in 1925. Because of the cable concession granted to the British by Spain before its loss of the Philippines, RCA could not connect to China from Manila until 1928, and then it was allowed entry only to Shanghai. Finally, in 1930, when the cable concessions lapsed, RCA was allowed to provide full service to China (Herring and Gross 1936:85).

At first it seemed that the lower costs and tariffs of wireless would drive the cable companies out of business.[14] But Western Union and the Commercial Cable's Postal Telegraph Company used their control of the "last mile" of the domestic telegraph network to block RCA. Both refused to collect or deliver traffic for RCA, forcing the company to establish offices in the major centers of New York, Boston, Washington, D.C., and San Francisco. Subsequently, Western Union agreed to collect and deliver cables for RCA's trans-Pacific service, but until 1931 Western Union and Postal Telegraph refused to collect traffic for the transatlantic service and refused to carry incoming traffic for it, except on the payment of retail rates by RCA. Postal Telegraph, whose offices were not as numerous as Western Union's, took the same line about delivery of transatlantic traffic and collected that traffic at only some of its offices. As a result of these interconnection bottlenecks, during its first nine years RCA delivered to the telegraph companies ten times as many transatlantic messages as it received from the companies (Herring and Gross 1936:262–63). The cable companies also controlled the capacity of the transatlantic radiotelegraph service by allowing congestion on the landlines between New York and Canada, over which their messages received priority. Coupled with the summer static that reduced transmission speed, it was not until 1923 that the one-third difference between cable and wireless transatlantic rates so eroded cable traffic that the cable companies felt compelled to drop their transatlantic charges (W. Baker 1970:124). The cable companies reacted by bringing RCA into the pool. Under an agreement of 1923, they reduced cable rates by 20 percent and raised radio rates so that there was no longer any rate differential (Schreiner 1924:222).

By the second year after this agreement the cable companies had brought their traffic back to the level of 1923, but part of the reason for cable's resurgence was the laying of a new Western Union "loaded" cable that nearly bankrupted the company (Brown 1927:97–98). The threat to Western Union's business was such that, during the 1920s, RCA and Western Union discussed the possibility that RCA would take over Western Union's international operations. But by then RCA's $4.8 million in international sales and services were only a small part of the company's gross income of $65 million, and it concluded that it should concentrate on domestic broadcasting (Sobel 1982:61).

International and Domestic Regulation, 1927–34

After World War I the State Department came under increasing pressure to rescind the 1916 Daniels circular to Latin American legations that had encouraged public ownership of radio. Among others, United Fruit had complained that the circular was hampering private enterprise, and both companies and associations of large users had come together to influence government policy (Schwoch 1990:293–94). But the circular had already taken root on a much-changed continent. In 1923 the Fifth International Conference of American States adopted a resolution recommending that states belonging to the Pan-American Union should be guided by the principle that international electrical communications were a public utility and should therefore be under government supervision. They also agreed that, insofar as internal communications formed a part of international communications, they should be regarded in the same way.[15] In 1924 at the Mexico City Conference on Inter-American Communications, fifteen Latin American states adopted further articles that contradicted the U.S. position.[16]

The 1924 conference also proposed that one international telegraph convention should govern both radio and telegraphs; that an inter-American union of electrical communications be established; that all communication facilities within each state be placed under one agency; that each state should construct additional landlines and wireless stations to interconnect with each other; and that governments should control broadcasting. Detailed regulations along the lines of the ITU regulations allowed senders to specify routes, and the signatories agreed to a coordinated plan in relation to tariffs that was based on that for postal services. The whole agreement was anathema to the Americans, who refused to sign.[17] Instead, the State Department used the occasion to underline its reversal of the 1916 Daniels circular supporting government ownership of radio facilities. The United States reaffirmed its commitment to "'private ownership and management'" and recommended "'private initiative and the investment of private capital'" as the best means of improving radio communications in the hemisphere.[18] Perhaps because of this public opposition by the United States, only four of the Latin American states had signed the agreement by the time of the Washington radio conference in 1927.

In Paris in 1926 the telegraph regulations were revised for the first time since before the war. Even though the United States was not a member of the International Telegraph Union and did not have the right to vote, it sent a large delegation with representatives from all the large U.S. companies (J. D. Tomlinson 1945:64). The conference agreed that the International Consultative Technical Committee on Long-Distance Telephone and a similar committee on the telegraph, set up the previous year with a permanent secretariat, should become part of the ITU. These bodies were subsequently to form the core of the organization's technical standardization work (Codding 1972:34–36). The conference also set up a preparatory committee to draw up a "more precise and universal set of telephone regulations" (Codding 1972:36).

At the 1926 Paris conference, following up on a decision made at the 1912 radiotelegraph conference in London to which the United States had entered no reservation, the articles of the telegraph convention were made applicable to radio, insofar as they were "not contrary to the provision of the Radio Telegraph Regulations" (J. D. Tomlinson 1945:65). Point-to-point communications via wireless therefore became subject to international regulations concerning charging and accounting between administrations. The decision did not find universal favor. Even a former British Post Office official, such as Frank James Brown, argued that the system of rate setting for the international telegraph, which depended on a division between intra- and extra-European and transit traffic, not distance, was irrational, inflexible, and a barrier to innovation (Brown 1927:129–30). Because the 1926 conference brought RCA and AT&T under the telegraph regulations, the United States had to get this position rescinded at the 1927 conference on radio communications in Washington, D.C.

Despite the chaos of competitive radio stations, in 1925 and 1926 the U.S. courts ruled that under the Radio Communications Act of 1912 no station could be refused a license. In response, only months before the long-delayed postwar conference on the international aspects of radio communications was to be held in Washington, President Calvin Coolidge proposed legislation that would assign the granting of licenses to a board that would meet whenever action became necessary (Luther 1988:27). Therefore the impossibility of operating a free market in the radio spectrum led to the acceptance of national regulation. The 1927 Radio Act established the five-member Federal Radio Commission (forerunner of the Federal Communications Commission) whose mandate had to be renewed annually; the board was to regulate "all forms of interstate and foreign radio transmission and communications within the United States, its territories and possessions" but did not have authority with regard to the Philippines or the Panama Canal Zone (Clark 1931:227). By passing overall responsibility from the navy's Bureau of

Navigation to the Department of Commerce, the act marked radio's move from primarily a marine matter to one of general commerce. In precluding the joint operation of wireless and cable, the act (sect. 17) followed the position that would be adopted at the international conference of 1927. This may have been an instance of the international's determining the domestic.

Preparations for the 1927 International Radiotelegraphic Conference began two years before with committees from the Departments of War, Navy, and Commerce working with technical experts from the industry (Clark 1931:229). As host country, the United States managed the conference, maneuvering to replace with more friendly faces the European nominees for chairs of committees put forward by the Berne secretariat (Tribolet 1929:26). In all, forty-one companies from eleven countries attended the conference, but only RCA and GE were actually directly represented within a government delegation (J. D. Tomlinson 1945:136n). As the assistant secretary of state later said of the convention: "'The radio companies practically wrote it'" (quoted in Clark 1931:195–96).

The most notable absentee was the Soviet Union. Although eligible to attend as a signatory of the 1912 London Radiotelegraphic Convention and interested enough to submit a whole new set of proposed service regulations, it was denied admission on the ground that the United States did not recognize the Soviet Union as a sovereign state. Because this allowed the USSR to develop its own radio system with more or less disregard for the international regulations, the decision had serious consequences for the future (J. D. Tomlinson 1945:60). In contrast, Germany demanded and was allowed the six votes that it had held through its colonies, thereby giving the Germans status equal to that of the United States, France, and Great Britain (Clark 1931:192).[19]

Given the U.S. government's previous attempts to exempt itself from specific aspects of international regulation to which its companies objected, the format of the final treaty was a matter of considerable importance. The 1926 decision to include radiotelegraph under the telegraph regulations created problems for the U.S. government if it wished to be a signatory. So that it could sign the convention but escape its rate regulation, the United States proposed that the convention and its regulations be divided into three classes of equal binding force on those states that were signatories to them. The convention itself would contain general provisions; the general regulations would include the provisions that all governments agreed that their operating agencies, whether publicly or privately owned, must follow in the public interest; and a second set of regulations in annex 2 would include all the rules that the countries adhering to the International Radiotelegraphic Convention and Regulations considered to be desirable among themselves—in other words, where government administrations operated radiotelegraph. The United States would not sign this second annex.

Later the U.S. delegation summarized all the provisions that had been adopted but that it was not prepared to accept and asked that they be included in this second annex. These included the provision that the telegraph regulations should apply to radio communications (J. D. Tomlinson 1945:66). In addition, although the United States had no intention of signing the second annex, its delegates softened the language of the regulations, replacing the word *must* with *should* and *obligation* with *suggestion* (Tribolet 1929:58–66).

One interpretation of the U.S. refusal to subscribe to the provisions on traffic and rates, made by a representative of the French Compagnie Générale de T. S. F., was that the U.S. companies wanted a free hand to compete with those that were bound by those regulations in the ship-to-ship and ship-to-shore mobile service (J. D. Tomlinson 1945:101). However, more important to the companies were the new shortwave long-distance services. The effect of placing the clause concerning the telegraph regulations in the additional regulations was that the radiotelephone was regulated only in Europe, and transatlantic telephone service was not subject to any international regulation, thereby benefiting AT&T (J. D. Tomlinson 1945:102).

The U.S. companies gained what they wanted from the conference—a lack of restriction on their operations. Under the new regulations the principle of obligatory interconnection was extended to the fixed service, thereby ensuring that government-controlled telegraph administrations could not lock out RCA. And the proposal to allocate wavelengths to specific services, rather than to states (which followed both the European agreement and that of RCA and Marconi in South America), allowed for the expansion of radio beyond national borders and therefore protected the interests of the U.S. companies in Latin America and Asia. In the words of Herbert Hoover, the president of the conference:

"In realization of the limited number of channels or wave lengths . . . at one time it was proposed that the use of these channels through the ether should be divided among the different countries of the world. . . . This Conference has found a basic solution by dividing the channels into groups, each being used for a particular variety in communication. To pursue the analogy further, the solution which all have happily agreed upon is that lanes are established across the sea which are devoted to specific types of service, all nations being free to engage in that special form of traffic upon these particular lanes." (quoted in Tribolet 1929:39)

Before the 1927 conference there had been only a rough allocation of wavelengths to mobile services in the Berlin and London regulations. A draft table of allocation of waves between 60 and 1,500 kilocycles per second (200 to 5,000 meters) was drawn up at the technical committee in Paris that followed the 1920 preliminary conference, which was held in preparation for the Washington conference of 1921. But the table was no more than a guide to governments, which tended to assign frequencies to favored national services without consideration of international consequences. This behavior was particularly common in Europe, where the major growth of radio had been in broadcasting, which was not covered in the London 1912 radiotelegraphic regulations (J. D. Tomlinson 1945:134).

A further problem in allocation was the existing capital investment by shipping in what had become technically outmoded spark transmitters that could use only a small number of frequencies in the medium and long waves. The lobby of the shipping owners, supported by the maritime powers (United States and Britain), conflicted with continental European broadcast interests. Further, the International Commission for Aerial Navigation asked for several small bands between 150 and 300 kilocycles per second (1,000 to 2,000 meters) for the aeronautical services, while the Germans and Japanese wanted extensive portions of long waves designated for military and naval services.

Negotiations about frequency allocation took place informally between the larger delegations, with the U.S. delegation presenting the eventual draft amid controversy. "The bitterness of certain countries which had been left out of the private negotiations helped to throw some light on how the agreement had been reached. The determination of the smaller European countries to fight for greater allocations to broadcasting services than had been included in the drafts, prevented any steamroller tactics of the great powers from forcing their draft upon them," J. D. Tomlinson reports (1945:141). The final compromise solution was to require all existing broadcasting stations outside the authorized bands to alter their wavelengths within one year and to allow no new long-wave broadcasting stations unless they caused no interference with existing stations. This solution immediately penalized those countries, such as Greece, which had not yet established a broadcasting service. Because the long-wave band assigned to broadcasting had room for only twelve stations, and there were seventeen operating outside that band that would have to shift into it, satisfying the broadcasting interests and the smaller countries in Europe was impossible (J. D. Tomlinson 1945:180). The failure of the conference to take into account the needs of smaller European countries led to separate European conferences.

Other conflicts at the Washington conference arose because the United

States was seeking to protect RCA and its mobile shipping service from the European radio companies, which wanted to reserve to fixed point-to-point services the portion of the long-wave spectrum that U.S. ships used to call home from Europe (J. D. Tomlinson 1945:150–51). Eventually, it was agreed that the table of allocations should apply to new but not existing services—thereby allowing existing services and the interference that they caused to continue.

The United States also insisted that, provided it did not cause interference to another country, each country should be free to assign any wavelength to any service. This provision left all problems of interference in Canada and Mexico to be sorted out bilaterally and proved unworkable in Europe (Luther 1988:29; J. D. Tomlinson 1945:159). The treaty also allowed regional agreements on allocation, thereby accepting that the western hemisphere would be treated separately from the eastern. The provision allowed U.S. companies to protect their investments in Latin America and to create a bloc with which to present their interests at future conferences (Luther 1988:31; Schwoch 1990:77).

Only on the question of an international technical consultative committee, demanded by Germany, was the alliance of the United States and Britain defeated on a vote (Tribolet 1929:37). British and U.S. opposition hinged on fears that such a committee would attempt to control the development of radio. However, although they lost on the general principle, they were able to rein in the committee's power by making it "newly constituted for each meeting," rather than a permanent body. In addition, so that the United States could be adequately represented at the technical committee's meetings, private companies were not only allowed committee membership in a consultative capacity but could also represent administrations and vote (Clark 1931:202). For the first time private companies gained voting privileges within an international body that would draw up regulations.

At the time one legal authority recognized the convention as "'the international expression of the national law,'" yet the description is not accurate (quoted in Clark 1931:229). The U.S. Radio Act of 1927 had introduced licensing and the power to withhold licenses. In the international sphere the system introduced was based on first come, first served, so the most advanced nations took the majority of spectrum, and research and development became the province of the private sector. Yet those principles, first adopted at the 1927 conference, remained unchanged into the twenty-first century.

In implementing the international convention, one of the first tasks of the Federal Radio Commission was to determine whether users might create their own private networks by using shortwave. The issue arose because of the assignments of frequencies for shortwave point-to-point communications made at the 1927 conference. The United States had laid claim to seventy-four of these frequencies; RCA applied for fifty-five and initially received fifteen. RCA's arguments were that shortwave frequencies were so scarce that only it and other common carriers should be allowed to use them. Although it gave frequencies to the press, the commission agreed that individual applications would not be allowed (Herring and Gross 1936:89–90).

As shortwave came on stream in 1930, the radio companies once again gained traffic at the expense of the cable companies (FCC 1940:467). Because revenue from radio transmission, unlike revenue from cable, was not shared with those telegraph agencies whose territory was crossed, and because governments often owned the radio transmitting stations, many foreign agencies favored radio over cable for point-to-point transmission. Western Union, heavily dependent on the transatlantic route, saw its revenue drop from $10 million to $4 million between 1930 and 1938 despite its new loaded cables. In 1938 the company posted a loss of $432,000 (FCC 1940:458). In contrast, RCA was protected from competition by monopoly contracts with European postal, telegraph, and telephone monopoly operators, and its international wireless service prospered (Herring and Gross 1936:87). By World War II, RCA had a worldwide service, linking the United States to forty-seven countries.

The Entrance of ITT

Meanwhile, a new company had come on the U.S. scene, a company that was perceived as the greatest threat to British interests. Sosthenes Behn, born to Danish and French parents in the Virgin Islands, which were then owned by Denmark, formed International Telephone and Telegraph in 1920 after he bought a small telegraph company in Puerto Rico, followed by another in Cuba. With help from the U.S. Commerce Department, International Western Electric Corporation (AT&T's manufacturer), and its U.S. bank, National City, which was then involved in restructuring Spain's debt, in 1923 ITT gained the concession to run the Spanish telephone service, against competition from Siemens of Germany and Ericsson of Sweden (Sobel 1982:38). With a commitment to local procurement, and a board that included political allies of Spain's dictator, Gen. Miguel Primo de Rivera, the Spanish company became the model for ITT's penetration of other countries. In return for a pledge that the Spanish telephone system would not be nationalized for twenty years, ITT promised to have it up and running within five years and accepted a rate of return of 8 percent. As far as is known, this is the first example of domestic rate-of-return regulation.

By 1924 ITT's annual report stated that it intended "'to develop truly national systems operated by the nationals of each country'" (quoted in Sampson 1973:23). However, the Spanish experience held other lessons—the importance of connecting the supply of equipment and operation. Control of local manufacture became paramount. So in 1925, when AT&T, anticipating antitrust action from a government concerned that domestic consumers were cross-subsidizing its international activities, split off some of its international manufacturing activities from its domestic, ITT bought International Western Electric for $30 million, thereby gaining factories in fifteen countries (Young 1983:52). By 1930, of the three major manufacturing groups in Europe—ITT, Ericsson, and Siemens (linked with AT&T)—ITT was the largest, with manufacturing subsidiaries in every country in Europe except Scandinavia, Poland, and Yugoslavia. ITT owned twenty-four factories outright and employed thirty to thirty-five thousand workers in Europe (Southard 1931:43–56). At a time when nationalistic governments were demanding local production, ITT's manufacturing companies became identified as "local" companies. In addition, in 1931 the company was successful in buying into Swedish Ericsson and carved up the supply of telephone equipment to Latin America through cartel arrangements with Siemens, Ericsson, and General Electric (Sampson 1973:25).

Nevertheless, by the mid-1920s, although ITT had grown in five years to a corporation with revenues of more than $17 million and assets of slightly less than $100 million, it was still basically a federation of national operating and manufacturing companies, not a multinational company. Just as AT&T had gained national dominance through the interconnection of local telephone companies, so ITT looked for a means of interconnection between its separated holdings and the United States. It looked to control of domestic operation and equipment supply, together with control of international communication, to provide the greatest profit potential.

The acquisition of All America Cables in 1926 created the means of interconnecting ITT's national operating companies and the United States in what became known as "the international system" (FCC 1940:454). The ownership of All America's system from Central America down the west coast to Peru operated as a beachhead into Latin America, giving Behn his introduction to governments. By the late 1920s ITT was perceived as the spearhead "for a vigorous, powerful and expanding American international capitalism" (Sobel 1982:47).

Behn's objective was to take over as many telephone companies as possible in Latin America and to displace the mainly British concessionaires. He was backed by two U.S. banks, Morgan Stanley and National City, that were

among the leaders of the U.S. financial institutions that were gradually replacing the British on the South American continent. Using the lure of local
manufacturing capacity, by 1929 ITT had taken over the domestic operators
in Mexico, Uruguay, Chile, Argentina, and Peru and a small company in Brazil. Each was then linked with the All America cable to funnel international
traffic to Europe through the United States. In other words, ITT used manufacturing jobs to create leverage for operational control of both domestic
and international communications (Sobel 1982:535). By the 1930s, as the
United States became mired in the depression, ITT was becoming entrenched
in Latin America as both manufacturer and operator. Because Western Union
had bought the Mexican Telegraph Company in 1926 and hooked up with
ITT's submarine cables down the west coast of South America, these two
companies operated a U.S.-controlled network that funneled traffic from
South and Central America to New York and London (Brown 1927:20–21).[20]
Toward the end of the 1920s ITT further expanded its international links to
South America by purchasing the French-owned United States and Haiti
Telegraph and Cable Company with cables from New York via Haiti to Ven-
ezuela and northern Brazil. With this move ITT gained an east coast route
and encircled South America (Brown 1927:21).

   ITT's international network was further extended by its acquisition of
Clarence Mackay's Postal Telegraph and Commercial Cable companies in
1928 (which in turn had bought the Federal Telegraph radio link to Hawaii
in 1927). Commercial Cable owned and managed seven transatlantic submarine cables and the trans-Pacific cable. Postal Telegraph was Western Union's
only domestic competitor. Although in 1927 its share of domestic traffic was
only 17 percent, acquiring Postal Telegraph gave Behn entry into domestic
operation (Sobel 1982:58–59). With control of sixty-three thousand miles of
submarine cable, ITT was in a better position to meet competition from the
British cable and wireless interests. By using shortwave radio it also competed
with the RCA-led combine in Latin America (Fejes 1986:23).

   In the late 1920s, after Western Union proposed to sell its international
business, RCA's banker, J. P. Morgan, suggested instead that RCA should help
create a major entity in international communications around ITT. The catalyst was the formation of the British Cable and Wireless and other similar
amalgamations in France, Germany, and Italy.[21] In 1928 negotiation between
the two companies began.

   But in the interests of competition the U.S. Radio Act of 1927 had forbidden the merger of radio and cable companies. Owen Young of RCA addressed
the Senate Committee on Interstate Commerce about lifting antitrust legislation to allow the merger. He argued from the point of view that "'in inter-

national communications the United States ought to be supreme,'" pleading with senators that "'if you have any hesitation about unifying our external communications in the hands of a private company, then I beg of you, in the national interest, to unify them under government ownership in order that America may not be left, in the external communications field, subject to the dictation and control of foreign companies or governments'" (quoted in Sobel 1982:65). But some members of Congress were against the merger, and in the meantime the stock market crashed. By then the potential threat of the British had also faded away. In 1931 the two companies, RCA and ITT, announced that they had called off their merger talks (Sobel 1982:66–67). Because ITT served U.S. interests, and its subsidiaries were wholly U.S. owned, Congress allowed the company to retain ownership of both cable and radio facilities, although four of the twenty-three directors of ITT's holding company and two of its twenty-two officers were foreigners and it was therefore in contravention of the intent of the Radio Act of 1927 (Sidak 1997:66). ITT, RCA, and Western Union all continued to provide international telegraph, and AT&T continued to provide international telephone communications.

The Senate may have refused to bless the merger of RCA and ITT because the senators did not accept that ITT, about one-fifth owned by foreign nationals (along the lines of Marconi of America), was an "American" company. This suspicion of ITT later was fueled by its connections to Nazi Germany. However, when these connections began, links between U.S. and German business were perfectly normal. In fact, German businesses had floated $826 million in bonds on Wall Street in the ten years before 1931, and many U.S. companies, including IBM and General Electric, had made investments in Germany. At one point General Electric had even attempted to take over Siemens. Thus when ITT and GE purchased three German equipment manufacturers in 1930 and placed them in a holding company, Standard Elektricitäts Gesellschaft (SEG), they were acting respectably. ITT's actions became suspect only after General Electric sold out and the Nazis came to power.

After suffering losses in 1932, ITT began to work with Hitler in 1933 in rearming Germany and appointed leading Nazis to its boards. ITT companies were declared "German" and therefore exempt from seizure of assets under Hitler's Custodian of Alien Property decrees (Sampson 1973:29). In Spain ITT sided with General Franco during the civil war, but after he won, the company had to pressure the State Department to prevent Franco from handing the telephone company to the Germans (Sobel 1982:87).

The beginning of World War II led Behn to draw back on the idea of an international system. He moved research facilities out of Paris before the

occupation and relocated those scientists to the United States, where he began manufacturing military, rather than telephonic, equipment. By 1945 ITT's
major business was manufacturing, and this U.S. bid to take on British hegemony over cable communications had ended (Sobel 1982:105).

Federal Regulation

President Franklin D. Roosevelt set up the interdepartmental committee that
recommended the establishment of the Federal Communications Commission (FCC) to unify the various separate systems of regulation and envisaged
that the FCC would fulfill a number of functions. It was expected to reduce
tariffs by regulating company profits and annual depreciation charges; control discrimination in favor of some customers and the exclusive contracts
that the companies had set up with hotels, railroads, and foreign countries;
prevent the "watering" of stocks (increasing debt, thereby devaluing current
shares); and create universal networks (Herring and Gross 1936:414). Congress had hurriedly approved the Communications Act of 1934, and it only
marginally expanded the provisions of the Radio Act of 1927, and of the
Mann-Elkins Act of 1910 as it applied to the Interstate Commerce Commission. The FCC gained responsibility for the regulation of cable rates, but the
president still held the right to delegate the issuing of cable landing licenses
under the 1921 Kellogg act. However, President Roosevelt had anticipated that
the new body might wish to alter the regulatory framework, and the Communications Act of 1934 gave the FCC the power to investigate the market
and recommend new regulatory arrangements to Congress (Herring and
Gross 1936:415).

But the FCC soon was seeking additional powers to oversee international
communications. It wanted to be able to insist that international consolidation did not prevent the expansion of international communications, which
meant that it could require such companies to install a radio or cable circuit
to wherever the FCC felt doing so was in the public interest. The FCC also
wanted the power to stop the dismantling of a cable or radio link. Behind
this proposal lay its problems with AT&T, which despite pressure from the
FCC, as well as the army and navy, refused to set up a direct telephone link
with Paris until 1935. The company had cited technical reasons for preferring
to have a link only with Britain (FCC 1940:476).

The technical problem was that the distance from Rugby, where the British Post Office had its transmitter, and the East Coast of the United States
was about the longest over which long-wave telephony was possible. Also,
available long waves were scarce. Shortwave was still unreliable because of

the transatlantic static. As with submarine cables, radio technology favored Britain's geographic location. Britain had no such technical problems in reaching the various parts of its empire.[22] As a result London was still the world's switching center and Rugby its chief relay station (Appleton 1933:11).

Tapping into a debate that had been going on since 1933—should radio-telegraph and cable companies merge?—the FCC was concerned that, where two or more U.S. companies competed for the business controlled by a single foreign administration (government-controlled telegraph and telephone agency), U.S. interests were endangered. It argued that competition between carriers placed them in a poor bargaining position with unified foreign carriers (such as British Cable and Wireless) and made them liable to pressure from foreign administrations to reduce tariffs, with the result that "effective regulation becomes practically impossible." The FCC wanted contracts between the carriers and foreign administrations to be subject to FCC approval, to prevent "whipsawing," by which British Cable and Wireless had reduced rates by 20 percent for Western Union but not other carriers (FCC 1940:479). Also, cables were in decline. The proportion of international traffic taken by radio had increased from 18 percent in 1930 to 32 percent in 1938. The FCC concluded that "the present unfavorable status of the cable carriers . . . indicates the desirability of some action looking toward elimination of destructive competition in this field" (FCC 1940:464). For these reasons, and on the basis that there was already a monopoly of domestic and international telephone, the FCC favored consolidation of the five U.S. cable carriers and seven radio international telegraph carriers into one carrier.

In addition, the Joint Board of the Army and Navy wanted the companies and the armed services to collaborate in research and development (Herring and Gross 1936:421). But the board would not contemplate sharing military secrets with companies that employed foreign nationals or in which they held voting stock. Bowing to these demands, the FCC recommended that the company formed from the existing companies should therefore exclude foreign nationals from employment and should have no more that 20 percent of its stock held by them.

That the FCC was unable to get its proposals off the ground can be regarded as partly the result of conflict within its own ranks and partly navy opposition. During congressional discussion of the financial restructuring of ITT, the U.S. Navy pressed for cable and radio to be completely separate. Its arguments were based first on the experience of British Cable and Wireless, where declining cable interests had become dominant in a unified system.[23] Second, it argued for separation on the basis that other countries could exercise control over cable communications that crossed their territory, which raised the possibility of "divided loyalty of employees" (FCC 1940:472–73). A majority of the FCC commissioners disagreed with the navy. But a minority, leaning more toward traditional concern with rates rather than strategy, disagreed with both plans. Instead, these commissioners preferred competition as the best way to reduce rates.

The FCC also acknowledged its problems in regulating international communications. It had even considered the possibility of placing government representatives on the board of the carriers "in order that it may participate in the management of these companies as a further means of protecting the national interest" but had decided against it (FCC 1940:479). Because of the companies' attitude toward international regulation, the majority of FCC commissioners were hostile to both AT&T and Western Union. "In the meetings that took place in the offices of the FCC during the two years prior to the Cairo conference [in 1932] these carriers used every available means to prevent any commitment by this Government with respect to participation in the regulations" (FCC 1940:476–77). Also, foreign nationals had represented both companies at international conferences.

The FCC's report to Congress concluded that "the national public interest can hardly be served by a continuance of the helter-skelter method of development with its lack of co-ordination, its weak bargaining position, its useless duplications, and its failure to supply a comprehensive unified plan of international communications" (1940:472–73). But with the navy and the companies against regulation, the FCC was unsuccessful in gaining legislation that would give it teeth. All such proposals were to be sidelined by the U.S. entry in World War II, when cables suddenly became important to security. In 1938 the U.S. government took control of the transatlantic cables. And, concerned that their government might merge them with the cables, the U.S. radio companies pressed the U.S. government for direct entry to the British colonies, which they eventually achieved in 1942.

International Regulation

The 1927 Washington conference, dominated by the U.S. radio companies, was a watershed in the international regulation of the radio spectrum. Increasingly, companies came to influence the debates. J. D. Tomlinson suggests that, although the language justifying this or that proposal was always in terms of the "public interest," it was difficult to actually pinpoint such occasions. In general, he says, nation-states used the international conferences to support the interests of their industry. The presence of companies at conferences gradually increased, from seven in 1912 to sixty-one in Cairo in 1932.

Companies could participate to the extent authorized by the chair of the committee or plenary, but J. D. Tomlinson suggests that their direct participation was less important than their influence on delegations (1945:260). He comments that "at both the Madrid and Cairo conferences direct participation of company representatives in the debates was not as much in evidence as at London and Washington, yet one has the impression that their interests were being cared for by the interested government delegations" (1945: 296). He cites a number of occasions where there was an evident synergy of interest between government and company—U.S., British, and French—but draws a distinction between governments that were acting in the "public interest" and those that were acting in direct response to the companies' private interests, as in the U.S. government's failure to sign the telegraph regulations (J. D. Tomlinson 1945:294–95).

From a European perspective, J. D. Tomlinson reports that at the 1932 Madrid conference foreign governments were especially concerned that U.S. commercial radio interests were attempting to dominate the world broadcasting spectrum. But from a U.S. point of view, Oscar Riegel, a U.S. sociologist attending the conference as an observer, saw it as weighted in favor of the large European powers by virtue of ""colonial"" voting. He also perceived the ""threat of a European raid upon channels previously allocated to the United States."" Although the U.S. companies had managed to have themselves excluded from ITU rate regulation, Riegel was additionally concerned that the conference had ignored the issue of ""free flow of news."" In view of the British government's continued censorship of cable communications, it is ironic that Riegel considered that only the British and Americans, the former protecting their overseas banking interests and the latter concerned for the U.S. news agencies, were worried about the ability of governments to legitimately intercept, censor, or interrupt international radio and telephone communications (Riegel 1934, quoted in Luther 1988:42).

In addition to bringing the U.S. companies into the forefront of determining international policy, the 1927 conference demonstrated a coherent U.S. policy toward radio that was based on a consensus with the industry that had been worked out over the previous eight years. That policy—"private ownership and management of facilities, non-adherence to international agreements, separate radio and cable agreements, representation of American business interests in delegations, government support of American commercial users and operators and a drive to obtain as much spectrum as possible"—then drove U.S. delegations to the international conferences (Schwoch 1987:297). For instance, in Madrid in 1932 it was agreed that the two bureaus for telegraph and radio should be brought together into the International

Telecommunication Union, but because of the objections of the United States and Canada the final convention had regulations for each service—telegraph, telephone, and radio communications. In fact, because the United States would not accept any international regulation of wireless rates, the additional regulations of the 1927 conference had to be carried over—so little changed, although the International Telecommunication Union was officially established in 1932. The provisions of the convention were made binding only for those services covered by the regulations to which the governments were parties (J. D. Tomlinson 1945:73). However, the U.S. delegation stated that it might adhere to the telegraph and telephone regulations once the U.S. government established a domestic agency to cover both radio and cable (1945:76).

Then, before the 1938 conference the United States weighted the proceedings against the Europeans by bringing a position to which all delegations from the western hemisphere had already agreed. According to J. D. Tomlinson, after the United States opposed the convention of the 1924 Inter-American Committee on Electrical Communications, the Mexican government invited North and Central American governments to a conference on radio communications in 1933. This conference also ended in disagreement (1945:246–47).

The Cuban government then organized a preliminary radiotelegraphic conference in the spring of 1937 to which it invited radio experts from the United States, Canada, and Mexico. The intention was to arrive at technical agreements for consideration by a general American conference later in the year. This first Inter-American Conference on Radio Communications, at which sixteen states were represented, was held in Havana in November 1937 under the hemispheric agreement of the 1927 Washington conference.

The ensuing convention was signed by all the participants except Argentina, but all signed an inter-American arrangement on radio communications, a regional agreement on broadcasting, and a final act embodying a number of propositions to be submitted to the international conference in Cairo (J. D. Tomlinson 1945:247). Although the Madrid International Radiotelegraphic Conference had not allocated any shortwave frequencies, the Inter-American Conference in Havana agreed that some should be allocated for "research and experimental use."

Although the inter-American agreement would not take effect until 1938 and had not been approved by all its signatories, the U.S. delegation to the Cairo conference used its shortwave allocation against the proposals made by the United Kingdom, France, and Germany. J. D. Tomlinson concludes that "the Havana allocations were made with a view to prevent a universal allocation of these frequencies which might be contrary to the interests of the United States" (1945:251). He comments that "the action of the American countries, and particularly the influence of the United States in using the Inter-American Conference as a lever for imposing its will on the Cairo Conference was resented by a number of European delegations at Cairo" (1945: 251n.5). Because it was impossible to reach universal agreement, one French delegate commented that the final spectrum allocation should read, "The Entire World minus the United States of America" (1945:176).

In addition, at Cairo the position within the ITU of the Consultative Committee on Radio was strengthened. The United States, Britain, and Italy joined together to oppose any overhaul of this committee's organization that would ensure continuity and coordination. But then Italy supported a provision that extended the committee's responsibility from the study of technical radio questions to questions of operation—thereby bringing within its purview the consideration of rates (J. D. Tomlinson 1945:274–75). Together the United States and Britain could not protect the interests of their companies against the combined voting power of the French, Germans, Italians, and the rest of the world.

Conclusion

This chapter illustrates how the overall ideology of U.S. administrations ebbed and flowed between free trade and mercantilism and how international and domestic politics were linked. Sometimes the two policies were played side by side, with demands for free trade in international forums at the diplomatic level and mercantilist responses by individual parts of the state at a lower level. For instance, in the immediate postwar Paris peace negotiations, while the State Department was attempting to liberalize submarine cable monopolies, the U.S. Navy, at the president's behest, was building RCA as a state-backed corporation and undertaking the expropriation of the assets of Marconi of America.

The latter policy resulted from naval coordination of patents in wartime and unsuccessful attempts by the navy and the State Department to nationalize wireless communications. It followed from their policy of pressing nationalization of radio on Latin America in order to prevent European control of the hemisphere's international radio communications. Once RCA had been created from the existing power bloc of manufacturing interests within the sector, and U.S. technical supremacy was seemingly assured, the navy and the State Department could return diplomatically to the policy of liberalization and private control of wireless.

Although RCA then defied that policy by forming a cartel with the British and Germans in South America, and only 25 percent of the resulting combine was U.S. owned, this did not prevent its backing by the new Harding administration. In general, during the early postwar period the actions of U.S. companies contradicted U.S. attempts at international diplomatic leadership.

International conferences, such as the preliminary conference in Washington, became part of the State Department's strategy to alter the balance of power in cable communications away from the British. When the Wilson administration's proposal for an electrical communications council failed because of U.S. companies' opposition, and because U.S. support for foreign liberalization contradicted government policy regarding the monopolies held by the Scrymser company, the Harding administration turned to opening up specific markets—South America, the Azores, and China. Yet in both the Azores and China the companies entered into joint ventures and cartels to gain entry—a policy directly contrary to that of the U.S. government. Eventually, the United States accepted cartels.

One might suspect that the U.S. communications companies at this point were almost impervious to political pressure, but that would not be correct. Western Union, which was closely linked to government in 1917, claimed that it undertook to create a submarine link with Brazil because of a specific request from the Wilson administration. But then, demonstrating the weakness of the U.S. political system in the face of strong business lobbies, Scrymser's company saw that its future as the main conduit from Brazil to the United States was threatened. The resulting scenario, in which Western Union challenged the power of the president of the United States in court, only to face armed militia preventing the landing of the Western Union cable, saw the company demonized as "British" (a form of regulation to increase the power of the state itself). Western Union and AT&T became so alienated that they were represented by the British delegation at the international conference in Cairo in 1932.

But eventually, the Harding administration was able to use the Kellogg Cable Landing Act of 1921 and a model landing license to impose free trade in third markets on U.S., as well as foreign, companies. Unilaterally applying legislation governing landing licenses did what the United States had failed to accomplish through multilateral conventions. Congress also learned from the experience of the Radio Communications Act of 1912, which introduced foreign ownership restrictions but failed to include any element of discretion or the concept of reciprocity in the process of granting a license.

The model landing license, introduced after the 1921 Kellogg act, brought international cable companies under common carrier regulation that was similar to that implemented by the Interstate Commerce Commission. But in order to avoid situations such as that in Brazil, where the links between the Eastern and Western Union had caused so much trouble, all such combines had to have prior state approval. It is not clear on what basis the U.S. government proposed to decide whether a foreign company might link with another or how the provisions of the U.S. Radio Act were implemented, but that power was not specifically mentioned in the Communications Act of 1934, much to the FCC's regret.

Despite this regulation of submarine cable, RCA not only formed a cartel in South America and China but also pursued a policy of not interconnecting with other systems and had monopoly agreements with European governments. And although the Radio Act of 1927 forbade the ownership of radio and cable facilities, ITT was allowed to operate both internationally. Thus the regulation of international cable and wireless was distinctly imbalanced.

In particular, ITT was to take on the mantle of Scrymser in demanding State Department support for its operations in foreign countries. This led to a dichotomy between the macrolevel policies of the U.S. government and those at the microlevel of the firm: free trade versus mercantilism, differentiated according to technology. Whereas in Britain radio was seen as the challenger to the more secure, strategically advantageous, cables and therefore to be held back, in the United States the navy, in particular, saw cable as a declining technology and radio as the technology of the future. Respective regulatory regimes seem to have reflected these priorities.

During this period domestic regulation through the Interstate Commerce Commission was not effective. Although its rulings on interconnection and leased lines were far ahead of any regulation in Britain, it fell down on lack of power to control tariffs. Also, the regulatory divide between the ICC and the regulation of radio allowed the cable companies to hamper the development of RCA's international traffic until 1928, when both the Federal Radio Commission and the provisions of the 1927 international convention on compulsory interconnection for point-to-point wireless systems came into being. In this case, international regulations, put forward to prevent discrimination against RCA by foreign governments, may have strengthened the company's position at home.

Where the United States was successful in international negotiations, it is evident that the companies were as eager as the administration to gain international regulation. So, for instance, the 1927 Washington convention was said to have been written by the companies, with years of planning going into the result. In this case, the companies wanted an institution and regulatory mechanism to oversee the global allocation and registration of wave bands to services. The U.S. administration might have been defeated by its own companies' opposition, as it was in 1921, if the convention had not been structured to allow the United States not to sign those regulations to which the companies objected. This was the first international convention that the U.S. companies dominated, but the experience gained here allowed them to lead U.S. policy at future conferences. And, by using the expanded powers of the Consultative Committee on Radio and the inter-American conferences to give it a voting bloc at ITU conferences, by the beginning of World War I the U.S. government had found a means to impose itself on what it continued to regard as a European organization. Yet, as was to become obvious later, this "power" was gained only at the expense of assuming a harmony of interests between the companies and the state. By 1939 one can see the frustration of the Federal Communications Commission in being able to call on no "national interest," other than the various companies' interests, in order to justify international action.

When the FCC was first created, the focus was on domestic, not international, regulation. Yet it soon wanted powers to plan overall international communications links. In common with national regulators in the 1990s, it found that, whereas it is possible to regulate tariffs, it is more difficult to produce the positive incentives to investment in particular places or networks. Partly because the companies had to work with foreign companies and administrations every day, their interests and those of the FCC diverged. Neither the FCC nor the armed services had the strategic power held by a body such as the British Cable Landing Rights Committee. The FCC could not order AT&T to invest in a telephone link to Paris, if in so doing the company perceived that it might offend the British.

What particularly concerned the FCC was a system of competition and separation of technologies when other countries were merging them. It therefore moved to a position of supporting the merger of all cable and radio telegraph companies into one company that would control both domestic and international telegraph infrastructure and transmission, along the lines of AT&T. In this way the FCC believed that it could end the European practice of playing one company off against another. The FCC reported, for example, that Cable and Wireless had offered Western Union a 20 percent discount on its international interconnection rates while refusing the same deal to ITT's Commercial Cable Company (FCC 1940:472). This practice, known as "whipsawing," was later banned by the FCC. In order to prevent foreign state monopoly administrations from gaining a competitive advantage, all United States domestic carriers were obliged to abide by the same terms of bilateral agreement as their overseas counterparts—they were not allowed to compete with each other in offering inexpensive interconnection rates for delivering international traffic. The effect was to institutionalize the dominance of Western Union within the U.S. international telegraph market and to increase the cost of international tariffs to consumers.

Also, the FCC found a fragmented industry impossible to regulate, and even considered placing political appointees on company boards in order to do so. The FCC evidently resented both Western Union's and AT&T's refusal to be formally governed by the International Telegraph Convention while accepting those international regulations in practice. The FCC failed in its proposal for a monopoly partly because of the navy's bias toward radio and partly because of the timing, coming as it did in 1939, at the beginning of World War II.

World War I had demonstrated the importance of the press and propaganda and the linkage between communications infrastructure and information transmission. Although the Associated Press was to argue that it alone was a nongovernment-supported press agency, and began a campaign in 1919 for "free flow of information" on that basis, the claim was actually untrue. The press subsidies on cables to South America in World War I were subsequently supplemented by subsidies through naval radio stations in the postwar period. And, unlike the press in the United Kingdom or on the European continent, the U.S. press had its own dedicated shortwave infrastructure and therefore paid at "cost" only. Thus in the interwar period control of information and transmission went hand in hand to ease penetration into Europe and South America.

To sum up, this chapter showed how U.S. policy moved from nationalization to free trade and then to the simultaneous implementation of mercantilist and free-trade ideology on a differential basis for U.S. companies and foreign, and for different technologies. It also showed that international and national markets and regulation were inextricably mixed, with companies pursuing their own interests, whether they conflicted with their government's policy or not. It was already evident that the weakness of the United States in international forums came from the fragmentation of the U.S. political system and the power that companies could wield in that system. Despite taking action against company interests in certain cases, it was primarily through war and the appeal to "national defense" that the U.S. state could gain the power to override those companies' commercial goals.

7. British Communications, 1919–40

During the interwar period the British government attempted to use the empire to boost its international status and trade against a continental Europe increasingly moving toward protection of agriculture and export subsidies. Having liquidated many of its Latin American assets during and immediately after World War I, British investment followed prewar trends, and from 1920 to 1929 almost 25 percent of all new capital issued in London went to various parts of the empire (Drummond 1972:29). Capital investment abroad in that period almost equaled investment at home but fell off during the depression of the 1930s.

Britain's strategic concerns with European stability worked against its commitment to its empire. Also, Britain's commitment to free trade and its need for low-cost raw materials worked against "empire preference," discriminatory tariffs in favor of empire members. Although "Empire Free Trade" was a rallying cry of the Conservative press, led by the newspaper tycoon Lord Beaverbrook, in effect it was no more than a preferential tariff system on a limited range of goods (Drummond 1972:34). The specter of mass unemployment at home led to the Empire Settlement Act of 1922, which assisted would-be emigrants with passage, and to the Colonial Development Act of 1929, which provided capital for infrastructure and the development of primary crops such as cotton.

In turn, as British goods lost their competitive edge, so the proportion of foreign goods imported by the colonies increased, and their overall importance to the British economy decreased. In the 1930s Britain became increasingly protectionist and favored empire-based supplies of agricultural products to those of previous suppliers, such as Argentina. But in 1938 foreigners still supplied more than 60 percent of all British imports (Drummond

1972:21). In the 1930s British capital investment turned inward. Controlled production of commodities, by both the British government and the mainly U.S.-based international cartels, became a factor in world trade in tin, tea, rubber, oil, and copper. Yet because of increasing cartelization and the division of the world market into spheres of activity, in certain industries such as chemicals, iron and steel, and telecommunications, the empire market remained of crucial importance.

Within the empire colonies gradually adopted new constitutional arrangements. As the political and economic futures of the dominions and India became increasingly tied to their regions, Britain allowed them to become more autonomous in their foreign relations. And, as the overall market share of British imports and exports within the empire fell, the empire countries became more integrated, supplying each other with about half of empire imports. Only in the period of 1929–33, when the economy of Britain suffered less from the slump than did the economies of other countries, did exporters within the empire find Britain more important than foreign countries (Drummond 1972:23).

By the 1930s, as the economic crisis hit, the dominions pressed for increased market share and prices for their commodities, but it became evident that Britain's market was not large enough to absorb the total production of their agricultural produce. In an attempt to make its manufactures competitive, Britain came off the gold standard in 1931, only for Canada to immediately impose an import tariff on British goods. The Ottawa conference of 1932, where Britain attempted unsuccessfully to mitigate the protectionism of the dominions, ended any sentimental view of the commonwealth. The British government blocked the establishment of import substitution industries in the dominions. And after 1938 the Anglo-American Agreement on trade meant that the United Kingdom had to absorb more manufactured U.S. goods, implying the end of the empire preference.

Yet despite these changes, British strategic interests demanded the retention of a unified empire. When communications technologies threatened to allow the dominions and colonies to pull further away from Britain, the British government's manipulation of those technologies during 1929–30 preserved the old centralized control until World War II. And this centralization of communications in turn preserved the European news agency cartel.

British Cable and Wireless

Even as World War I broke out, the concerns of the British were still with the costs of international communications and the cultural ramifications for the empire that less expensive telegraph communications could have. Experience in the war confirmed the strategic importance of cable communications. For instance, a new cable had been laid in 1915 to provide direct communication with Russia. Yet the question of the cost of communications within the empire was ever present. When in 1916 the Allies agreed in Paris to take steps to make themselves independent of enemy countries that had essential manufactures, communications, and maritime organization, they also spoke of lowering the cost of interallied transport, telegraphs, mail, and other communications (Drummond 1972:57n). And the Eastern came in for much postwar bitterness regarding the profits it had made on the transmission of lists of dead and wounded soldiers from the dominions (Mills 1924:n.83). In view of these concerns one might have anticipated a postwar welcome for the less costly radiotelegraphy. But this was not to be the case. In effect, the British Post Office's hostility to the Marconi company continued as it had before the war.

Britain ended the war with an additional government-owned transatlantic cable taken from the Germans. Nevertheless, this acquisition, followed by the government purchase of another cable in 1920 from the Direct United States Cable Company, also created problems for the future because the two transatlantic "imperial" cables were run by the Post Office, with British staff at both ends (Brown 1927:77). The operation of these cables was to place the bureaucratic Post Office, as both operator and regulator, in competition with the development of transatlantic radiotelegraphy and telephony.

During the four years of war no cables had been repaired and no new ones laid; with traffic more than doubled, considerable undercapacity afflicted the cable companies (Wilshaw 1939:6–7). The Eastern alone spent £3 million ($13 million) on new cables; the first one, completed in 1919, went to Brazil and Argentina to combat the U.S. challenge. Despite the strategic importance of cables, they were vulnerable to attack while they were being repaired; as a result the war had also spurred the development of wireless communications.

With its existing close relations to the Marconi company, at the outbreak of war the British Admiralty contracted for the construction and operation of thirteen long-range wireless stations that would allow it to communicate directly from London to the British navy around the world. By 1915 all but one of the stations were operational. But construction of the imperial wireless chain was halted in 1914, and the Marconi company was not paid for its work on the Cairo and Oxford stations. The Post Office also refused to pay the company for its war work in intercepting enemy wireless communications, and the matter had to go to arbitration, dragging out until the late 1920s. In 1919 a shortage of capital forced the company to sell its Latin American interests to the Pan-American Wireless and Telephone Company (the joint company that it had set up with Federal Telegraph to exploit South America) and to raise £3 million ($13.3 million) more by issuing shares (W. Baker 1970:178). Although the Foreign Office and the Admiralty argued that the company should receive a government subsidy so that it would not have to sell its rights and thereby jeopardize Britain's control of radio in the western hemisphere, the Treasury refused on the ground that the company was already borrowing from the Americans. The Treasury argued that it could hardly sanction the use of borrowed U.S. money to prevent the sale of the company's Latin American interests to Americans (Rosenberg 1982:95).

The idea of the imperial wireless chain was revamped in 1919. During the war it had seemed that the colonies, and in particular the dominions, were content with a subordinate role in which they contributed to British trade and the British army in return for a guarantee of defense. But even as early as 1917 the dominions were searching for a new relationship with Britain, and communications were considered crucial. The Dominions Royal Commission of 1917, the Imperial Conference of 1917, and the Imperial War Conference of 1918 all raised the issue.

The problem involved both high telegraph rates and the news agency system. High press rates for using the transatlantic cables controlled by U.S. companies meant that Canadian newspapers paid much less for news from the Associated Press in New York than they did for Reuters's news (Mills 1924:98). Long-distance point-to-point wireless promised less expensive communications directly from London. In 1918 "several of them [dominions] . . . objected . . . at the indifference of the British government to providing adequate imperial communication, which they defined as alternative means to communicate, lower rates for messages and news flows without 'foreign' intervention" (Fortner 1993:109). In addition, some areas of the empire, such as British Honduras and British Guiana, had limited external communications and received no service from private news agencies at all. Others, such as Jamaica, had to pay cable companies to supply news each day (Mills 1924:86–87).

In 1918 the Marconi company had reached Sydney directly by long wave from its Welsh transmitter (Sturmey 1958:130). The following year Marconi put forward a new proposal to the British government to establish direct wireless communications between Britain, South Africa, India, and Australia. Each would be linked to Britain by long wave, high-power transmitting stations, with less powerful stations feeding into these arteries from outlying areas.

However, domestic politics intervened once more. The telephone service had been nationalized in 1911, and the Post Office got a monopoly. So the Post

Office, now under the direction of the Imperial Wireless Committee, was given the responsibility for developing the chain. Under the "Norman" scheme—named after Sir Henry Norman, the committee chair—the Post Office planned eight stations of 500 watts each to be spread around the globe at a cost to the Exchequer of £850,000 ($3.9 million). Although large-valve transmitters had been developed by 1920 and the range of high-power stations had increased, the committee reported that direct communication with the colonies of Australia, India, and South Africa would be too expensive and that long-wave stations should therefore be built only two thousand miles apart with an intermediate station at Cairo for relay purposes (Wedlake 1970:143; J. D. Tomlinson 1945:52). In its report, issued in 1920, the committee proposed that the British Post Office and the post and telegraph authorities of the dominions should run these stations. The first two stations in the chain should be the existing stations at Leafield (Oxford) and Cairo.

But Australia objected to the idea of being at the end of a chain and preferred the Marconi idea of direct transmission from Britain. South Africa was similarly opposed. All the dominions and India also were opposed to paying for the stations from public funds (Mills 1924:184). Following objections voiced at the Imperial Conference of 1921, Winston Churchill, then the colonial secretary, distanced himself from the proposals (W. Baker 1970:206–7). Nevertheless, the conference reaffirmed commitment to the imperial wireless scheme and agreed to the completion of the two stations started in 1914. The Post Office opened Oxford in 1921 and Cairo a year later (Wedlake 1970:142).

For the Americans this imperial wireless chain was yet another attempt by the British to dominate world communications. In actuality the concept of centralized control of empire communications put forward by the Post Office's engineering bureaucracy was ill matched to the developing relations between Britain and the dominions, relations that increasingly paid lip service to equality. The dispute between the Post Office hierarchy and the Marconi company centered on two issues: whether there should be direct transmission to and from the dominions and India, and whether the service should be run by the Post Office.

Increasing the pressure on the British government to sanction direct transmissions to the dominions, British Marconi offered in 1922 to build a long-wave, high-power station for the South African government that it could pay for as revenue came in—an early build-and-operate scheme (Parliament 1924).[1] But in the same year another Imperial Wireless Committee made its report, which reiterated the Post Office line. Then the policy was suddenly reversed. In July 1922 the postmaster general announced that the government had become convinced that direct communication with India, South Africa, and Australia was the right course. The government would build and run a new high-power station, with others perhaps in Hong Kong and Singapore (Wedlake 1970:142). According to the Post Office, Marconi propaganda had suborned the colonies; although the model still was centralized and controlled by the Post Office, it did allow for direct transmission.

The press, which had sampled Marconi's direct telegraph transmission to Australia, was unhappy at the prospect of the Post Office's running the service to the colonies. Lobbying by the Empire Press Union and the Federation of British Industries against government ownership led to a further announcement in 1923, that, because of changes in the technology, private companies would be allowed to erect wireless transmitters in Britain for communication with the colonies. But the prime minister, Bonar Law, said that "'at the same time the government has decided that it is necessary in the interests of national security that there should be a wireless station in this country, capable of communicating with the Dominions and owned and operated by the State . . . available for commercial traffic as well as for service messages'" (quoted in Mills 1924:182). Once again the state was to control what could have been a private monopoly by setting itself up in competition.

As a result of the government's decision, the Post Office erected a giant station at Rugby that housed the world's most powerful transmitter for both worldwide telegraphy and telephony. Western Electric had effected the first transmission of voice through long-wave radiotelephony across the Atlantic in 1923. But only after the Rugby station began operation did two-way conversation become possible, and the service was not opened to the public until 1927 (Baldwin 1938:647).

The intention was that Rugby should be ready in 1925, but there were delays, caused—or so the Post Office thought—by the Marconi company's announcement of its shortwave breakthrough in 1924 (discussed shortly). The Post Office was so paranoid that it attributed the shortage of construction workers at Rugby to Marconi's announcement. The Rugby station, with masts 1.5 miles high, began operation in 1926 and could reach Australia directly. It could also communicate to ships and, for the first time, provided a British time signal and a broadcast news service (Wedlake 1970:143, 145).

But as some journalists pointed out, there was little or no chance that the station would pay its own way. Its main advantage was that "some important Imperial potentialities [were] bound up in such a peculiarly centralised station." One possibility was that the facility would be able to broadcast "news of Imperial significance simultaneously to every British Dominion and col-

ony throughout the world" (*Manchester Guardian,* Feb. 9, 1924). The original intention was that the company and the station would pool its telegraph
traffic, with two-thirds going to Marconi stations and one-third to Rugby.
But the Post Office had not given up its old ways. It attempted to use the
pooling policy to force the company to transfer all its current and future
patent licenses to the government without charge. The company refused. The
first Labour government then attempted to withdraw the domestic licenses
from the company (Mills 1924:187).

Challenged on the legality of this step, yet another committee was appointed; its 1924 report proposed that, with the exception of the Canadian route
on which competition would remain, the state should construct and run the
imperial chain. Private companies would be allowed licenses to develop communications with continental Europe and the rest of the world outside the
empire. But on Continental routes the companies would have to pay royalties to the Post Office to compensate it for lost cable traffic over the state-
run cables (United Kingdom 1924).

These proposals were still being debated in Parliament in 1924 when Marconi himself achieved a breakthrough in shortwave communications. In 1921
he had demonstrated that it was possible to connect telephone landlines to
shortwave wireless telephony links and thereby talk directly to the Continent
(*Times* of London, Dec. 19, 1921). In May 1924 he spoke to Sydney by direct
shortwave telephone (W. Baker 1970:220). Instead of long-wave stations,
Marconi offered the dominions considerably less expensive, and more effective, shortwave stations that could transmit telephone conversations as well
as the telegraph. Canada, South Africa, and Australia's acceptance of the
company's proposal to build these shortwave stations, rather than the long
wave for which it was under contract,effectively ended the argument.

In July 1924, in what was a commercial gamble, the Marconi company
entered into a contract with the Post Office to erect shortwave stations at
record speed for direct business news services to Canada, Australia, India, and
South Africa. The company was to receive a patent royalty on the traffic carried from the British end, but the Post Office was to operate the stations.
However, given permission to develop shortwave service from any part of the
empire, including Britain, to any place outside the empire, Marconi gained
control of the lucrative European traffic. The Canadian service opened in
1926, the others the following year. These "beam" stations could transmit by
using one-fiftieth of the power at three times the speed and one-twentieth
of the cost of long wave (Baglehole 1969:15).

But the Post Office had not finished with Marconi. The landing license that
it gave the Eastern in 1923 ran to nine pages, whereas Marconi's 1925 license
ran to twenty-two pages and included clauses on "British" control. These

clauses went further in limiting foreign participation in radio than did those of the U.S. Radio Communications Act of 1912. The directors of Marconi had to have been born Britons; so did those employed in radio stations in the United Kingdom, India, the colonies, and the dependencies, and foreigners were to hold no more than 25 percent of its shares.[2] Marconi himself could therefore not be a director.

The introduction of shortwave had profound implications for the organization of international communications. Instead of being an international matter, with telegraph companies exercising end-to-end control, long-distance telegraphy had become a national business. Speaking in 1930, Sir Basil Blackett, the chair of Imperial and International Communications Ltd., gave an overview of the situation:

> It is indeed becoming a matter of principle that the state in each country should have some measure of control or should require local ownership of the wireless stations within its borders, and this principle, once applied to wireless, is being extended to control over and operation of that portion of any submarine cable which lies within territorial waters. . . . For the future each nation is likely to insist on local control of its own international communications, whether telephonic or telegraphic, whether by cable or wireless. (1939a:57–59)

Wireless, with its low capital costs, allowed even small countries to afford their own wireless stations. They could not only charge lower rates than cables but could use their control of the inland telegraphs to feed their own international wireless systems. By doing so the dominions and colonies could create revenue for themselves because the sender and receiver split the revenues evenly. Whereas end-to-end control had given the Eastern all the revenues of international transmission, the colonies kept 50 percent of wireless revenue. The colonies could achieve high profits, even if they charged low tariffs, because the initial capital costs were so low.

Wireless rates were roughly one-third lower than cable's, and by the end of 1927 the cable companies on the routes served by shortwave—from Australia, South Africa, and India—had lost half their business (Wedlake 1970: 144). Only on the Canadian route, where RCA, Marconi, and the cable companies had agreed to a cartel, was there no crisis. The Pacific Cable Board faced an £80,000 ($388,800) drop in income in 1927–28, and because the dominion governments were subsidizing the Pacific cable, they asked the British government to appoint a committee to consider the situation (Baglehole 1969:15). In addition, the cable companies were threatening to either liquidate or sell their cables (the obvious beneficiary was International Telephone and Telegraph) if wireless competition was not reined in.

To sum up, the problem for the Marconi company during this period was that its wireless schemes threatened the secure prewar system of intraempire communications. Early in its development the Cable Landing Rights Committee had perceived that wireless would make cables, with their high rates, uneconomical. In altering the prewar model of international communications from one based on end-to-end British control to one based on national ownership, wireless held out the possibility of more autonomy within the dominions. Pressed as they were for revenue, dominion governments could be expected to link their domestic lines with the long-wave stations transmitting directly to Britain. They could be expected to bypass the Eastern's cables.

The various schemes put forward by the British government to deal with these problems were therefore designed to protect the submarine cables on which it had spent so much public money for security. Strategic concerns played against commercial realities in debates about how best to organize an intraempire wireless scheme and on public versus private ownership. One can view the first schemes as designed to slow transmission by wireless by relaying through a chain in order to prevent bypassing of the cables. But when it became evident that the dominions would not accept less than direct communications from Britain, the answer became public ownership of one large high-power station.

Then, following lobbying by the press and business, which were already dissatisfied with the behavior of the Post Office, the answer was deemed to lie in public competition with Marconi and a pool of the traffic between public and private. The British government's regulatory impulse once again was to use competition by the public sector in order to control the private. When this scheme failed because the Post Office tried to use it to gain access to all the company's patents without payment, the reaction of the new Labour government was to favor effective nationalization. Finally, the Marconi company gained the upper hand with its shortwave technology, and the British government acceded to direct transmission to the dominions and India. But the feared outcome occurred within one year of the services' opening. The Eastern's and the government-owned cables became uneconomical. The goal of government policy became one of preventing International Telephone and Telegraph (ITT) from snapping up those cables.

The Inauguration of Cable and Wireless

The British government called the Imperial Wireless and Cable Conference of 1928 to consider the competition of wireless with cable.[3] It dismissed the possibility of subsidizing the cables. Nor, given ITT's "attempt to build up an American communications Empire," was the British government prepared to see the cables sold to the United States (Blackett 1939b:59). Because of the security and secrecy afforded by submarine cables, the Conservative government proposed to create a national company that would merge cable and wireless interests. By doing so, the 1928 Report of the Imperial Wireless and Cable Conference stated that "'unity of control and unity of direction would be secured. The continuance of the cable system would be assured, economies could be effected, and the creation of a common purse and a common interest would leave the union free to devote its energies to resist encroachments on the part of foreign competitors'" (quoted in Blackett 1939a:42). The proposal mirrored that first aired by the Post Office in 1910.

During the ensuing conference, which was complicated by the number of interests represented, an agreement was reached in principle between the Eastern, its associated companies, and Marconi's Wireless Telegraph Company. Two companies were created—a holding company, Cable and Wireless Ltd., and a communications company, Imperial and International Communications Ltd. They shared a board of directors, but the chair of the communications company was appointed by the government. The two became jointly known later as Cable and Wireless Ltd. Because he had been the chair of the Eastern since 1917, John Denison-Pender would have been named to chair both, but he died soon after the agreement was signed.

The new holding company was capitalized with £53.7 million ($260.9 million); 56.25 percent of the voting power went to the cable group and 43.75 percent to the Marconi company. The communications company received the communications interests of Marconi, bought the loss-making imperial transatlantic cables from the Post Office for £450,000 ($2.19 million), paid £517,000 ($2.51 million), plus yearly payments of £77,000 ($374,220) for interest, to the Pacific Cable Board for the Pacific cable and a further £300,000 ($1.5 million) for the government-owned West Indies cables. The company also leased the loss-making Post Office beam stations for twenty-five years at an annual cost of £250,000 ($176.7 million). Of the total capital, £36.35 million (67 percent) was distributed to cable interests. W. J. Baker (1970:232) blames the Marconi board's lack of technical expertise—it was headed by an ex–postmaster general who had no business experience—and its failure to appreciate the potential of shortwave, for allowing it to sell the company short. Marconi, who had resigned as chairman in 1927 to devote himself to research and development, was the only technical member of the board.[4]

However, just when competition from wireless had started to reduce high cable rates, the colonial governments, particularly those of the dominions, did not look kindly on the prospect of a renewed monopoly. Therefore the conference agreed that the new company should be incorporated as a public utility. Profits were to be held to about 6.5 percent of the nominal capital of £30 million ($145.8 million), and this figure also acted as a target rate of return. Half of any surplus above this amount was to go to the company, with half put toward the reduction of rates or improvement in services. Two directors of the board were to be government appointees. The Imperial Communications Advisory Committee was set up with one representative each from the dominions and India and one representative for all the remaining colonies and protectorates, under the chairmanship of the British. It was to have veto power over any increase of tariffs, had control of half the profits over the 6.5 percent rate of return, and would be consulted on all matters of policy (Blackett 1939a:42–43). Members of the advisory committee were all based in London.

Just as in Victorian times when a subsidiary of the Eastern received a government subsidy, a government appointee was to sit on the company's board. But the mechanism of regulating tariffs by limiting the rate of return on capital (copied from the Americans) was a chimera. With cable interests and the government paid so much, the new company was overcapitalized, and it soon became evident that it could not make its expected return on capital.[5]

The situation was further complicated by Post Office actions. Under the new arrangements the overseas telephone service from Britain was to remain in the hands of the Post Office. In addition, if it wished, the Post Office had the right to use the Marconi beam stations for telephonic transmission to the dominions. In fact, the Post Office chose to develop an independent telephone network based on the Rugby transmitter in competition with Marconi (Brown 1927:103). This uneconomical development of a dual network kept international telegraph and telephone charges high. In addition, whereas radiotelegraphy to the Continent was the company's responsibility, the short-range cables to the Continent remained the responsibility of the Post Office, and the company had to compensate the Post Office for traffic that it lost to its competition.

Post Office behavior caused other problems. During the 1920s the Post Office began to use its power as regulator to prevent competition with its operations. It began to refuse U.S. cable companies' requests to lay their own cables from the United Kingdom to other European countries. It also refused requests from the financial sector for private wires to the Continent.[6] As a result it became inevitable that more transatlantic cables would go directly to the Continent from the Azores, which in turn meant that they evaded British censorship (Brown 1927:120–21).

An alteration also took place in landing licenses. These became more regulatory. Among other provisions, they allowed the postmaster general to take companies to the Railway and Canal Commission (a judicial body) if he considered cable charges were "'not just and reasonable.'"[7] Although it never used the provision, the commission had the power to fix charges as it saw fit "'after giving consideration to the cost of maintenance, operation and renewals'" and to other matters affecting the financial performance of the companies (quoted in Brown 1927:121).

Although the Imperial Communications Advisory Committee controlled the tariffs of Cable and Wireless Ltd., it did not regulate the Post Office. Whereas the Post Office previously rented landlines to cable companies as private wires on a flat-rate basis, just as it had to the press and to other businesses, after the merger it began to charge an annual rent plus a rate per word for all traffic. The companies, including Cable and Wireless, complained that the Post Office tariffs were out of proportion to the cost of the lines. The companies argued that other governments charged only a transit rate per word for interconnection. Brown suggests that by making an unreasonable profit the Post Office was imposing a "tax on communications" (Brown 1927:122).

The situation came to a head in the 1930s. Despite layoffs and economies, Cable and Wireless made a profit of only £75,000 ($340,500) in 1931, rather than the £1.865 million ($9.1 million) that the 1928 conference had envisioned. Negotiations with the Imperial Communications Advisory Committee resulted in new arrangements. The Post Office beam stations were sold to Cable and Wireless and closed down. Competition with the Post Office to the European continent was brought under a joint operating agreement for twenty-five years, and the rate of return was set at 4 percent, or £1.2 million ($5.45 million). In addition, to combat the growing competition from air mail, the Post Office introduced a flat rate for telegrams within the British Empire in 1938, followed by a "social rate" in 1939, and a flat imperial press rate of 2½ pence. These new rates expanded traffic to some extent (Baglehole 1969:20–21). But World War II brought about the major increase in traffic—from 231 million words (5 percent of which were from government) to 705 million in 1944, 38 percent of which were from government (Baglehole 1969:23–24). This expansion and its effect on profits, together with the increased need for wartime news, allowed the eventual introduction of an empire press rate of one penny per word in 1941, to be retained until the 1950s.[8]

Because of its debt load and its perpetual cost cutting, Cable and Wireless failed to become the dynamic entity that ITT had so feared but instead concentrated on servicing the dominions and colonies. In the 1930s the company began to build and operate domestic telephone systems overseas. In much the same way as ITT, it built systems in Turkey and Cyprus and most of the British colonies (Barty-King 1979:225). Even where domestic communications were state owned in the dominions and colonies, Cable and Wireless often controlled international communications. The Americans concluded that the merger had benefited cable interests and damaged radio technological development (Herring and Gross 1936:205). They were not alone in this conclusion. Blackett (1939a:45) comments that the Post Office's refusal to cooperate in radiotelephony had a negative effect on radio research by Cable and Wireless. However, given the dominance of cable within the company, Cable and Wireless continued to centralize the empire.

Sidelining wireless maintained London's position as a cable hub. As Lord John Cuthbert Denison-Pender, the chair of Cable and Wireless since 1932 (and grandson of John Pender), pointed out, "London is the centre of the world's switchboard." All calls from one colonial country to another went through London, thereby not only creating transit revenue for the Post Office but also centralizing communications (Denison-Pender 1939:105). In turn, this centralization through London was an obvious advantage to the intelligence services.

In 1920 the Official Secrets Act required cable companies to submit their traffic to the newly formed Government Communications Headquarters (GCHQ) within ten days of its receipt. According to West, "Most were returned for onward transmission, but a quantity of those believed to be of interest were duplicated and circulated to MI5, SIS [Secret Intelligence Service] or any other indoctrinated party." Later, Cable and Wireless "copied foreign traffic passing through its relay stations at Bermuda, Malta and Hong Kong and shipped carbon flimsies back by the diplomatic bag to London, where they were examined by teams of 'slip readers'" (West 1986:141). Alistair Denniston (who was head of GCHQ from 1921 to 1944) later boasted: "'Between us and the companies there has never been any question of why we wanted the traffic and what we did with it. . . . I have no doubt that the managers and senior officials must have guessed the true answer but I have never heard of any indiscretion through all these years with so many people involved'" (quoted in West 1986:142).

In 1938 GCHQ added a commercial section that "began work by collecting copies of internationally available codes, and progressed into the cryptographic field by solving a number of encrypted commercial telegrams sent by some of Japan's largest trading companies. The results were sufficiently impressive to ensure the Section's survival throughout the war" (West 1986:112). So although the U.S. companies may have been wrong in attributing commercial motives to the traffic monitoring of the British government in the 1920s, by World War II their suspicions were correct. In contrast, in 1929 President Herbert Hoover's new secretary of state, Henry Stimson, closed down the equivalent organization in the United States, the "Black Chamber," which had begun in 1917. Stimson commented that "'gentlemen do not read each other's mail'" (quoted in West 1986:84). The United States would have no such organization until 1941, when the Office of the Coordinator of Information, forerunner of the Office of Strategic Services (and then the Central Intelligence Agency), was established.

News Agencies

At the beginning of 1914 Reuters seemed all powerful. It sat "at the crossroads of the world of news and controlled traffic" (Cooper 1942:33). Despite its financial problems when the war began, Reuters became even more dominant in its immediate aftermath. The Versailles peace negotiations helped Reuters and Havas. In Paris, Kent Cooper of the Associated Press attempted to break up the consortium. He raised the question of the "inclusion of an article declaring for a free press and freedom of international news exchange" in the final treaty. But on raising the issue Col. Edward M. House, President Woodrow Wilson's closest adviser, was informed that "the matter had been taken care of privately." Cooper had the impression that Reuters would gain control of the territory previously supplied by Wolff and that proved to be the case (Cooper 1942:89–90). In an agreement of 1919 Havas and Reuters took the opportunity to limit Wolff to Germany and to take over its monopoly of the supply and collection of news in Scandinavia, Russia, and Austria. The result was a cordon sanitaire around Germany because Finland, Sweden, Norway, Denmark, Holland, Belgium, Switzerland, Austria, Czechoslovakia, and Poland, together with the Balkan states, were placed under the monopoly of either Havas or Reuters (Cooper 1942:106–7). Russia was also to join the consortium through a contract with Reuters in 1924.

But the consortium could work only if the means of transmission was under monopoly control. Once point-to-point radio telegraphy became available and competed in speed and price with the Eastern's cables, the alternative news agencies could prosper. The worldwide preeminence of Reuters, which had nearly been eliminated from South America by the end of World War I, came under attack until the late 1920s.

In the immediate postwar period Reuters faced financial pressure at home. The British Foreign Office decided in 1919 that it would run the British Official News Service that Roderick Jones had started during the war. Renamed the British Official Wireless Service, it broadcast daily for forty-five minutes, and overseas newspapers could use it for free. Although Reuters regarded the service as unfair competition, its complaints were limited lest the Foreign Office turn the service over to another agency. Further adding to Reuters's problems, the government shut down its Agence Service Reuter in 1919, despite Jones's arguments against its closure. And then in 1920 the Ministry of Information, itself facing closure, raised the possibility of a government-owned news agency. When the Empire Press Conference, an association of newspaper owners and editors, met that year, it vehemently opposed the idea, arguing that the problem of carrying British news was related to the costs of transmission. Newspapers throughout the empire wanted lower cable rates (specifically, a rate of one pence per word) subsidized by the British government (Mills 1924:119–20).

Instead, the Foreign Office agreed to use Reuters as its agent. Reuters was to circulate specific messages overseas for the Foreign Office, and the government would pay the cost of the additional wording. According to Donald Read (1992:148), the news agency attempted to maintain its stance of independence by agreeing to circulate only news "consistent with their independence and their obligations to newspapers." Renewed in 1921, this agreement and a similar one with the Indian Office remained in force throughout the interwar years. This kind of agreement, in which supposedly independent news was mixed with propaganda, and the commensurate direct subsidy, infuriated Kent Cooper, who, while ignoring the subsidies on transmission that the AP received, excoriated Reuters for being state owned and subsidized.

The Associated Press came increasingly to resent the British news agency. Short of money in 1920, Reuters rebuffed the AP when it attempted to gain additional freedom in dealing independently with newspapers in Europe (Cooper 1942:97–100). But as shortwave wireless lessened the cost of transmission after 1921, it became harder for Reuters to keep a lid on competition. Whereas Reuters and the Eastern had been able to control both the collection and transmission of information, with the advent of wireless neither could guarantee the other a monopoly.

Reuters was handicapped by Havas's casual attitude toward news gathering and its reliance on the old technology of cable. Delays from both were handicaps in a world where information quickly lost its value as a commodity. Also, the Foreign Office was uneasy at Havas's domination of news to and from Europe. This unease led to "a plan to make Berlin a centre for circulating British news supplied by Reuters, discussed with the Foreign Office in 1922," but this proposal came to nothing (D. Read 1992:149).

Nor did the British Post Office's jealous guarding of its monopoly of wireless transmission help Reuters. The company could not regain its nineteenth-century position as both a carrier and information provider. In 1921 its application for a license "to study the application of wireless to news dissemination" was seen by the Post Office as potential competition and was refused. At this time Reuters regarded Marconi's Wireless Press as its main domestic competitor and blamed its wartime monopoly of the reception of European continental news by wireless for giving Marconi an unfair advantage.

In fact, Marconi's Wireless Press was limited in the immediate postwar period by its agreement with the news agencies to prepare messages only for use aboard ship and to directly supply news only to newspapers that were published on board. Until 1922 the company acted as both news agency and carrier. Despite the Post Office's purchase of the company's ship-to-shore stations in 1909 and its ensuing monopoly of coastal wireless, Marconi distributed the service itself from its Irish transmitter. But in July 1922 the Irish Republican Army burned down the transmitter, so the Post Office took over the transmission of the news service.[9] In turn, until 1926, when the service was transferred to the newly constructed high-power long-wave station at Rugby, the company was unhappy with the range and quality of the service that it received in comparison to that received by its U.S. competitor, RCA.[10]

Despite its agreement with the existing news agencies, Marconi's Wireless Press was looking to expand into a full-fledged news agency. When Reuters began its "Trade Service" in 1920, distributing business news overseas by cable, the slowness of reception and delivery made it vulnerable to competitive pressure. Early in 1923 the Marconi company surveyed a number of companies in Britain and overseas with an offer to broadcast stock exchange information by wireless three times a day for £50 ($229) per year. The service depended on the ability of Marconi's Wireless Press to make arrangements with either the Post Office or the British Broadcasting Company (the forerunner of the BBC).[11] The news agencies—Reuters, the Press Association, the Exchange Telegraph Company, and Company News—immediately complained to the postmaster general that such a service would break the British Broadcasting Company's agreement not to distribute news until 7 P.M., in order to avoid competing with the press. Jones also argued, with considerable hypocrisy, that the proposal "seemed to contemplate that the Company responsible for the distribution of news should also collect it—an arrangement which the News Agencies considered highly objectionable in principle."[12] Only one week later, on March 2, Reuters was reported to be considering its own wireless station in order to broadcast to the Continent. Because of the Post Office monopoly Reuters was forced to settle for a "'service agreement'" for long-wave transmissions of "'circular toll broadcasts'" in Morse code to news agencies on the Continent.[13]

In fact, a J. M. McKay, who with the backing of a German news agency proposed a broadcast service of stock exchange information to Germany several times per day, had already approached the Post Office and the British Broadcasting Company. In the first evidence of "convergence" between data transmission and broadcasting, the British Broadcasting Company stated that it was prepared to transmit the service but was dependent on the Post Office's agreement. However, the Post Office and the Treasury saw in the proposed service a market opportunity that they could pirate.[14] The Post Office set about finding a British supplier of the business information. Reuters turned the approach down on the ground that the German agency Daheste was a competitor of Wolff's. And by the time the Exchange Telegraph Company had decided that it would undertake the collection of information, McKay had set up his own agency, Europradio, to do so.

The reaction to McKay's entry to the news agency business is indicative of British security concerns in this immediate postwar period and the corruption of news agency independence that was instigated by government ownership of Reuters. First, the government's Overseas Development Agency (ODA) asked the Post Office for confidential information about McKay, because there "was always the chance that some use may be made of the service for Government purposes and some control may be necessary over information distributed to European centers."[15] In other words, the government agency contemplated manipulating or censoring stock market information. Then pressure was brought to bear on the Post Office by the War Office and the ODA to reject McKay's proposals on the ground that he was unreliable. But the Post Office was not prepared to forgo the financial opportunity. Then, once the service had begun, the War Office demanded the codebooks. Even with these supplied, it was unable to decipher the messages, and when McKay left the company, the War Office tried (unsuccessfully) to gain the Post Office's help in interviewing him so that it might crack the code.[16]

When the existence of this service became public (perhaps from a Reuters leak), there was an outcry. One report pointed out that the existence of such commercial services conflicted with the lack of a public telephone service to Germany (*Halifax Daily Courier and Guardian,* Sept. 11, 1924). Reuters had once more rid itself of its competition in what was to become its primary profit-making activity.

Following McKay's initiative, in 1923 Reuters began its Continental Broadcasting Service, sending out price quotations and exchange rates at set hours seven times a day by wireless. Frequently expanded, according to Donald Read, it remained the leading business news service for Europe throughout the 1920s and 1930s and cross-subsidized Reuters's political news gathering. In 1925 "Special Broadcasting Services" (point to multipoint) were well enough established to have their own wave band included under the International Telegraph Union's regulations as agreed upon at the Paris conference. However, a review of wireless broadcast transmission of business and press news in Europe by the Post Office in 1926 suggested that "German developments are definitely challenging the prominent position held hitherto by this country."[17]

Because of the loss of their cables after the war, the Germans had developed wireless facilities superior to those in Britain. They had separate transmitters for point-to-point and data broadcast services, whereas the British transmitter in Oxford juggled the two. The Germans also had reserve transmitters, while the British had none. In addition, the German service was controlled from the office of the news agency, rather than from the transmitter, thereby cutting out time delays in broadcasting information. And whereas either wireless telegraphy or telephony was available to the German news agencies, Reuters could only use the telegraph.

The Post Office review suggested that Continental subscribers took the British service only for its information about the United States, that there were already signs that U.S. news agencies were about to supply information directly to Germany, and that Continental news agency subscribers preferred the less expensive German telephonic news service to the British telegraphic. In addition, the German administration was already testing a domestic facsimile service.[18] In other words, despite the intention of both Reuters and Havas to limit Wolff to Germany alone, by the mid-1920s, because of German state support of both the news agency service and wireless communications, Berlin was challenging London as the primary distribution center in Europe for press and business information.

Even after the Post Office review concluded that consolidation and development of the English services were necessary, the Post Office only offered the use of a shortwave transmitter and allowed keying from Reuters's offices, albeit by Post Office staff, from November 1929 (D. Read 1992:157). It was fortunate for Reuters as well as for the cable companies that direct wireless communications between the dominions and colonies of the British Empire and the United States were forbidden by the British government and that direct telephone communications between Germany and the United States were not available until the late 1930s. Instead, the merger of cable and wireless in 1929 allowed the European news agency cartel to work for a while longer (D. Read 1992:158).

During the interwar years Reuters was to ask the British government unsuccessfully on several occasions for a direct subsidy so that it could compete more effectively with the subsidized French and German news agencies. In particular, in 1927, on ending its South American agreement with Havas, Reuters requested £20,000 ($97,200) per year so that it might set up shop there. But the British government refused on the ground that subsidizing a private company was inappropriate (Taylor 1981:65). Reuters's request for a subsidy was also undermined by Foreign Office research that found that the local press in South America hardly used the German and Italian news services (Taylor 1981:211).

Reuters was subsidized throughout the 1920s by the low press rates of the domestic telegraphs and the submarine cables. But by the late 1930s, 90 percent of Reuters's news was being distributed by wireless. The Post Office refused repeated requests to reduce its wireless rates for Reuters's international financial news service (Brown 1927:148). The company was no more successful even in 1937, when the security situation in Europe led then foreign secretary Anthony Eden to support Reuters's application for a reduction (Taylor 1981:67). By 1938 Reuters was broadcasting its news to more than twenty destinations on the fringes of Europe and over the Middle East and Far East, including to India, Africa, and South America, but the cost was £5 ($24.50) per message (D. Read 1992:158). Because the Post Office continued to lose money on the domestic telegraph service, and particularly on overnight press transmissions, perhaps it concluded that the press already received enough subsidies from public funds. But it is not clear why the reduced press rates available under those regulations did not apply to the Post Office service, given that the International Telegraph Union's regulations were made applicable to wireless in 1912 and again in 1927.

To some extent Reuters came under pressure in the interwar years because it did not meet the needs of its clients. Limited editorial control of copy from countries where collection was the responsibility of Havas and Wolff meant that "news" reported from one country was not re-edited for different customers. Reuters was also the victim of increased nationalism in the United States and vulnerable to criticism that it delivered news biased toward British interests. Even within the empire the new, more autonomous relations of the dominions with the British government lent themselves to a less centralized organization. And the political situation in India, where demands for national independence were growing, made the production of "independent" news difficult and customer satisfaction problematic.

The Associated Press was not alone in its dissatisfaction with Reuters. In each case, Reuters's reaction was to set up a specialized press service for the country in question, beginning with an American service in 1924. Reuters's monopoly was challenged even within the empire. The Empire Press Union had long argued for more interchange between the constituent parts of the British Empire.[19] Within the dominions Reuters's links with South Africa were strongest and with Canada weakest. Perhaps the Canadians were influenced by their historic relations with the Associated Press and by Cooper's campaign, but the Canadians were the most antagonistic to links between governments and press. According to Donald Read (1992:164), they were deeply suspicious "about the attitude of Reuters to Canadian Government subsidies." Canadians received much of their foreign news from the Associated Press, including some originating with Reuters, but after the 1920 Imperial Press Conference, Reuters also provided a daily service of six hundred words of British and imperial news especially for Canada. Still dissatisfied but unable to break free, the Canadian press established its own bureau in Reuters's London headquarters in 1923.

In Australia, Reuters had never held a monopoly of foreign news. With communications to the United States eased by the Pacific cable from Vancouver, in the 1920s the Australian Press Association approached the Associated Press about an alliance that would bypass Reuters. By 1926, although the contract between Reuters and the major Australian newspapers was renewed, the Australians had joined the Canadians in editing their news in London (D. Read 1992:164–65). News of, and for, India continued to be handled by London, but Reuters could not combat the increasing demand for news of one dominion in another. So, for instance, by the 1920s Australian newspapers were in direct contact with South Africa (Mills 1924:130). Inexpensive direct point-to-point communications via wireless would have opened up those relations and necessitated the liberalization of Reuters's monopoly.

In 1927, in a move that Havas and Wolff apparently were unaware of, Reuters agreed that the Associated Press might enter Reuters's Japanese territory (Cooper 1942:172). Driven by domestic competition from United Press, the Associated Press set up bureaus in Tokyo, Shanghai, India, Australia, and South Africa, "because Reuters is not fast enough from these sections and has not our ideas as to what is news to meet our needs as against our competition" (Cooper 1942:194). The AP was still reliant on its alliance with Reuters and Havas; it did not begin serving Japan directly until 1930. Finally, in 1934, based on a policy of freedom in international news exchange, the AP signed a new contract with Reuters. The provision and dissemination of news became liberalized (W. Read 1976:101; Fenby 1986:49).

The 1930s were to prove a testing time for Reuters as income diminished and competition from government-subsidized agencies in France, Germany, Italy, Japan, and Russia increased. Walter Read suggests that, because of its links with Havas and Wolff, and because of a number of mistakes, the government no longer regarded Reuters as completely reliable. Some Foreign Office officials favored its competitors, British Official Wireless and Extel, and tried to find someone to replace Jones, whom they wanted to retire (D. Read 1992:181–82). But then, as propaganda took on a more important role during the Munich crisis of 1938, Reuters's news service was broadcast three times a day. The service was in plain language and could be used by anyone free of charge. The agreement between the British government and Reuters was for Post Office transmitters to carry 720,000 words per year at a cost of ½ pence per word, but the price also allowed for an insertion by the Foreign Office. Thus news agency and government once again entered an alliance in which news was deliberately manipulated for political or military ends (Wood 1992:21).

Conclusion

During the interwar years Britain's influence within world affairs came increasingly from the empire, which was necessary for both defense and trade. In terms of political, economic, and cultural influence, the British government virtually ceded South America to the Americans. Reflecting this shift in power, after a brief attempt to retain the Eastern's Brazilian monopoly, British government support for communications companies in South America ceased. The Marconi company sold its South American assets; the Eastern opened up its South American monopoly concessions, and Reuters was refused a subsidy to finance its penetration. Control of South American communications shifted to the United States after ITT bought out many British interests in the 1920s and linked the domestic operation of numerous South American telegraphs with the United States and after RCA formed its tripartite cartel to deliver radio communications. In light of a decrease in trade and international traffic, the competition to control the infrastructure of international communications faded into cartelization and acceptance of "spheres of influence." British concern with communications retreated to the empire.

The centralized system of communications via submarine cable, still largely in place after World War I, served Britain's strategic interests. By making Britain the hub for international cables, censorship and monitoring of political developments in foreign countries became routine. Messages from one dominion or colony to another also had to go through London, not only facilitating the process of monitoring but giving the Eastern all the revenue from its end-to-end control. The web of cables expanding outward from London also allowed Reuters to sit in the center, collecting and distributing "news." The dominions and colonies paid with high cable rates and through the slow distribution of news edited for readers elsewhere and in which their citizens were not necessarily interested.

In the prewar and postwar periods the dominions, which had sent their citizens to fight for British victory, demanded less expensive communications. Eventually, the Post Office reacted to this sustained pressure and made changes to cable landing licenses. These attempts to regulate submarine cable tariffs centered on a clause within the landing licenses that gave the government minister the power to refer the tariffs to a body—the Railways and Canals Commission—that had been resurrected from the Victorian age. The clause was never used. It was window dressing. One of the main reasons for the high cable tariffs was the behavior of the British Post Office as network operator and its demands for high interconnection charges. Throughout the period the Post Office, as dominant operator, stifled competition wherever it was able while acting as both policy adviser to the British government and regulator of the private companies. In some cases—for instance, when the Post Office refused landing licenses to foreign cross-channel cables—its actions were directly detrimental to British security interests. In others—as with its overt continuing hostility to the Marconi company and its subsequent refusal to collaborate on research and development into wireless—it damaged British leadership in that technology.

As Blackett, the head of Cable and Wireless, rightly foretold, wireless completely altered the model of international communications, from one based on end-to-end British control to one based on national ownership. In so doing, it not only held out the possibility of more autonomy within the dominions but threatened the security system of submarine cables. After years of attempting to find compromise solutions to this threat, deficits on the Pacific Cable and the potential sale of the Eastern to ITT spurred government action.

The resulting government-instigated merger of Marconi's Wireless Telegraph Company and the Eastern favored both the Eastern and the government, which unloaded many nonperforming assets on Cable and Wireless. Run by a board of dominion dignitaries resident in London, overcapitalized, setting a rate of return on that capital that was too high and with controlled tariffs, forced to pay the Post Office for the effect of its competition on Continental traffic, and doing business in an economic environment in which world trade was declining, Cable and Wireless was soon in financial trouble. It also had to compete with the Post Office's international telephone service. Given the scarcity of traffic, such overcapacity of infrastructure led the company to revert to a traditional pooling arrangement with the Post Office. Once the government openly took control, the inevitable political pressure for lower tariffs brought lower intraempire rates for social telegrams and the press (but not an instantaneous increase in traffic). World War II saved the company.

Censorship provided an additional reason for the establishment of Cable and Wireless. Throughout World War I, both the Eastern and the Marconi company had formed part of the system of British censorship. In view of the hostility displayed toward it, it seems unlikely that the Marconi company retained this role during the 1920s. However, for the cable companies of the Eastern, Western Union, and Commercial Cable (later ITT), censorship became a routine procedure. A clause was inserted in the U.S. companies' landing licenses in 1919 demanding that they hand over the telegrams transmitted; this was made absolutely obligatory by the Official Secrets legislation in 1920. Although these activities became public knowledge during congressional hearings about the Western Union drama in 1921, the regular censorship by the British of U.S. State Department telegrams seems to have been secret even after World War II began.

Under the Treaty of Versailles the Admiralty had wanted all commercial codes registered, so that it might hold the key. In the interwar years the interest in such codes increased, so that, as in the case of the German-backed transmission of industrial news, parts of the British state combined to get their hands on this information. Industrial espionage became part of the censorship fabric to which the companies adhered. However, had radio triumphed over cable, the numerous independent wireless companies in the dominions and colonies might have made such secrecy impossible.

As a by-product of the establishment of Cable and Wireless and the retention of the centralized system of communications, Reuters was also saved. Despite the dominions' demands from 1906 for an intraempire press service that would bring the empire together through horizontal communications between each member, and despite increasing dissatisfaction with its service, Reuters was able to retain control of its member press agencies by virtue of the communications system. Had wireless between the individual colonies been allowed to develop, competition in news agencies might have opened up, as happened in Europe and in the United States, and as the Marconi company attempted in Britain. Also, although the high rates imposed on Reuters by the Post Office handicapped it at home, as did the Post Office's refusal to issue Reuters a license for its own transmitters, the Post Office's control of wireless telegraph transmission, centralized through its long-wave Rugby transmitter, effectively prevented Marconi from competing with Reuters in transmitting business information. And, despite the better and faster technology available to German news agencies, Reuters was protected because there was only one direct telephone line from the United States—to Britain— until 1935, and the press in the United States tended to transmit via short-wave directly to Britain. Reflecting the commercial preeminence of the United States in the postwar world, it was Reuters's collection of business news from the United States that preserved its cartel in Europe until the 1930s. The Associated Press's defection, so that it might compete more effectively with United Press, began to spell the end of that cartel.

Reuters began to lose legitimacy once the British heard complaints about "foreign influence" on Reuters's political news, a "foreign influence" that was part of the cartel's structure. Like Cable and Wireless, Reuters was saved by World War II. Once denied subsidies by the British government, Reuters again became important for strategic ends and hidden propaganda.

To sum up, this chapter has again demonstrated the close linkages between international and national communications and between international relations and international communications. National wireless systems threatened the basis of the empire in terms of security and control of news and information. With so many established interests actively campaigning against wireless, it is not surprising that wireless was not allowed to remodel the empire before World War II. Instead, it introduced a new model, of national control of both domestic and international communications, both wireless and cable, that became the accepted norm in most of the world only after World War II.

8. Cultural Production and International Relations

During World War I the representation of the United States and the American way of life in the press of the Far East and Latin America became such an issue in Congress that it led directly to the opening of low-cost naval radio transmission of international news reports. Although Canada had grumbled about the Americanization of its culture, this congressional action was one of the first recognitions that culture and representation formed part of strategic relations. To the British the empire was both an economic outlet for British goods and the rationale for Britain's strategic importance in world affairs, so the penetration of cultural products became a sensitive issue. As the dominions pulled away from Britain, "British" culture came to be seen as a unifying force within the empire and "American" culture as a threat. On the other hand, for the Americans cultural products and equipment provided entry to an empire that it regarded as sealed. Americans companies saw the movies and radio as advertisements for the manufactured consumer products that would follow.

In turn, U.S. culture, epitomized first by Hollywood movies and then by advertising-led commercial broadcasting, became something for the British to resist. As Holland comments:

> Anti-Americanism and the Commonwealth idea . . . were closely related in that they were rooted in the determination of British policy makers to retain some unilateral initiative in world affairs. . . . The conflict of British and American interests was evident in almost all the main issues of the day—naval power, trade policy, access to raw materials, the containment of Japan, and so on. But its most characteristic expression was . . . the export of American culture and its head-

on clash with "British values." Post-war imperial rhetoric reached its most stri-
dent when it focused on these cultural questions. (1981:36)

Anti-Americanism became part of British political life.

Protectionism and quota restrictions followed. But the movie became a
"cultural product" that epitomized the particular characteristics of information—a product that can be enjoyed by large numbers of consumers without losing its value, whose high costs of creation are offset by the low costs of
distribution and exhibition, and for which the financial incentives of economies of scale act in favor of expansion to the largest audience possible (Garnham 1990).[1] It was inevitable that, having satisfied the domestic market,
movies would move into overseas markets. But that expansion was made
easier when the French stopped producing movies during World War I. That
war opened a vacuum to Hollywood movies, not only in South America but
in Europe and the rest of the world (Guback 1976:465).

This was also a period when international regulation was shown to be
weak. The Soviet Union refused to be bound by international frequency regulation. France and the United States backed the penetration of Britain by
commercial broadcasting. And attempts at the international regulation of
movie content demonstrated that it could not work without both the consensus of the industry and implementation by national governments. Consumer boycotts of specific movies reflected the lack of power of national
governments to alter U.S. commercial dominance.

In the late 1920s and the 1930s U.S. government policy became increasingly
dominated by its companies' interests. As its movie and radio companies
became stronger, both technically and in global penetration, U.S. policy in
international forums represented those interests in international expansion.
Yet this same dominance by its companies later handicapped the U.S. government in taking action against German and Italian propaganda in Latin
America. The domestic clash, between the commercial companies and those
wishing to see a more public corporate structure for radio and the commercial companies, was replicated at the international level within the intra-
American regional conferences and in relation to shortwave broadcasts. It
ended with the victory of the companies. The hesitance of even President
Franklin Roosevelt to fund the government takeover of shortwave transmitters until after Pearl Harbor reflects the power that the companies had accrued. Only where their interests were not affected, as in broadcasting within the European and Far Eastern theaters of war, was the government able
to develop its own "Voice of America."

Hollywood and Europe

Even before World War I, U.S. companies dominated the British film market, which they used as a distribution center for their European and South American customers. In 1911 U.S. films constituted 60 to 70 percent of films imported to Britain, but after World War I began in 1914, the penetration of U.S. films increased. In September 1914, one month after Britain declared war on Germany, *Moving Picture World* stated, "'Within the next year or so the demand for American films in Europe will be large enough to justify a greater "invasion" than Europe has ever known before'" (quoted in Thompson 1985:49). In fact, as the U.S. home market also expanded, the "invasion" took a couple of years to begin, both into European markets and into those of the empire.

Shortly after the Americans entered the war in 1917, the U.S. government introduced restrictions on exports of films. These restrictions were soon loosened, perhaps as a result of the industry's collaboration with the U.S. government's propaganda committee, the U.S. Committee on Public Information, which was known as the Creel Committee. Among other forms of propaganda, this committee used the film industry's development of the newsreel (Fielding 1972). The Association of the Motion Picture Industry set up a committee to work with government departments, to arrange films on wartime goals, and, at the president's behest, to organize the distribution of films in postwar France, Italy, and Russia (Puttnam and Watson 1997:90–91). In Woodrow Wilson's words: "'The film has come to rank as the very highest medium for the dissemination of public intelligence, and since it speaks a universal language, it lends itself importantly to the presentation of America's plans and purposes'" (quoted in Thompson 1985:94).

Wilson may have been primarily interested in exporting images of the U.S. way of life to advertise the benefits of its democracy. But from about 1912 exporters were also aware that the demand for U.S. goods followed films, so that even before the end of the silent era "the cinema had emerged as an effective way to persuade people to consume" (Izod 1988:63). Advertising, which began in movies in 1916, became big business, and the introduction of sound in 1927 further added to the movies' commercial potential (Izod 1988:63).

Control of the supply of Hollywood movies could be used to gain the cooperation of distributors in Europe. In return for expediting export licenses, the Creel Committee's film division gained the industry's cooperation in withholding movies from any theater in a neutral country that showed German films or that refused to show "educational films" that had the imprimatur of the Creel Committee. The so-called educational films comprised 20 percent of all export shipments (Thompson 1985:94) and were often little more than commercials for the products of the companies that donated them. The system ensured the increased distribution of U.S. commercial films in Sweden and Holland and in postwar Switzerland. The YMCA and the Red Cross acted as distributors in both Russia and South America. In August 1918 "the movie business was declared 'an essential business' enabling it to continue operating despite a shortage of materials" (Puttnam and Watson 1997:93).

However, claiming that the committee was competing with Hollywood in production and distribution, by 1918 the industry was demanding the closure of the Creel Committee's operations (Thompson 1985:99). Having paid $580,000 from its rentals to the U.S. Treasury, and assured the dominance of U.S. exports in Europe, the committee was closed down in February 1919. But relationships between Hollywood and the U.S. government remained close. In 1919 the first Fox News newsreel was accompanied by a letter from President Wilson praising its introduction (Fielding 1972:107).

The movie industry's expansion during and after World War I and the difficulty that the Europeans had in reentering the U.S. market were primarily due to the vertical integration of production and distribution within that market, to the cartelization of the major firms through the Motion Picture Producers and Distributors of America (MPPDA), and to support by the U.S. government in the penetration of overseas markets. Not only could the U.S. producers amortize their costs of creation in their home market, and therefore offer films for rent in Britain less expensively than their British counterparts, but they also controlled the European distribution system through block booking and "blind" booking, under which an exhibitor agreed to exhibit the whole of the year's production of a particular studio before it had been made (PEP 1952:38–41). Although such vertical integration was subject to antitrust legislation in the United States, the Webb-Pomarene Act of 1918 exempted overseas combines. The studio system also turned the movie into a manufactured product, and the star system acted as a form of branding that reduced marketing costs. Once worldwide revenues could be used to finance the production of movies, the capital investment required for production in turn precluded much competition.

By 1923 the British share of its home market had dropped to 10 percent, and by 1925 the twenty production firms of 1923 had declined to four or five. In Canada films from the United States took almost 98 percent of box office receipts in 1922 and 99 percent in 1926 (Jarvie 1992:49, 128). Nor were British films able to penetrate other empire markets. By 1917 India was dominated by U.S. films. In New Zealand the British share of the market between 1914 and 1918 fell from 44 percent to 4 percent, while that of Hollywood went from 32 percent to 92 percent (Thompson 1985:82).

Considerable resentment ensued, both at U.S. domination of the British film industry and in terms of the influence of the United States, through Hollywood, on the rest of the empire. Much of the resentment had to do with the way in which the movies catered to the tastes of the working classes, had a tendency to exaggerate class distinctions, and were often antiauthority. Ramsay McDonald was one of several British politicians to complain of the potential influence of Hollywood's love scenes on the perception of the "white man" in the Far East and the colonies.[2] The British political elite considered such public scenes of private passion to be offensive to Asian culture and as undermining the basis of white authority in the colonies.

As British industry struggled with tariff barriers in foreign markets, U.S. movies became seen as an adjunct to the penetration of U.S. manufactured goods into colonial markets. Lord Newton, in a House of Lords debate in May 1925, summed up the feeling of resentment: "'The fact is, the Americans realised almost instantaneously that the cinema was a heaven sent method for advertising themselves, their country, their methods, their wares, their ideas and even their language and they have seized upon it as a method of persuading the whole world, civilised and uncivilised, into the belief that America is really the only country which counts'" (quoted in Jarvie 1992:110–11).

The Federation of British Industrialists wanted the British film industry to export to the empire. But despite an investigation of the Indian market by a government committee, neither an "Empire quota" nor support for the Indian film industry was forthcoming (Jarvie 1992:110). In view of the political difficulties in India, it seems unlikely that the British government would have risked backing an Indian film industry. "British," not indigenous culture, was at risk. Holland comments, "Whenever the stimulation of a UK film industry was discussed in subsequent years, it was always placed in the context of shoring up British values in the face of cheap cultural competition from the U.S." (1981:36).

The content of Hollywood movies exercised other governments. France, Germany, Spain, and Mexico expressed outrage at the way their nationals were represented. Some attempted government-directed boycotts of U.S. films, but these countries' markets were not individually large enough to have an effect on the producers (Seabury 1929:77).

The British government also held strategic concerns. Prime Minister Stanley Baldwin announced to the House of Commons in June 1925: "'I think the time has come when the position of the film industry in this country should be examined to see if it is not possible, as it is desirable on national grounds, that a large proportion of films exhibited in this country are British, having regard to the enormous power which the film has developed for propaganda purposes, and the danger to which we allow that method of propaganda to be in the hands of foreign countries'" (quoted in Seabury 1929:26). After a year of consultations on a voluntary import agreement in which the larger distributors were at odds with producers, Parliament enacted the protectionist Cinematograph Films Bill in 1927. The act made blind booking illegal and imposed an annual quota of full-length British films on both renters and exhibitors. The act was criticized later for blocking the entry of U.S. films while not providing financial help for British production. As a result, with the quota increasing annually until 1935, the number of poor-quality British productions—"quota quickies"—increased, sponsored by the U.S. renters to fulfill their obligations (PEP 1952:50).

In 1925 Germany, Italy, and France also limited movie imports because of their concern about the representation of their nationals in Hollywood movies and because of the falling value of their currencies. Some imposed outright limits, and others set quotas for imports according to a pre-set proportion of local production. Both Germany and France saw attempts to link penetration of U.S. imports to reciprocal distribution in the United States of domestically produced films. At first these agreements were on a company-to-company basis but then became controlled by governments (Seabury 1929:66, 132; Southard 1931:97).

In turn, the threat of these quotas led to close cooperation between the film industry and the U.S. government. In the belief that "trade follows the film, rather than the flag . . . the screen acts as a voiceless salesman for the goods it pictures," Hollywood and the U.S. government saw import quotas for films as the precursor to import quotas for other U.S. goods (Luther 1988:181n.28). After a two-year lobbying campaign from Will Hays, president of the MPPDA, alleging an anti-American movement in Europe, the Department of Commerce established a motion picture section. Some section personnel may have accepted that the anti-American movement had its roots in the European perception that "through American motion pictures, the ideals, culture, customs and traditions of the United States are gradually undermining those of other countries." Nevertheless, they set out to win new markets for the movie industry (Thompson 1985:117).

Beginning in 1927 the Department of Commerce financed market surveys, first in Central Europe, Italy, and Spain, then in Scandinavia and the Baltic states, followed in 1929 by market research in Australia, New Zealand, Brazil, and Argentina (Thompson 1985:171). It also proselytized on behalf of Hollywood exports through articles in the European popular press and acted against copyright violations in Central America and the Far East (Thompson 1985:118). In addition, between 1926 and 1928 the U.S. government supported the movie industry in its opposition to the quotas imposed by the Europeans.

The U.S. government sent a note of protest to all those countries with film quota restrictions—Berlin, Rome, Madrid, Vienna, Prague, and Budapest—claiming that the restrictions were a violation of the Economic Convention of the League of Nations of 1927. It argued that this convention, to which the United States was a signatory, had been designed to abolish import and export prohibitions and restrictions (Thompson 1985:121). In July 1928 the U.S. ambassador to Switzerland presented to the league's 1928 Economic Conference the U.S. contention that the French imposition of quotas and reciprocity violated the 1927 convention. The U.S. government subsequently backed the MPPDA's withdrawal from the French market (Seabury 1929:142).

Proponents of the European quotas argued that the exceptions allowed under article 4 of the economic treaty—"public security," "moral or humanitarian grounds," and "public health"—covered the imposition of controls and the demands for reciprocity. The U.S. demand for reciprocity seems to have come from advice offered by Seabury, the former general counsel to the National Association of the Motion Picture Industry—a poacher turned gamekeeper (Seabury 1929:135). Supporting the French position, India then announced that it intended to adopt measures similar to those of France. But following U.S. diplomatic efforts, the French quota was raised in 1929 from four U.S. movies for every French movie to seven U.S. movies for every French movie (Southard 1931:99, 142).

The anxiety of the U.S. movie industry owed to its dependence on European receipts. In 1929, with an estimated annual net revenue of about $64 million, approximately 70 percent came from Europe (Southard 1931:94). In fact, quotas did rather little to help the French industry, primarily because its domestic distribution system was under U.S. control. And with little competition from the indigenous industry, U.S. producers were not motivated to set up production in Europe (Southard 1931:96). The direct effect of the British import controls of 1927 was to create something of a boom in British production; feature film production rose from 96 films in 1930 to 215 in 1935 and an attempt by British producers to again enter the world market. But U.S. producers had a home market more than twice the size of Britain's and took in $161.4 million per year, compared to the $14.7 million in revenue for British films. British expansion ended with bankruptcies and a slump in 1938 (PEP 1952:60, 69). Another British Cinematographic Act of 1938 followed, extending the earlier quotas.

Once talkies began in 1930, the production budgets required to compete with the U.S. film industry operated against the Europeans. Despite the challenge mounted by the German holders of patents on sound production equipment, in July 1930 they reached agreement with RCA and Western Electric to share the world market and the "interchangeability of films recorded on the different systems was made possible" (PEP 1952:53). Although facing problems created by language barriers, the U.S. movie industry continued to dominate the rest of the world through its vertical linkage of production and distribution. Only Germany, Japan, and India offered any real competition to U.S. dominance. In Germany state-backed production soon became the propaganda films of the Nazi era. In Japan vertical concentration of production, distribution, and exhibition kept U.S. imports low. And in India the addition of sound allowed the development of a specifically Indian version of the musical, and native producers were able to increase production dramatically. India got its own movie industry.

But the measures taken by other European countries also had an indirect effect on U.S. producers. As other export markets closed down, Hollywood became more dependent on the British market. Richards (1986:144) argues that this dependence led to U.S. producers' enthusiasm for colonial themes, where military heroism and implicit racism appealed to British and American audiences alike. Hollywood produced "empire movies" with themes similar to those made by British producers during the 1930s. Only after troops from the colonies joined whites in fighting the Axis did such themes become distasteful to the U.S. authorities (Richards 1986:157–58).

During the 1930s some governments tried to involve the League of Nations in the issue of movie content on the grounds that films could promote national antagonisms, racism, and war and that their content was insufficiently regulated. To protect children from unsuitable content most countries had forms of censorship, often, as in Britain and the United States, financed by the industry itself. But demand was growing for controls to prevent the showing of offensive movies. Because of the representation of Mexicans in U.S. movies, the Mexican government led an ineffective boycott of specific studios. But in a global market some argued that the problem was bigger than the nation-state, whose power was commensurate with its market size, and that the remedy was cooperation and agreement among nations.

In fact, the League of Nations held an international cinema conference under the auspices of the International Committee on Intellectual Cooperation in 1926 that was attended by 435 delegates from thirty-one countries. The MPPDA initially refused to attend, claiming that the conference ""might develop into an anti-American affair if we took part in it."'"[3] The conference was successfully limited to formulating and studying the problems of the film industry from an international perspective. Other European cinema trade personnel hijacked the conference, and the attempt to set up a permanent international committee of the League of Nations failed. Large numbers of resolutions were passed, but without any means to enforce them, they fell into obscurity.

Nevertheless, in 1927 Herbert Hoover, then the U.S. secretary of commerce, warned the industry of its obligation "'that every picture of South American life shown to our people and every picture of North American life shown to the South American peoples should carry . . . those ideals which build for that respect and confidence which is the real guarantee of peace'" (quoted in Seabury 1929:27). Fearing domestic regulation, the U.S. movie industry was moved the following year to reiterate its acceptance of the "eleven don'ts and twenty six be carefuls" to which it had first agreed in 1921. The don'ts included "'pointed profanity'"; licentious or suggestive nudity; depiction of illegal trafficking in drugs; inference of sexual perversion; white slavery; miscegenation; references to sexual hygiene and venereal diseases; childbirth; children's sex organs; ridicule of the clergy and "'willful offense to any nation, race or creed'" (quoted in Seabury 1929:201n.3).

Despite this code of practice, the U.S. Office of War Information banned reissues of *Gunga Din* and stopped Metro-Goldwyn-Mayer from making a film of Kipling's *Kim* after the United States entered World War II. For an industry desperate to keep up exports to those countries that were open to its films—Britain, Australia, New Zealand, and Canada—such old colonial themes were safe. But when Indians were fighting alongside the Allies, racial stereotypes had become an embarrassment, and strategic interest could override commercial concerns. Also, with an antitrust suit hanging over it, Hollywood was eager to cooperate. In effect, state-based regulation of markets and content by European governments, coupled with domestic problems, induced sufficient reaction within the U.S. government to improve the movie industry's self-regulation. In time of war, and with the threat of antitrust action, the U.S. government could stand up to Hollywood. But despite global penetration and the overriding dominance of Hollywood, no means had been found to regulate it worldwide.

Radio in Britain

The development of radio for broadcasting also raised the potential for its use for propaganda. It seemed possible that the new technology could establish a link with mass populations, particularly overseas, in a way that had previously been precluded by lack of literacy. Theoretically, whereas newspapers and news agencies spoke to a literate elite, radio, like movies, could be used to influence public opinion. The U.S. government recognized this potential of overseas broadcasting early.

President Woodrow Wilson was the first to use the radio for political purposes in a direct broadcast to the Asian, European, and American peoples promulgating his "Fourteen Points" in January 1918. And in July 1918 a direct transmission from the United States took the president's appeal for peace to the German people (Rosenberg 1982:93). But the efficacy of such appeals rested on the penetration of receiving equipment. In the early days international broadcasting was directed predominantly at the elites of foreign countries.

When World War I ended, British radio technology was ready to launch broadcasting, but the military and government considered that any such development would interfere with official transmissions and therefore opposed it. However, as in the United States, manufacturers had unused equipment left over from the war, and they exerted pressure on the government (Wedlake 1973:162).

RCA and the Marconi company had agreed to mutual access to each other's patents, and the Marconi company held the monopoly for radio equipment in Britain. The company's first experiment with radiotelephony was carried out in Ireland in 1919 and was followed by construction of a transmitter at Chelmsford, in the east of England, for which it was granted a temporary license in 1920. But the Post Office claimed a monopoly over radio transmission under the Telegraph Act of 1869 and the Wireless Telegraph Act of 1904 and regarded these broadcasts as frivolous.

Perhaps because it was the Marconi company, the Post Office banned any further broadcasts from Chelmsford in November 1920, ten months after they had begun. Then, after two years of being lobbied by amateurs and manufacturers, the Post Office allowed the company to resume broadcasts on an experimental basis. These ad hoc broadcasts were picked up by amateur radio enthusiasts (Eckersley 1942:39–47). Two other companies—Metropolitan Vickers, a valve manufacturer, and Western Electric (then a subsidiary of

AT&T)—applied for licenses. Eckersley suggests that the manufacturers wished to copy the U.S. system of broadcasting, where they would set up transmitters "so that they could make more money by selling wireless receivers" and sell "time on the air" to advertisers. He argues that "commercial broadcasting would undoubtedly have been instituted in Britain had it not been for the wavelength shortage" (1942:50).

In view of the problem of how to divide the few wavelengths among competing manufacturers, the government convened a conference of the manufacturers, armed services, the Board of Trade, and the Foreign, Colonial, and India Offices. Basing its arguments on the evidence of interference between competing stations in the United States, the Post Office suggested a single company for the purpose of broadcasting. Eventually, the British Broadcasting Company Ltd. was launched in October 1922 as an agent of the Post Office, with capital supplied by the manufacturers. The Post Office retained overall technical control, but gave the BBC a monopoly of all transmission of broadcasting in Great Britain and Northern Ireland. Broadcasts were allowed on the medium wave only between 5 P.M. and midnight.

The board of the British Broadcasting Company was made up of representatives of the radio manufacturers and included a representative of the Post Office (Wedlake 1973:165–67). The company was to gain revenue from a license fee charged to anyone with a receiver, to be collected by the Post Office and a portion transferred to the company. According to Eckersley (1942:53), the Post Office chose a license fee to generate revenue because it feared that the service would be unsuccessful. Advertising was not ruled out. But to protect the press, the BBC was forbidden to accept money for advertising. Nevertheless, broadcasting without advertising became perceived as the "British way," and it became elevated into a principle of high-quality broadcasting, in comparison to the low-quality commercial U.S. model. The U.S. model featured stunts, dance music, and "popular turns," rather than talks and drama, and despite a plethora of competing stations all U.S. programs were said to be of a similar type (BBC 1931:43–47; 1932:131–35).[4]

Marconi equipment became the de facto standard. In order to protect the four manufacturers' investment, the original license specified that only approved sets should be used. But these sets were too expensive for most people, and because many sets were homemade from foreign parts, the Post Office had to drop the requirement for "standard" sets (Wood 1992:32).

Broadcasting in Britain had to overcome the hostility of established interests, which ranged from the military and the civil service to the newspapers. Early in the negotiations the government stated that the BBC would not broadcast news that had not already been printed (Wedlake 1973:170). This edict protected both the press and Post Office revenue that derived from press telegrams. In particular, the press objected to the broadcasting of sports events, and although an agreement was eventually worked out that allowed Reuters to supply the BBC with news on a commercial basis, it could be broadcast only after 7 P.M. Until the end of 1926 the BBC was not allowed to broadcast sports events, and a separate news department was not set up until 1934 (Wedlake 1973:172–73).

In 1926 the BBC became a "public corporation." Instituted under the mechanism of a royal charter, its new status made it accountable to Parliament but allowed it an element of self-regulation, at arm's length from direct government intervention (Scannell and Cardiff 1991:7). As MacKenzie (1986:168) points out, the conservative nature of BBC broadcasts was partly due to the restrictions on what it could broadcast. "National" events, such as the Empire Exhibition of 1924 and Empire Day, were "therefore a convenient way in which the BBC could overcome these inhibitions on news gathering." The BBC's conservatism stemmed partly from its director, Lord Reith, a dour Presbyterian with a mission for broadcasting to "educate, inform and entertain." The conservatism was also due in part to the agreement at its inception that it should avoid controversy, an agreement that allowed the Post Office powers of censorship and that was not lifted until 1928. In general, the BBC did not become established as an institution or gain a reputation for editorial independence until the General Strike of 1926, during which newspapers were unable to print.

After 1921 shortwave technology also made possible international broadcasting. Reith saw that broadcasting could unify disparate communities and in 1924 had attempted "to get the India Office to take the potentialities of broadcasting seriously" but without effect (Reith 1949:113). By 1926 the BBC was broadcasting by medium and long wave, and the Post Office agreed that it might experiment with shortwave transmissions "in order to ascertain how far it would be possible—if such a course were found to be desirable—to establish a wireless link for the purpose of transmitting British programmes to the Dominions and Colonies." But these experiments had not begun in 1927, when an amateur radio association lobbied the Colonial Office to establish shortwave broadcasting from Britain to the colonies.[5] The group wanted the Colonial Office to finance the station, with revenue for programming coming from license fees in the colonies, and offered to act as the coordinator of the service. The Post Office rejected the suggestion, preferring the BBC.[6]

The upcoming 1927 Colonial Conference instigated a review of policy within the Colonial Office, which reached the conclusion that "in many of

the larger Colonies the stage has been reached in which it is necessary to formulate with care a policy in the matter of broadcasting as a channel of information and a means of entertainment."[7] The intention of the Colonial
Office was to ensure that the colonies adopted a scheme similar to that adopted in Britain, so each colony would have the equivalent of the British Broadcasting Corporation with a state monopoly funded by license fees from reception equipment. The conference heard from a number of colonies about
their establishment or proposed establishment of local radio stations.[8] The
Gold Coast could pick up U.S. broadcasts, and the Straits Settlements were
listening to the Dutch from Java. It was evident that a considerable demand
existed for shortwave broadcasts that could be relayed locally.

But the BBC was concerned that it should not rush in with a technically
poor service. "We should like to feel that the Conference appreciate the desire for careful thought and experiment and not just going in wildly ahead
in order to give the Colonies merely what you can receive from America on
the short waves, which is unsatisfactory and distorted," said Adm. Charles
Carpendale, the BBC controller. And because the BBC's revenue came from
listeners in England, he also wanted to know whether the colonies would be
prepared to share the cost (United Kingdom 1927:9).

But pressured to start a service, the BBC began experimental transmissions
in 1927 using the Marconi company's transmitter (Fortner 1993:110). Although
the Dominions Office saw the wireless as a means of rectifying a situation
where the general public in the dominions was ignorant of both Britain and
other parts of the empire, there were doubts about its efficacy. In the words
of one Whitehall official: "'If the British Official Wireless is to be widely and
regularly used (by the Dominions) the first essential is that it should be interesting. Could a daily supply of the right stamp be assured? It would not
do to give second-rate stuff, or to have to announce "Special Imperial Bulletin: no news tonight"'" (quoted in Holland 1981:34).

Such doubts and lack of enthusiasm from the dominions, coupled with
the general economic depression, led to further delays. Whereas by 1931 the
Netherlands, Germany, and France had all begun external broadcasting for
their expatriates, the British colonies had to wait. First, they had to apply to
establish transmitters and gain approval from the Imperial Wireless Committee, and then the Treasury had to approve their budgets. The BBC's experimental service continued for five more years and included the relay of
programs in the United States by the National Broadcasting Company. But
lack of funding for the colonies meant the idea of broadcasting within the
empire primarily for local relay had to be replaced with direct transmission
to listeners (BBC 1929:33–37; Appleton 1933:13).

Eventually, the BBC decided to pay for the service from its license fees, justifying the expenditure of income derived from domestic listeners on the ground that "'it seemed contrary to the interests of the listener, as a citizen, that Britain alone should be without a world-wide voice, seeing that it is both the focal point of a world-wide Empire and dependent upon world-wide exports and capital investments'" (quoted in Burton 1956:383). The BBC external services began on December 19, 1932, on Reith's personal initiative, under the title "Empire Service." Reith intended that the service should become "'a connecting and co-ordinating link between the scattered parts of the British Empire . . . dedicated to the best interest of mankind'" (quoted in Mansell 1982:2). Reaching to Australia, India, Africa, West Africa, and Canadian zones, its daily broadcasts rapidly expanded from ten to fourteen hours.

Eckersley, the BBC engineer responsible for the new service, described it as "'Empire consolidation by wireless'" (quoted in Mansell 1982:2). Some people within the BBC objected to the service's using English because many listeners would not understand it. Nevertheless, using domestic programming made the empire service inexpensive to run, so it consisted of the Home Service (broadcast in Britain), interspersed with the playing of phonograph records and light entertainment (BBC 1934:243–81; Gafatchi 1989).

Many specific features of the service concerned happenings related to the empire. Its inauguration in 1932 allowed King George V to make a Christmas Day broadcast for the first time to the empire—a broadcast that prompted two thousand lead stories in newspapers all over the world, including the United States (Reith 1949:169). But while Reith was "concerned to unite national and international audiences in imperial ritual," the image of the empire that the BBC portrayed was a mixture of the militarist and the peaceful internationalist, "both of which were out of tune with reality" (MacKenzie 1986:186). The service was aimed at expatriates and local elites, not the "man under the palm tree" (Briggs 1985:143).

Soon after its own national broadcasts began, the BBC had found its signals interrupted by interference emanating from the European continent. An informal meeting of broadcasters eventually instigated the creation of the International Broadcasting Union (IBU) in 1925 to consider the problem of mutual interference between European broadcasters. Chaired by a BBC man, with an administrative office in Geneva and technical office in Brussels, it was composed of European broadcasting organizations—public, semipublic, and private (BBC 1934:287–89). After much struggle between the members, in 1926 the technical committee of this organization drew up a plan, known as the Geneva plan, for the distribution of wavelengths to European stations (Eckersley 1942:86). The IBU then developed a "wave-meter," which determined how closely each station was operating to the wavelength assigned. The Geneva plan for broadcasting was what the 1927 Washington conference ignored in favor of the maritime interests of the major powers, leaving broadcasting problems in Europe to be addressed in Prague the following year (J. D. Tomlinson 1945:181).

At Prague the IBU became the official technical adviser to the International Telegraph Union (ITU) for the European broadcasting services, both public and private. And it was at this conference that twenty-eight European administrations first agreed on the allocation of specific wavelengths to individual broadcasting stations (J. D. Tomlinson 1945:187). However, from then on the plan became inflexible because the formality of the ITU overtook the informal IBU. And as broadcasting became linked to propaganda, the IBU became "the miniature battleground for international rivalries" (Eckersley 1942:100).

During the early, more cooperative, years of radio, the IBU "tried with some success to limit the power of stations situated near national frontiers. Some governments even forbade the broadcasting of any matter, which might give offense to nearby nations. Other countries, however exploited the advantage conferred on them by nature and began diffusing internal broadcasts obviously intended for foreign consumption" (Saerchinger 1938:251). In particular, the exclusion of the Soviet Union from the 1927 Washington conference had long-lasting implications. Although the Soviet Union attended IBU conferences, it refused to be party to European attempts to limit long-wave broadcasts or to reduce the power of its stations. It had seized the best long waves, kept them, and poured propaganda into Europe, inciting workers to rebellion.

The Soviet Union's behavior led the European broadcasting organizations to refer the matter of "spillover" of international broadcasting to the League of Nations. In turn, "all the international questions raised by the use of broadcasting in regard to international relations" were referred to one of the league's specialized committees—the International Institute of Intellectual Cooperation (J. D. Tomlinson 1945:227). A draft convention evolved over several years, and in September 1936 the council of the League of Nations convened the Intergovernmental Conference for the Adoption of a Convention Concerning the Use of Broadcasting in the Cause of Peace.

The final act required its signatories "'to agree to prohibit the kind of broadcasting into another state that would incite a population to acts incompatible with the internal order or security of that state, would constitute incitement to war, was harmful to good international understanding, or was known by the broadcaster to be false.'" It also bound the signatories to "'promote a better knowledge of the civilization and the conditions of life among the various countries, as well as their contribution to the organization of peace'" (quoted in Luther 1988:32). The convention was ratified by Brazil, the United Kingdom, Denmark, France, India, Luxembourg, New Zealand, the Union of South Africa, and Australia and took effect on April 2, 1938. But by then many of the European countries were defying the provisions of the convention. The league's own broadcasting service, Radio Nations, was also an abject failure (Rigby 1972:9).

The originators of the "politically ideological" external broadcast were the Soviets, who began broadcasting in foreign languages in 1929 (Cherry 1978:109). The dispersion of languages within Europe, with many states containing minorities speaking another language, could be used to justify broadcasting in foreign languages. Italy began broadcasts in Arabic in 1932 to its North African colony, Libya. The Germans followed suit shortly after with the 1933 "historic attempt of the Nazis to bring Austria into their political orbit" by using radio as an "offensive political instrument" through transmissions from Munich (Saerchinger 1938:253). Radio was also used to broadcast into Spain during the civil war in 1935.

The effect was to make Britain understand the need to project its interests. In 1936 a government committee recommended that the empire's English-language service be maintained and developed but, in the interest of British prestige and influence in world affairs, recommended the development of foreign-language broadcasts as well (Ullswater 1936). Belatedly, in 1935 the Treasury agreed to give the BBC the money to develop the Empire Service (Briggs 1985:141). That year the BBC started a relay service to the Gold Coast (now Ghana) (Gafatchi 1989:8). The BBC's second royal charter in 1937 then formalized the Empire Service by requesting that the corporation present "'programmes of broadcast matter for reception in His Majesty's Dominions beyond the seas and territories under His Majesty's protection'" (quoted in Burton 1956:388).

But the BBC's foreign-language broadcasting had a different genesis. When the long-wave transmitter at Rugby opened in 1926, the Foreign Office had begun transmitting the Official News Service from there each day in Morse code. Because the Foreign Office believed that news for distribution to the Arab world in Arabic needed "'special treatment of selection and omission,'" there was debate about whether foreign-language broadcasts would damage the BBC's reputation for impartiality (quoted in Taylor 1981:201). Then, during the Abyssinian crisis in 1935 the Italians began anti-British broadcasts to North Africa in Arabic. The Italian government's gift to Arab cafes of radios locked onto Italian frequencies motivated the Foreign Office to respond with its own Arabic broadcasts from Jerusalem on medium wave, operated under the British postmaster general of Palestine (Seif 1988:30–32; Saerchinger 1938:254). The Foreign Office then learned that the Middle East had more shortwave receivers than it had previously thought and considered siting a shortwave transmitter in Cyprus. When Cyprus proved to be too close to the Middle East for shortwave broadcasts, the Foreign Office tried to involve a reluctant Indian government in the scheme. Finally, when the Indian government demurred, the Foreign Office was obliged to use the BBC's shortwave transmissions from Britain (Taylor 1981:199).

In 1937 the BBC began broadcasts in Arabic to the Middle East. But in order to do so, and to gain financing for the service—although Reith continued to insist on independence of editorial control—the BBC came to a "gentlemen's agreement" with the government on the censorship of news, which led to different interpretations by each side (Walker 1992:31). The following year the BBC also began shortwave broadcasts to South America in Spanish and Portuguese. The aim of the new language broadcasts, according to the BBC, was "not to meet propaganda with counter-propaganda, but to secure a wider audience for a broadcast news service which has, in English, won a high reputation in all parts of the world for fairness and impartiality" (BBC 1938:52).

In truth, the broadcasts to South America were a smokescreen so that the Arab service would not antagonize Mussolini, then thought of as a potential ally (Walker 1992:31). But there had also been an increase in German propaganda into South America. With the intention that the Germans living in foreign countries should feel "united proudly with the Fatherland" (Grandin 1971:48), German shortwave broadcasts from Zeesen were directed at the more than seven million German nationals in the United States, 600,000 in Brazil, and 150,000 in Argentina. Broadcasts could be received on shortwave sets especially designed for the purpose and distributed by Nazi agents. But the Germans could reach a larger audience through local relays. In 1937 more than 235 German programs were rebroadcast by domestic radio stations free of charge in Argentina and two hundred in Brazil and Chile, compared to one rebroadcast of a British program. Reflecting government refusal to subsidize the Reuters service, some Latin American countries received no direct news service at all from Britain (Grandin 1971:47–49).

As the situation in Europe worsened, following the Munich crisis of 1938 the British government began to provide additional money to the BBC to broadcast in foreign languages to Europe. Transmission on medium wave began in 1938 in German, French, and Italian and in 1939 to Spain and Portugal. Shortwave broadcasts in Afrikaans to combat German propaganda to southern Africa became possible after a new transmitter was erected in 1939.

By 1940 the BBC also kept a representative in New York, and its Radio News-reel was broadcast regularly from London.

The BBC's shortwave broadcasts were indicative of the prewar increase in shortwave transmissions that were then unregulated. Based on evidence of increasing competition for these frequencies, the IBU recommended to the 1938 ITU conference in Cairo that it should develop a plan for the distribution of shortwave frequencies for long-distance broadcasting. In Europe television had begun in France, Germany, and the United Kingdom but on different bands and frequencies. And, in addition to overseas broadcasts, radio beacons for air and maritime service also used these frequencies in a number of countries. However, given the political nature of overseas broadcasting, and the U.S. delegation's opposition to an expansion of broadcasting bands at the expense of fixed services, the conference failed to address the problem of overseas broadcasts. For the first time the conference did reserve shortwave frequencies for intercontinental airplane communications (J. D. Tomlinson 1945:223).

In 1930 only three shortwave transmitters were used in Europe for international broadcasts. By 1939 this number had increased to forty. The Soviet Union alone transmitted in sixty-two languages. The war years saw further expansion. By war's end the BBC was broadcasting in forty-five languages and had extended the reach of its service far beyond the empire (Briggs 1985:225–26). In 1942 the United Kingdom was one of fifty-five countries, including the United States, that was involved in broadcasting into other countries—in violation of the League of Nations Convention (i.e., without permission) —in order to present national views to the world at large (Grandin 1971:44). These questions of sovereign rights were to arise again in the 1950s as the threat of broadcasting from satellites created pressure for a similar United Nations convention.[9]

Continental Broadcasts into Britain

Even before the outbreak of the European war, the British had had problems with broadcasts in English from the Continent. These were not political propaganda broadcasts but paid for by advertising, based on the U.S. model. The first, Radio Luxembourg, was a project of the Societé Française Radio-Électrique, a French company with a concession from Luxembourg. That state, in addition to the concession payments, also gained 30 percent of the station's profits. The station was conceived as a commercial enterprise to broadcast within Europe in French, English, and German. With programs sponsored by the International Broadcasting Company, owned by U.S. advertising interests based in London, the station, established in 1933, used a long-wave frequency outside the 1927 allocations. The station was to operate at 200 kilowatts, making it second to Moscow's 500 kilowatts in its power, at a time when the average station used 18 kilowatts (J. D. Tomlinson 1945:155).

Less concerned at the station's breach of technical standards than its carrying U.S.-style advertising, the British nevertheless used technicalities to try to close it. On the basis of its illegality, the BBC's Reith prevailed on the U.S. broadcasting networks not to cooperate with the station, but because of French support for Luxembourg at the ITU's 1932 conference in Madrid, the British were unable to limit its range, which was intended to reach Britain (J. D. Tomlinson 1945:209). The station was most popular in the early hours, before the BBC began transmitting, and on Sundays. It offered programs that advertised mainly U.S. food products that were "undemanding, but fun" (Walker 1992:18).

By the time of the Cairo conference in 1938, Radio Normandie, a private French station that had increased its transmitter power and targeted advertising in English at the United Kingdom, had joined Radio Luxembourg. Although the French government had stated in 1937 that it would introduce a bill forbidding private broadcasters to advertise in English, or use transmitter power exceeding that authorized in the international radio regulations, it took no such action (J. D. Tomlinson 1945:225n.4). Once again the British tried to use the station's frequency violations to get it outlawed. The delegation to the Cairo conference argued that "'at the present time two countries advertise in English; in some other countries, as a result of the important financial interests at stake, attempts are also being made towards being able to carry on similar publicity transmissions for British reception. This practice is of great profit both to the stations and the administrations. Consequently, if two countries profit thereby, why should not others do the same?'" (quoted in J. D. Tomlinson 1945:225).

Because the League of Nations had not considered commercial broadcasting as a "type of program harmful to good international understanding," the delegation asked the conference to rule on whether the broadcasting was legitimate (J. D. Tomlinson 1945:226). Without such agreement the Post Office's jamming of the signals would be illegal. Opposition from France (which had both a state and private radio system) and the votes of non-European delegations, such as that from the United States, led to a tied vote and no action. The failure of the British government to gain support in Cairo, and the public unpopularity of its stance against international commercial broadcasting, led to a reassessment of policy and an internal debate about advertising as a means of financing radio. The government began to play down its opposition, not raising the issue through Post Office delegates at the European Broadcasting Union's conference in Montreux. And as the international situation in Europe deteriorated, the British government used Continental stations to sponsor programs that aimed propaganda at Germany (Briggs 1985:368).

By 1938 Radio Luxembourg and Radio Normandie had been joined by others—Radio Lyons (1936) and Radio Toulouse (1937), both located in France, and Radio Athlone (1932), located in Ireland—sponsored by the same interests. Thus the years immediately before World War II saw the beginnings of a state-backed campaign by U.S. interests to liberalize, restructure, and commercialize the broadcasting market in Europe, a campaign that was to culminate with the introduction of commercial television in the 1950s in Britain.[10]

United States: Broadcasting

In the United States the passage of the Radio Act of 1927, the establishment of the Federal Radio Commission (FRC), and proper licensing procedures had helped to eliminate many of the competing radio stations of the 1920s. Commercial activity in the form of land-based transmission of programs via AT&T's landlines and, in 1926–27, the establishment of the two broadcasting networks, NBC (National Broadcasting Company)—owned by General Electric, Westinghouse, and RCA—and CBS (Columbia Broadcasting System), had also prevented much of the radio interference. Allocated clear channels by the FRC, network control of infrastructure and control of content went hand in hand. Radio had become big business. By 1928 the domestic sale of radio sets had reached $650 million (Wedlake 1973:158).

Advertising was first introduced in 1922 by AT&T in New York but did not attain the form we now recognize as "commercial advertising" until 1928 (McChesney 1994:150). Opposition from nonprofit stations and public interest groups ensured that the domestic debate about whether radio should be publicly or privately financed continued until the mid-1930s. McChesney (1994:30) reports that radio advertising, a marginal activity in 1927, accounted for $100 million in 1930 alone. By then advertising took up twelve to fifteen minutes of every hour, and the commercial advertising–based model of U.S. broadcasting was becoming accepted as the norm. The dominance of advertising led to concomitant problems in the private censorship of what were termed "controversial" opinions—any views contrary to the interests of advertisers. In this debate, from its establishment in 1927 the FRC was to act as a defender of the commercial broadcasting system (Schiller 1969:24).

The development of commercial radio led in turn to the creation of a mass market for music recordings. "Hand in hand with the development of entertainment broadcasting came the phonograph record, to create an industry that became the largest of its kind in the world, with such brand names as Columbia, Victor and Brunswick" (Wood 1992:14). Despite the 1932 antitrust consent decree against RCA that separated it from Westinghouse and General Electric, by 1933 and the election of Franklin Roosevelt the commercial system of broadcasting was well established. It was backed by the manufacturers of radio equipment and the producers of recorded music, financed by advertising-sponsored programs that in turn sold mass-produced products to a mass consumer society. In delivering audiences to advertisers, rather than programs to audiences, it posed a completely different model from the predominantly state-owned European model, or the voluntary association of the Dutch, or the "public service broadcasting" model of the BBC.

Internationalization of Commercial Radio

Radio's international commercial spread from the United States was initially limited by the technology. Using ground waves traveling along the surface of the earth, long-wave systems relied on high power and low frequencies to achieve distance. A limited number of usable channels prevented expansion. But, in contrast to Europe, where the small size of countries prevented the domestic use of shortwave for broadcasting, the large landmass of the United States allowed shortwave to be used during the 1920s to link radio stations that were far apart. Programs broadcast on medium wave at one station could be simulcast on shortwave, transmitted to another, and then rebroadcast on medium wave for local reception. When AT&T was seeking to enter the broadcast market to compete with RCA, Westinghouse, and General Electric, such a system bypassed AT&T's control of point-to-point transmission between radio stations. This issue was settled in 1926, when AT&T agreed to withdraw from broadcasting under government pressure and to lease long-distance landlines to the other broadcasting companies. Shortwave as a means of station-to-station interconnection was then banned by the FRC in 1929, and the commercial reason for its development was lost (Fejes 1986:47–49).

However, before this agreement a number of companies experimented with shortwave transmission. Companies such as General Electric and Westinghouse were primarily concerned with developing their radio equipment and better understanding the characteristics of the radio spectrum. By 1923 General Electric was rebroadcasting domestic programs to Latin America and Europe. In contrast, RCA's competition with AT&T for control of domestic broadcasting pointed it toward program exchanges. Because domestic regulation barred AT&T from any form of international broadcasting, RCA saw competitive advantage in bringing foreign programs to the United States (Fejes 1986:52).

However, RCA's suspicion of shortwave and preference for superpower long-wave transatlantic transmission, which proved unreliable, delayed its introduction of a commercial shortwave service between London and New York until 1927 (Fejes 1986:53). When that service in turn proved unreliable, RCA discontinued its shortwave broadcasting for two years while it explored and developed the technology. After further experimental transatlantic program exchanges, "the new era was inaugurated in late January 1930 with the proceedings of the London Five-Power Naval Conference transmitted to the United States and rebroadcast over the NBC and CBS networks" (Fejes 1986:56).

By 1931 exchanging programs with the BBC had become a standard part of U.S. broadcasting. But it was one-way traffic. "In 1931 while NBC rebroadcast 159 foreign program transmissions, equaling 73.5 hours, it only transmitted 24 programs to countries outside the United States, a total of 11.5 hours" (Fejes 1986:56). Imports from the BBC decreased during the late 1930s as the Foreign Office became sensitive to the possibility that BBC programs could be construed as propaganda and could antagonize the U.S. public (Taylor 1981:74–75). Nevertheless, the growth in shortwave broadcasts into the United States expanded the sales of shortwave receivers, which first appeared in 1933 (Fejes 1986:59).

Radio equipment exports became an important part of the postwar boom in U.S. international trade and foreign investment; the most important export markets in the late 1920s were Canada, Argentina, and Australia (Batson 1971:39–46). Aided by the market analyses and trade promotion of a much-expanded Department of Commerce under Herbert Hoover, exports of radio equipment amounted to nearly $60 million between 1920 and 1929. In most Central and South American countries the majority of receivers were American in origin, with the remainder primarily British and German. In 1930 shortwave sets were becoming increasingly popular even before the inauguration of French broadcasting to Latin America, a favorite among local elites (Batson 1971:48–65; Rigby 1972:9). U.S. international shortwave broadcasting was therefore closely tied to export markets for equipment.

NBC, Westinghouse, Crosley, and General Electric all were engaged in international commercial broadcasting during the 1920s. Although the FRC did not permit shortwave to take advertising specifically directed at third-country audiences, because most programming was simulcast, it contained domestic advertising. Writing its domestic regulation of international short-wave broadcasting in 1928 the FRC saw shortwave's future, not in direct broadcasting overseas but in the rebroadcast of exchanged programs by the receiving station on its regular frequency. As a result international shortwave broadcasting was defined as an "experimental relay" service. Claiming that further research was necessary, the FRC turned down both Westinghouse's and General Electric's 1930 applications for a commercial direct broadcast service to Latin America (Fejes 1986:59).

This decision partly reflected the prevailing attitude toward Latin America following the stock market crash of October 1929. With Latin America gaining importance for strategic resources, such as oil, the 1920s had seen U.S. financial institutions investing heavily in Latin American bonds. But as the depression took hold, U.S. policy became increasingly protectionist. A U.S. drive for exports and an Open Door overseas went hand in hand with high tariffs to protect the national market. That protectionism was in turn an incendiary to Latin American economic nationalism, evident in the upsurge in labor movements demanding social reform and national control of resources. Suspicion of the United States and its policy in radio had already been voiced at the 1924 Mexico conference when, according to the U.S. delegate William Vallance, "'the United States has been charged with having in mind nearly complete control of communication facilities in this hemisphere, so that in case of difficulties it could stop the cable and radio stations and isolate any unruly country'" (quoted in Fejes 1986:n. 67).

The Department of Commerce encouraged U.S. companies to advertise directly on Latin American radio stations, which it saw as a way to reach the elites who might buy luxury goods. A survey in 1930 found that radio stations in Argentina, Bolivia, Brazil, Chile, Colombia, Peru, Uruguay, and Venezuela accepted advertising (Schutrumpf 1971:9–10). The markets where advertising was allowed were also those with the highest penetration of radio sets. The 1931 survey estimated 400,000 radio sets in Argentina, 190,000 in Brazil, 70,000 in Peru, 60,000 in Uruguay, 35,000 in Chile, 5,000 in Colombia, and 2,500 in Venezuela but fewer than 200 in other countries. In Central America only Mexico with 100,000 and Cuba with almost 29,000 radios had penetrations worthwhile to advertisers (Schutrumpf 1971:30).

Mostly, stations played sponsor-produced programs and advertising announcements, rather than their own programming. Although the Department of Commerce was eager to promote the use of phonograph records made in the United States, it pointed out that these needed to be at 78 rpm, not 33⅓ rpm, because only older equipment was available. Also, because stations would not use records in English, the market was limited to dance music, said to be particularly successful in Cuba (Schutrumpf 1971:21).

As a result of domestic regulation of international shortwave transmission, by the mid-1930s the private companies had realized that the commercial broadcasting application of this technology was limited, and they reduced their shortwave activities significantly. This reduction coincided with the realization by the U.S. government of "the capability of short wave to help achieve foreign trade and policy goals" and its potential in South America (Fejes 1986:5). The change in policy toward international shortwave broadcasting followed the inauguration of Franklin D. Roosevelt as president in 1933 and his institution of the "Good Neighbor" policy, with its emphasis on reciprocal trade agreements and its refutation of armed intervention in Latin America. The Good Neighbor policy in turn allowed the resumption of exports from Latin America financed by the Export-Import Bank, thereby improving relations.

In 1933 the Montevideo Inter-American Conference called for a Pan-American system of cultural broadcasting. The idea had arisen within the Pan-American Union as a result of the broadcasting, in 1924, of the union's programs of music and addresses to Latin America over the transmitter of the commercial radio station WRC in Washington, D.C., by the U.S. government. This first transmission was followed by the navy's 1927 agreement to transmit the programs by long wave. Then President Calvin Coolidge allocated three shortwave frequencies to the navy in 1929 for the specific purpose of these broadcasts, and President Hoover added two more. But nothing happened. Gregory suggests that the navy was deliberately stockpiling the frequencies to prevent their use by others (Gregory 1970:1–5, cited in Fox 1997:17).

But the proposal was also directly contrary to Hoover's policy of using private companies and the FRC's close relations with the networks. In any case, the FRC, asked for advice by the State Department, replied that any service on these frequencies would not be considered inter-American but U.S. based, with spare time used for domestic broadcasts. The Pan-American Union then abandoned the idea of a Pan-American radio station (Fejes 1986:81–82).

This was a period when U.S. security and commercial interests ruled. After the failure of the 1932 Madrid conference to resolve the problem of allocation of wavelengths within the western hemisphere, a separate North American radio conference was called for the summer of 1933 in Mexico City, where it was hoped that the United States, Mexico, Canada, Cuba, and the

Central American governments could agree to a regional allocation of the spectrum (McChesney 1994:155). At this point the United States had complete or partial control of ninety of the ninety-six available channels. The question was whether the United States would be willing to offer additional channels to other North American countries. Reflecting the continuing debate about public versus private control of radio within the United States, Armstrong Perry, an official of the U.S. National Committee on Education by Radio, a group of higher education organizations devoted to promoting educational broadcasting, helped draft the Latin American proposals demanding twelve clear channels. When the United States made it clear that it was prepared to relinquish only three or four channels—at the most—Latin American delegations were incensed, and the conference ended without an agreement. But Perry's involvement in the international sphere provided the material for a backlash by the commercial broadcasters within the domestic debate (McChesney 1993:158).

The proposal for Pan-American broadcasting reappeared in a different guise in the first years of the Franklin Roosevelt administration. In the face of increased broadcasting into Latin America by the Europeans, the Pan-American Union now suggested a U.S. government-funded Pan-American radio station. But Congress never approved the funding because of opposition from the commercial radio companies and limited presidential support (Gregory 1970:2–17, cited in Fox 1997:17). Nevertheless, the Roosevelt administration became increasingly concerned with cultural matters, agreeing to support an inter-American exchange program and setting up a division of cultural relations within the State Department in 1938 (Fejes 1986:74).

While the U.S. broadcasters were scaling back their shortwave broadcasts, the lack of power in their transmitters, together with atmospheric interference over the equator, made reception of their programs unreliable. But the Germans were expanding their broadcasting to German communities in North and South America. This German propaganda included free news agency copy and local radio programming extolling the virtues of German goods. Because Germany was prepared to exchange manufactured goods with the impoverished Latin American governments for raw materials, rising economic nationalism could have caused Latin America to ally itself with the Axis. The U.S. government became more interested in the potential of international broadcasting, both as a medium for advertising of consumer goods and as a means of combating German penetration.

In 1936 the Federal Communications Commission, successor to the FRC, redefined international shortwave broadcasting as "'the experimental transmission of broadcast programs for direct international public reception,'" thereby bringing the definition into line with actual practice (quoted in Fejes 1986:87). However, the technical characteristics of shortwave transmission meant that frequencies needed changing as climatic conditions changed, and German and Italian stations could broadcast on six frequencies, whereas the U.S. stations broadcast on only one or two frequencies at a time. Worried that failure might lead to government intervention in shortwave, which might then give legitimacy to intervention in the domestic market, the broadcasters upgraded their international output, with high power of 50 kilowatts and directional antennas. In return for that upgrading, the ban on advertising in international broadcast programs was lifted in 1939.

Even when commercial advertising was allowed, the U.S. radio companies had difficulty gaining sponsors. The problem was that they had little knowledge of who the Latin American listener was, and they were competing with agencies that placed U.S. advertisements on local radio stations. The broadcasters were faced with a drop in revenue. By 1942 only NBC had any substantial income from sponsorship.

In view of the poor response by U.S. advertisers to direct international broadcasting, the broadcasters turned to building networks of affiliated Latin American stations. By 1941 CBS had sixty-four, Crosley had twenty-four, and NBC had 117 affiliates (Fejes 1986:128). But after the fall of France in 1940, the U.S. government became more active within international broadcasting.

In 1940 a special Latin American division of the State Department became the Office of the Coordinator of Inter-American Affairs. Established at the suggestion of Nelson Rockefeller and then led by him, it was responsible for propaganda and cultural aspects of relations with Latin America. The Office of War Information was subsequently established in 1941; after a period of bureaucratic in-fighting it coordinated actions in Europe and Asia, while Rockefeller's group remained responsible for Latin America (Pirsein 1979:18–20). But at its inception the Inter-American Affairs office, with jurisdiction during the war over broadcasts to Latin America, faced numerous problems. These included a lack of coordination between the existing twelve shortwave stations, which had been used "for some fitful and half-hearted attempts at foreign language broadcasting" (Hale 1975:32).

Lack of power, wide beams, and weak signals prevented good reception. Lack of receivers in Latin America and the poor content of programs compounded Rockefeller's problems (Pirsein 1979:5–7). Attitudes had to change—radio had to become something other than "merely a profitable vehicle for advertisements" and had to move away from "the all-American cycle of isolationism and commercialism" (Hale 1975:32). Given the technical problems, the Inter-American Affairs office worked first with the commercial companies and emphasized the rebroadcasting of news programs, with CBS providing the news, AT&T delivering the signal to Latin America, and ITT distributing it to local stations (Pirsein 1979:15).

By mid-1941 broadcasts by all the stations totaled thirty-six hours a day in English, twenty-three hours per day in Spanish, seven and a half hours per day in Portuguese, and six hours per day in English and Spanish. Of those totals, news programming, prepared by the Inter-American Affairs office, amounted to thirteen hours each day (Pirsein 1979:11). After a period in which more powerful transmitters were built and the Roosevelt administration toyed with the idea of establishing a state-owned corporation to undertake its own international shortwave broadcasting, a compromise was reached (Weldon 1988:83). The government both leased the broadcasters' facilities and commissioned programming from the two major networks. But the problems were not solved.

In 1942, when the government leased the broadcasters' shortwave facilities and took control over programming, six private companies were broadcasting internationally to Latin America.[11] Shortwave facilities to Europe, Asia, and Africa were coordinated in one operation known as "the Voice of America," which began broadcasting two months after Pearl Harbor. In Latin America CBS and NBC were allowed to broadcast in a competitive manner. In effect, CBS and NBC were given the frequencies of the other stations to administer, but programs were put out under the call signs of the old stations. Behind this arrangement was the determination of CBS to preserve its Latin American network for its postwar business, but the effect was to hide the government control of both programming and transmission. The signature "Voice of America" was not used in Latin American broadcasts (Pirsein 1979:30).

But research showed that competition would split the audience, so in 1943 the two networks became one. Even after this concentration, the lack of audiences led the Inter-American Affairs office to supplement direct shortwave broadcasting and rebroadcasting. Local radio broadcasts were organized according to transcriptions, which the Inter-American Affairs office supplied, and local committees of the Inter-American Affairs office, consisting of U.S. radio company representatives, organized the transmission of local live productions (Fejes 1986:156; Pirsein 1979:24).

Further, to aid penetration the Inter-American Affairs office followed Italian precedent and put one million low-priced receivers on the Latin American market (Rolo 1943:189). But once the United States had entered the war, subsidizing radio penetration ended because of the need to conserve raw materials for armaments. In 1943 the Inter-American Affairs office began to focus on the expansion of advertising by U.S. corporations and gathered information about all the Latin American media markets. Because tax deductions from the U.S. government subsidized American companies' advertising on Latin American radio, by the end of the war the U.S. government, through the Inter-American Affairs office, was the largest radio time user and revenue producer of Latin American broadcasters (Fejes 1986:199). The Inter-American Affairs office not only structured the market by pulling advertising from stations that aired Axis propaganda but re-created Latin American radio broadcasting in the image of the U.S. market, with program formats such as quiz shows borrowed from U.S. stations.

In this way, by the end of World War II the communications industry had not only increased Latin America's dependence on the United States but also had effectively restructured the radio market along the lines of the "American model." After the war, as the networks focused on developing television, the government's lease of the stations was extended, and they became the basis of the state-owned Voice of America. But the entrenched model of commercial broadcasting in Latin America, subsidized by the U.S. government during the war years, then eased the penetration of U.S. network television (Fejes 1980:46).

In contrast, the Voice of America (VOA) programming directed at occupied Europe and the Far East was centralized under government control in 1940. The programs were prepared in-house for western Europe and were initially rebroadcast by the BBC. The bulk of the programming was news donated by the Associated Press (Renaud 1985:15). A gradual centralization took place, with a news file moving from a central VOA source to the language desks, so that eventually the language desks were primarily engaged in translation. In turn, the conflict between centralization and autonomy created tensions within the organization that persisted throughout the postwar years (Pirsein 1979:74).

Direct radio broadcasts to Europe encountered technical problems. Deterioration of the transmission occurred near the northern auroral zone and produced a shielding effect that prevented reception in a geographic arc extending from central and eastern Europe through the Near and Middle East, including parts of Southeast Asia and the Far East (Pirsein 1979:160–61). High power was also needed to get around signal jamming. For these reasons the VOA had to rely on relay stations from which it could rebroadcast, although by the end of the war the U.S. government had constructed nineteen short-wave transmitters at a cost of $5 million (Pirsein 1979:78). These were set up first in North Africa, then in the Pacific. Then, during 1943, rather than use the BBC relay service, the American Broadcasting Station in Europe was established "using transmitters shipped in from the United States of America and with studios in London. It became a relay-program center" (Pirsein 1979:82). In addition to news and entertainment, it broadcast coded messages to Resistance forces (Pirsein 1979:83). But the U.S. service had problems in its content. As one commentator put it: "'It can be said without hesitation, that American strategic propaganda, especially in broadcasting, seldom attained the high standards set by the British. . . . There were many reasons for this comparative inferiority . . . but the most important was American remoteness from the . . . audience'" (Wallace Carroll, quoted in Pirsein 1979: 99). Thus in yet another field the stage was set for Anglo-American competition in international communications in the postwar world. But unlike U.S. overseas broadcasting to Latin America, that of the VOA in Europe did not itself effect a restructuring of European domestic broadcasting.

Conclusion

The movie industry and the news agencies were among the first industries in which the economics of information became evident. Because of its large home market the U.S. movie industry was able to undercut its competitors overseas, to gain global revenues, and to thereby invest to upgrade the technical quality of its movies. The studio system treated the movie as a manufactured product, and the branding of the star system was an inexpensive means of marketing, affording the product instant recognition. Control of the means of distribution then ensured that a less attractive movie could be cross-subsidized by a more attractive one, thereby reducing the risk attached to creation and preventing the exhibition of competitors' products. Simply because of its large home market, and its domination of distribution, the same system of U.S. domination of the global movie market continued throughout the twentieth century.

In these circumstances, then as now, consumers were the main way to prevent Hollywood from exploiting its monopoly. Governments in Europe were to find little success in their attempts to bolster their movie industries through quotas based on "cultural policy." Reciprocity, when attempted by the Europeans, failed because they did not have the products. Although there were exceptions, the U.S. consumer, accustomed to Hollywood's offerings, generally did not find British and French films appealing.

When movies were first introduced into the class-based society of post–World War I Britain, they were seen as threatening the status quo. They attracted the working classes at a time when working-class political parties were rising, filled people's heads with ideas, seemed to glorify crime, and generally advertised U.S. lifestyle products. The movies threatened the glue of British "culture" that held the empire together.

That Hollywood movies often were offensive in their representation of other nationalities may have had much to do with their being made primarily for the home market and then "dumped" elsewhere (i.e., rented at a lower price than in the domestic market). In the 1930s there is some evidence that the product was adjusted for the British market, but by then the social attitudes of the Americans in terms of race were incompatible with Allied wartime politics. While governments might attempt to temper the number of movies entering their economies, the question of representation was much harder to regulate.

International regulation failed to get off the ground, and it is hard to see how it could have worked—the idea was to have a world combine of companies—even if the MPPDA and the U.S. government had not objected. Government-led boycotts, as in the small market of Mexico, were simply ignored by the industry, but they were the forerunner of the consumer boycotts of today, perceived as the only way to prevent such global monopolies from exploiting their position.

Broadcasting in Britain was also seen as a frivolous activity that had to be curtailed in favor of serious matters of naval communications. That it was accepted eventually had much to do with the way in which its director, John Reith, worked within the limitations set. Its development into a more or less independent broadcaster, rather than one that was the mouthpiece of the government (as in France or Germany), was the result of his vision of the potential of broadcasting in terms of "education, information and entertainment." The BBC's conservatism and Christianity made it acceptable to the powerful. In contrast, U.S.-based commercial radio, with advertising mixed in with programming, was the antithesis of these values. Radio Luxembourg threatened not just the BBC monopoly but English culture. Its early morning advertising jingles competed with the BBC's *Daily Prayers.*

But, again, international regulation was shown to be weak. Regulation had to come from the country where the international transmission took place. If that country was not prepared either to insist on a legal wave band or reduce the power of transmission so that it did not cross borders, the ITU regulations and the League of Nations Convention had no power. The British could do nothing about the commercial radio transmissions from outside its borders. Similarly, once the Soviet Union had been excluded from the 1927 Washington conference, other European countries had no way to control its broadcasting. Ironically, the British government, accepting its defeat on Radio Luxembourg transmissions, used the weak international regulation to sponsor propaganda on Continental radio stations to combat that of Germany. Security concerns overruled culture-based opposition to commercial broadcasting.

The British themselves were late to develop overseas broadcasting. The BBC's Empire Service came at the request of the colonies, many of whose expatriate residents could then tune in to poor-quality U.S. broadcasts. But as with the development of wireless infrastructure, the British Treasury was unwilling to provide financing for developments that would aid the restructuring of the empire. The eventual model of centralized direct broadcasting to individuals, rather than to local relay stations, did not threaten the status quo. This then shaped the broadcasting that developed in the colonies, both institutionally and in terms of content.

But the British government did not trust the BBC's "objectivity" when it came to foreign-language broadcasting. The Foreign Office's attempts to bypass the BBC led eventually to an uneasy relationship in which the Foreign Office attempted to control overseas broadcasting through its subsidies. Broadcasting in foreign languages at a time of deteriorating international relations brought the BBC into the realms of propaganda and politicization. The introduction of programming in foreign languages, particularly Arabic, created a tension with the Foreign Office regarding editorial control. However, although the government introduced overt propaganda into Reuters's news items, the BBC demanded independent editorial control, and government influence was evidenced mainly through the organization's self-censorship of programming. As with Reuters, competition made the BBC more customer friendly and more sensitive to local cultures. Following the successful model of the Germans, the BBC's move to tailor material for consumers made it more successful than the Voice of America in Europe. The U.S. service found that centralized production and problems of transmission favored uniformity of product, not consumer interaction. And distance produced its own problems in tailoring VOA programming to local audiences.

For the Americans, broadcasting to Latin America in order to gain exports of equipment followed the model of the development of radio at home—from equipment sales to programming to advertising. By the mid-1930s, despite the domestic debate concerning the funding and content of broadcasting, and the role that it should play in a democratic society, the commercial model of broadcasting was institutionalized. Thus even when those companies used domestic content ineffectively to broadcast inexpensively overseas, because of their political clout Franklin Roosevelt was not prepared to press hard for a public corporation to manage overseas shortwave broadcasts. Overall, the period demonstrates the increasing power of the major U.S.

companies, both within domestic debates, where they controlled the infrastructure, content, and access to debate, and within international markets.

Even the structure of international broadcasting was determined by the companies' concern at the positioning of their networks in the postwar world. Rockefeller's office worked around the companies, using local committees and radio stations in Latin America as much as working with the companies. But the companies were the major beneficiaries in that their prewar Latin American networks were strengthened by government actions in reshaping the structure and content of Latin American broadcasting in the U.S. image. The very argument against advertising-controlled media used by its opponents within the United States—that it precluded any "controversial" material from being broadcast—was used as a way to ensure that the Allied, rather than Axis, message prevailed in Latin America. Content followed finance. Despite the entrance of directly controlled broadcasting via the Voice of America in 1942, one can argue that the most important development with future structural implications for the communications industry in Latin America was the U.S. subsidy of advertising through the tax system.

To conclude, we can see in the stories of the penetration of movies and broadcasting into Latin America and Europe during these interwar years the forerunners of the issues raised by Latin American attacks on the "cultural imperialism" of news flows and broadcasting in the 1970s and 1980s. In turn, the "flavorization" of cultural products—the alteration of cultural products to suit local audience tastes—that began with Nazi radio was the precursor of the "glocalization-homogenization" debate of today.[12] Today, as then, regulation of overseas broadcasting, whether state owned or commercial, has to come from the country where it is broadcast. The problems of regulation of overseas broadcasting documented here reflect the concerns of the Europeans and others regarding the regulation of satellite broadcasting from the 1990s.[13] The cinema quotas imposed by European governments in the 1930s were the precursor of today's European Union broadcasting quotas and the exclusion of free trade in cultural products from the 1994 World Trade Organization agreement. Today, as then, European and other film producers must combat U.S. ownership of distributors and exhibition outlets. Today, as then, the seemingly ineffectual regulation of the behavior of international companies leads to consumer boycotts.

In sum, we can view the beginnings of international market restructuring in favor of Western, and particularly U.S., cultural products and formats as the direct antecedent of the liberalization and commercialization of broadcasting in Europe and the rest of the world that has been taking place since the 1990s. The happenings of the 1930s led directly to the global media and global branding of today.

Conclusion

THIS BOOK BEGAN by asking a number of specific questions about international communications and its relationship to international relations and domestic politics. The intention was to explore the dynamics of international and domestic communications in the nineteenth and early twentieth centuries, when the infrastructure and content of international communications were last under the control of private companies. The purpose was to see how communications developed and how governments set out to control international companies and whether any parallels exist today.

The book was written as a counterpoint to both neorealists and regime theorists who see international regimes as resulting directly from domestic politics. Instead, the theoretical framework adopted suggested that international and domestic communications and regulation were intrinsically linked with each other, both in terms of company strategy and government policy. The book is based on the ideas of Susan Strange, who wrote in the 1990s on the expansion of government-to-company relations, and of Vincent Mosco, who writes about the legitimacy of regulation. The book argued that regulation was part of a complex policy process in which governments were involved at one and the same time in international and domestic negotiations with governments and companies

The historical research reported here has highlighted the various strategies and mechanisms used by companies and governments at different times during the one hundred years that this book considers. Often the U.S., German, and British governments espoused free-trade ideology at the diplomatic level yet at the same time adopted mercantilist policies at the company level. Debates about public versus private ownership affected domestic politics in both the United States and Britain in a variety of ways and then spilled over into the international. Regulation varied from solely domestic to the use of international regulation in lieu of domestic regulation to the unilateral transposition of domestic regulation to the international to one mode of regulation for foreigners and another for domestically owned companies. In other words, international regulation did not simply come about through international regimes. It was also the product of domestic regulation, its influence extending beyond the initiating state. And underlying such changes in regulation, in international regulatory regimes, and in the structuring of those regimes and institutions, was the struggle for control of international communications. Such control was perceived as a strategic and commercial resource.

Whereas the original development of transatlantic submarine cables was a matter of cooperation between the U.S. and British governments, which were eager to link financial and commodity markets, that cooperation survived little beyond the laying of the first transatlantic cable. Ownership of patents, control of the raw material for insulation, the geographical position of the British Isles and London's financial hegemony, the numbers of small islands within the British Empire on which to land cables, shipbuilding and engineering expertise all contributed to the dominant market position of British cable companies.

These factors gave British companies first mover advantages. They gained preferential concessions within the British Empire and monopoly concessions in South America. From that point on, the U.S. government struggled to overcome these advantages for primarily commercial reasons. For the British government strategic motives were always more important than commercial ones. The Indian Mutiny, the Crimean War, the American Civil War, the Boer War, World War I, and the possibility of a second world war instigated the expansion of the submarine cable system, backed by British government subsidies, and then its defense.

After the failure of the first transatlantic cable, government losses led the U.S. government to subsidize the expansion of the domestic network and, during the Civil War, to its decision to back a proposal for a land-based cable through China. Although the British government cooperated by allowing Western Union a concession in British Columbia, the U.S. government overrode that agreement with its own demands, giving a first demonstration of its competitive nationalism. The attempt to reach Europe via China also appears to have been sold to the public as a U.S. proposal to ring the world with cable. Therefore by the 1860s a mercantilist bias already had begun to infect U.S. attitudes toward international communications, a bias that was aggravated by failure to do anything about the British monopoly concessions in South America. That was when the U.S. Congress awarded its first monopoly concession.

The mercantilist bias of the United States became increasingly evident once a company financed with British capital had laid the 1866 transatlantic cable. Americans' experience of railway pools and the high tariffs they engendered fed the U.S. hostility toward British cable dominance. The failure of Napoleon III and the continental Europeans to include those countries with domestic telegraph networks run by private companies in the first international conferences may have instigated the unsuccessful U.S. attempt to initiate an international treaty to prevent monopoly concessions. The domestic debate about whether to nationalize the telegraphs may also have been affected by the prospect of being an outsider to international regulation. But by the time of the St. Petersburg Convention in 1875, Western Union was a domestic monopoly. It may well have refused to be bound by international regulations in 1875 because to do otherwise would have given legitimacy to the arguments for domestic nationalization.

Then, once Jay Gould had laid his own transatlantic cables, from the 1880s on the company's resistance to international regulation was primarily commercial. International telegraph regulations held down profits. And as Western Union and AT&T grew in size and power, the ability of the U.S. government to override them, except in wartime, decreased. Contrary to later accounts, it appears that in 1898 the U.S. government may have wished to be part of the international convention and, despite not being a signatory, accepted its provisions regarding censorship. Some evidence appears to say that as late as the 1930s the U.S. president would have signed the international telecommunications convention in its entirety were it not for U.S. telegraph companies and their lobbying of Congress against ratification.

Yet the original concerns of the U.S. government were that its own dispatches and commercial communications might be locked into a high tariff by the British submarine cable cartel. The U.S. concerns were quite different from those of the landlocked European countries, which wanted to standardize tariffs throughout a fragmented Continent. In the European context standardizing tariffs, including transit charges, was a way of standardizing interconnection rates. Its parallel is the 2001 decision by national regulators in Europe to begin to standardize their regulatory practices (Hills 2001). However, from the outside the division of traffic into intra-European and extra-European, with intra-European defined as including those other countries (i.e., colonies) that the member states wished to include, looked like a European cartel. Again, the perception of the 1870s resonates more than a century later in U.S. fears of a Fortress Europe.

After the British government nationalized its telegraphs, joined the continental Europeans in the International Telegraph Union, and agreed to regulations that legitimized the interception of traffic, the U.S. government became primarily concerned at the lack of secure communications and the potential for foreign-owned cartels. Even before any U.S. companies had transatlantic cables, Washington acted to ensure that the Europeans would not be able to block the expansion of U.S. cable laying. Not being a party to international regulation increased the need for domestic policy. By 1875 the main principles of that policy had been laid down: Reciprocity, which combined demands for liberalization abroad with protection at home, became a major factor in U.S. control of landing rights. In the early 1890s Secretary of State James G. Blaine extended the policy to include the liberalization of third markets and then to withhold interconnection for those companies that held monopoly concessions of any kind. The policy allowed discretion on a case-by-case basis and was applied selectively to best advance the interests of U.S. companies. Thus reciprocity, which became a regulatory feature of U.S. policy in the twentieth century, can be said to be a traditional mechanism of U.S. international relations.

This pattern of behavior was to repeat itself in the Wireless Ship Act of 1910, the Kellogg Cable Landing Act of 1921, and subsequent landing licenses. First, the U.S. government entered into international negotiations. When the negotiations failed, either defeated within the international forum or rejected by an isolationist Congress, there followed domestic legislation or regulation with unilateral international effects. Cable, over which the British held a monopoly, was more strictly regulated than wireless, a field that U.S. companies led after World War I. And domestic antitrust legislation was made inapplicable to international combines through the Webb-Pomarene Act of 1918.

Instead of cooperating with the British, the U.S. government engaged in head-to-head competition with the British government on behalf of U.S. communications companies. The Americans became protectionist at home but the advocates of liberalization of cable concessions in third countries. The British, free traders in domestic and colonial landing rights, became defenders of monopoly concessions elsewhere. Although there were exceptions, both countries played out this dichotomy in ideology and practice within different parts of the state and in their relation to business. Throughout, the attitude of the U.S. executive branch, which focused more on international free trade, contrasted with the mercantilist and nationalistic viewpoint of Congress. This dichotomy became evident even before the transatlantic cable was laid. Whereas the president was demanding liberalization from the British and French, Congress was granting a monopoly concession to A. J. Scrymser's International Ocean Telegraph Company.

In particular, the Spanish-American War of 1898 was a watershed. The U.S. government was suddenly made to recognize its dependence on the good nature of the British for communications to other parts of the world. And to the British, congressional backing for the cutting of British cables was a shock. The British then included the Americans in war scenarios. U.S. expansion into colonization was partly occasioned by the need for cable landing bases in the Pacific. And U.S. censorship gave legitimacy to that practiced later by the British.

This combination of U.S. nationalism and financial stringency led eventually to the failure of thirty or more measures to subsidize a U.S.-owned Pacific cable. In 1902 the American John W. Mackay's Postal Telegraph Company formed a joint venture with the Eastern and Great Northern—two British companies—to lay a Pacific cable; the participation of the British companies, which owned the concessions from the Philippines to China and within China, was known to President Theodore Roosevelt but was kept from Congress for twenty years. Later, in 1919, Woodrow Wilson was demanding liberalization of markets from the Allied participants in the Versailles negotiations, while his navy was instigating the creation of RCA. Point-to-point wireless was regarded as a technological means to defeat the British cable monopoly, but in practice its expansion involved RCA in a worldwide cartel with British, French, and German companies and in monopolistic agreements with western European governments. Thus the U.S. policy of liberalization became in practice one of mercantilism.

It was evident quite early on in the development of telegraph networks that in a free-market environment the companies regarded expansion overseas as a means of reinforcing their position in their domestic market. In Britain in the mid-nineteenth century the Magnetic and Electric companies physically interconnected their domestic and cross-channel cables. To U.S. domestic companies, such as Cyrus Field's American Telegraph Company in the 1850s, Commercial Cable in the 1880s, and AT&T in 1911, international and national networks were one and the same. In recognition of this perception, when Mackay first invested in a transatlantic cable in the 1880s, it was physically connected to his Postal Telegraph Company's domestic network so that international and domestic worked as one. Realizing the advantage that such direct transmission gave its competitor, AT&T (which then owned Western

Union) followed suit in 1912. The companies wanted to run their international cables as they ran their domestic—for the greatest profit. End-to-end control, with domestic collection at one end and domestic delivery at the other, gave them 100 percent of the revenue. Thus they got the best returns in liberalized markets, which allowed them to advertise and collect traffic overseas. In contrast, international regulations reduced companies' profits.

The way in which these companies conceptualized the international was therefore quite different from that of the European states. Europeans perceived "international" communications as that part of the network outside the physical boundaries of each state-owned telegraph system. The politics of international communications in Europe were based on the nation-state and state ownership. In this scenario physical interconnection between domestic and international networks could occur only if both were state owned. Yet because state-owned cables would not have been allowed entry to another country, state ownership of international telegraph cables was not possible. For that reason, even the most dirigiste of countries, France, created state-backed private international companies. But at a time when the majority of traffic was domestic, the split between domestic and international networks meant that low flows of international traffic had to pay off the initial high investment charges and therefore carried high tariffs.

In turn, overcapacity in infrastructure led to the failure of competition, cartelization, and pooling of revenue, as, for example, on the India route, between government and private companies. Overcapacity may be one reason why British manufacturers of the capital equipment, rather than the operators, received high profits. Liberalization, coupled with private ownership of infrastructure, benefited the suppliers. This lesson was to be learned later by European governments, which established their own telephone manufacturers, and by ITT, a company that made its profits through the supply and operation of national domestic networks. As the British Treasury recognized in the nineteenth century and the Federal Communications Commission was to find in the twentieth, such vertical integration also hides "costs" and makes regulation difficult. Strangely, even by the 1930s the United States had no manufacturing capacity, so AT&T passed to the British its research into and development of the practical application of cable technology.

By the 1880s interconnection had already emerged as the prime mechanism to be used by dominant companies to prevent competition and enforce pooling of revenue. It was used both in the domestic context and in the linkage between national and international networks. Over the years Western Union, AT&T, the British Post Office, the Marconi company, and German companies refused interconnection in domestic networks to potential competitors. Once Western Union got its own transatlantic cables in the 1880s, the British Eastern's dependence on interconnection for the collection and delivery of its traffic in the United States gave it no alternative but to accede to Western Union's power and to join its pool. In contrast, the U.S. companies were allowed to establish their own offices and advertise for traffic within Britain. Eventually, in 1911 the U.S. companies were able to use this imbalance in interconnection rights to freeze the British out of the U.S. market and to take over the British cables. Yet there is no evidence that any British government ever contemplated retaliation by using the concept of bilateral reciprocity.

In general, with minimal domestic U.S. regulation of the telegraph and interstate telephone, the commercial interests of first Western Union and then AT&T prevailed. At home both were allowed to provide leased lines to large users below cost, and, after the takeover of the British cables, they also provided private lines across the Atlantic. Nevertheless, when World War I began and with it the nationalization of AT&T, the ensuing price hikes to domestic subscribers led to the perception that a public monopoly was even less regulated than a private one. The experience virtually ended any further advocacy of state ownership.

Although the development of wireless seemed to offer a way to bypass the British control of the international submarine cable network, a British company dominated the world market, first in marine wireless and then in point-to-point long-distance wireless. Marconi's wireless hegemony came from de facto standardization and a refusal to share the technology that would allow other companies' equipment to be compatible with its own. As it had in regard to submarine cables, the U.S. government originally attempted to gain liberalization through a multilateral international convention. As with submarine cables, the emphasis was on interconnection.

The history of the Marconi company's relations with the British and U.S. governments provides a good illustration of the interdependency of international and national regulation. The U.S. Navy was the foremost opponent of the Marconi company. At the behest of the German government, the U.S. Navy first used domestic regulation, introduced in 1887, to bar Marconi from operating the Nantucket lightship. Although Congress had not ratified the 1903 and 1906 conventions because of corporate opposition, the navy was able to use those conventions to advance its domestic and international agenda. Even before the 1912 convention, the very fact of the international conference had led to the Wireless Ship Act of 1910, under which the navy gained additional domestic powers and resources. Marconi was forced to interconnect its equipment through the imposition of domestic legislation that had extraterritorial effects. This act also first introduced foreign ownership restrictions on wireless licenses—a feature of domestic regulation that remained in force in the development of radio communications in the late twentieth century. Using these powers, the U.S. Navy planned to buy out Marconi's ship-to-shore stations in 1917, got the Alexander Bill introduced in Congress, and used "neutrality" at the start of the European war to expand naval control over wireless. The U.S. Navy also was responsible for the expropriation of the interests of the Marconi Wireless Telegraph Company of America in the postwar period and for establishing RCA.

In fact, although the 1906 radiotelegraphic convention set out the principles of subsequent international radio regulation (frequency allocation to services, avoidance of interference, and registration of frequencies), it demonstrated that international regulation is effective only so far as the member states implement that regulation. It is evident that the British did not impose the 1906 regulations on shipping interests. Nor did they regulate Marconi's activities in third markets. Nor did the Germans carry through on the convention that they had initiated. As soon as the Marconi International Marine Communication Company formed a joint company with Belgian and German manufacturers, the joint operation maintained a policy of noninterconnection that was supported by the German government.

The U.S. Navy developed the policy in South America that shifted the control of radio communications away from the Europeans before World War I. Competition against the British in cables focused on Brazil, where the U.S. government tried to break the British monopoly from the 1870s through to 1919. Despite the emphasis placed on communications hegemony in South America, the only congressional subsidy was for a strategic cable from Panama to the United States. But when the British threatened to gain wireless concessions, not only was all available diplomatic pressure brought to bear in favor of U.S. companies, but to stop the British, the navy developed a wireless policy advocating the creation of state-owned domestic wireless networks by the South American republics. That policy was lifted in favor of private enterprise in 1924, when U.S. radio companies found it a handicap.

However, it would be wrong to suggest that the United States was universally successful in gaining the policy outcomes that it wanted. Although the navy was instrumental in creating RCA as a flagship wireless company, the company soon embarked on a policy of market sharing and patent exchange with the Marconi company and then with German Telefunken. It carved up the markets of South America and China despite presidential opposition. The experience of the Harding administration was that neither radio nor cable companies could be forced into free trade against their will.

If anything was different in British and U.S. policy between the wars, it was that the British conceded South America to the United States. Britain officially recognized the Monroe Doctrine within the Versailles Peace Treaty, and by the mid-1920s U.S. telephone and telegraph investment in South America had largely replaced British investment. Marconi sold its Latin American interests, cable monopolies were opened up, U.S. movies dominated the market, and U.S. news agencies were widely represented.

During World War I the U.S. government actively used propaganda to try to change Latin American perceptions of the United States. In view of the domination of the French news agency Havas in the region, and the Associated Press's arrangements with that agency, the U.S. government actively supported United Press in penetrating South America. In turn, UP's activities forced the AP into loosening its links to the worldwide news agency cartel. That the news agencies could expand their activities internationally was itself dependent on the preexisting expansion of U.S.-owned cables, on subsidies to press transmission through those private cables, and on navy radio stations organized by the U.S. government. Yet Latin Americans' interest in U.S. news was small compared to their interest in the U.S. movie industry. Forced to distribute directly from the United States, rather than through Europe, Hollywood opened the way for U.S. radio and advertising interests in the postwar period. The primary factor in shifting influence in South America away from the Europeans to the United States was World War I.

Again in the years preceding World War II, the anti-American propaganda of German overseas broadcasting into Latin America raised the importance of content and propaganda to a strategic level. But U.S. government intervention was handicapped by the domestic power and existing interests of the radio companies. Whereas overseas broadcasting to Europe was done through a government organization, Voice of America, government intervention in Latin America was through the companies as agents. This arrangement was a further demonstration of the weakness of domestic regulatory power.

This weakness was first displayed in the hostile name calling of Western Union in the immediate postwar period and by the decision of that company (together with AT&T in 1932) to have its interests represented by the British at the international radiotelegraphic conferences of 1927 and 1932. With virtually no domestic regulation of their activities in the interwar years, communications companies became almost impossible to regulate, according to the fledgling FCC. Although the fragmented regulation of telegraph cables via the Interstate Commerce Commission and of point-to-point wireless and broadcasting via the Federal Radio Commission were integrated into the FCC, the regulatory powers that had accrued through landing licenses were not initially available to the FCC. Its establishment seems to have lost to the executive branch the efficacy that the 1921 landing license regulation had given in terms of reciprocity and powers over investment. The international dimension of regulation was subordinated to the domestic.

In contrast to the primarily commercial concern of the Americans, during the prewar period British concern focused on the security, rather than commercial, aspects of the British cable network. Following a somewhat unsuccessful attempt at protectionism in the later years of the nineteenth century, the British moved to a free-trade ethos in relation to landing licenses. Such free trade coincidentally benefited security interests. London became the hub of a vast web of cables under the control and censorship of the British government. Fears that cables could be cut in time of war led to a preoccupation with routes that avoided potentially unsympathetic governments and to the development of an "All-Red," deepwater, state-owned Pacific cable. In contrast to its German enemy, Britain could use cable cutting and censorship as strategic resources in World War I, and in contrast to the United States, Britain emerged stronger in cables from that war.

Because of the public subsidies that the private submarine cable companies received, regulation of their activities developed earlier in Britain than in the United States. But the various mechanisms tried, ranging from parliamentary regulation to Treasury control of purchasing to government appointments to their boards, were ineffective. For a period of thirty years the British then relied on including a clause within licenses for landing rights that specified that companies should abide by the international regulations. In a period of free-trade ideology, when regulation of private property rights had little legitimacy, international regulations developed by a mercantilist continental Europe substituted for domestic regulation.

However, from the early years of the twentieth century the British government followed U.S. precedents and began to use the British cable landing licenses of the U.S. companies to demand interconnection in third markets. Despite its fears that it would be vulnerable to a monopoly, the British government's primary concern with the strategic importance of cables precluded more effective mechanisms for regulating its own companies. Therefore it returned in the early 1900s to funding public competition against the Eastern in order to gain a reduction in tariffs on the Australia route. Only after World War I did the British use the cable landing licenses of the private companies to control tariffs and even then never used the archaic mechanism of regulation that the government chose.

In general, the British government was able to use its voting power within the International Telegraph Union to keep its companies under control. International companies needed the government to avoid regulations that they did not want. In turn, the International Telegraph Union's regulations were modeled on the British Telegraph Act of 1869. The regulations stipulated reduced tariffs for the press and the right of the press to lease lines overnight and excluded private leased lines from regulation. These points reflected the British government's need to compromise between defense of its dominance of international communications and defense of a similar hegemony within international news agencies. The European news agencies, helped by their privileged status under the 1875 convention, cartelized the world market. In contrast, U.S. newspapers and news agencies were handicapped by the costs of international collection and distribution of news and by the primacy of the commercial interests of the telegraph companies.

The original intention of the International Telegraph Union was to formalize cartelization between a number of countries. It was intended to end competition and to equalize tariffs. That was why only government-owned telegraph administrations were eligible for representation. Nevertheless, telegraph companies were allowed entry to the discussions starting in 1871 and, although not allowed to vote, were present when regulations affecting them were made. In contrast, the first radiotelegraphic conventions excluded the Marconi company and forcibly demonstrated that effective regulation requires the cooperation of the regulated company.

In the case of wireless, there was an evident interplay between the domestic interests of the British Post Office, its desire to provide wireless communications itself, and the international regulations that it supported. The 1903 Berlin convention provided the rationale for the British Wireless Act of 1904, under which the government would later nationalize Marconi's marine wireless business. And, despite a conflict with the Admiralty that forced some compromise, the 1906 convention again strengthened the British government's hand domestically by limiting the frequency spectrum that the Marconi company might use and led to its nationalization. For many years the Post Office's intention was to place Marconi in a position that would force it to sell its technology to the government for a low price; the relevant technology was first marine wireless, then long-wave technology.

That Marconi survived was due first to the strategic interests of the Admiralty, the company's foresight in not patenting its long-wave technology, then its legal action to defend its patents, and finally its threat to collaborate with German Telefunken. Only in the years immediately before World War I did the company begin to gain the diplomatic support of the British government.

Ironically, the Marconi company's development of shortwave technology spelled its end. For the British these interwar years were characterized by increasing dependence on their empire for retaining their political and economic influence in world affairs. Therefore, when the introduction of shortwave radio appeared both to open the door to both low-cost intracolonial communications and a realignment of the prewar centralization of the empire, it was rejected in favor of cable. The Americans initially viewed with alarm the ensuing creation of Cable and Wireless as a British national company, but it was dominated by the slow and expensive cable interests and loaded with debt; it soon became little more than an empire-based government communications agency. In effect, ITT and Cable and Wireless operated in their own spheres of influence, with ITT concentrating on western Europe and South America and Cable and Wireless to the east.

In Britain the regulation of domestic and international communications was handicapped by the position of the Post Office as both operator and regulator. Successive governments interpreted the founding legislation of the Post Office's monopoly as meaning that as an operator it could provide no special services, such as leased lines, for business. Its control of two transatlantic telegraph cables and those to the European continent gave the Post Office the incentive to preclude competition from U.S. companies. As a domestic regulator, it shored up its losses by preventing competition. Yet, ironically, the Rugby transmitter, which had threatened to be a white elephant, became the means by which Britain once more centralized its telephone communications. Thanks to the transmitter's geographic location, and the Post Office's refusal to allow independent communication to the colonies, all telephonic communications to the United States had to go through Britain. Nor was a transatlantic telephone cable, the U.S. technology for which was available in the 1930s, allowed to compete. As a result the United States entered World War II as it entered the first war—dependent on British control of international communications links. Only in 1942, one year after Pearl Harbor, did the British government allow U.S. radio companies direct access to the empire.

Radio itself altered the conceptualization of international communications. Radio enabled governments to control their own infrastructure. And because the initial capital costs of shortwave were low, 50 percent of the revenue accrued to the government, and because governments could interconnect with their domestic networks, radio became the preferred means of international communication. As Blackett anticipated in 1930, the national ownership of communications established by wireless transposed itself into the ownership of cables. After World War II the European state-based concept of international communications took hold throughout the world.

War was also to increase the importance of government propaganda and therefore the influence of the news agencies and broadcasting. In order not to inhibit the seeming independence of Reuters, the British government effectively but secretly nationalized it. Reuters survived the diminution of its communications business by receiving subsidies from government. In contrast, Marconi's Wireless Press, which received news directly from the Continent via wireless, was able to carve out a niche for itself. But because of government hostility to the company, it was not allowed to take over Reuters.

All international companies suffered during the depression of the 1930s as world trade fell away. But as a by-product of the establishment of Cable and Wireless and the retention of the centralized system of communications, Reuters was saved. Despite dominion demands from 1906 for an intraempire press service that would bring the empire together through communications, and despite increasing dissatisfaction with its service, Reuters was able to retain control of its member press agencies by virtue of the communications system. Had wireless between the individual colonies been allowed to develop, competition in news agencies might have opened up. And despite the better and faster technology available to German news agencies, Reuters was protected by the fact that until 1935 all telephone communications still went through Britain. Reflecting the commercial preeminence of the United States in the postwar world, Reuters's collection of business news from the United States preserved its cartel in Europe until the 1930s. The defection of the Associated Press to meet domestic competition from United Press presaged the end of the international cartel.

War also aided the penetration of Hollywood movies into Europe and Latin America. Aided by President Wilson's desire to spread U.S. values, the movies became part of the propaganda initiatives of the U.S. government during World War I and filled the film void left by the withdrawal of the French from the movie export business. The movies were the first cultural commodity and means of communication over which U.S. industry gained dominance. The British profoundly resented the postwar infiltration of U.S. popular culture and its threat to the status quo of class and intraempire relations. Hollywood's virtual monopoly of the European market created protectionist policies of quotas. Yet that protectionism had little effect in the face of the large U.S. home market and U.S. companies' vertical ownership of creation and distribution outlets. Nor were international efforts at regulation of content effective against opposition from the industry and the U.S. government. Only U.S. government interest in the problem promoted more effective self-regulation.

Similarly, regulation of overseas broadcasting proved impossible. As the European countries edged toward war, politically controlled broadcasting became too sensitive for even technical regulation. And where it was commercially controlled, the profits to the transmitting states outweighed international opprobrium. It became evident that the only mechanism for controlling such broadcasts was through regulation by the state in which the transmission took place. Without that, international regulation was powerless. Such problems of the permeability of the nation-state to external broadcasting and difficulties of regulation beset satellite broadcasting today.

Both world wars increased the strategic relevance of representation and content. In Latin America and Britain broadcasting by foreign states led to a postwar restructuring of state broadcasting in favor of commercial interests. Those foreign state broadcasters began the packaging of Western cultural products to align with local cultures now practiced by commercial global media companies.

Finally, the internal structure of international organizations became part of the struggle. When the first international telegraph convention was held, the agreement reached had to be completely changed at the subsequent conference. Starting in 1875 it consisted of a convention that governed general principles and regulations that covered specifics. The convention could be changed by infrequent plenary sessions of member states, whereas the regulations could be changed by administrative conferences. In 1920 the British and French attempted to introduce both a combined telegraph and radio-telegraphic convention and international council, based on the League of Nations structure. Although the United States accepted this innovation, U.S. companies rejected it and proposed a structure that would allow the United States to be part of the international regime. That structure, inaugurated in 1927, finessed the problem by putting regulations to which the U.S. companies objected in a section titled "Additional Regulations"; it outlasted the later decision to have one convention. At the same time the international regime was altered to give companies more power within the technical committees, and they played a greater role within national delegations. In other words, private ownership of transmission infrastructure demanded an international regulatory regime with greater participation from the private operators.

What specific lessons does this historical analysis offer that are relevant to international and domestic communications today? Perhaps first is that international communications are most profitable to private companies when liberalized markets allow end-to-end control of collection and delivery. But allowing private companies to control both ends presents a built-in challenge to the authority of the nation-state. Companies will seek to control infrastructure and content, creation and distribution, and distribution and manufacturing supply on a global basis. In such an environment they will enter into international discriminatory arrangements with other companies—pools, cartels, trusts, interconnection agreements, proprietary standardization, and much more—in order to reduce costs and risk. Competition will not flourish unless governments take action to ensure that it does.

Also, the flip side of easier international communications is the increased risk to national security that governments perceive. Such anxieties as currently inflict regulation of the Internet are nothing new. We can see that a strengthening of state censorship goes hand in hand with liberalization of international communications.

In terms of the specific mechanisms of regulation, parallels between the research reported here and those of today are obvious. Licensing was and still is the primary regulatory tool, defining those parameters of company behavior that are acceptable to the government. Interconnection was and is a principal means of preventing competition. Vertical integration can disguise "costs." New competitors can cream skim by offering deals to large users. Companies must be able to accept the legitimacy of regulatory authority: Hostility between regulator and regulated demonstrates weakness in the regulatory agency. And today, as then, failure of international and national regulation can lead to consumer boycotts and protectionism.

If these regulatory lessons were known before the beginning of World War II, they got lost in the next fifty years. After that war the almost immediate entry into the cold war and the burgeoning independence of former colonies pushed international communications back into the state-based, state-owned conceptualization of the Europeans of the nineteenth century. From the 1940s to the 1980s international communications reverted to state ownership. In freezing out new technologies and competition, the ensuing dual role of the Post, Telegraph, and Telephone Administration as operators and regulators replicated the pattern of behavior of the British Post Office. Although satellite communications in the 1960s threatened to alter this state-centric pattern and once more give the U.S. government an alternative technology by which to attempt to gain international hegemony, only at the end of the twentieth century, with the demise of the Soviet Union and growing internationalization of large user companies, did international communications move to the nineteenth century's end-to-end conceptualization of the telegraph companies.

Since the early 1990s most countries have moved, or are in the process of moving, from state-owned telecommunications and broadcasting to private provision. As the industrialized countries allowed competition within their domestic telephone networks, the liberalization of international communications in the 1980s began on a company-to-company basis. The 1997 telecommunications agreement of the World Trade Organization formalized the rules to be followed in the opening of domestic markets to foreign competitors and outlined a regulatory framework for licensing and interconnection to be implemented at the national level. In that context, as private equity in domestic networks has replaced state ownership, national regulation has become increasingly important to the assertion of public priorities over corporate profit. In turn, because of the penetration of international regimes into the national and the interdependence of international and domestic regimes, governments are still working toward a commensurate reworking and restructuring of domestic regulation.

At the same time international regimes and institutions are once more being restructured to give private companies more power. In turn, this trend has continued the diminution of the sovereignty and bargaining capacity within international institutions of the formerly colonized southern hemisphere. The West may not now have colonial votes, but the dominance of international regulatory decisions by the industrialized countries produces the same effect today.

If this book has an overall message, it is that the privatization and liberalization of international communications requires individual state administrative capacity—that is, although international and domestic regulation are inextricably linked, national regulation must implement the international rules. History teaches that "international" regulatory regimes are subject to continuous redefinition through bilateral and unilateral pressure by the most powerful states. In a worldwide liberalized communications environment, separating the interests of industrialized countries from those of their companies becomes difficult—free trade can become the ideological vehicle for hiding protectionism, mercantilism, and neocolonialism. These ideologies may coexist at different levels of the state in forms of the "liberal developmentalism" of the nineteenth century. Above all, the research reported here teaches us that national regulation is the bulwark of sovereignty.

Notes

Those documents denoted PO are to be found in the BT Archives and Historical Information Centre, Holborn Telephone Exchange, High Holborn, London. Documents denoted PRO are to be found in the Public Record Office, Ruskin Avenue, Kew, Richmond, Surrey.

Introduction

1. For examples of unilateral and bilateral action by the United States, see Hills (1998b, 2001). On reciprocity see Hay and Sulzenko (1982).

2. Exceptions to this generalization include Nier and Butrica (1988) and Standage (1999).

3. Canada received full self-government in 1840, becoming a dominion in 1867. New Zealand gained responsible government in 1852, with New South Wales, Victoria, Tasmania, and South Australia following in 1855–56 and Cape Colony in 1872.

4. The terms *pooling* and *joint purses* were used to describe a form of cartelization. Companies agreed to place all revenues in a common pool and then share them according to the amount of traffic each cable carried. Pooling also led to each company's charging similar tariffs. Lack of competition thereby hurt customers.

5. See J. C. Lamb, third secretary of the General Post Office, in evidence to Pacific Cable Committee, 30 Nov. 1896, PO 83/94.

6. Although subsequently criticized as inaccurate in its time frame, for our purpose the concept of "formal" and "informal" (trading) empire makes a useful distinction between foreign rule and economic penetration.

7. Codding (1972:41n.184) quotes a Russian complaint of 1897 that Great Britain controlled thirteen votes and Russia only one.

8. Half the stock of the Commercial Pacific Cable Company was owned by the British Eastern, one quarter by the Anglo-Danish Great Northern Company, and one quarter by

John Mackay's Commercial Cable Company, the American firm that ran a successful transatlantic cable (Tribolet 1929:190).

9. In 1932 Americans controlled approximately 90 percent of ITT's outstanding shares. Foreigners comprised four of ITT's twenty-three directors and two of its twenty-two officers (Sidak 1999:66).

Chapter 1: Infrastructure and Information in the United States and Britain, 1840s–1890

1. The British monetary system of pence, shillings, and pounds had twelve pence to one shilling and twenty shillings to one pound.

2. See Foster (1992:17–43) on the history of parliamentary regulation and the railways. A maximum dividend of 10 percent was imposed for the first time on a telegraph company in the 1855 Consolidation Act, which created the Electric Company (Kieve 1973:53).

3. The Electric Telegraph Company was founded by William Cooke in 1846. According to Bright (1898a:16), it merged with the International Telegraph Company in 1853 to become the Electric and International Telegraph Company. The English and Irish Magnetic Telegraph Company, founded in 1850 by a group of Manchester and Liverpool merchants, including John Pender, merged with the British Telegraph Company in 1856 to become the British and Irish Magnetic Telegraph Company (Barty-King 1979:11).

4. The four were the Telegraph Construction and Maintenance Company (Telcon); Siemens Brothers, a subsidiary of the German Siemens & Halske company; Messrs. Silver & Company, known as the Silvertown Company; and W. T. Henley, which became W. T. Henley's Telegraph Works Company in 1880. In 1864 the India-Rubber, Gutta Percha and Telegraph Works Company Ltd. took over the Silvertown Company (Bright 1998a:156–57).

5. In 1901 the Associated Companies, or "Eastern" group, consisted of the Eastern Telegraph Company (cables between England and India); Eastern Extension and Telegraph Company (cables between India and the Far East; India and Australasia; Durban, South Africa, and Australia); Eastern and South African Telegraph Company (cables between Luanda, Angola, and Cape Town; Aden and Durban; Zanzibar, the Seychelles, and Mauritius); West African Telegraph Company (cables between Senegal and Sierra Leone; Grand Bassam, Ivory Coast, and Luanda); Europe and Azores Telegraph Company (cable between Lisbon and Azores); Western Telegraph Company (cables between Lisbon and Pernambuco, Brazil); West Coast of America Telegraph Company (cables between Chorillos, near Lima, Peru, and Talcahuano, Chile); African Direct Company (cables between Cape Verde Islands; Bathurst, Gambia; Sierra Leone; the Gold Coast; and Lagos, Nigeria); Pacific and European Telegraph Company (a landline); London Platino-Brazilian Telegraph Company; Anglo-American Telegraph Company (transatlantic cables); Direct United States Cable Company (transatlantic cable); and four West Indian companies. See Balfour Committee (1902). Sir John Pender was chairman of the Eastern group until his death in 1896.

6. Palmerston to Electric Telegraph Commission, 4 July 1851, PRO, FO97/197.

7. Post Office to Board of Trade, 1 Sept. 1899, PO 30/574A.

8. Post Office to Board of Trade, 23 Oct. 1894, PO 30/573.

9. Post Office to Treasury, 12 Aug. 1884, PO 86/016.

10. This form of regulation through potential buy-back was similar to that which W. E. Gladstone attempted to exert over the railways when he was president of the Board of Trade in 1844. See Foster 1992:23–28.

11. The company established by Gisborne and later acquired by Field was called the New York, Newfoundland, and London Telegraph Company. This company's concession was transferred for five years to Field's Atlantic Telegraph Company in 1856 but reverted to the New York, Newfoundland, and London Telegraph Company in 1862. A new company, the Anglo-American Telegraph and Cable Company, was formed by Cyrus Field in 1866. The Atlantic Telegraph and Anglo-American Telegraph and Cable companies merged in 1873 and took over the New York, Newfoundland, and London Telegraph Company (Bright 1898a:16n).

12. Charles Bright comments that Sir James Anderson, the managing director of the Eastern, had proposed "the joint working, under international control, of all the cables of the world" but that "such a telegraphic millennium still looks very remote" (1898a:177n).

13. Because of offshore currents the DUS Cable Company was also forced to land in Canada and link to New York by landline (Scott 1958:75).

14. Barty-King refers to "AT&T," not to Gould's Atlantic Telegraph and Cable Company, but this seems to be a mistake because Gould did not take over AT&T until later (1979:58).

15. Under the Post Roads Act of 1866 before a telegraph company could take advantage of rights-of-way along public roads, it had to provide the postmaster general with written acceptance of the law's conditions concerning government rates and interconnection, but the law appears to have provided for no enforcement mechanism other than the courts. See Herring and Gross (1936:210).

16. The new measure from Congress was the Government-Aided Railroad and Telegraph Act, August 7, 1888. See Herring and Gross (1936:210).

17. Australia's five colonies were Tasmania, Queensland, South Australia, Western Australia, and Victoria.

18. Memorandum from Zongli Yamen, 6 June 1870, quoted in Baark (1997:81).

19. Post Office memorandum, 11 Aug. 1899, PO30/378A.

20. Fish to Motley, 23 Nov. 1869, quoted in Clark (1931:140).

21. Regulation XXVII, first adopted in 1868 (Post Office memorandum on International Telegraph Convention, 9 Feb. 1901, PO30/1208). The name of the International Bureau of Telegraph Administrations changed in 1906 to International Bureau of the Telegraph Union (Codding and Rutkowski 1982:9).

22. "Intra-European" was deemed to include the French colonies in North and West Africa.

23. The 1879 regulations have seven British signatures, including two from India and one from New Zealand, compared to three from France; two each from the Ottoman Empire, Austria, and Belgium; one from Germany; and one each from Hungary, Denmark, Spain, Japan, Norway, Holland, Portugal, Roumania, Serbia, Sweden, and Switzerland.

24. See, for instance, the complaints of James Anderson (1872) about the lowering of rates to India by the International Telegraph Conference (Anderson 1872:37–39).

25. Postmaster general to Treasury, 15 Mar. 1883, PO30/378A.

Chapter 2: Following the Flag

1. Calleo and Rowland (1973), table 1, shows British investment in the empire as rising from 36 percent of all investment in the 1860s to 47 percent in the 1880s, falling slightly in the period 1900–1913 to 46 percent. During the same period British investment in Latin America rose from 10.3 percent to 20 percent to 22 percent.

2. Quoted in Post Office memorandum, 17 Aug. 1900, PO30/1208.

3. Opinion of the Solicitor to the Post Office, 18 Dec. 1891, PO30/815.

4. Eastern to Post Office, 2 Feb. 1899, PO30/815.

5. Acting Manager, Hong Kong, to Eastern, 14 May 1898, PO30/815.

6. John Denison-Pender to Foreign Office, 7 June 1898, PO30/815.

7. Post Office to J. H. Carson, Anglo-American Telegraph Company, 30 Mar. 1899, PO30/815.

8. J. H. Carson to Post Office, 4 Apr. 1899, PO30/815.

9. Post Office memorandum, 10 Apr. 1899, PO30/815.

10. Post Office to J. H. Carson, Anglo-American Telegraph Company, 30 Mar. 1899, PO30/815.

11. Interdepartmental Committee on Cable Communications (Balfour Committee), Second Report, draft, 21, PO30/1209.

12. J. C. Lamb, Evidence to Lord Balfour's Committee, 11 June 1901, PO30/1209.

13. War Office to Post Office, 10 Apr. 1899, PO30/850C. The term *All-Red* may have arisen from the pink that atlases of the time used to denote British possessions.

14. PRO, Cab. 37/49/15, 6 May 1899, quoted in Kennedy (1971:738).

15. Balfour Committee, Second Report, draft, 20.

16. Board of Trade to Treasury, 7 Mar. 1900, PO30/1208.

17. Colonial Office to Treasury, 22 Feb. 1900, PO30/1208.

18. Treasury to Colonial Office, 5 Feb. 1900, PO30/1208.

19. Treasury to Lord Balfour of Burleigh, 19 Feb. 1901, PO30/1208.

20. Balfour Committee, Second Report, draft.

21. Report of Meeting of Cables Committee, 15 Feb. 1900, PO30/999B.

22. Minutes of Committee on Submarine Cable Landing Rights, 28 May 1901, PO30/999B.

23. Committee on Landing Rights for Submarine Cables Meeting, 23 Oct. 1902, PO30/999B.

24. Post Office memorandum, 21 Aug. 1901, PO30/999B.

25. France had acquired the colony of New Caledonia off the west coast of Australia in 1891.

26. Pacific Cable Committee Report, 1897, ¶1786, PO83/94.

27. A memorandum to Treasury from Postmaster General, 11 Aug. 1899, PO30/378A, makes clear that the landing rights for the Eastern in Hong Kong were not "exclusive" but "preferential."

28. Pacific Cable Committee, 1900, 6, PO83/94.

29. Ibid., 7.

30. Correspondence between Post Office and Treasury, PO 30/1209.

31. 1896 Report from U.K. delegation to ITU Convention, 11, PO83/24.

32. The comment about the International Bureau in Berne comes from J. C. Lamb in regard to a letter from the International Bureau to the Eastern, 20 Dec. 1900, PO30/1930.

Chapter 3: Wireless and the State

1. Sir Oliver Lodge, Fellow of Royal Society (1851–1940) and a physicist, later became president of the British Association, a government-financed organization that promotes science and whose members are the elite of the scientific community. Marconi established his first company, Wireless Telegraph and Signal Company, in 1897 and was the the main shareholder. In 1900 the name was changed to Marconi's Wireless Telegraph Company.

2. Henry Jackson was to become first sea lord of the Admiralty in 1915 and to fight in the Battle of Jutland in World War I (Kaufman 1974:6–7).

3. Post Office memorandum, 20 Aug. 1909, PO30/2184.

4. Memorandum of Agreement between Marconi International Marine Communication Company Ltd. and Lloyd's, 26 Sept. 1901, PO30/1488B.

5. See Austen Chamberlain's speech to House of Commons and Marconi company replies, PO30/1298.

6. See correspondence between Postmaster General and Marconi's Wireless Telegraph Company, 1902–3, PO33/1298.

7. Post Office memoranda, 1899–1906, PO30/850C.

8. Agreement between Admiralty and Marconi's Wireless Telegraph Company, 24 July 1903, London, clause 9, PO30/1913A.

9. See correspondence between Admiralty and Post Office, 1909–10, PO30/1913A.

10. The company formed by the alliance was named Gesellschaft für Drahtlose Telegraphie.

11. On the question of a private monopoly see correspondence between H. Babington Smith and H. Cuthbert Hall, July–Aug. 1905, PO30/1346.

12. "Return Relative to the Working of the Wireless Telegraph Act for the First Three Months of the Year from the 1st Day of January to the 31st March 1905," House of Commons Papers, July 1905, PO30/1346.

13. Government-Aided Railroad and Telegraph Act, 7 Aug. 1888.

14. Post Office memorandum on third meeting of British delegates to the International Radiotelegraphic Conference, 2 Aug. 1906, PO30/1346.

15. On these altercations see files on 1906 Berlin conference, PO30/1298/1299/1344/1346/1347/1348.

16. License to Establish a System of Wireless Telegraphy for Commercial Purposes, n.d. (ca. 1906), PO30/1157B.

17. Allgemaine Elektricitäts Gesellschaft to Sir Edward Grey, Foreign Office, 8 May 1906, PO30/1344.

18. British delegates to Sir Edward Grey, Foreign Office, Oct. and Nov. 1906, PO30/1346.

19. Draft Evidence of Babington Smith to House of Commons Select Committee, 22 Feb. 1907, PO30/1488B.

20. Post Office memorandum for Cabinet on Radiotelegraphic Select Committee Report, 11 July 1907, PO30/1346.

21. Correspondence between William Preece and Oliver Lodge, 1911, PO30/878B.

22. Post Office memorandum of Meeting with Sir John Denison-Pender, 6 Aug. 1909, PO30/2184.

23. Post Office memorandum on Lloyd's, 20 Aug. 1909, PO30/2184.

24. "Report on Applications from Eastern Telegraph Company and Marconi Company for Permission to Establish Wireless Telegraph Stations in Various Colonies," 27 Sept. 1909, PO30/2184.

25. Committee on Landing Rights for Submarine Cables, "Report on the Question of the Provision of Ship and Shore Commercial Wireless Stations at Gibraltar, Singapore and Hong Kong," 19 Feb. 1912, PO30/2184.

26. Downing Street to governor of Singapore, 16 Feb. 1912, PO30/2184.

27. Correspondence between Admiralty and Post Office, April 1909–December 1910, PO30/1913A.

28. Godfrey Isaacs to Admiralty, 17 Nov. 1910, PO30/1913A.

29. Post Office to Admiralty, 22 Feb. 1911; Post Office to Treasury, 6 Jan. 1912, both in PO30/1913A.

30. Post Office memorandum of meeting with Godfrey Isaacs, 17 Jan. 1911, PO30/2274.

31. The U.S. delegation arrived with the intention of claiming six votes for its possessions but was denied because of failure to notify the convention six months in advance.

32. Meeting with French and German delegates at Paris, 26 and 27 Apr. 1912, PO30/2272B.

33. In the meeting before the conference the Germans said they opposed the merger of the two bodies because it was premature. They claimed it "should be deferred until it is possible to dispense with Naval and Military delegates at Radiotelegraph Conferences" (meeting with French and German delegates at Paris, 26 and 27 Apr. 1912, PO30/2272B). The German opposition may have resulted from German collaboration with the Americans who, because of U.S. cable companies' antagonism to international regulation, wished to keep the two bodies separate.

34. Radio Communications Act of Aug. 13, 1912, Pub. L No. 62-264, 37 Stat. 302 (1912), quoted in Sidak (1997:25).

35. Godfrey Isaacs to Admiralty, 17 Nov. 1910, PO30/1913A.

36. The twenty-two stations were Alexandria, Aden, Mombasa, Natal, Cape Colony, Bombay, Colombo, Singapore, Hong Kong, North Australia, Sydney, New Zealand, St. Helena, Sierra Leone, Bathurst, British Guiana, and the West Indies, with additional stations in Mauritius, Nelson Island, Nairobi, Singapore, and Poona.

37. Godfrey Isaacs to Colonial Office, 10 Mar. 1910, PO30/2184.

38. Report, Cable Landing Rights Committee Meeting, 27 Apr. 1910, PO30/2184.

39. Post Office memorandum, 17 Jan. 1911, PO30/2274.

40. Report of Interdepartmental Committee, 2 Feb. 1911, PO30/1913A.

41. Memorandum, Cable Landing Rights Committee, 8 Mar. 1911, PO30/2274.

42. Post Office memorandum of discussion at Cable Landing Rights Committee, 11 Mar. 1911; Post Office memorandum of Meeting with Admiralty, 4 Apr. 1911, both in PO30/2274.

43. Godfrey Isaacs to Post Office, 13 Apr. 1911, PO30/2274.

44. Telegram: Eastern Extension Australasia and China Telegraph Company to London HQ, 28 Oct. 1909, PO30/2184.

45. Internal company memorandum, ca. 1916, Marconi Company Archives, GEC-Marconi Research Centre, Essex, U.K.

46. "Wireless station at Chapultec," translation of article in *El Universal,* 19 June 1920, PO30/1819B.

47. House Committee on the Merchant Marine and Fisheries, *Government Control of Radio Communication: Hearings on H.R. 13,159, a Bill to Further Regulate Radio Communication,* 65th Cong., 3d sess., Dec. 12, 13, 17, 18, 19, 1918, p. 9, quoted in Tribolet (1929:201).

Chapter 4: The United States, Trade, and Communications, 1890s–1917

1. See Gen. Smedley R. Butler's comments on links between armed intervention and American business, quoted in Pearce (1981:20).

2. U.S. companies had invested $618 million in Canada, $587 million in Mexico, $573 million in Europe, $371 million in Central America and the Caribbean, $323 million in South America, $17 million in Oceania, and $13 million in Africa.

3. Post Office memorandum, 30 Jan. 1897, PO30/793C.

4. Cited in *Electrical Review,* 9 Oct. 1896 PO30/790C. The U.S. government sued Compagnie Française des Câbles Télégraphiques, the United States and Hayti [*sic*] Telegraph Cable Company, and the United States and Hayti [*sic*] Cable Company. Ahvenainen quotes the *New York Herald* of December 3, 1896, which refers to these two companies as the United States and Haiti Telegraph and Cable Company. This company, although a subsidiary of the French company, had American directors who were also directors of the Commercial Cable Company (Ahvenainen 1996:100).

5. Post Office memorandum 30 Jan. 1897, PO30/793C.

6. Evidence of J. C. Lamb to Pacific Cable Committee, 30 Nov. 1896, PO83/94.

7. Similar discrimination against radio competition is documented for the first ten years of its existence, 1919–29, when RCA delivered ten times as many transatlantic messages to Western Union and the Postal Telegraph Company as it received for transmission abroad. See Herring and Gross (1936:203).

8. The vacuum tube repeater was introduced in 1915, making transcontinental speech possible, but even in the 1930s only 1.4 percent of AT&T's traffic was interstate.

9. The ICC's ruling may be found in *Private Wire Contracts,* 50 I.C.C. 731 (1917).

10. Japan's exports had grown from £2.7 million ($13.1 million) in 1888 to £54 million ($262 million) by 1902. See Peel (1905:274).

11. *New York Journal of Commerce,* 6 Apr. 1915, cited in Schwoch (1987:60n).

12. Post Office memorandum, 16 Dec. 1918, PO33/1938.

13. Eastern Telegraph to manager, Gibraltar, 25 Nov. 1898, PO30/815.

14. Report and Minutes of Proceedings, Pacific Cable Committee, Colonial Office, Mar. 1897, ¶27, PO83/94.

15. C. H. Mackay to Hon. Norman Davis, chairman of the American delegation to the Preliminary Communication Conference of Washington, 15 Nov. 1920, quoted in Tribolet (1929:12).

16. Report, Commission of Enquiry into the Organisation and Methods of the American Telegraph Companies, Feb. 1929, PO33/2519.

Chapter 5: South America

1. In 1897 British investment in Latin America totaled $2.06 billion, whereas France had invested $628 million and the United States, $308 million. In 1914 Britain's investment there had increased to $3.7 billion, France's to $1.2 billion, the United States's to $1.7 billion, and Germany's to $900 million (Petras et al. 1973:93, table 2).

2. The International Union of American Republics became the Pan-American Union in 1910. See Harrison (1997:15).

3. Cayenne Concession from French Government, 4 Apr. 1874; Notes on Original Brazilian Concession for Cables along West of Brazil, 25 Mar. 1970; Notes on Original Concession from Brazil for Cable from Rio De Janeiro to States of Rio De La Plata, 16 May 1871 and 25 Oct. 1871, all in PO30/815.

4. The War of the Triple Alliance was waged by Argentina, Brazil, and Uruguay against Paraguay from 1865 to 1870.

5. Post Office to Western and Brazilian Company, 15 Dec. 1897, PO30/815.

6. Notes on original Portuguese Concession, 12 Nov. 1872, PO30/815.

7. On the history of the telegraph in the Caribbean, see Dunn (1991) and Ahvenainen (1996).

8. Baur (1994:13); see also Post Office Memorandum, 11 Nov. 1897, PO30/789.

9. The secretaries of state were William H. Seward, Thomas F. Bayard, James G. Blaine, Frederick T. Frelinghuysen, John Hay, Elihu Root, Philander C. Knox, William Jennings Bryan, and Robert Lansing.

10. This 1890 French cable was what led the United States to extend its landing-rights policy.

11. Post Office to Foreign Office, 30 Dec. 1911, PO30/2359B.

12. *Le Bulletin Hebdomaire,* Paris, 6 Apr. 1905, PO30/2359B.

13. British Legation, Panama, to Foreign Office, 20 Sept. 1910, PO30/2359B.

14. Post Office Memorandum, 19 Oct. 1912, PO30/2359B.

15. Ibid.

16. Post Office to Foreign Office, 30 Dec. 1911, PO30/2359B.

17. Cable Landing Rights Committee Report, 6 Mar. 1906, PO30/1817. On the Guatemala–San Salvadore war see Scrymser (1915:83–84).

18. British Legation, Mexico, to Foreign Office, 11 Oct. 1913, PO30/1819B.

19. British Legation, Panama, to Foreign Office, 1 Aug. 1903, PO30/3657A.

20. British Legation, Ecuador, to Foreign Office, 30 July and 15 Sept. 1913, PO30/2359B.

21. Cable Landing Rights Committee Report, 21 July 1909, PO 30/1817.

22. *Morning Post,* United Kingdom, 28 Nov. 1914, PO30/2110A.

23. Godfrey Isaacs to Colonial Office, 7 July 1911, PO30/2110A.

24. Paraphrase in English was made by the Brazilian government of the *note verbale* from the U.S. State Department to the Brazilian ambassador in Washington, D.C., Nov. 1916, for transmission to Brazilian government. Enclosed in letter from British legation, Petropolis, Brazil, to Foreign Office, London, 16 Feb. 1917, PO30/2359B.

25. The navy subsequently withdrew its support when it learned that Federal Telegraph would control only one-quarter of the combine, with the rest split between the American and British Marconi companies. See Hogan (1977:142n).

26. Post Office Memorandum, n.d. (ca. 1919), PO30/1018C.

27. Translation of article in *El Universel,* 19 June 1920, PO30/1819B. See also Schwoch (1990:44–45).

28. *Electrical Engineer,* United Kingdom, 21 Apr. 1911, PO30/2359B.

29. The name of the Central and South American Telegraph Company was changed to All America Cables, Inc., in 1920. The Mexican Telegraph Company remained separate and was sold to Western Union in 1926.

30. Post Office Memorandum, 19 Oct. 1912, PO30/2359B.

Chapter 6: The United States

1. The U.S. government had also intercepted and deciphered telegraph messages both before and during World War I, such as those from Siemens Schuckert Ltd. in Argentina sent through the Swedish legation during 1916–17. See PO30/1081C.

2. Testimony by Clarence H. Mackay, president, Commercial Pacific Cable Company, before the Subcommittee of the Committee on Interstate Commerce, U.S. Senate, *Cable Landing Licenses: Hearings,* 10 Jan. 1921, 263–81, cited in Tribolet (1929:189).

3. The League of Nations did develop its own radio service, but it was geared to the bureaucracy. See Rigby (1942:9).

4. Woodrow Wilson to Senator Hitchcock, 22 Oct. 1918, cited in Stannard Baker (1923, 2:413).

5. Sir Hubert Llewellyn Smith to Bernard Baruch, American member of the Economic Drafting Committee, 2 Feb. 1919, cited in S. Baker (1923, 2:415).

6. Tribolet (1929:55n.17) suggests that in refusing to back the "spheres of influence" proposal, the State Department may have been retaliating for Western Union's charging the U.S. government twice what it charged the British government for messages, and because Western Union insisted that the U.S. government pay cash up front before it would transmit government messages.

7. Western Union operated eight transatlantic cables in 1920: two leased from AT&T until 1932; five leased from Anglo-American for ninety-nine years; one (the cable formerly owned by Direct United States Cable) bought by the British government in 1920 and leased to AT&T with a requirement of six months' notice to end the lease. See Shreiner (1924:105).

8. The Wireless Specialty Corporation, bought in 1912 by United Fruit, controlled the patents for the radio crystal detector. See Schwoch (1990:21).

9. David Sarnoff, commercial manager of RCA, testimony to U.S. Congress, House of Representatives, Report No. 10003, 66th Cong., 2d sess., 1920, cited in Tribolet (1929:209).

10. British Legation, Buenos Aires, Letter and Memorandum to Department of Overseas Trade, 26 Feb. 1925. A handwritten note attached to records of Marconi's Argentinean company comments that the record "makes clear that they never intended the Argentine company for any other than a Stock-Exchange counter" (both in PO30/1081C).

11. "Federal Trade Commission Report on the Radio Industry" in response to HR548, 67th Cong., 4th sess., 1924, cited in Tribolet (1929:60).

12. Owen D. Young to James R. Sheffield, 7 Dec. 1921, quoted in Tribolet (1929:61).

13. This company already had a strong prewar relationship with the U.S. Navy, which subsequently promoted it as an "American" company that could act as an alternative supplier to RCA.

14. A high-power radio station with a range of about three thousand miles was estimated to cost $1 million to $1.5 million to build in the 1920s, with annual operating costs of about $100,000 for the two stations. Compared to the costs of cable, which for the same distance would need $7 million in capital, with annual operating costs of about $60,000, the new technology was low cost. See Schreiner (1924:149).

15. Charles E. Hughes, Department of State, to H. M. Lord, Department of State, 1 Feb. 1924, PO33/1442B.

16. The fifteen states were Argentina, Brazil, Colombia, Costa Rica, Cuba, Salvador, Mexico, Guatemala, Nicaragua, Panama, Paraguay, Peru, Santo Domingo, the United States, and Uruguay.

17. Department of State, Report on Inter-American Committee on Electrical Communication, 12 Aug. 1924, PO33/1442B.

18. Letter from Charles Warren, Chairman, American Delegation, to Secretary of State, 17 July 1924, quoted in Hogan (1977:145).

19. Italy and the Netherlands had three votes; Belgium, Spain, and Japan had two.

20. The Mexican Telegraph Company was Scrysmer's old company. It ran submarine cables from Texas to Vera Cruz (Mexico) and landlines from Vera Cruz to the Pacific coast.

21. In France the French wireless companies Compagnie Générale de Télégraphie sans Fils and the Compagnie Radio-France merged with the French cable company. A similar amalgamation took place between the Italian wireless company and the Italian cable company. And in Germany the Telefunken Company, owned by Allgemaine Electricitäts Gesellschaft and the Siemens-Halske Company, entered into a working arrangement with the German cable company. See Brown (1927:114).

22. In 1930 direct shortwave telephone service was available from the British Isles to Australia, Canada, Egypt, India, and South Africa (Appleton 1933:12).

23. This was the conclusion of the U.S. Interdepartmental Radio Advisory Committee, appointed in 1933. See Herring and Gross (1936:205).

Chapter 7: British Communications, 1919–40

1. This station was never built.

2. Cable Landing License, 28 Sept. 1923; Marconi License, 31 Dec. 1925, with Supplements, 14 Jan. 1928, all in PO33/5903.

3. Report of Imperial and Wireless and Cable Conference, 1928, PO33/5903.

4. The new companies had Sir Basil Blackett as chairman, John Cuthbert Denison-Pender (grandson of John Pender) and F. G. Kellaway as managing directors, and Edward Wilshaw as general manager and secretary. Blackett, Denison-Pender, and Wilshaw all came from the Eastern, and Kellaway was a one-time politician, so the new communications company was run by cable men. Denison-Pender became chairman in 1932.

5. Marconi's entertainment interests were sold to the gramophone company His Master's Voice, but it kept its manufacturing and research in radio, producing radio sets and telecommunications equipment.

6. See Post Office memoranda 1899–1926 on private wire agreements, PO30/826.

7. Quoted in Brown (1927:121). The Railway and Canal Commission had been established in 1888 and had the authority of a high court. A judge and two lay assessors presided over the commission, and barristers argued the cases. See Foster (1992:48).

8. Garratt (1950:41). Press traffic remained at 10 percent of the total international traffic from 1913 to 1929; slightly less than 50 percent was intraimperial, 25 percent was sent from the empire to a foreign nation, and 25 percent was sent between foreign nations. See Blackett (1939a:47).

9. Marconi International Marine Communication Company to Post Office, 4 Aug. 1922, PO33/1223.

10. Post Office and Wireless Press Correspondence, 1922–25, PO33/1223.

11. The British Broadcasting Company Ltd. became the British Broadcasting Corporation (the BBC) on December 31, 1926.

12. Post Office memorandum, 20 Feb. 1923, PO33/1069.

13. Post Office memorandum, 2 Mar. 1923, PO33/1223, cited in Donald Read (1992:157).

14. Post Office to Treasury, 14 Aug. 1923, PO33/1223.

15. Overseas Development Agency to Post Office, 8 Mar. 1923, PO33/1223.

16. War Office to Post Office, 3 July 1924, PO33/1233.

17. Post Office memorandum, ca. 1926, PO33/1069.

18. Ibid.

19. The first Imperial Press Conference in 1909 was organized in London in the Foreign Office and was chaired by Lord Crewe, the colonial secretary. Out of this conference came the Empire Press Union, an association of newspaper owners and editors. A second conference was held in Ottawa in 1920. See Mills (1924:112–13).

Chapter 8: Cultural Production and International Relations

1. See Litman (1998) on the specific economics of the movie industry.

2. Ramsay MacDonald in opposition to British Cinematograph Film Bill, 16 March 1927, *Parliamentary Debates,* Commons, 5th series, vol. 203 (Feb. 28–March 18 1927): 27.

3. Will H. Hays, quoted in *New York Times,* 1 July 1926, quoted in Seabury (1929:150).

4. See, for instance, British prime minister Ramsay MacDonald to John Reith, reported in Reith (1949:177).

5. Colonial Office memorandum C.O. 5 for Colonial Office Conference, 1927, PO33/1441B.

6. The Wireless Association of Great Britain, begun in 1926, was one of several associations of amateur wireless enthusiasts. On the amateur associations see Pegg (1983).

7. Colonial Office memorandum, 19 May 1927, PO33/1441B.

8. The colonies that reported efforts to establish local broadcasting were Ceylon, Straits Settlement, Gold Coast, and Kenya (Colonial Office Memorandum C.O. 5 for Colonial Office Conference, 1927, PO33/1441B).

9. On later debates see, for instance, UNESCO (1968) and Gerbner and Nordenstreng (1981).

10. On the introduction of commercial television broadcasting in Britain, see Skornia (1965) and Wilson (1961).

11. The six private companies were NBC, CBS, Westinghouse, General Electric, Cros-

ley Corporation, and the Worldwide Broadcasting Foundation. Associated Broadcasters, Inc., also received a license from the FCC to set up a station in San Francisco to blanket the Pacific and Latin America in six languages for sixteen to twenty hours per day. The transmitter that it used was government owned but was operated by Associated Broadcasters (Rolo 1943:185; Pirsein 1979:29).

12. On the "cultural imperialism" thesis and subsequent debates, see, for instance, Hamelink (1983); Herman and McChesney (1997); Mattelart (1979); Schiller (1969, 1976); Sinclair et al. (1996); and J. Tomlinson (1991).

13. On the issues raised by satellite broadcasting, see Sakr (2001).

References

Ahvenainen, Jorma. 1981. *The Far Eastern Telegraphs.* Helsinki: Suomaleinen Tiedeakatemia.
————. 1996. *The History of the Caribbean Telegraphs before the First World War.* Helsinki: Suomaleinen Tiedeakatemia.
Aitken, Hugh G. J. 1976. *Syntony and Spark: The Origins of Radio.* New York: John Wiley
 and Sons.
Alexander, W. D. 1911. "The Story of the Trans-Pacific Cable." In *Development of Subma-
 rine Cable Communications.* Ed. Bernard S. Finn. Vol. 1:50–80. New York: Arno Press.
Anderson, Sir James. 1872. *Statistics of Telegraphy.* Read before the Statistical Society, 18
 June 1872. London: Waterlow and Sons.
Appleton, E. V. 1933. *Empire Communication.* Norman Lockyer Lecture. London: British
 Science Guild.
Attman, Artur, Jan Kluse, and Ulf Olsson. 1976. *L. M. Ericsson.* Vol. 1: *The Pioneering Years:
 Struggle for Concessions Crisis, 1876–1932.* Stockholm, Sweden: L. M. Ericsson.
Baark, Erik. 1997. *Lightning Wires: The Telegraph and China's Technological Modernization,
 1860–1890.* Westport, Conn.: Greenwood Press.
Baer, George W. 1994. *One Hundred Years of Sea Power.* Stanford, Calif.: Stanford Univer-
 sity Press.
Baglehole, K. G. 1969. *A Century of Service: Cable and Wireless Ltd., 1868–1968.* London:
 Cable and Wireless Ltd.
Baker, Stannard R. 1923. *Woodrow Wilson and World Settlement.* Vols. 1–3. London: Wil-
 liam Heinemann.
Baker, W. J. 1970. *A History of the Marconi Company.* London: Methuen and Co.
Baldwin, F. G. C. 1938. *The History of the Telephone in the United Kingdom.* London: Chap-
 man and Hall.
Barnouw, Eric. 1970. *The Image Empire: A History of Broadcasting in the United States.* New
 York: Oxford University Press.

Barty-King, Hugh. 1979. *Girdle round the Earth: The Story of Cable and Wireless and Its Predecessors to Mark the Group's Jubilee, 1929–1979.* London: Heinemann.

Batson, Lawrence D. 1971. *Radio Markets of the World* (1930). U.S. Department of Commerce, Bureau of Foreign and Domestic Commerce, Trade Promotion Series No. 109. In *World Broadcast Advertising: Four Reports.* 1–108. Reprint, New York: Arno Press.

Baur, Cynthia. 1994. "The Foundations of Telegraphy and Telephony in Latin America." *Journal of Communication* 44 (Autumn): 9–25.

BBC (British Broadcasting Corporation). 1929. *BBC Handbook, 1929.* London: BBC.

———. 1931. *BBC Yearbook, 1931.* London: BBC.

———. 1932. *BBC Yearbook, 1932.* London: BBC.

———. 1934. *BBC Yearbook, 1934.* London: BBC.

———. 1938. *BBC Handbook, 1938.* London: BBC.

Becker, William H. 1982. *The Dynamics of Business-Government Relations: Industry and Exports, 1893–1921.* Chicago: University of Chicago Press.

Benians, E. A. 1959. "Imperial Finance Trade and Communications, 1870–95." In *The Cambridge History of the British Empire.* Ed. E. A Benians, J. R. M. Butler, P. N. S. Mansbergh, and E. A. Walker. Vol. 3:181–229. Cambridge: Cambridge University Press.

Berthold, V. M. 1922. *Of the Telephone and Telegraph in Brazil, 1851–1921.* New York: AT&T.

———. 1924. *A History of the Telegraph and Telephone in Chile.* New York: AT&T.

Blackett, Sir Basil P. 1939a. "Address to the Fourth Imperial Press Conference, June 1930." In *The Cable and Wireless Communications of the World: Some Lectures and Papers on the Subject, 1924–1939.* Ed. Cable and Wireless Ltd. 39–54. London: Cable and Wireless.

———. 1939b. "Address to the Royal Empire Society." In *The Cable and Wireless Communications of the World: Some Lectures and Papers on the Subject, 1924–1939.* Ed. Cable and Wireless Ltd. 55–60. London: Cable and Wireless.

Blondheim, Menahem. 1994. *News over the Wires: The Telegraph and the Flow of Information in America, 1844–1897.* Cambridge, Mass.: Harvard University Press.

Braisted, William Reynolds. 1958. *The United States Navy in the Pacific, 1897–1909.* Austin: University of Texas Press.

Bresnahan, Mary I. 1979. "English in the Philippines." *Journal of Communication* 29 (Spring): 64–71.

Briggs, Asa. 1985. *The BBC: The First Fifty Years.* Oxford: Oxford University Press.

Bright, Charles Sir. 1898a. *Submarine Telegraphs: Their History, Construction, and Working.* London. Reprint, New York: Arno Press, 1974.

———. 1898b. "The Extension of Submarine Cable in a Quarter Century." *Engineering Magazine* (December). In *Development of Submarine Cable Communications.* Ed. Bernard S. Finn. Vol. 1:417–28. Reprint, New York: Arno Press, 1980.

———. 1911. *Imperial Telegraphic Communication.* London: P. S. King and Son.

———. 1914. "Imperial Telegraphy and Inter-Imperial Telegraphy" *Quarterly Review* 220:134–51.

Bright, Edward B., and Charles Bright. ca. 1898. *The Life Story of Charles Tilston Bright.* Vols. 1–2. London: Archibald Constable.

Brock, Gerald W. 1982. *The Telecommunications Industry: The Dynamics of Market Structures.* Cambridge, Mass.: Harvard University Press.

Brooks, John. 1975. *Telephone: The First Hundred Years.* New York: Harper and Row.

Brown, Frank James. 1927. *The Cable and Wireless Communications of the World.* London: Sir Isaac Pitman and Sons.

Burton, Paulu. 1956. *British Broadcasting: Radio and Television in the United Kingdom.* Minneapolis: University of Minnesota Press.

Calleo, David P., and Benjamin M. Rowland. 1973. *America and the World Political Economy: Atlantic Dreams and National Realities.* Bloomington: Indiana University Press.

Cannadine, David. 1983. "The Context, Performance, and Meaning of Ritual: The British Monarchy and the 'Invention of Tradition,' 1820–1977." In *The Invention of Tradition.* Ed. Eric Hobsbawm and Terence Ranger. 101–65. Cambridge: Cambridge University Press.

Cell, J. W. 1970. *British Colonial Administration in the Mid-Nineteenth Century: The Policy-making Process.* New Haven, Conn.: Yale University Press.

Cherry, Colin. 1978. *World Communications—Threat or Promise? A Socio-technical Approach.* London: Wiley.

Clark, Keith. 1931. *International Communications: The American Attitude.* New York: Columbia University Press.

Clarke, Geoffrey R. 1927. "Post and Telegraph Work in India." *Asiatic Review* 23:79–108.

Codding, George Arthur, Jr. 1972. *The International Telecommunication Union: An Experiment in International Cooperation.* New York: Arno Press.

Codding, George Arthur, Jr., and Anthony M. Rutkowski. 1982. *The International Telecommunication Union in a Changing World.* Dedham, Mass.: Artech House.

Connell-Smith, Gordon. 1974. *The United States and Latin America: An Historical Analysis of Inter-American Relations.* London: Heinemann Educational Books.

Cooper, Kent. 1942. *Barriers Down.* New York: Farrar and Rinehart.

Danelian, N. R. 1939. *AT&T: The Story of Industrial Conquest.* New York: Vanguard.

Denison-Pender, John Cuthbert. 1939. "Lecture to the Officers of the Royal Corps of Signals, January 1934." In *The Cable and Wireless Communications of the World: Some Lectures and Papers on the Subject, 1924–1939.* Ed. Cable and Wireless Ltd. 101–6. London: Cable and Wireless.

Douglas, J. Susan. 1985. "Technological Innovation and Organizational Change: The Navy's Adoption of Radio, 1899–1919." In *Military Enterprise and Technological Change.* Ed. Merritt Roe Smith. 117–73. Cambridge, Mass.: MIT Press.

———. 1987. *Inventing American Broadcasting, 1800–1922.* Baltimore, Md.: Johns Hopkins University Press.

Drummond, I. M. 1972. *British Economic Policy and the Empire, 1919–39.* London: Allen and Unwin.

Du Boff, Richard B. 1982. "The Telegraph and the Structure of Markets in the United States, 1845–1890." In *Research in Economic History: A Research Annual.* Ed. Paul Uselding. Vol. 8:253–72. Greenwich, Conn.: JAI Press.

———. 1984. "The Rise of Communication Regulation: The Telegraph Industry, 1844–1880." *Journal of Communication* 34 (Summer): 52–66.

Dunn, Hopeton. 1991. "Telecommunications and Underdevelopment: A Policy Analysis of the Historical Role of Cable and Wireless in the Caribbean." Ph.D. diss., City University, London.

Earl of Jersey. 1894. *Report of Colonial Conference at Ottawa 1894.* London: HMSO.

Eckersley, P. P. 1942. *The Power behind the Microphone.* London: Scientific Book Club.

Esthus, Raymond A. 1967. *Theodore Roosevelt and Japan.* Seattle: University of Washington Press.

Federal Communications Commission. 1940. "Report on the International Telegraph Industry." Submitted to the Senate Interstate Commerce Committee Investigating Telegraphs. Reprinted in *Development of Submarine Cable Communications.* Ed. Bernard S. Finn. 450–81. New York: Arno Press, 1980.

Fejes, Fred. 1980. "The Growth of Multinational Advertising Agencies in Latin America." *Journal of Communication* 30 (Autumn): 36–49.

———. 1986. *Imperialism, Media, and the Good Neighbour: New Deal Foreign Policy and United States Shortwave Broadcasting to Latin America.* Norwood, N.J.: Ablex.

Fenby, Jonathan. 1986. *The International News Services.* New York: Schocken Books.

Fieldhouse, D. K. 1965. *The Colonial Empires: A Comparative Survey from the Eighteenth Century.* London: Macmillan.

Fielding, Raymond. 1972. *The American Newsreel, 1911–1967.* Norman: University of Oklahoma Press.

Foreman-Peck, James. 1995. *A History of the World Economy: International Economic Relations since 1850.* New York: Harvester Wheatsheaf.

Fortner, Robert. 1993. *International Communication.* Belmont, Calif.: Wadsworth.

Foster, C. D. 1992. *Privatisation, Public Ownership, and the Regulation of Natural Monopoly.* Oxford: Blackwell.

Fox, Elizabeth. 1997. *Latin American Broadcasting: From Tango to Telenova.* Luton, U.K.: John Libbey Media.

Gafatchi, John. 1989. "A Review of the Development of the BBC African Service—Policy Perspectives." Master's thesis, City University, London.

Galbraith, J. K. 1994. *The World Economy between the Wars: A Personal View.* London: Mandarin.

Gallagher, J. A., and R. E. Robinson. 1953. "The Imperialism of Free Trade." *Economic History Review,* 2d ser., 1:1–15.

Garnham, Nicholas. 1990. *Capitalism and Communication.* London: Sage.

Garratt, Gerald R. M. 1950. *One Hundred Years of Submarine Cables.* London: HMSO.

Garvin, J. L. 1905. "The Maintenance of Empire: A Study of the Economic Base of Political Power." In *The Empire and the Century.* Ed. Charles Sydney Goldman. 69–143. London: John Murray.

Geddes, Keith. 1974. *Guglielmo Marconi, 1874–1937.* London: HMSO.

Gerbner, George, and Kaarle Nordenstreng, eds. 1981. *The Global Media Debate.* Norwood, N.J.: Ablex.

Goodwin, W. D. 1996. *One Hundred Years of Maritime Radio.* Glasgow, Scotland: Brown, Son and Ferguson.

Grandin, Thomas. 1971. *The Political Use of Radio.* New York: Arno Press.

Gregory, Bruce N. 1970. *The Broadcasting Service: An Administrative History.* Special Monograph Series No. 1. Washington, D.C.: U.S. Information Agency.

Grodinsky, Julius. 1957. *Jay Gould: His Business Career, 1867–92.* Philadelphia: University of Pennsylvania Press.

Guback, Thomas H. 1969. *The International Film Industry.* Bloomington: Indiana University Press.

———. 1976. "Hollywood's International Market." In *The American Film Industry.* Ed. Tino Balio. 463–86. Madison: University of Wisconsin Press.

Hale, Julian. 1975. *Radio Power.* London: Paul Elek.

Hall, Cuthbert H. ca. 1906. "The Marconi System and the Berlin Conference." *Empire Review.* Reprinted for company distribution. Marconi Archives, GEC—Marconi Research Centre, Essex, U.K.

Hamelink, Cees. 1983. *Cultural Autonomy in Global Communications.* New York: Longman.

Harcourt, Edgar. 1987. *Taming the Tyrant.* Sydney: Allen and Unwin.

Harrison, Lawrence. 1997. *The Pan-American Dream.* New York: Basic Books.

Harvey, David. 1990. *The Condition of Postmodernity.* Oxford: Blackwell.

Hay, Keith A. J., and B. Andrei Sulzenko. 1982. "U.S. Trade Policy and 'Reciprocity.'" *Journal of World Trade Law* 16 (November–December): 471–80.

He, Zhou. 1997. "A History of Telecommunications in China: Development and Policy Implications." In *Telecommunications and Development in China.* Ed. Paul S. N. Lee. 55–87. Cresskill, N.J.: Hampton Press.

Headrick, Daniel R. 1981. *Technology and European Imperialism in the Nineteenth Century.* New York: Oxford University Press.

———. 1988. *The Tentacles of Progress: Technology Transfer in the Age of Imperialism.* New York: Oxford University Press.

Herman, Edward, and Robert McChesney. 1997. *The Global Media: The New Missionaries of Corporate Capitalism.* London: Cassell.

Herring, James M., and Gerald C. Gross. 1936. *Telecommunications: Economics and Regulation.* New York: McGraw Hill.

Hills, Jill. 1993a. "Regulation, Politics, and Communications." In *Deregulating the Regulators.* Ed. J. P. Chamoux. 99–117. Amsterdam: IOS Press.

———. 1993b. "Back to the Future: Britain's 19th Century Telecommunications Policy." *Telecommunications Policy* 17 (April): 186–99.

———. 1994. "U.S. Hegemony and GATT." *Review of International Political Economy* 1 (Summer): 257–77.

———. 1998a. "Liberalization, Regulation, and Development." *Gazette* 60 (December): 459–76.

———. 1998b. "International Accounting Rates: The Process of Demise of an International Regime." *Communications and Strategies* 30 (2d quarter): 241–69.

———. 2001. "The WTO Reference Paper: Telecommunications Restructuring and Telecommunications Regulation." Paper presented at the Sixth Asia Pacific Regional Conference of the International Telecommunications Society. Hong Kong University of Science and Technology. 5–7 July.

Hobsbawm, Eric, and Terence Ranger, eds. 1983. *The Invention of Tradition.* Cambridge: Cambridge University Press,

Hogan, Michael. 1977. *Informal Entente: The Private Structure of Cooperation in Anglo-American Economic Diplomacy, 1918–1928.* Columbia: University of Missouri Press.

Hoida, Jason A. 1997. *American Telephony: 120 Years on the Road to Full-Blown Competition.* Oslo, Norway: Tano-Aschehoug.

Holland, R. F. 1981. *Britain and the Commonwealth Alliance, 1918–39.* London: Macmillan.

Horowitz, Robert B. 1989. *The Irony of Regulatory Reform.* Oxford: Oxford University Press.

Howeth, L. S. 1963. *History of Communications: Electronics in the United States Navy.* Washington, D.C.: Government Printing Office.

Hudson, M., and J. Stanier. 1997. *War and the Media: A Random Searchlight.* Stroud, U.K.: Sutton Publishing.

Hurd, Percy. 1896. "Our Telegraphic Isolation." *Contemporary Review* 69:899–908.

Hynes, William G. 1979. *The Economics of Empire Britain: Africa and the New Imperialism.* London: Longman.

Innis, Harold. 1972. *Empire and Communications.* Toronto: University of Toronto Press.

Izod, John. 1988. *Hollywood and the Box Office, 1895–1986.* Basingstoke, U.K.: Macmillan.

Jarvie, Ian. 1992. *Hollywood's Overseas Campaign: The North Atlantic Movie Trade, 1920–1950.* Cambridge: Cambridge University Press.

Johnson, George, ed. 1903. *The All Red Line: The Annals and Aims of the Pacific Cable Project.* London: Edward Stanford.

Jolly, W. P. 1972. *Marconi.* London: Constable.

———. 1974. *Sir Oliver Lodge.* London: Constable.

Josephson, Matthew. 1934. *The Robber Barons.* New York: Harcourt, Brace and Co.

Kaufman, Burton I. 1974. *Efficiency and Expansion: Foreign Trade Organization in the Wilson Administration, 1913–21.* Westport, Conn.: Greenwood Press.

Kennedy, P. M. 1971. "Imperial Cable Communications and Strategy, 1870–1914." *English Historical Review* 86 (October): 728–52.

Kieve, J. L. 1973. *Electric Telegraph: A Social and Economic History.* Newton Abbott: David and Charles.

Kirwin, Harry W. 1953. "The Federal Telegraph Company: A Testing of the Open Door." *Pacific Historical Review* 22:271–86.

Krasner, Stephen D., ed. 1983. *International Regimes.* Ithaca, N.Y.: Cornell University Press.

———. 1985. *Structural Conflict: The Third World against Global Liberalism.* Berkeley: University of California Press.

Lawford, G. L., and L. R. Nicholson, eds. 1950. *The Telcon Story, 1850–1950.* London: Telegraph Construction and Maintenance Co.

Lindblom, Charles E. 1977. *Politics and Markets.* New York: Basic Books.

Litman, Barry L. 1998. *The Motion Picture Mega Industry.* Needham Heights, Mass.: Allyn and Bacon.

Lukes, Steven. 1974. *Power: A Radical View.* London: Macmillan.

Luther, Sara Fletcher. 1988. *The United States and the Direct Broadcast Satellite.* Oxford: Oxford University Press.

McChesney, Robert W. 1994. *Telecommunications, Mass Media, and Democracy: The Battle for Control of U.S. Broadcasting, 1928–35.* Oxford: Oxford University Press.

McCormick, Thomas. 1967. *The China Market: America's Quest for Informal Empire, 1893–1901* Chicago: Quadrangle Books.

Mackay, Corday. 1946. "The Collins Overland Telegraph." *British Columbia Historical Quarterly* (July): 187–215.

MacKenzie, John. 1986. *Imperialism and Popular Culture.* Manchester, U.K.: Manchester University Press.

Mansell, Gerald. 1982. *Let Truth Be Told.* London: Weidenfeld and Nicolson.

Mattelart, Armand. 1979. *Multinational Corporations and the Control of Culture.* Brighton: Harvester Press.

May, Stacy, and Galo Plaza. 1958. *The United Fruit Company in Latin America.* Washington, D.C.: National Planning Association.

Mende, T. 1973. *From Aid to Recolonisation: Lesson of a Failure.* London: Harrap.

Mills, John Saxon. 1924. *The Press and Communications of the Empire.* London: W. Collins Sons.

Morris, James. 1979. *Pax Britannica: The Climax of the Empire.* London: Penguin.

Mosco, Vincent. 1988. "Towards a Theory of the State and Telecommunications Policy." *Journal of Communication* 38:107–24.

Moyal, Ann. 1984. *Clear across Australia: A History of Telecommunications.* Melbourne: Nelson.

Neering, Rosemary. 1989. *Continental Dash: The Russian-America Telegraph.* British Columbia: Horsdal and Schubart.

Nier, Keith A., and Andrew J. Butrica. 1988. "Telegraphy Becomes a World System: Paradox and Progress in Technology and Management." In *Essays in Economic and Business History.* Ed. Edwin J. Perkins. 211–25. Los Angeles: History Department, University of Southern California.

Nordlinger, Eric A. 1981. *On the Autonomy of the Democratic State.* Cambridge, Mass.: Harvard University Press.

Pastore, J. O. 1964. *The Story of Communications.* New York: McFadden Bartell.

Pearce, Jenny. 1981. *Under the Eagle: U.S. Intervention in Central America and the Caribbean.* London: Latin American Bureau.

Peel, George. 1905. "The Nerves of Empire." In *The Empire and the Century.* Ed. Charles Sydney Goldman. 249–87. London: John Murray.

Pegg, Mark. 1983. *Broadcasting and Society, 1918–1939.* London: Croom Helm.

PEP (Political and Economic Planning). 1952. *The British Film Industry: A Report on Its History and Present Organisation, with Special Reference to the Economic Problems of British Feature Film Production.* London: Political and Economic Planning.

Petras, James, H. Michael Erisman, and Charles Mills. 1973. "The Monroe Doctrine and U.S. Hegemony in Latin America." In *Spheres of Influence and the Third World.* Ed. Vladimir Dedijer, Bipan Chandra, Malcolm Caldwell, James F. Petras, H. Michael Erisman, Charles Mills, and Edward W. Said. 38–54. Nottingham, U.K.: Spokesman Books.

Petrazinni, Ben. 1995. *The Political Economy of Telecommunications: Reform in Developing Countries.* New York: Praeger.

Pirsein, Robert. 1979. *The Voice of America: A History of the International Broadcasting Activities of the U.S. Government, 1940–62.* New York: Arno Press.

Porter, Glenn. 1973. *The Rise of Big Business, 1860–1910.* New York: Thomas Y. Crowell.

Puttnam, David, with Neil Watson. 1997. *The Undeclared War: The Struggle for Control of the World's Film Industry.* London: HarperCollins.

Rantanen, Tehri. 1990. *Foreign News in Imperial Russia: The Relationship between International and Russian News Agencies, 1856–1914.* Helsinki: Suomaleinen Tiedeakatemia.

———. 1992. *Mr. Howard Goes to America: The United Press Associations and Foreign Expansion.* Roy W. Howard Monographs, No. 2. Bloomington: Indiana University.

Read, Donald. 1992. *The Power of News: The History of Reuters.* Oxford: Oxford University Press.

Read, Walter. 1976. *America's Mass Media Merchants.* Baltimore, Md.: Johns Hopkins University Press.

Reith, J. C. W. 1949. *Into the Wind.* London: Hodder and Stoughton.

Renaud, J. L. 1985. "U.S. Government Assistance to Associated Press's Worldwide Expansion." *Journalism Quarterly* 62:10–16.

Richards, Jeffrey. 1986. "Boys Own Empire: Feature Films and Imperialism in the 1930s." In *Imperialism and Popular Culture.* Ed. John Mackenzie. 140–65. Manchester, U.K.: Manchester University Press.

Riegel, Oscar. 1934. *Mobilizing for Chaos: The Story of the New Propaganda.* New Haven, Conn.: Yale University Press.

Rigby, C. A. 1972. *War on the Short Waves.* 1942. Reprint, New York: Arno Press.

Rippy, J. F. 1946. "Notes on the Early Telephone Companies of Latin America." *Hispanic American Historical Review* 26:116–18.

Rolo, Charles J. 1943. *Radio Goes to War.* London: Faber and Faber.

Rosen, Philip. 1980. *The Modern Stentors: Radio Broadcasters and the Federal Government, 1920–34.* Westport, Conn.: Greenwood Press.

Rosenberg, Emily. 1982. *Spreading the American Dream: American Economic and Cultural Expansion, 1890–1945.* New York: Hill and Wang.

Rossi, John P. 1985. "A 'Silent Partnership': The U.S. Government, RCA, and Radio Communications with East Asia, 1919–1928." *Radical History Review* 33:32–52.

Saerchinger, César. 1938. "Radio as a Political Instrument." *Foreign Affairs* 16 (Autumn): 244–58.

Sakr, Naomi. 2001. *Satellite Realms: Transnational Television, Globalization, and the Middle East.* London: I. B. Tauris.

Sampson, Anthony. 1973. *The Sovereign State: The Secret History of ITT.* London: Hodder and Stoughton.

Scannell, Paddy, and David Cardiff. 1991. *A Social History of British Broadcasting.* Oxford: Basil Blackwell.

Schiller, Herbert. 1969. *Mass Communications and American Empire.* New York: A. M. Kelley.

———. 1976. *Communications and Cultural Domination.* New York: M. E. Sharpe.

Schreiner, George. 1924. *Cable and Wireless and Their Role in the Foreign Relations of the U.S.A.* Boston: Stratford Co.

Schutrumpf, E. D. 1971. *Broadcast Advertising in Latin America* (1931). U.S. Department of Commerce, Bureau of Foreign and Domestic Commerce, Trade Information Bulletin No. 771. In *World Broadcast Advertising: Four Reports.* 1–30. Reprint, New York: Arno Press.

Schwoch, James. 1987. "The American Radio Industry and International Communications Conferences, 1919–1927." *Historical Journal of Film, Radio, and Television* 7 (Sept.): 289–309.

———. 1990. *The American Radio Industry and Its Latin American Activities, 1900–1939.* Urbana: University of Illinois Press.

"Singapore: Early Days." 1937. Extracts from "100 Years of Singapore Being Some Account of the Capital of the Straits Settlement, from Its Foundation by Sir Stamford Raffles on the 6th February 1819 to the 6th February 1919." In *British Malaya: the Journal of the Association of British Malaya*. Reprinted in *Intermedia* 19 (August–September 1991): 12.

Scott, J. D. 1958. *Siemens Brothers, 1858–1958*. London: Wiedenfeld and Nicholson.

Scrymser, James A. 1915. *Personal Reminiscences of James A. Scrymser in Times of Peace and War*. Easton, Pa.: Eschenbach.

Seabury, William Marston. 1929. *Motion Picture Problems: The Cinema and the League of Nations*. New York: Avondale Press.

Seif, Ahmed. 1988. "Broadcast to and in the Arab World." Master's thesis, City University, London.

Sidak, J. Gregory. 1997. *Foreign Investment in American Telecommunications*. Chicago: University of Chicago Press.

Sinclair, John, Elizabeth Jacka, and Stuart Cunningham, eds. 1996. *New Patterns in Global Television: Peripheral Vision*. Oxford: Oxford University Press.

Skornia, Harry J. 1965. *Television and Society: An Inquest and Agenda for Improvement*. New York: McGraw Hill.

Smith, Willoughby. 1891. *Rise and Extension of Submarine Telegraphy*. London: J. S. Virtue.

Sobel, Robert. 1982. *ITT: The Management of Opportunity*. London: Sidgwick and Jackson.

Southard, A. 1931. *American Industry in Europe*. Boston: Houghton Mifflin.

Standage, Tom. 1999. *The Victorian Internet*. London: Phoenix.

Sternbridge, Stanley R. 1982. *Parliament, the Press and the Colonies, 1846–1880*. New York: Garland Publishing.

Stewart, Watt. 1946. "Notes on an Attempt to Establish Cable Communications between North and South America." *Hispanic American Historical Review* 26:118–20.

Storey, Graham. 1951. *Reuters' Century, 1851–1951*. London: Max Parrish.

Strange, Susan. 1996. *The Retreat of the State: The Diffusion of Power in the World Economy*. Cambridge: Cambridge University Press.

Stuart, Campbell. 1920. *Secrets of Crewe House*. London: Hodder and Stoughton.

Sturmey, S. G. 1958. *The Economic Development of Radio*. London: Gerald Duckworth.

Taylor, Philip. 1981. *The Projection of Britain: Britain Overseas Publicity and Propaganda, 1919–39*. Cambridge: Cambridge University Press.

Thompson, Kristin. 1985. *Exporting Entertainment: America in the World Film Market, 1907–34*. London: British Film Institute.

Thornton, A. P. 1978. *Imperialism in the Twentieth Century*. London: Macmillan.

Tomlinson, J. 1991. *Cultural Imperialism: A Critical Introduction*. Baltimore, Md.: Johns Hopkins University Press.

Tomlinson, J. D. 1945. *The International Control of Radio Communications*. Ann Arbor, Mich.: J. W. Edwards.

Tribolet, Leslie Bennett. 1929. *The International Aspects of Electrical Communications in the Pacific Area*. Baltimore, Md.: Johns Hopkins University Press.

Tulchin, Joseph. 1971. *The Aftermath of War: World War I and U.S. Policy towards Latin America*. New York: New York University Press.

Ullswater Broadcasting Committee. 1936. *Report of the Broadcasting Committee, 1935.* Cmd. 5091. London: HMSO.

UNESCO (United Nations Education, Scientific, and Cultural Organization). 1968. *Communication in the Space Age: The Use of Satellites by the Mass Media.* Paris: UNESCO.

United Kingdom. 1906a. *Agreement between the Postmaster General and the Marconi's Wireless Telegraph Company Limited and the Marconi International Marine Communication Company Limited. 11th August 1904 with Reference to Wireless Telegraphy.* London: HMSO.

———. 1906b. *Agreement between the Admiralty and the Marconi Wireless Telegraph Company. 24 July 1903.* London: HMSO.

———. 1927. *Colonial Office Conference, 1927: Summary of Proceedings.* Cmd. 2883 London: HMSO.

———. 2000. *Florence Nightingale and the Crimea, 1854–55.* London: HMSO.

———. Balfour Committee. 1902. *Interdepartmental Committee on Cable Communications.* Second Report. Cd. 1056. London: HMSO.

———. Joint Committee. 1861. *Report of the Joint Committee of the Lords of the Committee of the Privy Council for Trade and the Atlantic Telegraph Company to inquire into the Construction of Submarine Telegraph Cables.* London: HMSO.

———. Parliament. 1924. *Report of the Imperial Wireless Telegraphy Committee, 1924.* Cmd. 2060. London: HMSO.

Vevier, Charles. 1959. "The Collins Overland Line and American Continentalism." *Pacific Historical Review* 28:237–53.

Walker, Andrew. 1992. *A Skyful of Freedom: 60 years of the BBC World Service.* London: Broadside Books.

Wedell, E. G. 1968. *Broadcasting and Public Policy.* London: Michael Joseph.

Wedlake, G. E. C. 1973. *S.O.S.: The Story of Radio Communication.* Newton Abbott, U.K.: David and Charles.

Weinthal, Leo. 1923. *The Story of the Cape to Cairo Railway and River Route from 1887 to 1922.* London: Pioneer Publishing.

Weldon, James O. 1988. "The Early History of U.S. International Broadcasting from the Start of World War II." *IEEE Transactions on Broadcasting* 34 (June): 81–86.

West, Nigel. 1986. *GCHQ: The Secret Wireless War.* London: Weidenfeld and Nicholson.

Williams, William Appleman. 1969. *The Roots of American Empire.* New York: Random House.

Wilshaw, Sir Edward. 1939. "Speech to the Country Conference of the Chartered Institutes of Secretaries, Manchester, May 1924." In *The Cable and Wireless Communications of the World: Some Lectures and Papers on the Subject, 1924–1939.* Ed. Cable and Wireless Ltd. 1–15. London: Cable and Wireless.

Wilson, H. H. 1961. *Pressure Group: The Campaign for Commercial Television.* London: Secker and Warburg.

Winston, Brian. 1998. *Media Technology and Society: A History—From the Telegraph to the Internet.* London: Routledge.

Wood, James. 1992. *History of International Broadcasting.* London: Peter Peregrinus.

Young, Peter. 1983. *Power of Speech: A History of Standard Telephones and Cables, 1883–1983.* London: Allen and Unwin.

Index

JILL HILLS is a professor in the School of Communication, Design, and Media at the University of Westminster, London. She is the author of *Information Technology and Industrial Policy* (1984) and *Deregulating Telecoms* (1986) and coeditor of *Feminism and Political Theory* (1986).

The History of Communication

The University of Illinois Press
is a founding member of the
Association of American University Presses.

_____

Composed in 10.5/13 Adobe Minion
with Adobe Minion display
at the University of Illinois Press

Manufactured by Thomson-Shore, Inc.
University of Illinois Press
1325 South Oak Street
Champaign, IL 61820-6903
www.press.uillinois.edu